SECOND EDITION

The Basics of Paralegal Studies

David Lee Goodrich
Member of the Florida Bar

PRENTICE HALL PARALEGAL SERIES

Prentice Hall
Upper Saddle River, New Jersey 07458

Library of Congress Cataloging-in-Publication Data

Goodrich, David Lee.
   The basics of paralegal studies / David Lee Goodrich. — 2d. ed.
     p. cm.
   Includes index.
   ISBN 0-13-568189-8
   1. Legal assistants—United States.
KF320.L4G66 1996
340′.023′73—dc20   90-21870
                                     CIP

Acquisitions Editor: Elizabeth Sugg
Director of Production and Manufacturing: Bruce Johnson
Managing Editor: Mary Carnis
Editorial/Production Supervision and
   Interior Design: Inkwell Publishing Services
Cover Director: Jayne Conte
Manufacturing Buyer: Edward O'Dougherty

 © 1997, 1991 by Prentice-Hall, Inc.
A Simon & Schuster Company
Upper Saddle River, New Jersey 07458

Printed in the United States of America

10 9 8 7 6 5 4 3 2 1

ISBN 0-13-568189-8

PRENTICE-HALL INTERNATIONAL (UK) LIMITED, *London*
PRENTICE-HALL OF AUSTRALIA PTY. LIMITED, *Sydney*
PRENTICE-HALL CANADA INC., *Toronto*
PRENTICE-HALL HISPANOAMERICANA, S.A., *Mexico*
PRENTICE-HALL OF INDIA PRIVATE LIMITED, *New Delhi*
PRENTICE-HALL OF JAPAN, INC., *Tokyo*
PRENTICE-HALL OF SOUTHEAST ASIA PTE. LTD., *Singapore*
EDITORA PRENTICE-HALL DO BRASIL, LTDA., *Rio de Janeiro*

To my wife, Gail
for her love,
support, and encouragement

Contents

2
The Reading and Briefing of Cases   *29*

3
Legal Analysis *64*

4
Legal Research *82*

5
Writing Skills   *129*

6
Ethics   *138*

7
Substantive Civil Law and Procedure 175

8
Civil Discovery 223

9
Criminal Law, Discovery, and Procedure   257

10
Real Estate *273*

11
Decedents' Estates   *315*

12
Domestic Relations   *337*

13
Contracts   *366*

14
The NALA CLA Examination 393

Preface

The Basics of Paralegal Studies is designed to introduce the layperson to the field of paralegal assisting. It is specifically written for people who would like to know more about the field, but have no background in the area. The intent is to provide not only an overview of the legal principles in a variety of areas of the law, but also to give a practical introduction to the kinds of duties and responsibilities that may face a paralegal in the workplace. The contents of the book prepare students for the NALA CLA examination.

This new edition maintains and improves the benefits of the first: readable, in-depth explanations of courts and the sources of law. We have added coverage of torts, contracts, and expanded information on corporations and agency. We have strong organization geared to a practical approach.

While this book is designed to be used as a text in an introductory course for paralegal assisting, the book's structure, organization, and content qualify it as a comprehensive reference that will continue to be valuable to anyone working in the paralegal field. Members of the general public will also find it informative in gaining insight into general subject areas of the law as they affect the paralegal profession.

The names used in the forms, examples, and questions are purely fictional, and resemblance to any person living or dead, or any legal action in any jurisdiction, is purely coincidental. Similarly, information in questions concerning the existence of jurisdictional limits of specific courts in particular states is totally fictional and given for instructional purposes only.

ACKNOWLEDGMENTS

Many of our current text users provided insight that went into the preparation of this edition. It was with their help and the help of expert reviewers, such as Joyce Lynn Wood of Anne Arundel Community College; Brian McCully of Fresno City College; and Jan Halverson of Pierce College, that we were able to include so many significant improvements to this edition.

I would like to gratefully acknowledge the assistance of my parents, Dr. and Mrs. Albert Goodrich, who spent countless hours in the preparation of this manuscript for publication. I also want to thank attorneys Perry Hodges, Robert Wills, Thomas A. Goodrich, Darcee Siegel, and William G. Crawford, Jr., as well as Dr. James S. Goodrich and Bernita N. Blanton for their contributions to the book.

My wife, Gail Goodrich, has both assisted and been a constant source of encouragement, and I will always be deeply grateful for her support.

DAVID LEE GOODRICH

1 *Introduction*

CHAPTER OVERVIEW

SEC. 1-1
WHAT IS A PARALEGAL?

A. Definition

The term *paralegal* is often used interchangeably with the term *legal assistant,* and it is intended to refer to a class of individuals who are not attorneys, but who are nevertheless highly knowledgeable in certain areas of the law. Although they may be very skilled and may perform many of the functions that attorneys might otherwise handle, they are prohibited from rendering legal advice or representing clients in court.

In 1986, the American Bar Association agreed on the following definition for a legal assistant:

> A legal assistant is a person, qualified through education, training, or work experience, who is employed or retained by a lawyer, law office, governmental agency, or other entity in a capacity or function which involves the performance, under the ultimate direction and supervision of an attorney, of specifically-delegated substantive legal work, which work, for the most part, requires a sufficient knowledge of legal concepts that, absent such assistant, the attorney would perform the task.[1]

It is not necessary for a paralegal to obtain a special license or certification in order to claim paralegal status. *Licensing* refers to the procedure by which a governmental agency establishes minimal standards that must be met before an individual will be allowed to engage in a particular business. The primary reason that licensure has not been required in the past is that the paralegal must work under the supervision of an attorney who in turn must already have a license to practice law.

Licensing must be distinguished from certification. *Certification* refers to the process by which an organization acknowledges that an individual has met certain minimal qualifications and can therefore claim that he or she is certified by that group as having attained a certain level of competence. The term "certification" implies by its very nature that such recognition is not mandatory for the individual to be able to practice in the field. Proof of competence in the field of legal assisting may be shown by passing a written test given by the National Association of Legal Assistants, one of the primary organizations of paralegals. While taking such an examination is voluntary, it is arguable that doing so forces paralegals to increase their overall knowledge. Passing it may put paralegals in a stronger position to obtain a good job or ask for a salary increase. Furthermore, those who favor certification see the process as a means of increasing the status of the profession.

The memberships of the other paralegal organizations have differing views with regard to the certification issue. The other groups include the National Federation of Paralegal Associations (NFPA); the American Association for Paralegal Education (AAfPE), which was formed primarily for paralegal educators; and more recently, the Legal Assistant Management Association (LAMA). Opponents of certification argue, among other things, that certification is premature in this field when even the definition of a paralegal is subject to debate. They argue that there is no consensus among the legal community as to the minimal educational requirements or experience and that it may be difficult, if not impossible, to devise a test that can accurately measure competence in the field.

In the 1970s, Oregon instituted a voluntary certification program, but it was subsequently dropped because of minimal involvement by the paralegal community. On the other hand, the state of Texas created a voluntary certification program for legal assistants in 1994 and is the only state that currently has such a state-sponsored certification.

In 1985, the American Bar Association considered the issues of both the licensure and certification of legal assistants, but it ultimately declined to support either one.

B. Key Components of the Definition

1. Legal Skills

The individual must have certain legal skills, such as researching the law, investigating background information about parties or witnesses, drafting documents, interviewing witnesses, organizing evidence for trial, and performing many other functions. The exact skills required may depend upon where the paralegal is working. In a law office that specializes primarily in wills and trusts, for example, a large percentage of the paralegal's time will probably be spent in the preparation of documents.

2. Under the Supervision of an Attorney

The paralegal must operate under the ultimate supervision and direction of an attorney. This does not mean that he or she is supervised on a minute-by-minute basis by an attorney. It does mean, however, that the work product of a paralegal must generally be approved by the attorney before it is given to or used on behalf of the client.

3.   *Not an Attorney and Not Practicing Law*

Paralegals do not take the bar exam and are not generally authorized to do many of the kinds of activities that attorneys perform, such as represent clients in court. In addition paralegals may not do what attorneys themselves may not do, such as violating the confidences of office clients.

C.   *Different Meanings of the Word "Paralegal"*

Especially in light of the fact that legal assisting is a relatively new occupation, the term *paralegal* (or *legal assistant*) has come to represent different meanings to different people. There are some people claiming to be paralegals who are in fact only highly skilled legal secretaries. True paralegals perform many more functions than the typical legal secretary and should be paid accordingly for their superior skill. While it is not necessary to take a national or state exam at the present time in order to claim the status of a paralegal, there is always the possibility that this kind of proof of competence may be required in the future.

SEC. 1-2
WHY DO ATTORNEYS AND OTHER EMPLOYERS USE PARALEGALS?

While members of other professions, such as doctors and dentists, have used paraprofessionals for many years, attorneys and other employers in law-related fields have only recently realized the value of using paralegals in their offices. Attorneys discovered that if they could delegate certain kinds of tasks to employees who were not attorneys, they could spend more time on matters that required the expertise of an attorney and thereby increase their billable hours.

To illustrate, assume that an attorney was handling a probate matter that required approximately 10 hours of work. If the office billed at a rate of $100 per hour, the law office could receive $1,000 for the legal services rendered. Assuming four of the 10 hours could be delegated to a competent paralegal who was being paid at a rate of $18 per hour, the attorney could afford to charge considerably less. The attorney could still make a substantial profit by billing the client for $800 rather than $1,000 and spending the extra four hours on another case at a substantial hourly rate. The client would also benefit, since the client would save $200 on what would otherwise be a bill for attorneys fees in the amount of $1,000. Under these circumstances, both the attorney and the paralegal could make substantial incomes, the client could benefit from reduced attorneys fees, and the law office could profit from dramatically increased productivity.

As a result of the obvious advantages of employing paralegals, more and more firms in recent years have chosen to hire paralegals. Legal assisting has become one of the fastest growing professions in the country, and there is every reason to believe that the market will be a continually expanding one in the coming years.

SEC. 1-3
WHAT FUNCTIONS DO PARALEGALS PERFORM?

The duties of a paralegal differ significantly from one office to another and, as noted above, generally depend upon the type of law being practiced by the paralegal's employer. The areas of law listed below are followed by examples of duties typically performed by paralegals in offices with these specializations. The list is not intended to be complete and it does not represent all activities that might be the responsibility of the paralegal. All documents drafted by the paralegal in connection with any of the following types of practices would have to be approved by the attorney before they were turned over to the client.

A. Real Estate

In offices that represent clients at real estate closings, paralegals might be involved in the handling of those closings (under the supervision of the attorney) from start to finish. During the initial stages of the attorney's representation, the paralegal could be responsible for obtaining the legal description of the property, ordering the abstract, and starting to build a file that included all information relevant to the closing such as the names, addresses, and telephone numbers of the parties, the names of any existing or new lenders, and the names and telephone numbers of any real estate agents involved. Such a file would also include other general information such as the purchase price, approximate amount of cash needed by the buyer to close, and the last possible date for closing under the terms of the contract.

The paralegal might also be responsible for the preparation of the closing documents, although the documents would have to be approved by the attorney before they could be executed by the parties at the closing. The documents prepared would include a closing statement indicating who was responsible for the various costs associated with the sale and purchase of the real estate, how much the buyer had to bring to the closing, and how much the seller was to receive. It might also be the responsibility of the paralegal to ascertain whether the taxes have been paid on the property and whether the roof, termite, and swimming pool inspection reports have been submitted. Paralegals with significant real estate experience and training may even be able to assist the attorney with the title search of the property.

Once all of the documents have been prepared and the parties are ready to close, it may be the responsibility of the paralegal to contact all of the parties, the real estate agents or brokers, and the lenders to set the final date and time for the closing. When the closing finally does occur, the paralegal may be present and assist the attorney, although the paralegal cannot ethically give any clients direct legal advice.

In law offices that specialize more in real estate management and landlord/tenant matters, paralegals might be involved in the preparation of lease agreements, eviction notices, or pleadings that result from lawsuits filed in connection with any such contractual agreements between the parties.

B.   Probate and Estate Planning

(See the "Decedents' Estates" chapter of this book for a discussion of the meaning of this specialization.) Paralegals in offices with this specialization would probably assist in the drafting of wills and/or trusts. For estates which are being probated or administered, the paralegal might be assigned to prepare a file using the basic background information concerning the estate such as the date of death, the location of any will (if one exists), the names, addresses, and telephone numbers of all apparent heirs or beneficiaries, and a description and location of all estate assets. The paralegal might also assist in preparing documents to be filed with the probate court such as a petition for administration, an accounting, or an inventory, as well as obtaining various documents relevant to the estate including tax statements, death certificates, and insurance policies.

C.   Personal Injury

The number of potential duties that a paralegal may have in this specialization is so great that any individual paralegal may not be responsible for handling all paralegal functions in a particular case. Some paralegals may be responsible for the interviewing of the client and witnesses, while others may be assigned general investigative functions such as searching public records or tracking down tangible evidence.

Paralegals may be heavily involved in the preparation of court pleadings. Many pleadings, such as notices of hearing, are relatively routine and demand little creativity on the part of the person preparing the document. Other pleadings, however, require a substantial knowledge of both procedural and substantive law, and the paralegal who is able to help draft these kinds of documents should be in great demand.

Personal injury cases may also involve a substantial amount of research. While the ability to research is a talent that requires a significant amount of practice, the paralegal can reach a level of expertise that can be of substantial benefit to a law firm. Those who research and who have strong writing skills may also be called upon to draft extensive memoranda on specific points of law.

Another major contribution of the paralegal in personal injury cases may be in the area of discovery (see the "Civil Discovery" chapter of this book for a discussion of the meaning of this specialization). Paralegals may be involved in the preparation of deposition or interrogatory questions. The choice of questions to be asked during discovery may require a substantial degree of legal judgment and discretion, however, and it is not regarded as ethical for the paralegal to ask questions at a deposition. Once the answers to interrogatories are received from the opposing party, or the depositions are received from the court reporter's office, it may be the responsibility of the paralegal to summarize the answers to those interrogatories or depositions.

Prior to trial, the paralegal may be called upon to locate and contact all witnesses as well as to organize all of the court pleadings, depositions, interrogatories, and tangible evidence into a systematic order so that the attorney can use them at trial. The paralegal may actually be requested to accompany the attorney to trial in order to help with the exhibits, although the paralegal will not usually be permitted to speak before the court on behalf of any client. If any appeals are taken from the decision of the trial court, the paralegal may be asked to order the transcripts from the lower court.

Personal injury specialization involves such major subject areas as discovery and civil procedure. Whole chapters of this book are devoted to these topics. A knowledge of the court procedural rules in these civil actions may often be as critical to the success of the paralegal as a knowledge of substantive law.

D. *Criminal Law*

Paralegals working in a criminal law practice may do many of the same kinds of functions performed by those in personal injury or general civil litigation practices. (For an understanding of the difference between civil and criminal cases, please see Sec. 1-7.) Paralegals working in this specialization are usually found in private law firms, prosecutors' offices, or public defenders' offices.

They are often called upon to draft pleadings, trial briefs, and motions as well as summarize depositions and organize the attorney's file into a systematic order so that it may be used at trial. Paralegals may also be called upon to do the kind of extensive research needed to support effective criminal litigation and prepare extensive memoranda of law based upon the research done.

E. *Family Law*

This specialization includes a wide variety of subject areas including:

1. those that pertain to marriage itself, such as suits for dissolution of marriage;
2. those that pertain to children, including child custody matters, child support, adoption, and questions involving visitation rights; and
3. those that involve the appointment of a guardian or conservator.

In many family law matters, the responsibilities of the paralegal focus on investigative functions such as the location of assets. They may also include interviewing or drafting skills.

F. *Corporate Law*

Most of the work done by a paralegal in a firm that specializes in corporate law involves the preparation of paperwork. When a corporation is initially formed, it may be the responsibility of the paralegal to ascertain whether the name that the client has chosen for the corporation is available, because a corporation will not be allowed to do business under a name that is deceptively similar to one that is already in use in the state. Articles of incorporation will have to be prepared and filed with the appropriate legal authorities so that the corporation can be properly chartered. Corporate bylaws, resolutions, minutes, and annual reports may need to be prepared for continuing clients.

SEC. 1-4
WHERE ARE THE EMPLOYMENT OPPORTUNITIES?

The variety of opportunities for paralegal employment is great and constantly growing, but at the present time, most openings are found in the following places:

A.   *Private Law Firms*

At the present time, there are substantially more employment opportunities in private practice firms than in any other sector.

B.   *U.S. or State Prosecutors' and Public Defenders' Offices*

A state court prosecutor, known in some areas as the *District Attorney* or the *State Attorney,* is responsible for the prosecution of criminal cases under state law. The prosecutor in federal criminal cases is known as the *U.S. Attorney.* The office of the U.S. Attorney handles civil matters as well. The state *Public Defender* represents criminal defendants in state courts when they cannot afford to pay for legal representation. The U.S. *Public Defender* represents similar clients in federal court.

C.   *Banks, Insurance Companies, and Other Corporations*

Most paralegal positions available in banks can be found in their trust departments, while paralegals in insurance companies are generally used in claims work. Any business that has a legal department may have employment opportunities for competent paralegals.

D.   *The Government*

Since 1975, the federal government has advertised job openings under the new employment category of "legal assistant." All three branches of state and local government have a need for paralegals. On the federal level, the greatest number of positions will generally be found either in the legal departments that advise members of the cabinet or in the Justice Department. One advantage to working for the government is that paralegal positions are generally civil service jobs and the salaries are often higher than those for comparable ones in the private sector.

E.   *Legal Aid Offices*

These offices represent clients who cannot afford their own representation in civil cases. Because of the limited funding available to those working in legal aid offices, paralegals in these offices tend to have lower paying positions.

F.   *Freelance Opportunities*

There is a growing trend for legal assistants to work in differing legal environments on an as-needed basis. Groups of paralegals have combined into business entities for the purpose of providing such services as independent contractors. Law firms needing the skills of a legal assistant with a specialization in a particular area of law can often fulfill their needs by contacting such companies for short-term projects to be performed under the supervision of an attorney.

A distinction should be drawn between freelance paralegals who work for attorneys and paralegals who are rendering legal services while not operating under the supervision of an attorney. Individuals in the latter category are potentially subject to prosecution for the unauthorized practice of law.

SEC. 1-5
SOURCES OF LAW, THE RELATIONSHIP BETWEEN THOSE SOURCES, AND THE EFFECT OF A VETO

A. Sources of Law

While there are many sources of law, the primary ones include:

1. Statutes

Statutes are legislative acts passed by either the federal legislature (the Congress) in Washington D.C. or the state legislatures. The U.S. government has a *bicameral* (two chamber) legislature composed of a House of Representatives and a Senate. Representation of each state in the House of Representatives is based upon population, while in the Senate, each state has two representatives regardless of geographical size or population. A federal statute generally must be passed by a majority of both houses of Congress before it can become law. An example of a statute is any law passed by Congress that outlaws the interstate transportation of prohibited narcotics.

Statutes can be distinguished from ordinances, which are rules passed by local legislative bodies.

2. Constitutions

As in the case of statutes, there are both federal and state constitutions. Constitutions generally deal with broad principles that pertain to issues of governmental organization, governmental powers, and basic human rights.

a. U.S. Constitution.   When the U.S. Constitution was originally proposed, there was strong opposition to various parts of it by representatives of the colonies. In order to obtain a document acceptable to all parties, certain amendments were proposed. Ten amendments to the Constitution were ratified approximately two years after the main document was signed, and they are known collectively as the *Bill of Rights.* These 10 amendments address issues involving the basic rights of the individual such as the right to exercise free speech, the right to be secure against unreasonable searches and seizures, the right to be free from double jeopardy, and the right to refuse to testify against oneself. Many of these rights are stated in abstract terms, and it has fallen upon the courts and the legislature to determine how the abstract concepts are to be applied to various specific situations (see Sec. 1-5, subsection A.5).

b. State constitutions. Most state constitutions are modeled after the U.S. Constitution, although each state's document may have its own unique features.

3. *Administrative Regulations*

Within the last 75 years, a new body of law has been created in the form of *administrative regulations.* These rules come from administrative agencies such as the Federal Communications Commission, the Environmental Protection Agency, the Federal Trade Commission, the Small Business Administration, and other similar governmental bodies. These agencies have been created by Congress, and other similar agencies have been established on the state level by state legislatures. The purpose and scope of authority for each agency has been established in the act creating it. Legislatures clearly have the power to create such organizations, and the contention that they are without authority to delegate their rule-making power to other bodies has been rejected by the U.S. Supreme Court. Since the early 1930s, the number of administrative agencies has grown so large that the business of the administrative wing of the government on both the state and federal levels comprises a substantial portion of the government's business.

Like the federal government, each administrative agency is divided into three branches:

1. the legislative,
2. the executive, and
3. the judicial.

The legislative branch functions in a rule-making capacity, the executive branch involves investigation and inspection, and the judicial branch engages in court-like activities. The powers exercised in each branch are designed to complement each other. For example, the FDA (Food and Drug Administration) may issue a rule that prohibits the inclusion of certain dye colors in preserved foods because the dyes have been shown to cause cancer in rats. In issuing such a ruling, the agency is exercising its legislative function. This rule is just as binding upon food manufacturers and processors as if it were passed by a legislative body.

If the agency has reason to believe that the rule is being violated by a particular individual or group, it then has the power within its executive branch to investigate and determine whether the charges are true. An investigation may generally be initiated either by the agency itself, or as a result of a complaint filed by a private citizen or group. In conducting investigations, administrative officials are subject to many of the same search and seizure restraints under the Constitution as are police officers.

Each administrative agency generally has a judicial branch which is empowered to handle cases involving violations of its administrative rules. Administrative courts appear to be similar to state courts, but there is no right to trial by jury and decisions are rendered by those with expertise in the field. There are also courts to which one can appeal within the agency in the event that the party charged with violating agency rules wishes to contest the decision of the lower administrative court.

4. Treaties, Executive Orders, and the Like

Treaties signed by the President of the United States are also part of the general body of law of this country once they are ratified by Congress. With regard to executive orders, the President also has innate powers to issue certain kinds of executive orders without legislative approval. Such orders are also included in the general body of law.

5. Case Law

Even though court decisions are by their very nature directed to the immediate parties, the rules of law that come from cases may serve as precedent in subsequent legal proceedings. The body of all court decisions is known as *case law* and is another primary source of law. It includes court decisions interpreting the federal and state constitutions, statutes, administrative regulations, and other materials. The rulings of the highest courts, of course, carry the greatest weight.

To illustrate, if the U.S. Supreme Court is asked to rule on a case involving the use of alleged excessive corporal punishment by a teacher against a student, the Supreme Court will carefully consider not only any statute governing the question, but also the interpretation that has been given to that statute by other courts. When courts follow the precedent that has been established in previous cases, they are said to be applying the doctrine of *stare decisis*. If the courts were not to give deference to court precedent, our system of laws would be much less stable. It would also be more subject to the whims of the judge who happened to be presiding over a particular case. If, however, court precedent was always followed, the laws would never change, and the legal system would become inflexible in the face of changing times. It is the responsibility of the courts to strike the appropriate balance between these two extremes.

The flexibility of the legal process can be seen in the way that the courts have handled cases involving obscene materials. It has been affirmed by the U.S. Supreme Court that *obscenity* is not protected speech under the First Amendment to the U.S. Constitution.[2] It has been less clear, however, exactly what kinds of materials fall within the definition of obscenity. The Supreme Court has, on occasion, modified the rules and definitions used in previous cases as social attitudes change. In the 1957 case of *Roth v. United States*,[3] for example, the Court ruled that matter could be regarded as obscene if the average person, applying contemporary community standards, would find that the work taken as a whole, appealed to the person's prurient interest. In 1973, the Court, in the case of *Miller v. California*,[4] added two elements to the definition of obscenity:

1. "the work depicts or describes, in a patently offensive way, sexual conduct specifically defined by the applicable state law"; and

2. "the work, taken as a whole, lacks serious literary, artistic, political, or scientific value."

A change in the definition of obscenity was probably necessitated not only because of the vagueness of the *Roth* test, but also because the whole perception of what constituted obscene matter had changed significantly during the interim between the *Roth* and *Miller* cases.

Courts are generally free to overrule their own prior decisions or those of lower courts. They must, however, follow the decisions of higher courts.

a. Mandatory precedent.   When the ruling of another court must be followed by the present court, the prior court decision is referred to as *mandatory precedent*. Courts are required to follow the decisions rendered by higher courts within the same court system. For example, a trial court in Florida must follow the decisions of the Florida Supreme Court. Similarly, a federal court in a particular state is bound by the decisions of higher federal courts within the same circuit. Federal courts interpreting state constitutional or statutory provisions must reflect the prior decisions of the state's courts.

In a state court system in which there are two levels of appeals courts, a middle-level appeals court in one part of the state is not obligated to follow the decision of another middle-level appeals court in that same court system. Any apparent conflict between the decisions of the two would have to be resolved on appeal to a higher state court.

While it may be apparent that a state court must follow previous decisions that emanate from higher state courts, it may be less clear whether the set of facts in a particular case is similar enough to the facts of the previous case to make the previous decision a mandatory precedent. If a court determines that the facts are not sufficiently similar, it need not regard the higher court's decision as mandatory authority. If one of the parties feels that mandatory precedent exists, he or she may choose to appeal the court's ruling. When an attorney is faced with case law that the court may consider to be mandatory precedent, one of two strategies is usually employed. The attorney may attempt to distinguish the facts of the two cases and argue that the previous case is, therefore, not binding upon the present case. The attorney may also argue that the former case may be mandatory precedent with regard to a particular legal issue that is present in both cases, but that the issue is not the determinative one in the present case.

b. Persuasive precedent. Court precedent that is not mandatory may be regarded as *persuasive*. A decision, for example, from an Arkansas state court would be regarded as only persuasive in a Montana state court since the ruling did not come from a higher court within the Montana state court system. Also included in the category of persuasive precedent are the decisions of a federal Circuit Court of Appeals in federal circuits other than the one in which a particular case is being heard. Law review articles and textbooks are additional sources of persuasive authority. In general, courts may regard as persuasive any authorities that they may find as convincing but are not obligated to follow.

B. Relationship Between the Sources of Law

To illustrate the relationship between the U.S. Constitution, statutes or administrative regulations, and case law, an example may be helpful.

The Eighth Amendment to the U.S. Constitution prohibits the infliction of "cruel and unusual punishment," but it does not indicate what type of punishment falls within that category. Assume a state legislature has passed a statute providing for the death penalty in cases involving first degree murder. Since the individual legislators agree to uphold the Constitution of the United States when they take office, the majority of legislators have apparently come to the conclusion that the death penalty is not in violation of constitutional standards.

John Smith is convicted of first degree murder and is sentenced to death. He claims in his ultimate appeal before the U.S. Supreme Court that, regardless of the fact that a death penalty statute has been passed in the state, the statute violates the Eighth Amendment to the U.S. Constitution and, therefore, should not be enforced. One of several things may happen at this point.[5]

1.   *The Statute Is Declared Unconstitutional*

If the U.S. Supreme Court agrees that the law is unconstitutional, the ruling of the court will effectively strike down the penalty statute and it cannot be enforced against the defendant. The ruling of the court with regard to the unconstitutionality of the death penalty in the case of *State v. Smith* becomes a precedent to be followed in future cases.

a. The legislation is modified.   If the decision indicates that the statute might have been acceptable if altered in some way, the state legislature may choose to reenact the statute with language modified to comply with the Supreme Court decision. Any new statute will not, however, affect Smith. This is because Article I, § 9 of the U.S. Constitution specifically prohibits the passage of *ex post facto laws,* which are laws attempting to hold the perpetrator responsible for violating a law that was not in force at the time of the purported violation.

b. The Constitution is amended.   The people can amend the Constitution and thereby effectively override the ruling of the Supreme Court in similar future cases. The U.S. Supreme Court could not, for example, declare that the infliction of the death penalty was cruel and unusual punishment if the U.S. Constitution was amended to provide that the states could enact death penalty legislation. It would be implicit that by amending the Constitution in this manner, the people intended to override the more general reference in the Constitution to "cruel and unusual punishment."

The process that must be followed in order to amend the Constitution is relatively cumbersome and, as a result of the difficulty in the amendment process, the Constitution has only been amended 27 times since its enactment. Article V of the U.S. Constitution indicates the manner in which the Constitution can be amended. This provision states that

> The Congress, whenever two thirds of both Houses shall deem it necessary, shall propose Amendments to this Constitution, or, on the Application of the Legislatures of two thirds of the several States, shall call a Convention for proposing Amendments, which, in either Case, shall be valid to all Intents and Purposes, as part of this Constitution, when ratified by the Legislatures of three fourths of the several States, or by Conventions in three fourths thereof, as the one or the other Mode of Ratification may be proposed by the Congress....

2. *The Statute Is Upheld*

If the Court finds that the law is constitutional, it will uphold the statute. It is not, however, the position of any court to act as a second legislature, and the court should, therefore, uphold a statute even if the individual members of the court do not agree with the legislation. Their function in the *Smith* case would be to determine the constitutionality or unconstitutionality of the death penalty. Assuming that the statute is found to be constitutional and all other arguments on appeal have been exhausted, the death penalty can then be imposed on Smith.

a. The possibility of a pardon for the defendant.   Even if the highest court has upheld the constitutionality of the legislation, the chief executive still has the power to pardon a defendant and thereby nullify the effect of the statute with regard to a particular defendant. The power to pardon applies only to defendants in criminal, as opposed to civil, cases. For example, when President Richard Nixon was pardoned, he was effectively shielded from criminal prosecution for the period during which he served as President. Numerous civil suits against him, however, were unaffected. The authority for the presidential pardon can be found in Article II, § 2 of the U.S. Constitution.

C. *Effect of a Veto*

If the President does not agree with legislation that has been passed by a majority of the members of both the House of Representatives and the Senate, the President may then prevent the act from becoming law by vetoing it. While it is possible for Congress to override the veto, a two-thirds vote rather than a simple majority vote of each house of Congress is required. The authority for the presidential veto and the ability of Congress to override it are powers that are expressly created in Article I, § 7 of the U.S. Constitution.

SEC. 1-6
THE COURT SYSTEM

A. *The Role of Trial and Appellate Courts*

1. *Trial Courts*

If the case is before a jury, the judge will determine questions of law, and the jury will decide questions of fact. *Questions of law* include such technical legal questions as whether a statement should be admitted into evidence. *Questions of fact,* on the other hand, pertain to what actually happened in the case, and the jurors' ultimate determinations on these questions will generally lead to a verdict in favor of one party or other. If the case is not being heard before a jury, the judge will be responsible for determining questions of both law and fact. If the judge makes an error in admitting certain statements or materials into evidence, this could obviously have an effect on the jury's ultimate verdict in the case and could be grounds for appeal.

2.   Appellate Courts

Appeals are generally heard before a panel of justices. The number of justices for an appeal may vary from state to state, but it is usually odd in number in order to avoid tie votes. In appeals cases, a majority vote of the justices will prevail. It is extremely difficult to win an appeal on a question of fact. Once a jury has spoken, an appeals court will not usually overturn the jury's finding of fact unless it determines that there is no evidence supporting the verdict. This is true even if the court is of the opinion that the jury finding was erroneous.

On the other hand, appellate courts may be more inclined to consider appeals based on alleged errors made by the judge concerning questions of law. If the appeals court becomes convinced that the jury's ultimate verdict in the case might have been different if the trial court judge had ruled differently on a question of admissibility, for example, the appellate court might consider overruling the previous decision.

The appellate court has to be convinced not only that an error was made, but that such an error ultimately affected the outcome of the trial. Harmless errors are not generally grounds for reversal of the trial court determination.

In many kinds of cases, appellate courts are not required to hear all of the appeals brought before them. In such situations, the party filing the appeal, also known as the *appellant,* seeks a *writ of certiorari,* which is a document from a higher court that essentially initiates appellate proceedings by ordering a lower court to provide it with a pending pleading.

B.   The State and Federal Court Systems

Paralegals should be thoroughly familiar with both the state and federal courts in their area. State court systems vary from state to state, but they tend to follow certain basic organizational patterns. The organization of the federal court system, as explained in this subsection, is applicable in all sections of the country.

1. **The State Court System**

    a. The various levels in the state court system

    (1) *Courts of original jurisdiction.* These courts handle the legal matters of the parties for the first time. There are various kinds of courts of original jurisdiction.

    (a) *Courts not of record.* Some states have courts that are included in this category. No permanent record is maintained of the court proceedings, and appeal from a decision of such a court is therefore virtually impossible. Justice of the peace courts are included in this division.

    (b) *Courts of general jurisdiction.* These courts handle a wide variety of cases. Many states have two levels of original jurisdiction courts. Often, one court has a civil branch that includes monetary suits up to a certain amount, such as $15,000, and a criminal branch that handles the less serious crimes known as *misdemeanors*. The other court might include a civil branch that handles monetary suits greater than a certain amount and a criminal branch that deals with the more serious crimes known as *felonies.*

    (c) *Courts of limited jurisdiction.* Courts with limited jurisdiction only have the power to rule over specific kinds of cases, such as traffic or dissolution of marriage matters.

    (2) *The middle-level appellate courts.* These courts generally exist only in the larger states. Whether one has the right to appeal to these courts may be discretionary with the appellate court in certain kinds of cases under the state rules. (See the discussion of writs of certiorari in Section 1-6, subsection A.2.)

    (3) *The highest-level appellate court.* This is the court of last resort and it is referred to as the *Supreme Court* in most states.

    b. Selection of judges. Judges in state courts are chosen by a variety of different plans. In some states, they are elected. In others, they are appointed by the governor. Such appointments may require approval by the legislature or by a judicial nominating commission. It is also possible that the selection process may dictate that the governor make all appointments from a list of candidates supplied by a judicial nominating commission. Commissions created for this purpose are often composed of both attorneys and lay people, and the purpose of such committees is to help ensure that members of the judiciary are selected on a non-partisan basis.

2.   *The Federal Court System*

A federal court system is created in the U.S. Constitution, but the only court that is specifically established in that document is the U.S. Supreme Court. Article III, § 1 of the Constitution provides that Congress shall have the power to create "inferior Courts as the Congress may from time to time ordain and establish." Based on this authority, Congress has over the past 200 years created the U.S. District Court and the U.S. Circuit Court of Appeals systems. The question of whether a case may be heard in federal court is a very complex one, and it is not one that is made by the paralegal.

a. The three levels of federal courts.   There are three levels of courts in the federal system. They are the U.S. District Courts, the U.S. Circuit Courts of Appeal, and the U.S. Supreme Court.

> **(1)** *The U.S. District Courts.* These are the main trial courts for the federal system. The 50 states, the District of Columbia, and the U.S. territories have been divided into 93 individual districts. The U.S. territories include the Virgin Islands, Puerto Rico, Guam, and the Northern Mariana Islands. The number of judges allocated to each district has been determined largely by the size of the case load. Some districts have only one judge, while others may have several dozen. In any one case, however, only one judge will be presiding.

> **(2)** *The U.S. Circuit Courts of Appeal.* The Circuit Court is an intermediate appellate court. There are 13 circuits in the federal judicial system; 11 of them handle appeals from District Courts and administrative tribunals of the 50 states as well as from the U.S. territories. The Twelfth Circuit Court of Appeals has been established solely for the purpose of handling appeals from the District of Columbia judicial system. The Thirteenth Circuit Court of Appeals is a court of limited jurisdiction and only handles appeals from the Court of International Trade, the Patent and Trademark Office, the U.S. Claims Court, and other specialized administrative offices. The Court of International Trade considers rulings made with regard to the valuation of imported goods for the purposes of imposing customs duties. The U.S. Claims Court renders decisions concerning claims filed against the United States.

> A map showing the geographical boundaries of the District and Circuit courts can be seen in Figure 1-1.

> **(3)** *The U.S. Supreme Court.* This is the highest court in the country. It is the appellate court of last resort for appeals from either federal circuit courts or the highest court in any state. There are also a few circum-

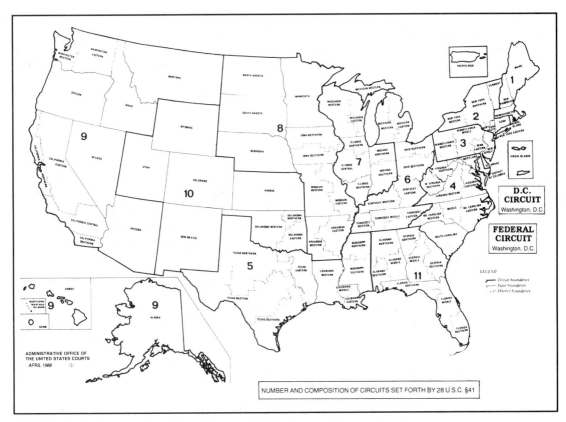

FIGURE 1-1. Geographical boundaries of U.S. Court of Appeals and U.S. District Courts.

stances in which the U.S. Supreme Court has original jurisdiction. In other words, although the vast majority of the cases heard by the Supreme Court are cases that are being heard on appeal, there are some that are heard for the very first time by this court. The U.S. Constitution directly addresses this issue in Article III, § 2, which states:

> In all Cases affecting Ambassadors, other public Ministers and Consuls, and those in which a State shall be a Party, the Supreme Court shall have original Jurisdiction …

b. Selection of judges.   Federal judges on all three levels are appointed by the President of the United States for life, but such appointments must be ratified by Congress before the appointments become effective. As a result, vacancies generally occur only when a judge dies, resigns, or commits an impeachable offense that results in his or her conviction.

SEC. 1-7
CIVIL V. CRIMINAL LAW

The entire body of law can be divided into two primary parts: civil law and criminal law.

A. Two Important Divisions of the Law

1. Civil

Civil suits involve the adjudication of private rights between two or more parties. If, for example, John Smith intentionally injures Sam Jones, Jones has a legal right to sue Smith for the loss that he has suffered. Small claims suits are *civil actions*. Other examples of actions that might be heard in a civil court are negligence, libel, slander, breach of contract, infliction of mental distress, and civil fraud.

The body of civil law is itself divided into two subdivisions: law and equity.

a. Law.   While the term "law" can obviously refer to the entire subject matter addressed in this text, it also has a different and more specific meaning. In a suit in a "law" court, the claimant is generally suing for a monetary amount, which is otherwise referred to as a *suit for damages*. Three kinds of damage suits may be raised: those for compensatory damages, punitive damages, and nominal damages.

When one sues for compensatory damages, the plaintiff is asking to be awarded money for claims based on medical bills, lost wages, property damages, or pain and suffering. An award of such damages is designed to place the claimant in the financial position that was occupied prior to sustaining any harm.

Suits for punitive damages serve an entirely different purpose, which is to punish the wrongdoer for intentionally wrongful or grossly negligent conduct. They would not be appropriate in cases of ordinary negligence. To illustrate the concept of punitive damages, consider a case in which one party maliciously strikes another with a baseball bat. A court might award a plaintiff $10,000 for compensatory damages plus an additional $30,000 in punitive damages. Since the purpose of the $30,000 award would be to punish the defendant rather than compensate the plaintiff, such an award would amount to a windfall for the plaintiff. When the amount of punitive damages is way out of proportion to the amount of compensatory damages awarded in a particular case, an appeals court may be inclined to reduce the punitive damages awarded.

The term "nominal damages" comes from the Latin term for "name," and it is defined as damages awarded in name only. For example, when a plaintiff who sued for $20,000 is awarded only one dollar, the court is implicitly saying that the plaintiff won the case, but was unable to prove an actual loss for which compensation should be made. The court is therefore awarding a token amount to signify that the plaintiff has won in principle even though no actual damages were granted.

b. Equity.   When civil courts were created in the earliest times, not all remedies were available to the parties filing suits. Courts were often willing to award monetary amounts to aggrieved parties, but were not willing to grant them other forms of relief. For example, if one was trespassing on a person's property, the property owner might be more interested in obtaining a court order prohibiting future intrusions than in securing monetary damages.

In order to accommodate the need for different remedies, a new system of courts, called *equity courts,* arose. Any individual filing a case in equity had to allege a need for something other than a monetary recovery.

Injunctions and orders of specific performance are typical remedies in equity courts. An *injunction* is a court order prohibiting a party from doing a particular act such as an order to enjoin a person from entering upon the land of another. An *order of specific performance* is a court order requiring a party to do a particular act. It might be appropriate, for example, if the owner of a parcel of real estate refused to transfer title of the property to another party in accordance with the terms of a signed agreement between the parties.

As more and more cases were heard, matters brought before equity courts were eventually governed by what were called *maxims in equity,* which were principles based upon fundamental fairness. They included principles which were general in nature, such as "Whoever comes into equity must come with clean hands." This particular maxim means that a suing party cannot expect to obtain relief from an equity court without having personally acted in an honest and forthright manner.

In modern times, equity courts have merged with the "law" (nonequity) courts in most states, so that if one serves as a judge of the "law" court at a particular jurisdictional level, that person may be authorized to act as "chancellor" or judge over equity matters. A typical example of an equity case would be a dissolution of marriage suit, since the petitioning party is primarily seeking a court order to dissolve the marriage, even though financial issues may also be involved. In a case that is purely equitable in nature, there is no general right to a jury trial.

2. Criminal

In contrast to civil law, criminal law involves punishment for acts that have been deemed to be contrary to standards imposed by society. Such punishment may include imprisonment, fines, restitution for the victim, or even execution. While civil actions are initiated by private parties, criminal actions generally begin with issuance of an arrest warrant or an actual arrest. The state is therefore a party to any criminal case involving a violation of state criminal law, and the United States is a party to federal criminal cases. For a more detailed discussion of the subject of criminal law in general, see Sec. 9-1, subsection A. in the "Criminal Law, Procedure, and Discovery" chapter.

Crimes are generally categorized as either felonies or misdemeanors.

a. Felonies. A *felony* is an act that has been defined by the legislature as a serious crime. The maximum penalty for a felony is generally greater than one year of incarceration. Examples of felonies are murder, possession of large amounts of illegal narcotics, assault with a deadly weapon, burglary, and arson. Since each state determines whether a particular act will be regarded as a felony or misdemeanor (see subsection A.2.b following immediately), an act may be a misdemeanor in one state and a felony in another.

b. Misdemeanors. A *misdemeanor* is an act that has been defined by the legislature as a crime that is less serious than a felony. In most states, the penalty for a misdemeanor is generally no greater than one year in jail. A fine may also be imposed. Two examples of crimes regarded as misdemeanors in most states are possession of less than one ounce of marijuana and shoplifting of items worth less than a certain specified amount, which in many states is $200 or $300.

B. Civil and Criminal Cases Based on the Same Facts

Sometimes, one factual situation can give rise to both civil and criminal actions. For example, if Kelly drives while she is intoxicated and carelessly runs over Thomas, Kelly could be arrested for the crime of driving while intoxicated or driving under the influence. She could also be sued by Thomas for the civil wrong called negligence. The name of the criminal case would be *State v. Kelly*, while the name of the civil case would be *Thomas v. Kelly*. Since the court requires a higher standard of proof in a criminal case than it does in a civil case, acquittal on the criminal charge does not conclusively establish that the wrongdoer would not be liable to the injured party in a civil case. Furthermore, the fact that one can be both sued civilly and charged criminally in connection with the same activity is not a violation of the double jeopardy clause in the Fifth Amendment to the U.S. Constitution since the amendment only prohibits a second prosecution of a defendant for the same criminal offense. It was not written to restrict the filing of a civil law suit after a criminal prosecution of the defendant.

SEC. 1-8
BASIC TERMINOLOGY

A. Plaintiff

A *plaintiff* is the party who files suit in a civil (nonequity) action.

B. Petitioner

A *petitioner* is the party who files suit in an equity action. In a totally different context, it can also refer to a party who files an appeal, or in general, to a person who is simply requesting a court ruling.

C. Defendant

A *defendant* is the party who is either sued in a civil (nonequity) action, or one who is charged in a criminal action.

D. Respondent

A *respondent* is the party who is sued in an equity action. It can also refer to the party against whom an appeal is taken.

E. State Attorney or District Attorney

The *State Attorney* or *District Attorney* is the prosecutor in a state criminal action. In states in which this person is elected, the position may primarily require the administration of an office composed of numerous attorneys who are actually handling the individual cases. That chief administrator of the office may also personally prosecute several cases. The lawyers who are routinely trying the cases on behalf of the office are referred to as Assistant State Attorneys or Assistant District Attorneys. For federal court matters, the chief supervisor of the office is known as the *U.S. Attorney.* The office of the U.S. Attorney handles civil matters as well. Assistant U.S. Attorneys, like their counterparts in the state courts, have the responsibility for dealing with individual cases.

F. Public Defender

The *Public Defender* is an office of attorneys paid by the government to represent defendants who cannot afford private counsel in criminal cases. In order for a defendant to be entitled to a Public Defender, it must be established that the defendant has insufficient financial assets to obtain adequate legal representation. In states in which the Pubic Defender is elected, this person generally supervises Assistant Public Defenders who try the cases on a day-to-day basis. The U.S. Public Defender has similar responsibilities for criminal defendants in federal court.

G. The Office of Legal Aid

This office represents people in civil matters, such as landlord/tenant actions, when they cannot afford the expense of an attorney. The office of *Legal Aid* is to be distinguished from that of the Public Defender, which is responsible for criminal matters only. Like the Public Defender's office, however, it must be established that the defendant has insufficient financial assets to obtain adequate legal representation.

H. Clerk of the Court

The *clerk of the court* is the individual in charge of all record-keeping functions for the courts.

I. Bailiff

The *bailiff* is the person responsible for assisting the court in maintaining order. The bailiff also has responsibility for the custody of prisoners while in court and the custody of jurors.

J. Jurisdiction

Jurisdiction is the power of a court to hear a case. The judge in a traffic court, for example, has no jurisdiction to handle a dissolution of marriage suit. A transfer of a case, however, from one small claims court judge to another would not be regarded as a change of jurisdiction.

1. Original Jurisdiction

Original jurisdiction is the power of a court to hear a case for the first time. Even the Supreme Court of the United States has original jurisdiction in a few limited situations. [See Sec. 1-6, subsection B.2.a.(3).]

2. *Appellate Jurisdiction*

Courts having the power to review cases that have already been heard before another tribunal are said to have *appellate jurisdiction.* Most cases heard by the U.S. Supreme Court, for example, fall within its appellate jurisdiction. The federal Circuit Courts of Appeal, except for the thirteenth circuit, have such jurisdiction over matters initially heard in the District Courts within their respective circuits. The thirteenth circuit has appellate jurisdiction over specialized matters, such as those pertaining to patents and trademarks. The U.S. Supreme Court, in turn, has the power to review the decisions of federal appellate courts, although it may in its discretion choose not to hear all cases that are brought before it.

K. *Venue*

Venue is the geographical location where a case is heard. A *motion for change of venue* may be justified when a different location would be more convenient for the parties and witnesses involved. Such a motion would be particularly appropriate in large states where a small population is scattered over a relatively large area, such as in Wyoming. A change of venue might also be proper when pretrial publicity in a particular area may prevent a fair trial.

L. *Guilty*

The term *guilty* refers only to responsibility for criminal acts.

M. *Liable*

The term *liable* refers to a responsibility for civil wrongs. It should not be confused with the term *libel,* which refers to the civil wrong of written defamation.

REVIEW QUESTIONS

1. The U.S. Congress passes legislation which provides penalties for desecration of the American flag. Smith is arrested for violating that statute.
   a. If the President opposes the legislation that has been passed, what options does he have?
   b. What options does the Congress have if it wishes the legislation to remain in force despite the opposition of the President?
   c. Assuming that Smith admits that he actually burned an American flag, what possible argument can he raise in his defense in a court of law?

d. In the event that Smith is convicted and his appeals are unsuccessful, can the President intervene to nullify the effect of the court decision?

2. Discuss the federal court system with regard to the following issues:

   a. Name the three main levels of courts in the federal system.

   b. Explain how the jurisdiction of the twelfth and the thirteenth circuits differs from that of the other circuits.

   c. Discuss the manner of selecting judges for each of the above-named courts.

3. Discuss the state court system in your state with regard to the following issues:

   a. Name each primary court that forms part of the state court system.

   b. Discuss the manner of selecting judges for each of the above-named courts.

   c. Indicate the jurisdiction of each court.

   d. Name the court that hears equity cases. Define equity.

4. Discuss the difference between the licensing and certification of legal assistants. Should there be licensing of legal assistants? Why has licensing generally not been required in the past?

5. On what basis does one determine whether court precedent is mandatory or persuasive?

6. The U.S. Congress passes legislation outlawing the sale and distribution of pornography. When Penrod is convicted of violating the statute, she takes her case through the appellate system to the U.S. Supreme Court. The Court rules that the statute is unconstitutional and that Penrod's conviction should be reversed. Is there any way for the U.S. Congress to counterbalance the ruling of the Court with respect to similar future cases? Can the U.S. Congress effectively reverse the ruling of the Court in any way with respect to this particular defendant?

7. Name three factual situations in which a party could be sued civilly by the victim and charged criminally by the government for the same act.

FOOTNOTES

[1]Copyright by American Bar Association. All rights reserved. Reprinted by permission.

[2]*Roth v. United States*, 354 U.S. 476, 77 S.Ct. 1304, 1 L.Ed.2d 1498 (1957).

[3]See the previous endnote.

[4]*Miller v. California*, 413 U.S. 15, 93 S.Ct. 2607, 37 L.Ed.2d 419 (1973).

[5]It should be noted that the U.S. Supreme Court has in fact upheld the death penalty in a number of cases, such as *Furman v. Georgia*, 408 U.S. 238, 92 S.Ct. 2726, 33 L.Ed.2d 346 (1972).

2 *The Reading and Briefing of Cases*

CHAPTER OVERVIEW

a. Damages

b. Injunction

c. An order of specific performance

2. The Need for Brevity

3. The Absence of a Remedy in Criminal Cases

C. The Cause of Action

  1. Examples

    a. Negligence

    b. Breach of contract

    c. Defamation

    d. Infliction of mental distress

    e. False imprisonment

    f. Any act constituting a crime

  2. The Need for Brevity

D. The Facts

  1. Avoidance of Excessive or Insufficient Facts

  2. Avoidance of Confusing Names

E. The Procedural History

F. The Issue

  1. Caution with Regard to "Given Issues"

  2. Key Questions to Consider When Formulating an Issue

    a. Are both procedural and substantive issues to be examined?

    b. Will the answer to the issue have applicability to future cases?

    c. Does the question call for a "yes or no" answer?

G. The Finding

H. The Reason

2-3 Examples of Briefs

A. *Smith v. Jones*

  1. The Brief

  2. Comments Concerning the Brief

    a. An orderly format

    b. The identification of the plaintiff and the defendant

    c. The identification of the remedy and the cause of action

    d. The framing of the issue for general applicability

    e. Focus on the primary issue

    f. Avoidance of unaddressed causes of action

B. *State v. Gleason*

  1. The Brief

C. *Townes v. State*

  1. The Brief

SEC. 2-1
LOCATING A CASE AND UNDERSTANDING ITS BASIC COMPONENTS

This section will briefly explain how cases are located in a law library and then analyze the basic components of a case as it might be recorded in the West Publishing Company National Reporter System. The case of *Florida Bar v. Furman*, which can be seen in Figures 2-1a through 2-1e, will be used as an example.

A. Locating Cases

In order to locate a case, one must look at the case citation that follows the case name. The citation for this particular appeal[1] of the *Furman* case is 376 So.2d 378, which means that the written opinion of the court can be found in volume 376 on page 378 of the set of books known as *Southern Reporter, Second Series.* This set contains the state appellate court decisions in Florida, Alabama, Louisiana, and Mississippi, but it does not include either federal court decisions in those states or state trial court cases. There is a corresponding set for each region of the country. The regional reporters only include the decisions of the state appellate courts.

Other sets of books, collectively known as *Federal Case Reporters,* include both the decisions of the federal trial courts (the U.S. District Courts) and those of the federal appellate courts (the U.S. Circuit Court of Appeals and the U.S. Supreme Court). See the "Legal Research" chapter of this book for further information regarding the use of these sets.

B. The Basic Components of a Reported Case

The following numbers correspond to the circled numbers on the decision in the *Furman* case.

1. The Style

The *style* is the name of the case. It can appear in various forms such as *State v. Smith, Williams v. Johnson, In re: the Marriage of Park and Park,* or in other forms.

2. The Docket Number

The number listed is an internal docket number rather than the one assigned to the case when it was originally filed.

3. The Name of the Court Rendering the Decision

4. The Date of the Present Court Decision

This includes information such as the date of any rehearing of the matter if one took place.

5.   *A Brief Summary of the Case*

This summary, which is generally only one or two paragraphs in length, is prepared by the publisher and not by the court.

6.   *A Notation of Concurring and Dissenting Opinions*

When decisions are rendered by a group of judges, the judges may not all agree with the conclusions or reasoning of the one writing for the majority. A judge who agrees with the outcome of the majority ruling but disagrees with the reasoning in the opinion may write a *concurring opinion*. A written opinion of any judge that disagrees with the conclusion reached by the majority is known as a *dissenting opinion*. It is possible to concur in part and dissent in part. Concurring or dissenting opinions will appear after the majority opinion.

7.   *Headnotes*

Points of law drawn from the case by the publisher are called *headnotes*. They are organized by topic and can give the reader an insight into the contents of the case. In the *Furman* case beginning in Figure 2-1, there are two headnotes. The first is entitled Injunction key number 131, and the second has three separate titles, which are Attorney and Client key number 11(3), Constitutional Law key numbers 90.1(1) and 230.3(9), and Injunction key number 89(5). Since headnotes are from the publisher and not the court, it is necessary to verify that a point made in a headnote is accurate. For a complete explanation of how headnotes and key numbers can be used to find further law on the subjects discussed in the case, see the "State Digests" section (Sec. 4-3, subsection D) in the "Legal Research" chapter of this book.

8.   *The Names of the Attorneys Involved in the Appeal*

In the *Furman* case, the reader will note that the names of the primary attorneys are followed by a reference to "William H. Adams, III, Jacksonville, for amicus curiae." An *amicus curiae brief* is a "friend of the court" brief filed by one who has no right to appear before the court, but who nevertheless wishes to bring to the court's attention legal arguments relevant to the resolution of the case. In the present case, while Adams did not represent either party in this matter, he wanted the court to consider certain arguments that were relevant to the issues addressed. It is, of course, within the discretion of the court to accept or reject such arguments, but the court will at least consider the arguments made in amicus curiae briefs.

9. *The Name of the Justice Writing for the Majority Opinion*

In the *Furman* case, one can see the words "PER CURIAM" where the name of a specific justice would ordinarily appear. A *per curiam decision* is an opinion coming from the entire court, as opposed to the opinion of only one judge or justice. For an example of a case where the decision emanates from one justice, see Figures 4-1b, 4-1c, and 4-1d in which Justice Adkins wrote for the majority in the case of *Alexander v. State.*

10. *The Body of the Decision*

In the main part of the court decision, there are paragraphs that begin with bracketed numbers, such as [1] and [2]. The paragraph beginning with [1] deals directly with the material found in the first headnote. In the *Furman* case, for example, [1] is found in the first complete paragraph of the second column on page 379 of the decision. The material in that and the following paragraphs deals with the legal point in the first headnote, which is Injunction 131. As with the headnotes, the bracketed numbers are supplied by the publisher rather than the court. With this organizational format, it is easy to find the portion of the case that is of particular interest.

11. *The Names of All Justices Joining in the Majority Opinion*

The letters "C.J." before a name refer to the fact that the named individual is the Chief Justice of the court. The "J." is an abbreviation for Justice (or Judge), and the letters "JJ." are an abbreviation for Justices (or Judges).

12. *Concurring and Dissenting Opinions*

See Section 2-1, subsection B.6.

Edward MERCER, Petitioner,

v.

Louie L. WAINWRIGHT, Respondent.

No. 52231.

Supreme Court of Florida.

Sept. 28, 1979.

Appeal from District Court of Appeal, Fourth District; Richard H. Cooper, Judge.

Michael Sigman, Richard E. Mandell, Orlando, for petitioner.

Richard L. Jorandby, Public Defender, Kenneth G. Spillias, Asst. Atty. Gen., West Palm Beach, for respondent.

ORDER

This cause having heretofore been submitted to the Court on jurisdictional briefs and portions of the record deemed necessary to reflect jurisdiction under Fla.R. App.P. 9.120, and it appearing to the Court that it is without jurisdiction, it is ordered that certiorari is denied.

No Motion for Rehearing will be entertained by the Court. See Fla.R.App.P. 9.330(d).

ADKINS, Acting C. J., and BOYD, OVERTON, SUNDBERG and ALDERMAN, JJ., concur.

KEY NUMBER SYSTEM

THE FLORIDA BAR, Petitioner,

v.

Rosemary W. FURMAN, etc., Respondent.

No. 51226.

Supreme Court of Florida.

May 10, 1979.

On Rehearing and Opinion Clarified Nov. 1, 1979.

Petition was filed to enjoin non-lawyer from unauthorized practice of law. The Supreme Court held that nonlawyer's preparing papers considered by her necessary for filing and securing dissolution of marriage, and holding conferences with and asking questions of her customers in connection therewith, constituted unauthorized practice of law and would be enjoined despite contention that such result violated First Amendment by restricting her right to disseminate and right of her customers to receive information and would deprive indigent citizens of equal protection.

Ordered accordingly.

Alderman, J., filed opinion concurring in part and dissenting in part.

1. Injunction ⟐131

In proceeding to enjoin alleged unauthorized practice of law, referee's findings must be approved unless they are erroneous or wholly lacking in evidentiary support.

2. Attorney and Client ⟐11(3)
Constitutional Law ⟐90.1(1), 230.3(9)
Injunction ⟐89(5)

Nonlawyer's preparing papers considered by her necessary for filing and securing dissolution of marriage, and holding conferences with and asking questions of her customers in connection therewith, constituted unauthorized practice of law and would be enjoined despite contention that such result violated First Amendment by restricting her right to disseminate and right of her customers to receive information and would deprive indigent citizens of equal protection. West's F.S.A.Const. art. 5, § 15; 32 West's F.S.A. Integration Rule of the Florida Bar, art. 16, subd. I et seq.; U.S.C.A.Const. Amend. 1.

Bernard H. Dempsey, Jr., Chairman, Standing Committee on Unauthorized Practice of Law, Orlando, Lacy Mahon, Jr., Bar Counsel, Jacksonville, and H. Glenn Boggs, II and John A. Weiss, Asst. Staff Counsels, Tallahassee, for petitioner.

FIGURE 2-1a

Albert J. Hadeed, Southern Legal Counsel, Inc., Gainesville, and Alan B. Morrison, pro hac vice, Washington, D. C., for respondent.

William H. Adams, III, Jacksonville, for amicus curiae.

PER CURIAM.

The Florida Bar has petitioned this Court to enjoin Rosemary W. Furman, d/b/a Northside Secretarial Service, from unauthorized practice of law in the State of Florida. Our jurisdiction to rule in this matter is provided by article V, section 15 of the Florida Constitution and by The Florida Bar Integration Rule, article XVI. We find the activities of the respondent to constitute the practice of law and permanently enjoin her from the further unauthorized practice of law.

The Florida Bar alleged, through an amended petition dated September 23, 1977, that Furman, a non-lawyer, engaged in the unauthorized practice of law by giving legal advice and by rendering legal services in connection with marriage dissolutions and adoptions in the years 1976 and 1977. The bar specifically alleges that Furman performed legal services for at least seven customers by soliciting information from them and preparing pleadings in violation of Florida law. The bar further contends that through advertising in the *Jacksonville Journal*, a newspaper of general circulation, Furman held herself out to the public as having legal expertise in Florida family law and sold "do-it-yourself divorce kits." The bar does not contend that Furman held herself out to be a lawyer, that her customers suffered any harm as a result of the services rendered, or that she has failed to perform the services for which she was paid.

In describing her activities, Furman states that she does not give legal advice, that she does prepare pleadings that meet the desires of her clients, that she charges no more than $50 for her services, and that her assistance to customers is in aid of their obtaining self-representative relief from the courts. In general, the respondent alleges as a defense that the ruling of this court in *Florida Bar v. Brumbaugh*, 355 So.2d 1186 (Fla.1978), violates the first amendment to the United States Constitution by restricting her right to disseminate and the right of her customers to receive information which would allow indigent litigants access to the state's domestic relations courts. She alleges that our holding in *Brumbaugh* is so narrow that it deprives citizens who are indigent of equal protection of the laws as provided by the Florida and United States constitutions.

[1] When this case was at issue, we referred it to retired Circuit Judge P. B. Revels of the Seventh Judicial Circuit, one of Florida's most experienced trial judges, to serve as referee. The referee has filed his report which, in pertinent part, indicates:

A. That the Respondent, Rosemary W. Furman, d/b/a Northside Secretarial Service, is the sole proprietor and owner of said secretarial service. The Northside Secretarial Service has never registered under the fictitious name law.

B. Respondent has never received any legal training or education; is not now nor ever been a licensed attorney of law of the State of Florida or elsewhere; that she is not now and never has been a member of The Florida Bar.

•   •   •   •   •   •

D. That the Respondent under the guise of secretarial services for a fee prepares all papers considered by her to be necessary for the filing and securing a dissolution of marriage, as well as detailed instructions as to how the papers should be filed, service secured, hearings set and a briefing session as to the questions and answers to be offered at the trial of the case before the Court and for entry of Final Judgment of Dissolution.

E. The Respondent admitted, when a person comes to her place of business, they state they want to get a divorce or they want her to help them get a divorce, although many of the people deposed insisted that they only asked that she type

FIGURE 2-1b

papers to enable them to obtain the divorce. So after some discussion, the customer is provided with the appropriate intake sheet for the facts listed at the first visit—either Respondent's Exhibit 11 or 12. In addition to the intake sheet the Respondent furnishes papers outlining the legal steps, the law and the procedures, as shown by Respondent's Exhibits 13, 14 and 15, advising them to read the matter and it will help them in filling out the intake sheet.

F. The Respondent admits that the customer returns with the intake sheet not completed, because the people are unfamiliar with the legal terms and some are illiterate and, of course, she then proceeds to ask questions to complete the intake sheet for preparing the Petition for Dissolution of Marriage. Then after she types the Petition for Dissolution of Marriage, she advises the customer to take the papers for filing to the Office of the Clerk of Circuit Court, and Respondent follows the progress of the case every step of the way until it is at issue. She then notifies the customer to come in for a briefing session preferably the day before the date set for trial. In the course of briefing Respondent furnishes the customer with a diagram of the Court chambers and where to find the Judge to which that particular case has been assigned. A copy of the diagram of chambers that she furnishes to the customer is shown by Respondent's Exhibit 10. She also explains the full procedure that will take place before the Judge, including the questions the customer should ask the customer and the resident witness. A copy of same is shown by Respondent's Exhibit 20. The facts in the record of this case establish very clearly that the Respondent performs every essential step in the legal proceedings to obtain a dissolution of marriage, except taking the papers and filing them in the Clerk's office and going with the customer to the final hearing and interrogating the witness.

*   *   *   *   *   *

H. Respondent admitted that she could not follow the guidelines as set forth in the *Florida Bar v. Brumbaugh*, Supreme Court Opinion, for the reason that the customers who come to obtain her services are not capable for various and sundry reasons, mainly not being familiar with legal terminology or illiterate, and were unable to write out the necessary information. Therefore, she was compelled to ask questions and hold conferences with her customers.

I. Pre-trial Stipulation, Joint Evidentiary Exhibit 1, briefly enumerates the factual situation in each of the cases which I believe I can state the substance of the Stipulation, even though there are some varying circumstances in each case, for the purpose of my findings without quoting the Stipulation in full. The cases involved were *Green vs Green, Ammons vs Ammons, Kirkby-Petition for Adoption, Howland vs Howland, Mayden vs Mayden, Holmes vs Holmes,* and *Touchton vs Touchton.* The substance of this Stipulation is as follows:

The factual information contained in the pleadings was obtained by Respondent from the customer as a result of oral questions asked by Respondent and answered by the customer, which information was written upon Respondent's standardized intake sheet. Respondent by both oral and written instructions informed the customer as to the procedures to be followed in filing the pleadings and in processing the same to final hearing. Respondent specifically informed customers that she was not an attorney nor licensed to practice law in the State of Florida and at no time did the customers believe that the Respondent was an attorney or licensed to practice law. In paragraphs 16 and 17 of said stipulation the parties agreed that the customers did not think or know that they had suffered any damage as a result of Respondent's services; that they did not think that the Respondent gave them legal advice or engaged in legal counseling.

The referee made the following findings:

1. The foregoing facts show by a great weight of the evidence, Rosemary

FIGURE 2-1c

W. Furman, shielded behind the cloak of Northside Secretarial Service, has been engaged in the unauthorized practice of law for approximately three years.

2. That the Opinion in *Florida Bar v. Brumbaugh* is being interpreted by many as a license to individuals, who are trained and experienced in secretarial work, to practice law. This creates a grave danger to the citizens of Florida.

•   •   •   •   •   •   •

11. Rosemary W. Furman should be adjudged guilty of contempt of the Supreme Court of Florida, and permanently enjoined from engaging or pursuing any course of action personally or in her secretarial service that touches or resembles in any way the practice of law. She should be prohibited from typing legal papers of any kind, filling blanks on any legal forms, or giving oral or written advice or directions. The fact she is an expert stenographer does not give her any legal right to engage in divorce and adoption practice anymore than a nurse has the right to set up an office for performing tonsillectomy or appendectomy operations or a dental assistant to do extractions or fill teeth.

The referee's findings must be approved unless they are erroneous or wholly lacking in evidentiary support. *Florida Bar v. Wagner*, 212 So.2d 770 (Fla.1968).

We do not write on a clean slate in this case. Last year we took the opportunity to clearly define to non-lawyers the proper realm in which they could operate without engaging in the unauthorized practice of law. In *Brumbaugh*, we clearly stated what services a similar secretarial business could lawfully perform. We said:

We hold that Ms. Brumbaugh, and others in similar situations, may sell printed material purporting to explain legal practice and procedure to the public in general and she may sell sample legal forms. To this extent we limit our prior holdings in *Stupica* and *American Legal and Business Forms, Inc.* Further, we hold that it is not improper for Marilyn Brumbaugh to engage in a secretarial service, typing

such forms for her clients, provided that she only copy the information given to her in writing by her clients. In addition, Ms. Brumbaugh may advertise her business activities of providing secretarial and notary services and selling legal forms and general printed information. However, Marilyn Brumbaugh must not, in conjunction with her business, engage in advising clients as to the various remedies available to them, or otherwise assist them in preparing those forms necessary for a dissolution proceeding. More specifically, Marilyn Brumbaugh may not make inquiries nor answer questions from her clients as to the particular forms which might be necessary, how best to fill out such forms, where to properly file such forms, and how to present necessary evidence at the court hearings. Our specific holding with regard to the dissolution of marriage also applies to other unauthorized legal assistance such as the preparation of wills or real estate transaction documents. While Marilyn Brumbaugh may legally sell forms in these areas, and type up instruments which have been completed by clients, she must not engage in personal legal assistance in conjunction with her business activities, including the correction of errors and omissions.

355 So.2d at 1194.

Our directions could not have been clearer.

[2] Before the referee and before this court, Furman admitted that she did not abide by the dictates of *Brumbaugh*. She says that it is impossible for her to operate her "do-it-yourself divorce kit" business in compliance with this court's ruling in that case. The bar alleges that Furman has engaged in the unauthorized practice of law as previously defined by this court. The referee so found. She so admits. We believe the referee's findings are supported by the evidence.

In other portions of the referee's report, he urges that as part of our disposition in this case we require the bar to conduct a

FIGURE 2-1d

study to determine how to provide effective legal services to the indigent. Without question, it is our responsibility to promote the full availability of legal services. We deem it more appropriate, however, to address this issue in a separate proceeding. By doing so under our supervisory power, we insure a thorough consideration of the overall problem without delaying the present adjudication.

Devising means for providing effective legal services to the indigent and poor is a continuing problem. The Florida Bar has addressed this subject with some success. In spite of the laudable efforts by the bar, however, this record suggests that even more attention needs to be given to this subject.

Therefore, we direct The Florida Bar to begin immediately a study to determine better ways and means of providing legal services to the indigent. We further direct that a report on the findings and conclusions from this study be prepared and filed with this court on or before January 1, 1980, at which time we will examine the problem and consider solutions.

Accordingly, we find that Rosemary Furman, d/b/a Northside Secretarial Service, has been guilty of the unauthorized practice of law by virtue of the activities recited herein and she is hereby permanently enjoined and restrained from further engaging in the unauthorized practice of law in the State of Florida.

It is so ordered.

ENGLAND, C. J., and ADKINS, BOYD, OVERTON, SUNDBERG, HATCHETT and ALDERMAN, JJ., concur.

ALDERMAN, J., Concurring in part, dissenting in part.

I concur in the revision of the original opinion, but I would also tax the costs of this proceeding against the respondent, Rosemary W. Furman.

The Florida Bar properly brought to the attention of this Court the respondent's unlawful activity. As a result, the respondent has been found guilty of the unauthorized practice of law. There has been no wrongdoing on the part of the Bar. The culprit in this case is Rosemary W. Furman. If she had not violated the law, it would not have been necessary for The Florida Bar to bring this action. The respondent is the guilty party, and she is the one who should pay the costs that were necessarily incurred by The Florida Bar to stop her illegal activity.

Edward J. BROWN, Petitioner,

v.

STATE of Florida, Respondent.

No. 53782.

Supreme Court of Florida.

June 14, 1979.

Rehearing Denied Nov. 27, 1979.

Defendant was convicted on a plea of nolo contendere in the Circuit Court, Dade County, Ellen Morphonios, J., of unlawful possession of marijuana, and he appealed. The District Court of Appeal, 355 So.2d 138, affirmed, and defendant filed petition for writ of certiorari. The Supreme Court, Sundberg, J., held that: (1) a plea of nolo contendere which is made subject to condition that defendant be allowed to file an appeal is permissible only when legal issue to be determined on appeal is dispositive of case, and (2) a confession may not be considered dispositive for purpose of applying rule.

Writ discharged; decision of District Court of Appeal approved, and cause remanded with directions.

Hatchett, J., dissented and filed opinion.

FIGURE 2-1e

SEC. 2-2
BRIEFING A CASE

A paralegal involved in research may be asked to "brief" cases. A brief is a short summary of a case with its primary points of law organized into a certain format. It is imperative that such a summary remain brief, since otherwise it would be just as easy for the attorney to read the entire case.

The format used in various classes or employment situations may differ, but whatever format is preferred by the employer or teacher is the one that should be used. It is likely to include a case name and citation, remedy, cause of action, facts, procedural history, issue, finding, and reason. While reading this section, it may be helpful to refer to the sample briefs in Sec. 2-3 following.

A. The Case Name and Citation

The *citation*, or location where the case may be found, must be included with the title of the case. The case name is usually centered at the top of the page, with the citation centered on the page directly below the name. In the following examples, citations will not appear under the titles of any cases when the written decisions are based upon fictitious circumstances and no actual decision exists.

B. The Remedy

The *remedy* is the type of recovery being sought by the plaintiff or petitioner and it often can be found in the first several lines of the decision.

1. Examples

Some typical examples of remedies are:

a. *Damages.*   A suit for *damages* is a suit asking for a monetary amount.

b. *Injunction.*   An *injunction* is a court order in equity directing one to refrain from performing a particular act. (See the first chapter of this book for a detailed discussion of equity.)

c. *An order of specific performance.*   An *order of specific performance* is a court order directing one to perform a particular act. Like an injunction, it is an equitable remedy.

2.   *The Need for Brevity*

When listing a remedy in a brief, it is generally not necessary to use full sentences such as "The Plaintiff is seeking damages in the amount of $23,500." Writing the word "damages" will suffice.

3.   *The Absence of a Remedy in Criminal Cases*

When the format for briefs used in this book is utilized, there is never any remedy per se in a criminal case since the state attorney or prosecutor is always seeking the same basic end result, which is the punishment of the defendant by fine, imprisonment, or other means. Since there is no remedy in these cases, one should leave out the whole category rather than write something such as "Remedy: none."

C.   *The Cause of Action*

The *cause of action* is the legal theory upon which the plaintiff or petitioner has based the original suit.

1.   *Examples*

The following are examples of causes of actions:

a. Negligence. This civil cause of action pertains to cases in which the defendant damaged the person or property of the plaintiff as a result of the defendant's failure to use the degree of care that would be exercised by a reasonable person under the circumstances. For example, careless driving that results in the personal injury of another could give rise to a negligence action.

b. Breach of contract. One can be sued for breach of a contract whether it is oral or written, or even when it is implied by the circumstances.

c. Defamation. There are two kinds of defamation: libel, which generally pertains to written disparagement, and slander, which concerns oral disparagement.

d. Infliction of mental distress. This is a recognized civil cause of action, and it may be either intentional, or negligent and unintentional.

e. False imprisonment. This civil cause of action pertains to the unintentional and unprivileged detention of an individual without his or her consent. *Un-*

privileged means that the defendant does not fall into the category of individuals, such as police officers and security guards, who have the right to detain others. *Detention* does not require that a person be physically imprisoned. Leaving him or her in a position with no means of escape is sufficient.

f. Any act constituting a crime.   In a criminal case, the crime (such as murder, rape, robbery, kidnapping, or grand larceny) is regarded as the cause of action under one method of briefing. The focus of the case may also be regarded as the cause of action when the crime itself is not central to the main legal point of the case. For example, *search and seizure* might be viewed as the cause of action if the main issue deals primarily with the limitations of a search regardless of whether a murder, narcotics violation, or other crime was involved.

2.   *The Need for Brevity*

As in the case of the remedy, the cause of action in a brief is not generally written in full sentences such as "The cause of action in this case is negligence." Writing a single word, like "negligence," is acceptable.

D.   *The Facts*

This section contains background information that formed the basis for the original suit or charge. Special care should be taken to avoid the use of an inappropriate number of facts or to refer to the parties with confusing names.

1.   *Avoidance of Excessive or Insufficient Facts*

The facts should be reduced to a minimum so that the benefit of briefing the case will not be lost. On the other hand, care should be taken to include necessary background information so that the reader can have the facts vital to an understanding of the case. All information needed to formulate the legal issue must be included.

2.   *Avoidance of Confusing Names*

Case decisions may refer to the parties involved by various names. It is always best to use the terms *plaintiff* or *defendant* in civil matters. In a criminal case, the government is referred to as the *state* or the *U.S.* While the terms *appellant* and *appellee* are certainly applicable and in common usage, they can be confusing in a brief when there have been several levels of appeals. The appellant is the party who files an appeal, while the appellee is the party against whom an appeal is taken. The appellant may or may not be the one who "lost" in the lower court, since the "winning" party may have appealed only one particular aspect of the case (such as the amount of damages). In order to avoid any confusion, it is best, therefore, to avoid the use of these terms altogether when writing a brief.

Regardless of whether there have been counterclaims made by the defendant against the plaintiff after the case has been filed, the plaintiff can always be identified as the one who filed suit. In criminal cases, the defendant is the party charged with the crime, while generally the other party will be either the U.S. or the state.

E.   *The Procedural History*

This should include the outcome of lower court proceedings as well as the results of any appellate proceedings that have occurred prior to the present hearing of the case. It should also include any other critical procedural matters that may form the basis for the present appeal (such as a denial of a key motion). The purpose of this section is to tell how the case came before the present court.

F.   *The Issue*

The *issue* is the main legal question in the case. It is always stated either in the form of a question or in the form of a clause beginning with the word "whether." Often, a particular sentence in the decision can be reworded into the form of a question and stated as the issue. On the other hand, the issue can sometimes be formulated only by using totally original language that takes into account all aspects of the case.

1.   *Caution with Regard to "Given Issues"*

Sometimes a decision includes a statement that "The issue in this case is ..." One should be cautious of such statements, since they may pertain to procedural matters when one is attempting to focus on substantive issues, or vice versa. (See Sec. 2-2, subsection F.2.a.) Furthermore, the question may not be formulated for general applicability (see Sec. 2-2, subsection F.2.b), or it may be in the form of an open-ended question (see Sec. 2-2, subsection F.2.c).

2. *Key Questions to Consider When Formulating an Issue*

a. Are both procedural and substantive issues to be examined? Procedural issues are so labeled because they deal only with procedure and the manner in which a case is handled by the judicial system. One example is a question such as "Did the defendant answer the plaintiff's complaint within the allotted 20-day time period if the answer was mailed and postmarked within that period?" Other questions are known as substantive issues because they deal with the actual substance of legal rights. They often address certain aspects of the cause of action. In an assault case, an example of a substantive issue might be "Can an assault be committed against another without actual physical contact?" If an attorney is asking the paralegal to brief a number of cases dealing with the elements of assault, the attorney is clearly looking for the substantive issues in the cases. If it is unclear whether the substantive or procedural issues are to be examined, the paralegal should check with the person requesting the briefs.

b. Will the answer to the issue have applicability to future cases? Issues such as "Was the defendant guilty?" or "Was the defendant negligent?" are poor because the answer to these questions only tells the reader of the outcome in this one particular case. A question like "Did Sam Smith hit John Jones with the pipe?" is also inadequate for the same reason. If one has difficulty eliminating the names of individual parties from the issue, then the issue has probably been incorrectly framed.

c. Does the question call for a "yes or no" answer? While others might disagree, the author believes that it is useful to frame the issue in the form of a "yes or no" question to avoid problems associated with open-ended issues. For example, if one poses a question such as "Under what circumstances does one have the right to conduct a warrantless search of a person's home?", the answer to this issue might require hundreds of pages and would, therefore, be of no value to the one requesting the brief. Compare, however, the following question: "Do policemen without warrants have the right to seize property inside a person's home when they are in hot pursuit of an owner who has apparently committed a crime and is apparently about to destroy evidence of that crime?" A simple "yes or no" answer to this question establishes exact circumstances under which such a seizure may be justified.

G. *The Finding*

The *finding* is the decision that the court rendered in the case being briefed. If one of the parties won the case outright, all that is necessary for this section is an identification of the prevailing party. If the court grants a judgment in favor of one of the parties, but it renders specific instructions with regard to the future disposition of the case, those instructions may have to be included. For example, if the appellate court *remands* the case and thereby orders the case to be returned to a lower court for further action in accordance with the appellate decision, that fact should be noted in the brief.

H.   The Reason

In this section, the person briefing the case explains why the court reached its conclusion. Generally, this should require only a few sentences.

SEC. 2-3
EXAMPLES OF BRIEFS

Below are three cases each of which is followed by a brief. The first is the fictitious civil case of *Smith v. Jones,* which will be followed in Sec. 2-3, subsections A.1 and A.2, respectively, by a sample brief of the case and comments concerning that brief. The cases in subsections B and C are from actual appellate decisions.

The cases found in this section and in the review questions have been created in shortened form to simplify analysis and briefing. Cases that are considerably longer should be anticipated by the legal assistant during actual paralegal practice.

A.   Smith v. Jones

Smith v. Jones

This was a suit for damages by Samuel Smith against Arthur Jones for trespass to land. The lower court record reflects that the underlying circumstances were essentially undisputed by the parties.

The appellant and the appellee own adjoining parcels of real estate and have been neighbors for more than 18 years. On or about January 21, 1996, the appellee began the construction of a stone wall that was to run along the boundary line between the property of the two parties. During the three-day period that it took to complete the wall, the appellee and his assistants worked on the appellant's side of the boundary line even though the appellant repeatedly requested that the appellee and his workers refrain from doing so. The appellant even threatened one of appellee's workers with a baseball bat, but the workers ignored him.

The lower court dismissed the appellant's complaint for damages and discharged the jury on the basis that no evidence had been introduced to show that damage had been done to the property and that a suit for trespass would, therefore, not lie. The First District Court of Appeals affirmed the ruling of the lower court and the appellant now brings the matter before the present body.

SLEEPER, J.

The lower court was clearly in error in ruling that a case for trespass to land did not exist as a matter of law. If the presence of the workers on the property of the appellant was unauthorized, an action for trespass would exist whether damage to the property was or was not proven. The degree of injury to the property only bears on the issue of damages and there was, therefore, no justification for dismissal of the complaint. The law will assume at least some minimal degree of damage by the mere fact of unauthorized entry.

The judgment is reversed and a new trial is ordered.

1. The Brief

Smith v. Jones
Remedy: damages

C/A: trespass to land

Facts: The plaintiff and the defendant owned adjoining parcels of real estate. The defendant and his workers repeatedly entered the property of the plaintiff during the construction of a wall on the boundary line between the two properties despite the plaintiff's objections.

Proc.: The lower court dismissed the complaint, and the dismissal was upheld by the First District Court of Appeals.

Issue: Is it necessary to prove property damage in order to establish a case of trespass to land?

Finding: Plaintiff. Reversed and new trial ordered.

Reason: The degree of injury to the property only bears on the amount of damages to which the petitioner may be entitled. It is not relevant in determining whether a legally prohibited trespass took place.

2. Comments Concerning the Brief

a. An orderly format. The order of the categories and the overall appearance of the brief are very important. The categories should be easily differentiated and the material for each category should be set out separately. If the content is obscured by the format, the brief will not be useful to the attorney.

b. The identification of the plaintiff and the defendant.   Since the case involves trespass, the owner of the property on which the trespass took place is the plaintiff. He is referred to as the appellant in the fourth line of the decision and is also implicitly identified as the plaintiff at the beginning of the third paragraph where it states that the appellant filed the suit. The other party is, therefore, the appellee/defendant.

c. The identification of the remedy and cause of action.   Both the remedy and the cause of action are identified in the first sentence of the case.

d. The framing of the issue for general applicability.   Because the issue in this case has been framed properly, the answer to the issue in this brief will clearly have relevance to future cases dealing with the general subject matter of trespass.

e. Focus on the primary issue.   Unlike the present case, some cases may have more than one issue. In general, however, only the primary relevant issues should be listed in the brief. If one is briefing a case involving burglary, arson, and false imprisonment charges, and the employer is requesting the brief in connection with a burglary case, it should be evident that the burglary issue should be regarded as the primary one.

f. Avoidance of unaddressed causes of action.   In the above case, we are told that the appellant threatened one of the workers with a baseball bat. While it is possible that assault charges against the appellant might be appropriate, the present case does not address that particular question, and it is, therefore, not pertinent to the primary issue in this case.

B.   State v. Gleason[2]

State v. Gleason
431 N.W.2d 363 (Iowa 1988)

JORDAN-MAYS, J.
… In January 1986 Patricia Schuler, who was living with Gleason, reported to the Waterloo, Iowa police that he had assaulted her and that he had been involved in a number of recent thefts. The police then obtained a search warrant for Gleason's residence, but before they could execute it on January 10, they received a call from Gleason. In the course of this conversation, Gleason was advised the search warrant had been issued and was requested to meet the officers at his residence so it could be served on him. He agreed to meet them there. When Gleason had not arrived at the residence within an hour, the officers served the search warrant on his father, who owned the house. While the officers were conducting the search, Gleason telephoned the residence. He was again requested to meet the officers there, but he declined to do so, stating he

would come to the police station the next day, a Saturday. The officers then informed him he should wait until the beginning of the next week, as the investigating officers would not be in on the weekend.

Saturday morning, January 11, 1986, Gleason telephoned the police station to ascertain whether a warrant had been issued for his arrest. He was informed a warrant had not yet been issued, but that he would probably be arrested when he came to the police station. Gleason then indicated he would wait until Monday morning to turn himself in, since he did not want to spend the weekend in jail. In truth, Gleason left for Colorado that weekend. A warrant for his arrest was ultimately issued on January 29, 1986. Gleason was apprehended in Arvada, Colorado on May 17,1986.

Gleason was thereafter convicted of violating IOWA CODE § 719.4(4) (1985), which provides:

> A person who flees from the state to avoid prosecution for a public offense which is a felony or aggravated misdemeanor commits a class "D" felony.

Gleason, noting chapter 719 does not provide a definition for the term "prosecution," asserts the general definition found in § 801.4(12) applies. This section provides:

> "Prosecution" means the commencement, including the filing of a complaint, and continuance of a criminal proceeding, and pursuit of that proceeding to final judgment on behalf of the state or other political subdivision.

[IOWA CODE § 801.4(12) (1985)] It is Gleason's contention that application of this definition to § 719.4(4) requires the State to prove, as an element of unlawful flight to avoid prosecution, that a prosecution of the underlying offense had commenced by the time the defendant left Iowa ...

Although we agree the definition of "prosecution" in § 801.4(12) applies to § 719.4(4), we are not persuaded its application has the effect Gleason suggests. In our view, it is quite possible to avoid "the commencement ... and continuance of a criminal proceeding" (to use the language of § 801.4(12)) before filing a criminal complaint ...

The words used in a statute should be given their ordinary meaning, absent a legislative definition or a particular and appropriate meaning in law. *State v. Bessenecker,* 404 N.W.2d 134, 136 (Iowa 1987); *State v. Bartusek,* 383 N.W.2d 582, 583 (Iowa 1986). The statute prohibits an otherwise lawful act, leaving the state, when that act is performed for an unlawful purpose to avoid prosecution ... Thus, one form of unlawful flight would be that which was to prevent even the occurrence of prosecution. By definition, this type of flight would occur in the absence of any previously filed criminal complaint.

Identical language in the federal unlawful flight statute has been similarly construed: "The words 'to avoid a *pending* prosecution.'" *United States v. Bando,* 244 F.2d 833 (2d Cir. 1957). Thus, the scope of the federal statute is not limited to cases where the offender's crossing of the state border is delayed until after the offended state has commenced a prosecution. *Lupino v. United States,* 268 F.2d 799, 801 (8th Cir. 1959); *Bando,* 244 F.2d at 843; *Miller,* 76 N.M. at 66–67, 412 P.2d at 243.

We conclude the reasonable interpretation of § 719.4(4) is that it does not require the State to prove a prosecution had commenced before the defendant fled Iowa. Adoption of Gleason's contrary interpretation would allow the validity of an unlawful flight charge to depend on whether the prosecutor could race to the courthouse to file a formal complaint faster than the accused could exit the state with knowledge of its filing. The main purpose of § 719.4(4) is to encourage the accused to remain in the state by exacting a penalty for leaving to avoid prosecution. Clearly this purpose would be thwarted by an interpretation which actually provided an incentive to flee as soon as possible ...

AFFIRMED ...

1.   *The Brief*

State v. Gleason
431 N.W.2d 363 (Iowa 1988)

C/A: unlawful flight to avoid prosecution

Facts: Patricia Schuler, who was living with the defendant, notified the police that she had been assaulted by the defendant and that the defendant had been involved in a number of recent thefts. The defendant left the state at a time when he knew that no arrest warrant had been issued, but that one was going to be served on him within the next few days. He was subsequently arrested in Colorado and returned for trial in Iowa.

Proc.:   The defendant was convicted in the District Court and his appeal in this case was heard before the Iowa Supreme Court.

Issue: Must the state prove that a prosecution had commenced prior to the time when the accused left the state before it can establish a case of unlawful flight to avoid prosecution under Iowa Code § 719.4(4) (1985)?

Finding: State; affirmed.

Reason: The state need not prove that a prosecution had commenced prior to the time when the accused left the state before it can establish a case of unlawful flight to avoid prosecution under Iowa Code § 719.4(4) (1985). To hold otherwise would mean that the legitimacy of the charge would depend upon whether the prosecutor could file a formal complaint faster than the accused could leave the state with knowledge of its filing.

C. *Townes v. State*[3]

Townes v. State
314 Md. 71, 548 A.2d 832 (1988)

McAuliffe, Judge

In 1980, Lewis Townes negotiated a plea agreement. In return for his plea of guilty to the second count of a two-count indictment, the State agreed to enter a *nolle prosequi*[4] as to the first count, as well as to related charges in separate indictments, and to recommend a suspended sentence with probation. A judge of the Circuit Court for Baltimore City accepted the plea and the recommendation, and suspended the execution of a three and one-half year sentence upon condition of a three-year probation. Within 18 months, Townes was thrice haled into court on charges of violation of probation. On each of those occasions the court found a violation, but declined to strike the suspension of sentence. However, a fourth allegation of violation of probation followed and, after finding a violation had been proven, the trial judge struck the suspension and sentenced Townes to serve two years of the original sentence.[5] Unhappy with this turn of events, Townes appealed to the Court of Special Appeals ... We issued a writ of certiorari before consideration of the appeal by the immediate court.

The facts underlying the charges against Townes are these. Townes learned that the owner of a 1975 Lincoln automobile was in arrears on his payments and wished to have the car "stolen" so that he could collect its fair market value from Government Employees Insurance Company (GEICO) pursuant to his insurance coverage for theft. Townes conspired with the owner and others to carry out this plan, and to thereby defraud GEICO. Additionally, Townes was to profit by dismantling the Lincoln and selling its various parts, with the assistance of the co-conspirators. Pursuant to the plan, the owner left the Lincoln in a designated parking lot from which it was taken by Townes. The owner reported the car stolen and filed a claim with GEICO. Aided by a tip from an informant, the Baltimore City Police Department exposed the scheme and arrested the conspirators before GEICO made payment. Various charges of conspiracy and theft were brought against Townes in four indictments. In the indictment with which we are concerned, the first count charged conspiracy to obtain money from GEICO by false pretenses, and the second count, to which Townes pled guilty, charged conspiracy to *attempt* to obtain money from GEICO by false pretenses …

Townes argues that people ordinarily do not conspire merely to attempt to commit a crime, and therefore the law does not recognize as a crime a conspiracy to attempt to commit a criminal offense. In addressing the related question of whether there may be an attempt to attempt a crime, the Supreme Court of Colorado cogently stated the rationale underlying Townes' argument:

> Perhaps philosophers or metaphysicians can intend to attempt to act, but ordinary people intend to act, not to attempt to act. *Allen v. People,* 175 Colo. 113, 485 P.2d 886, 888 (1971).

We had occasion to outline the elements and characteristics of the crime of conspiracy in *Mason v. State,* 302 Md. 434, 444–45, 488 A.2d 955 (1985). A criminal conspiracy consists of the combination of two or more persons to accomplish some unlawful purpose, or to accomplish a lawful purpose by unlawful means. The essence of a criminal conspiracy is an unlawful agreement. The agreement need not be formal or spoken, provided there is a meeting of the minds reflecting a unity of purpose and design. In Maryland, the crime is complete when the unlawful agreement is reached, and no overt act in furtherance of the agreement need be shown.

A conspiracy to commit a crime exists as an offense separate and distinct from the substantive crime that is the object of the conspiracy …

An attempt to commit a crime is, in itself, a crime. A person is guilty of an attempt when, with intent to commit a crime, he engages in conduct which constitutes a substantial step toward the commission of that crime whether or not his intention is accomplished. *Cox v. State,* 311 Md. 326, 329–31,534 A.2d 1333 (1988); *Young v. State,* 303 Md. 298, 311, 493 A.2d 352 (1985) …

Townes' argument is … that persons who conspire to commit a crime intend to complete that crime, and not to stop short of completion. Therefore, he argues, it is logically inconsistent to charge one with conspiracy merely to attempt a crime.

Townes' argument fails to take into consideration an established principle of Maryland law. In this State, unlike a minority of other states, failure to consummate the intended crime is *not* an essential element of an attempt. *Young v. State, supra,* 303 Md. at 302, 493 A.2d 352 (1985); *Lightfoot v. State,* 278 Md. 231, 237–38, 360 A.2d 426 (1976).

The logical inconsistency postulated by Townes simply does not exist in this State. A person intending to commit a crime intends also to attempt to commit that crime. The intent to attempt is viewed as correlative to and included within the intent to consummate. Accordingly, one who conspires to commit a crime concurrently conspires to attempt to commit that crime. Judgment affirmed; costs to be paid by appellant.

1.   *The Brief*

Townes v. State
314 Md. 71, 548 A.2d 832 (1988)

C/A: conspiracy to obtain, and conspiracy to attempt to obtain money from an insurer by false pretenses

Facts: The defendant, Townes, agreed with another individual that he, Townes, would "steal" the other person's car so that the other person could make a claim against the insurer of the vehicle. Aided by a tip from an informant, the police arrested both parties before the insurer made payment.

Proc.:   The defendant was convicted in the Circuit Court of Baltimore City. When a suspended sentence was stricken, the defendant appealed to the Court of Special Appeals and a *writ of certiorari*[6] was issued.

Issue: 1. When two or more parties agree to commit a crime, must there be an overt act in furtherance of the agreement in order to prove a conspiracy under Maryland law?

2. Can one be held responsible under Maryland law for conspiring to *attempt* to commit a crime?

Finding: State; costs to be paid by the defendant

Reason: 1. A conspiracy requires an agreement by two or more parties to commit a crime, and no act in furtherance of the agreement need be shown. It is the agreement itself that constitutes the conspiracy.

2. One can be held responsible under Maryland law for conspiring to attempt to commit a crime. An attempt to commit a crime is itself a crime. If a conspiracy involves an agreement to commit a crime, and an attempt may itself constitute a crime, then it follows that one can be guilty of conspiring to attempt to commit a crime.

REVIEW QUESTIONS

Note: With the exception of the last case, all of the following cases, along with their case citations and statutory references, are fictitious, and they are used for illustrative purposes only. Furthermore, the student should note that the following cases are condensed and are considerably shorter than most appellate decisions. Some cases are preceded by information that may be helpful in understanding the court's decision, and any such information should be read prior to reading the case itself.

1. Please brief the following case:

Hargrave v. Brock

WELCH, J.

Hargrave filed this false imprisonment case against Brock for damages. The circumstances that originally resulted in this case being brought before the Superior Court are as follows:

In March of 1996, Hargrave and Brock arranged to go out on a deep sea fishing trip for purely recreational purposes. Although the trip was originally canceled due to inclement weather, the two parties ultimately made the trip in April of 1996. They chose to rent a rowboat that was owned by the Surf and Sand Corporation of Newport, Rhode Island. While the record is somewhat unclear as to exactly what happened next, it appears that Brock had arranged to have a motorboat drive by and pick him up—and leave Hargrave stranded. Brock not only jumped into the water and boarded the other boat, but he also threw the oars to the rowboat into the water so that Hargrave could not control the rowboat. Furthermore, Hargrave could not swim, and Brock was aware of that fact. Brock left Hargrave more than 25 miles from shore in the rowboat without oars. Hargrave was eventually rescued by the Coast Guard 14 hours later.

While Hargrave sued Brock on various grounds, it is his claim against the defendant for false imprisonment that is the subject of this appeal. Hargrave won a judgment against Brock in the amount of $110,000, and Brock has now appealed his case to the present court.

It is Brock's contention that Hargrave was in no way "imprisoned" and that Brock should therefore have prevailed as a matter of law. In any false imprisonment case, the plaintiff must prove an intentional, unprivileged detention without consent. In the present case, attorneys for Brock have focused on the element of detention and pointed out that no walls were used to prevent Hargrave's movement. This, however, misses the point. The essence of this kind of case is a prevention of freedom of movement. This court has ruled in the past on numerous occasions that this cause of action can exist wherever freedom of movement is restricted. It is not necessary to show that the defendant used walls to prevent that freedom of movement.

Affirmed.

HARVEY and **HOXIE, JJ.** concur.

2. Please brief the following case:

Collings v. Wentworth

JESSICA, J.

In this case, the appellant is seeking an order of specific performance for the purpose of compelling the appellees to transfer title to their house in accordance with a contract signed on February 18, 1997.

Back in December of 1996, the appellees placed their house on the market and hired a real estate agent to find a buyer for them. While they had several likely prospects in the first several weeks, no offers were made until February of 1997. At that time, the appellant presented a written contract to the appellees for a prospective purchase price of $92,500 and told them that they would have a definite deal if they would simply sign the document and return it to him. On February 18, the appellees signed the contract upon the receipt of a $6,000 deposit. The deposit was held by the real estate agent.

On February 24, the appellees notified the appellant that they had changed their minds and that they no longer intended to sell the property. They indicated to the appellant that they would direct the real estate agent to release the $6,000 deposit. The appellant said that the return of his deposit was not sufficient and that, if necessary, he would file suit in court in order to compel the appellees to abide by the terms of the contract. When the parties came to an impasse with regard to the conflict, the appellant filed suit in Carson County Circuit Court for breach of contract in order to obtain an order of specific performance to transfer title. The District Court of Appeals reversed the decision. The case has now reached the present court for consideration.

In any case in which one of the parties is seeking an order of specific performance, the petitioner must show that the property that is the subject of the potential order must be unique. The appellees contend that there are literally hundreds of other pieces of property of the same size and shape within the very same development and that the appellant therefore cannot establish the requisite uniqueness of the property. This argument, however, overlooks one very important factor. Every piece of real estate is by definition unique, because every piece of land has a unique location. It would be improper for the appellate court to force upon the appellant a different piece of property when the appellant entered into a contract for the very purpose of acquiring the land in question. In light of this fact, orders of specific performance in these kinds of cases will always be appropriate.

Judgment for the appellant. The District Court of Appeals decision is reversed.

WATKINS and **HORNUNG, JJ.** concur.

3. Please brief the following case:

State v. Rockhold

KRANNERT, J.

This is a criminal action in which the defendant is being charged with robbery. The facts of the case are as follows. On or about September 23, 1997, John Patterson, Philip Benjamin, and Peter Marlowe were engaged in a poker game at the Seabreeze Hotel just outside Mellon Beach. Robert Rockhold broke the lock and burst into the room while brandishing a sawed-off shotgun. The three card players were forced to stand facing the wall while Rockhold stole the $2,356.71 that was on the table. Rockhold threatened to come back and kill them if any one of them called the police. He then proceeded to the parking lot where he escaped in his blue 1995 Cadillac. Three hours later, he was apprehended by the police. Rockhold was subsequently identified by all three victims. The minimum sentence for robbery in this state is three years. Rockhold was tried in Circuit Court, convicted, and sentenced to nine years in jail, or the minimum of three years for robbing each of the three victims. The case now comes before this court on appeal.

It is the contention of the attorney for the defendant that it was improper to sentence the defendant to any more than one three-year term since only one act of robbery occurred. With this contention we cannot agree. When sentences are handed down by the court for defendants charged with multiple counts of criminal law violations, it is within the discretion of the court to decide whether the sentences should run consecutively or concurrently. The attorneys for the defendant never questioned the right of the court to sentence their client to consecutive sentences. They are contending, however, that such sentencing would be improper in this case because the defendant really committed only one crime at one moment in time against three different victims. They argue that a single act of robbery occurred in this case and that the defendant should only be subject to a single minimum three-year penalty. This court simply cannot accept this argument. If there were ten victims, the court would be justified in sentencing the defendant to the three-year minimum for each one of the ten victims. If the defendant chose to rob all of the victims in the room, the court has the right to render a separate sentence against the defendant for each act of robbery, and the three-year minimum sentence can run consecutively for each one.

Affirmed.

GATES and HARTFIELD, JJ. concur.

4. Please brief the following case:

Peterson v. Jungclaus

DONOVAN, J.

Susan Peterson was a 21-year-old student at Fairlane College who lived most of her life on her family farm in Minnesota. Although she was a dean's list student during her first year, her academic performance declined after she became deeply involved in an international religious cult organization known as The Source. Near the end of her junior year, her parents became alarmed by the changes in Susan's physical and mental well-being and concluded that she had been "reduced to a situation of psychological bondage by The Source." They sought help from Kathy Mills, a self-styled "deprogrammer" of minds brainwashed by cults.

On May 24, 1996, Norman Jungclaus, Susan's stepfather, picked up Susan from Fairlane State. Instead of returning home, they went to the residence of Kathy Mills, where Ms. Mills attempted to deprogram Susan. While Susan was skeptical, she willingly consented to the stay at the Mills residence. For the first few days of her stay, Kathy was unwilling to discuss her involvement with The Source, but she was friendly and communicative with her father. Susan also went roller skating and played softball at a nearby park over the following weekend. During the next week, she spoke daily by telephone with her fiance, a member of The Source, who begged her to return to the cult. Susan expressed the desire to get her fiance out of the organization, but a meeting between them could not be arranged outside the presence of The Source. After nearly 16 days of "deprogramming," Susan left the Mills residence and returned to her fiance and The Source. Upon the direction of The Source, Susan brought this action for damages in the State Superior Court against her parents for the tort of false imprisonment. The defendant prevailed.

Judgment for Mr. and Mrs. Jungclaus. The key to this decision rests on the fact that Susan willingly remained in the company of her parents during her 16-day visit. She also had several reasonable and safe opportunities to escape while playing softball or while roller skating. Under such circumstances, Susan agreed to the restrictions placed upon her, and the suit for false imprisonment must therefore inevitably fail.

Affirmed.

GONZALEZ and **O'DONALD, JJ.** concur.

5. Please brief the following case:

Katko v. Briney

BRINDELL, J.

Briney owned a large farm on which was located an abandoned farmhouse. For a ten-year period the house had been the subject of several trespasses and burglaries. In an attempt to stop the intrusions, Briney boarded up the windows and doors and posted "no trespassing" signs. After one break-in, however, Briney set a spring gun in a bedroom. It was placed over the bedroom window so that the gun could not be seen from outside. No warning of its presence was posted. The gun was set to hit an intruder in the legs. Briney loaded the gun with a live shell, but he claimed that he did not intend to injure anyone.

Katko and a friend of his, McDonough, had broken into the abandoned farmhouse on an earlier occasion to steal old bottles and fruit jars for their antique collection. On the night of October 12, 1997, they returned for a second time after the spring gun had been set, and Katko was seriously wounded in the leg when the gun discharged as he entered the bedroom. He then brought this action for battery, and claimed damages in the amount of $17,000. He won in the Circuit Court, but the defendant appealed.

Judgment for Katko. Katko and McDonough committed a felony when they broke into and entered Briney's farmhouse. Although Briney is privileged to use reasonable force in the protection of his property, he could not use such means of force as would take human life or inflict great bodily injury. The use of a spring gun constitutes such force. Its use would be justifiable only if the trespasser was committing a felony of violence, a felony punishable by death, or any act endangering human life. In other cases, such as that of Katko's theft in an abandoned farmhouse, the law places a higher value on human safety than upon mere property rights. As such, Briney's use of a spring gun constituted excessive force in the defense of property and was not justifiable.

Affirmed.

MARCOS and SCHWEIDER, JJ. concur.

6. Please brief the following case. Information helpful for briefing the case includes the following:

    a. Contributory negligence and comparative negligence are defenses that can be raised by the defendant in a negligence case.

    b. From a reading of the case, it should also be evident that no state can have both defenses since they would lead the court to contrary results.

Sarbanes v. Arcuro

CZERNY, J.

Sarbanes filed this present negligence action against Arcuro for damages. The circumstances that originally resulted in this case being brought before the Circuit Court are as follows:

Sarbanes was driving his red Saturn eastbound on Chester Road as he approached the intersection of Chester Road and Wildwood Drive. Arcuro was driving northbound on Wildwood in his new Buick Regal. There was a traffic light at the intersection, and it showed a red light for Arcuro and a green light for Sarbanes. Arcuro went through the red light without even slowing down and was hit broadside by Sarbanes. Sarbanes, however, had approached the intersection at more than 55 miles per hour in what was a 25 mile-per-hour zone. In the Circuit Court, a judgment was rendered in favor of the plaintiff in the amount of $85,000. Arcuro then appealed to this court.

It is necessary for us to determine whether it is proper for Sarbanes to recover damages when Sarbanes was to some degree negligent himself. In the past, courts in this state have ruled that if the plaintiff was at all negligent, the plaintiff could recover nothing. This has proven to lead to some rather harsh results. For example, a blind application of this doctrine would deny recovery to a plaintiff who was only 5 percent responsible for the injuries sustained even though the defendant bore 95 percent of the responsibility. In 1995, the Supreme Court of this state reconsidered this harsh doctrine in the case of *Rinaldi v. Patt* and other cases [citations omitted].

Since 1995 it has become firmly established in this state that the previous doctrine known as contributory negligence has been replaced by the more realistic concept of comparative negligence. The adoption of this concept is now in line with the position held by the vast majority of states. According to the recently adopted jury verdict form used in this state, the jury found that the total damages in this case were $100,000. They also found, according to that form, that the defendant was 85 percent responsible for the accident and the plaintiff was 15 percent responsible. The jury therefore concluded that damages should be awarded to the plaintiff in the amount of $85,000. The jury verdict form clearly shows that the current law was correctly applied in this case. The decision in this case is directly in keeping with the law adopted by *Rinaldi,* and there is no reason for this court to reconsider the issue or reiterate all of the various supporting reasons for that decision at this time.

Affirmed.

KOENIG and **FONG, JJ.** concur.

7. Please brief the following case:

State v. Cantor

CHRISTIE, C.J.

In the lower court, the appellant was prosecuted for violation of STATE STATUTE § 144.34, which states that "Anyone who commits an act of robbery shall be guilty of a third degree felony and shall be punishable by a maximum penalty of no more than a $5,000 fine or 5 years incarceration."

The essential facts of the case are not in dispute. On the night of February 16, 1997, the appellant entered the 7-11 on the corner of Hilton Drive and Farmouth Avenue in downtown Fairfield. He threatened the cashier with a handgun and demanded all the money in the cash register. There were 17 other people in the store, and the appellant demanded that everyone lie down on the floor with his or her face down. Furthermore, he said that anyone would be shot if he or she moved. Once the cash register was cleaned out, the appellant ran out of the store, jumped into a late model Chevrolet, and vanished. None of the people in the store was injured in any way, and he escaped from the store with approximately $975 in cash. The appellant managed to get about 10 miles away before he was apprehended by a police officer who had heard of the robbery on an all-points bulletin in his police car. Eleven of the people in the store subsequently identified the appellant in a line-up. The appellant was later convicted in District Court.

The attorney for the appellant contends for the purposes of argument that her client may have been guilty of larceny, but he was not guilty of robbery. She furthermore argues that since robbery is larceny with violence, and that since the appellant never actually injured the cashier, there is no criminal responsibility here. With this contention we cannot agree. One can be responsible for robbery if the state is able to prove that the wrongdoer actually committed an act of violence or placed the victim in apprehension of violence. When the appellant entered the store and waved the gun at the cashier, that act alone would create a reasonable apprehension of violence.

AFFIRMED.

MILLER and **SANDSTONE, JJ** concur.

8. Please brief the following case. Information helpful for briefing the case includes the following:

   a. An executor is sometimes referred to as a personal representative. The primary functions of a personal representative are to make an inventory of the estate assets, to pay creditors of the deceased, and to distribute the property and money of the deceased to the rightful beneficiaries.

   b. When a will has been *executed*, it has been signed by the maker as that person's last will and testament.

c. When a will is *probated,* the court accepts the will as the last will and testament of the deceased, and it appoints a personal representative to perform the tasks indicated above (among many others).

d. *Testamentary capacity* refers to an individual's mental capability to execute a will.

In re: the Estate of Bennington

MORRIS, C.J.

This is an appeal taken by Margaret Weathers, personal representative for the estate of Catherine Bennington, from an award of attorneys fees granted to Andrew Bennington. The facts giving rise to this appeal are as follows:

In the fall of 1994, Catherine Bennington executed a will that left $4,000 to the American Society for the Prevention of Cruelty to Animals, $7,000 to the American Cancer Society, and the remainder of the estate totaling almost $2,500,000 to Andrew Bennington, the son of Catherine Bennington.

In April of 1997, Catherine Bennington executed a second will leaving the entire estate to the American Cancer Society. Catherine Bennington died within six weeks of the signing of the second will.

When a probate of the estate was opened, Andrew Bennington challenged the validity of the 1997 will on the grounds that his mother, Catherine, lacked sufficient testamentary capacity to execute the will. He therefore maintained that the 1994 will was the last valid one executed by the deceased and that the earlier will should therefore be the proper subject of probate proceedings. Margaret Weathers, the personal representative for the estate, staunchly supported the validity of the 1997 will.

In January of 1998, a hearing was held before the Honorable Susan Mackey to determine the validity of the 1997 will. The probate court ruled that Catherine Bennington did in fact possess testamentary capacity at the time of the execution of that will, and that the 1997 will would be admitted to probate. One month later, Andrew Bennington petitioned the court to reimburse him for attorneys fees incurred in challenging the will. When the court granted Andrew Bennington's petition, the estate appealed, and that appeal is presently being heard by this court.

The probate court granted attorneys fees on the basis of STATE STATUTE § 744.23, which states that "... those who have the right and responsibility to defend a will on behalf of the estate, or those who challenge the validity of a will offered for probate, shall be allowed reasonable fees and expenses associated with such a right or responsibility." It is obvious from the case law of this jurisdiction that such a claim is not absolute or unqualified (see *In re: the Estate of Tyler, In re: the Estate of Kuchen,* and others [citations omitted]). The right to claim attorneys fees when challenging the validity of a will rests with the court, and the court's decision will depend on whether the court perceives that the petitioner was acting in good faith. In this case, the record supports a finding of good faith on the part of the petitioner.

This rule exists to encourage a legitimate search for the truth in probate proceedings when there are reasonable grounds for challenging or defending the will.

Affirmed.

Schotz and Cicchese, JJ. concur.

9. Please brief the following case. Information helpful for the briefing of the case includes the following:

a. A *grand jury* is a jury assembled for the purpose of hearing evidence and determining whether there is sufficient probable cause to formally charge or indict the accused (as opposed to determining the ultimate guilt or innocence of a defendant who has already been charged).

State v. Generis

Glenn, J.

In December of 1994, the Honorable James Kardin was appointed to investigate fraud, corruption, and patient abuse in connection with the state Medicaid program. A grand jury was formed, and the order creating it specifically directed the grand jury to "make inquiry to determine whether one or more crimes within the jurisdiction had been committed." In October of 1998, the grand jury subpoenaed records from Dr. Jonah Generis, a state Medicaid provider, and demanded that he produce certain specified documents pertaining to patient treatment for the period from July of 1996 through October of 1998. The parties agree that none of the material requested concerned the period prior to December of 1994. Dr. Generis refused to comply with the subpoena, and the court then issued an order to show cause why Dr. Generis should not be held in contempt of court.

At the hearing on the contempt citation, the attorneys for Dr. Generis indicated that their client refused to comply with the demand for production on the grounds that the demand was beyond the scope of the grand jury's authority. The basis for this contention was that the records requested dated from a time during which the grand jury had no authority. The court nevertheless found the doctor in contempt. This court, however, agrees with the contention of the doctor's attorneys, and this court is now lifting the contempt citation and quashing the subpoena.

Since a grand jury has no common-law power, its authority over specified matters can emanate from only two possible sources. One is the enabling statute that allows for the creation of grand juries in this state. The pertinent language of that statute (State Statute § 832.41) indicates that grand juries may conduct investigations "to determine whether crimes within the jurisdiction have or have not been committed." The second is the order creating the grand jury with regard to this particular investigation.

In the case of both the statute and the order, it is clear that authority was granted only to investigate past conduct. As far as the statute is concerned, if the legislature had decided to give grand juries ongoing authority to investigate matters postdating the empanelment of the grand jury, it could have done so as other states have done [citations omitted]. In addition, the case law of this state clearly demonstrates that they have authority only to investigate matters that predate the jury's creation (see *State v. Monroe, State v. Safferin,* and others [citations omitted]).

The subpoena is quashed, and the lower court ruling is reversed.

WESTMINSTER, CARTLY, EASTERLIN, MINTON, VORHEIS, and FRANCISCUS, JJ. concur.

10. Please brief the following case. Information helpful for the briefing of the case includes the following:

a. The term *consortium* refers to love, affection, or companionship. When a person files suit against a party for loss of consortium because of an injury to his or her spouse, the implication is that the suit includes a claim for loss of sexual relations as well.

b. A *tortfeasor* is a person who commits a tort, which is a civil wrong other than breach of contract. Examples of torts are negligence, libel, slander, and fraud.

Pierce v. Casas Adobes Baptist Church

HOWARD, Presiding Judge.

James Anthony Pierce (Tony) was severely injured on June 15, 1984, in a motor vehicle accident while on a church-sponsored outing. At the time he was 17 years of age. He suffered a ruptured spleen, ruptured liver, a concussion, bruised heart and lungs and his back was broken in two places. After four days in the Gila General Hospital to stabilize his internal injuries, he was evacuated by air to Tucson Medical Center where he remained hospitalized for another 24 days ...

Tony and his parents brought suit against the church and the driver of the vehicle. Liability was admitted and the issue of damages was tried to the court. The court awarded Tony $1,320,742. This sum included $265,000 for loss of earning capacity, $155,742 for future medical expenses, and $900,000 in damages. The court awarded his parents $42,638.51 for medical expenses and $25,000 for lost wages and expenses in caring for Tony until he recovered. The court denied the parents' claim for loss of consortium. Appellants contend that the trial court erred in this regard. We do not agree and affirm....

In this case, the record shows that the parents have not lost the love, affection, or companionship of their son as a result of the injuries, and also shows that Tony completed high school after the accident, is not confined to a wheel chair or bed, and is capable of obtaining gainful employment. Nevertheless, the parents contend that they are entitled to recover for loss of consortium because of the emotional effect upon them in seeing Tony's injuries and their effect on Tony, and in seeing a happy, healthy, active 17-year-old ... [face] a future dramatically different than the one they had hoped and reasonably expected for him. In essence, what the parents are seeking to recover is damages for their own pain, suffering, and mental anguish, and *not* for loss of consortium.

The parents contend that the *Frank* case[7] supports their claim. They base this conclusion on language in the *Frank* case quoted from a law review note that "[t]he true significance of a parent's action under modern practice is that it compensates the parents' *emotional losses* when their child is injured." 150 Ariz. at 232, 722 P.2d at 957, quoting, Note, *The Child's Right to Sue for Loss of A Parent's Love, Care, and Companionship Caused by Tortious Injury to the Parent*, 56 B.U.L. REV. 722, 731–732 (1976). (Emphasis added.) We do not agree with the parents' conclusion. The note is referring to "emotional losses" from the deprivation of their child's society, companionship, love, and support and not the parent's emotional distress caused by observing their child's injuries. In Arizona, an action for mental distress for negligent injuries to another is limited to the witnesses of an accident. See *Keck v. Jackson,* 122 Ariz. 177, 593 P.2d 671 (1978).

Frank makes clear what damages are recoverable:

> In conclusion, we believe parents should have a remedy in damages against a negligent tortfeasor whose actions have so severely injured the parents' adult child that they are deprived of their child's society, companionship, love and support—in short, of the child's consortium.... 150 Ariz. at 234, 722 P.2d at 759.

There was no such deprivation here.
Affirmed.
LACAGNINA, C.J., concurs.
[The dissenting opinion of Judge Hathaway has been omitted.]

FOOTNOTES

[1]Further proceedings concerning this case can be found at 451 So.2d 808 (Fla. 1984). Reprinted with permission from 376 *Southern Reporter, Second Series,* page 378 *et seq.,* copyright © 1979 by West Publishing Co. For a discussion of subsequent proceedings in the case, see Sec. 6–5 in the "Ethics" chapter of this book.

[2]Reprinted with permission from 431 *North Western Reporter, Second Series,* page 363 *et seq.,* copyright © 1988 by West Publishing Co.

[3]Reprinted with permission from 314 *Atlantic Reporter, Second Series,* page 832 *et seq.,* copyright © 1988 by West Publishing Co.

[4]*Nolle prosequi* (or *nolo prosequi*) means the dropping of charges against the defendant by the prosecution in a criminal case.

[5]MARYLAND CODE (1957, 1987 REPL. VOL.) Art. 27, § 642 provides that, upon a finding of violation of probation, a judge may "sentence the person to serve the period of imprisonment prescribed in the original sentence or any portion thereof …"

[6]A writ of certiori is a writ of a higher court ordering a lower court to provide it with a pending pleading, thereby resulting in the initiation of appellate proceedings.

[7]*Frank v. Superior Court of Arizona,* 150 Ariz. 228, 722 P.2d 955 (1986). The citation was given in a portion of the case that was edited out of this textbook.

3 *Legal Analysis*

CHAPTER OVERVIEW

SEC. 3-1
IN GENERAL

A paralegal must have the ability to analyze statutes, subdivide them into their component parts, and then apply them to specific factual situations. Unlike briefing, which pertains to court cases, the legal analysis addressed in this chapter deals primarily with statutes and procedural rules.

The skills learned in this chapter should be useful in any situation requiring statutory analysis. If, for example, an office client is charged with the violation of a particular statute, and the attorney wants an initial assessment of the strengths or weaknesses of the case based upon the statutory language, the following approach should be helpful.

SEC. 3-2
BASIC FORMAT

Formal analysis of the relationship between the facts of a given case and a particular statute or rule includes sections dealing with the statute, the facts, the questions, the analysis, and the conclusion.

A. Statute

The relevant statute or rule must be quoted verbatim.

B. Facts

These are the background facts that will be compared and contrasted with the requirements of the statutory language. This section will be similar to the "Facts" portion of a brief, and only the essential circumstances should be included.

C. Question

Unlike the briefing of a case, the analysis should be based upon a given question, and the question will often include named parties.

D. Analysis

The analysis is separated into two main parts: subdivision of the statute into elements and application of the facts to each element.

1.   *Subdivision of the Statute into Elements*

The statute or rule must be broken down into its component parts. Suppose, for example, that one is asked to analyze NEW YORK PENAL LAW § 244(3), which states that

> A person who ... strikes, beats, or willfully injures the person or apparatus of any news reporter or news photographer during the time when such reporter or photographer is engaged in the pursuit of his occupation or calling in any public place or gathering ... is guilty of assault in the third degree.

The key elements that must be shown in order to establish a violation of this criminal statute are:

1. strikes, beats, or willfully injures
2. the person or apparatus;
3. of any news reporter or news photographer;
4. during the time when such reporter or photographer is engaged in the pursuit of his occupation or calling; and
5. in any public place or gathering.

Each one of the five elements will have to be proven in the defendant's case if he is to be found guilty.

Several points should be noted with regard to the subdivision of any statute:

a. Some elements must be stated in the alternative.   In the statute above, for example, it is not necessary to establish that the defendant struck, beat, *and* willfully injured the person or apparatus. It is sufficient to demonstrate that any one of the three acts occurred, so the three alternative acts must be combined into one element (as they have been in the first element above).

b. Language pertaining to penalties is not generally included.   A penalty section, which is often included in the substantive part of a statute, is not broken down into elements since nothing in that section needs to be established in order to demonstrate that the substantive law has been violated.

c. The subdivision of the statute does not depend on the facts of any given case.   The subdivision of a statute is based solely on an examination of the statutory language; it is not dependent upon what did or did not occur in a particular case.

The facts are analyzed as explained in Sec. 3-2, subsection D.2. immediately following, after the elements of the statute are established.

2. *Application of the Facts to Each Element*

This part of the analysis can be explained most clearly by illustration. Suppose, for example, that Arthur Stone, a member of one of the city planning boards, is approached by reporters and photographers as he leaves his house on April 4, 1997. In moving through the crowd, Stone pushes aside one of the news photographers who is trying to take his picture and the photographer falls to the ground. The photographer suffers no personal injury, but his camera is damaged. Assume for the present example (as well as all others in this chapter) that all of the given facts can be proven. The paralegal is asked to look up the statute, see what the elements of the offense are, and make an initial assessment of Stone's case.

First, the five key elements of this particular statute are listed, and a space is left below each element.

Next, each element is examined in light of the facts of the present case. The analysis might indicate that an element is obviously present or absent, that further factual information is needed, or that research will be necessary with regard to that element. Below is a brief analysis of the present case.

a. "strikes, beats, or willfully injures" (the person or apparatus)

Debatable. Stone did not strike or beat the photographer. We need more information to ascertain whether the pushing by Stone was aggressive enough to constitute willful injury. Whether Stone's pushing action constituted "willful injury" to the photographer's camera (apparatus) is open to question. Does this statute mean that Stone could only be convicted if it could be shown that he *intended* to damage the camera, or is it sufficient to show that he intended to push the photographer, and that the camera was damaged in the process? Research is needed.

Note that in this particular set of facts, several of the elements of the offense tie in together. For example, with regard to the present element, "strikes, beats, or willfully injures" can only be understood if it is known what the object of such striking, beating, or willful injury is. It is, therefore, best if the object ("the person or apparatus") is included in parentheses with the first element so that the context of the element is clear. However, it is still also imperative that the element of "the person or apparatus" be analyzed separately.

b. "the person or apparatus"

Clearly established. The photographer's camera would almost certainly qualify as an "apparatus" in the context of this statute.

c. "of any news reporter or news photographer"

Clearly established.

d. "during the time when such reporter or photographer is engaged in the pursuit of his occupation or calling"

Clearly established.

e. "in any public place or gathering"

Debatable. More information is needed to ascertain whether the incident took place on Stone's property, on the street, or elsewhere. Research is needed to determine what the law is concerning the meaning of "public gathering."

E.   *Conclusion*

Finally, a brief conclusion must be drawn. It might be assumed by the one requesting the analysis that basic legal research would be done prior to drawing any conclusions. If the Conclusion section were to be prepared prior to an opportunity for researching any relevant issues, that section might indicate that the likelihood of conviction would depend on (1) whether pushing the photographer and thereby damaging the camera amounts to "willful injury" within the meaning of this statute, and (2) whether the incident occurred in a "public place or gathering." The conclusion section would have to note that research and more information would be needed as to both issues.

SEC. 3-3
ANALYSIS OF HYPOTHETICAL FACTS IN RELATIONSHIP TO SPECIFIC STATUTES

The following are examples in which case facts have been applied to the elements of given statutes:[1]

A.   *Former N.Y. Penal Law § 1294 (McKinney 1994)*

Note: The current larceny penal law in the state of New York (§ 155 et seq.) has eliminated virtually all of the problematic language found in former N.Y.

PENAL LAW § 1294, but the former law is being used because it better suits the analysis discussion of this chapter.

1. Statute

Former N.Y. PENAL LAW § 1294 states that "A person is guilty of grand larceny in the first degree, who steals, or unlawfully obtains or appropriates ... (2) property of a value of more than $25.00, by taking the same in the night time from any dwelling-house, vessel, or railway car...."

2. Facts

Nancy Edwards owns a gift shop in a building that is floating on a raft anchored in New York City harbor. The store closes at 5:00 P.M. At about 11:30 P.M., the police arrest William Reynolds inside the store. They conduct a personal search of Reynolds and find a ring in his pocket. The ring has a price tag on it from the gift shop. While the tag lists a price of $29.95, the ring was actually on sale for $24.75. When the police ask Reynolds for a receipt proving that he owns the ring, he refuses comment and demands to speak to his attorney.

3. Question

Is Reynolds likely to be convicted of violating § 1294?

4. Analysis

a. "steals, or unlawfully obtains or appropriates"

Probably established. There is strong circumstantial evidence to suggest a wrongful taking.

b. "property of a value of more than $25.00"

Debatable. Should the price tag amount, the sale price amount, or the wholesale cost be used? If the sale price is the one to use, does the dollar amount referred to in the statute include tax?

c. "In the night time"

Clearly established.

d. "From any dwelling-house, vessel, or railway car ..."

Probably not established. The shop was clearly neither a dwelling-house nor a railway car. While research could be done to verify the meaning of the word "vessel" in the context of this statute, it seems unlikely that this element is present.

5. Conclusion

Whether Reynolds is likely to be convicted of § 1294 probably depends upon (1) whether the price tag amount, the sale price amount, or the wholesale amount is to be used, (2) whether tax is to be included in the amount, and (3) whether the shop was regarded as a "vessel" within the meaning of this statute. It would appear that Reynolds is likely to win, especially with regard to the third issue, although further research is necessary.

B. PENAL LAW § 1053-c

1. Statute

PENAL LAW § 1053-c states that "Any person who while engaged in hunting shall discharge a firearm or operate a long bow in a culpably negligent or reckless manner, whereby a human being is killed, is guilty of criminal negligence while engaged in hunting."

2. Facts

Susan Armstrong uses a crossbow to hunt bears in the forest. She is aware of the fact that many other hunters are regularly in the forest. One day, she shoots her crossbow without carefully checking the landscape and wounds another hunter, Tom Walton. Walton is in the hospital for more than nine months before he dies of the pneumonia that he contracted from one of the other patients in the hospital.

3. Question

Is Armstrong likely to be convicted of violating § 1053-c?

4. Analysis

    a. "Person engaged in hunting"

        Clearly established.

    b. "Discharges a firearm or operates a long bow"

        Debatable. Is a crossbow classified as a "long bow" within the meaning of this statute? Research is needed.

    c. "In a culpably negligent or reckless manner"

        Probably established. While the question of culpable negligence may require complex analysis, the facts would seem to suggest that Armstrong's conduct was at the very least reckless.

    d. "Whereby a human being is killed"

        Debatable. While Walton did die after being shot by Armstrong, two questions arise: (1) Does the victim have to die within a certain time period from the date of the shooting in order for Armstrong to be responsible? (2) Does the intervening cause of death (pneumonia) provide a possible defense for Armstrong? Does it make any difference whether the victim was exposed to the intervening cause only because he was in the hospital as a direct result of Armstrong's actions? Research is needed.

5. Conclusion

Before one can determine whether Armstrong is likely to be convicted of violating § 1053-c, further research will be required to determine (1) whether a crossbow is classified as a "long bow" within the meaning of this statute, (2) whether the victim had to die within a certain time period from the date of the shooting in order for Armstrong to be responsible, and (3) whether the intervening cause of death (pneumonia) provides a possible defense for Armstrong. The attorney may also wish to personally examine the issue of whether there was culpable negligence or recklessness.

C. MO. REV. STAT. § 305.090 (1995)

1. Statute

MO. REV. STAT. § 305.090 provides that "Any person who shall tamper with any aircraft or put into motion the engine of such aircraft without the permission of the owner shall be punished by imprisonment in the penitentiary for a period not to exceed five years or by imprisonment in a county jail for a period not to exceed one year or by a fine not to exceed one thousand dollars, or by both such fine and imprisonment."

2. Facts

While visiting the Air and Space Museum at Cooperstown, Missouri, Karen Ferndon sees a full size mock-up of the space shuttle. Even though visitors are only permitted to look into the cabin area, she decides to crawl into the craft. As she sits in the cockpit, she throws a number of switches on the dashboard and actually breaks off one piece before she is pulled out by a security guard.

3. Question

Is Ferndon likely to be convicted of violating § 305.090?

4. Analysis

  a. "any person"

   Clearly established.

  b. "tamper with any aircraft, or put into motion the engine of such aircraft without the permission of the owner"

   (1) "tamper with any aircraft"

    (a) "tamper with"

     Debatable. What constitutes "tampering"? Did the breaking off of a piece on the dashboard amount to such tampering? Research is needed.

    (b) "aircraft"

     Probably *not* established. The term "aircraft" probably only includes crafts that can actually fly and, therefore, eliminates full-size mock-ups or models of aircraft. Another possible issue is whether the term includes spacecrafts, although that seems likely. Research might verify these conclusions.

  or (2) "put into motion the engine of such aircraft without the permission of the owner"

     Clearly *not* established. Does the question of putting the engine into motion suggest that the use of the term "aircraft" in this statute may refer only to crafts that can be flown?

5. Conclusion

While research may need to be done as to the meaning of the terms "tamper with" and "aircraft," it would appear from the context of the second part of the statute that only crafts capable of flying are included, and that Ferndon is, therefore, *not* likely to be convicted of violating § 305.090.

D. *S.C. CODE ANN. § 16–17–520 (Law. Co-op. 1994)*

1. *Statute*

S.C. CODE ANN. § 16–17–520 states that "Any person who shall (a) willfully and maliciously disturb or interrupt any meeting, society, assembly or congregation convened for the purpose of religious worship, (b) enter such meeting while in a state of intoxication or (c) use or sell spirituous liquors, or use blasphemous, profane or obscene language at or near the place of the meeting shall be guilty of a misdemeanor and shall, on conviction, be sentenced to pay a fine of not less than twenty nor more than one hundred dollars, or be imprisoned for a term not exceeding one year or less than thirty days, either or both, at the discretion of the court."

2. *Facts*

During a meeting of the Metaphysical Society for the Pursuit of Truth and Enlightenment, Samuel Penz jumps up from his seat and cuts off the speaker who is at the podium. Penz says that he finds the teaching of the group to be "garbage," and he pleads with the members to disavow their support of the group. He continues to disrupt the meeting until the police come and take him into custody.

3. *Question*

Is Penz likely to be convicted of violating § 16–17–520?

4. *Analysis*

    a. "any person"

        Clearly established.

    b. "willfully and maliciously disturb or interrupt any meeting, society, assembly or congregation convened for the purpose of religious worship, *or* enter such meeting while in a state of intoxication *or* use or sell spirituous liquors, *or* use blasphemous, profane or obscene language at or near the place of the meeting"

        (1) "willfully and maliciously disturb or interrupt any meeting, society, assembly or congregation convened for the purpose of religious worship"

            (a) "willful and malicious"

                Clearly established.

(b) "disturb or interrupt"

Clearly established.

(c) "meeting, society, assembly or congregation"

Clearly established.

(d) "for the purpose of religious worship"

Debatable. Is the Metaphysical Society for the Pursuit of Truth and Enlightenment engaged in a meeting of "religious worship"? Are there any spiritual aspects, as opposed to those that are purely intellectual or social, that are associated with the society's activities? Is it relevant whether the Internal Revenue Service recognizes the organization as a religious organization for tax exemption purposes?

or **(2)** "enter such meeting while in a state of intoxication"

(a) "enter such meeting"

Clearly established.

(b) "while in a state of intoxication"

Probably not established. Nothing in the facts suggests that Penz was intoxicated, although it might be prudent to confirm this.

or **(3)** "use or sell spirituous liquors (at or near the place of the meeting)

Probably not established. Nothing in the facts suggests that Penz was using or selling liquor, although it might be prudent to confirm this.

or **(4)** "use blasphemous, profane or obscene language" (at or near the place of the meeting)

Probably not established. Nothing in the facts suggests that Penz used such language, although it might be prudent to confirm this.

5. *Conclusion*

It would appear that the defendant's responsibility may depend upon how the term "religious worship" is defined within the meaning of this statute, and whether the activities of the Metaphysical Society are included within that definition. If Penz was intoxicated at the time, or was using or selling spirituous liquors, that could also bear on his responsibility. More information is needed to ascertain whether he was using "blasphemous, profane or obscene language" at or near the place of the meeting, and if so, research must be done as to the meaning of that phrase.[2]

E.   KY. REV. STAT. ANN. § 525.110 (Michie/Bobbs-Merrill 1995)

1.   Statute

KY. REV. STAT. ANN. § 525.110 provides that "(1) A person is guilty of desecration of venerated objects in the second degree when he intentionally: (a) desecrates any public monument or object or place of worship; or (b) desecrates in a public place the national or state flag or other patriotic or religious symbol which is an object of veneration by the public or a substantial segment thereof."

2.   Facts

While Cynthia Carton is visiting a privately owned museum that is open to the public, she sees a modern art sculpture called "The American Collection" that is composed of a conglomeration of various pieces of property. One of the components of this sculpture is a portrait of James Madison. Cynthia is caught scratching her name across the Madison portrait with a knife.

3.   Question

Is Carton likely to be convicted of violating § 525.110?

4.   Analysis

   a.   "any person"

   Unquestionably established.

   b.   "desecrates any public monument or object or place of worship; *or* desecrates in a public place the national or state flag or other patriotic or religious symbol which is an object of veneration by the public or a substantial segment thereof"

   (1) "desecrates any public monument or object or place of worship"

   (a) "desecrates"

   Probably established, although one might research the meaning of the term in the context of this statute.

(b) "any public monument or object or place of worship"

    (a) "public monument"

        Clearly not established.

or **(b)** "object"

        Probably not established, since the context of the statute seems to suggest an object similar in some way to a public monument. Research is needed.

or **(c)** "place of worship"

        Clearly not established.

or **(2)** "desecrates in a public place the national or state flag or other patriotic or religious symbol which is an object of veneration by the public or a substantial segment thereof."

    (a) "desecrates"

        Probably established, although one might research the meaning of the term in the context of this statute.

    (b) in a "public place"

        Probably established, since the museum was open to the public, but research should be done to determine if it makes any difference that the museum was privately owned.

    (c) "national or state flag or other patriotic or religious symbol which is an object of veneration by the public or a substantial segment thereof"

        (a) "national or state flag"

            Clearly not established, since even if such flags were part of the exhibit (which the facts do not suggest), the information does not seem to indicate that any flags were desecrated by Carton.

        or **(b)** "other patriotic or religious symbol which is an object of veneration by the public or a substantial segment thereof"

            Debatable, since it is unclear what the definition of a "patriotic symbol" is in the context of this statute, and what the basis is for determining whether a particular symbol is an object of veneration by the public or a substantial segment thereof. Does it make any difference that portraits of Madison are not generally venerated, or is the issue whether it is an object of veneration simply because it is a portrait of a United States president? Does it make any difference that people would tend to view the portrait differently if, as in this case, it was part of a work of art? Research is needed.

5.   Conclusion

Whether Carton is likely to be convicted is debatable, since it is unclear what the definition of a "patriotic symbol" is in the context of this statute and what the basis is for determining whether a particular symbol is "an object of veneration by the public or a substantial segment thereof." Research is needed. Also, since the act had to occur in a "public place," research should be conducted to verify that a privately owned museum that is open to the public is a "public place" within the meaning of this statute.

F.   MICH. COMP. LAWS ANN. § 750.197c (West 1995)

1.   Statute

MICH. COMP. LAWS ANN. § 750.197c provides that "A person lawfully imprisoned in a jail, other place of confinement established by law for any term, or lawfully imprisoned for any purpose at any other place ... who, without being discharged from the place of confinement, or other lawful imprisonment by due process of law, through the use of violence, threats of violence or dangerous weapons, assaults an employee of the place of confinement or the custodian knowing the person to be an employee or custodian or breaks the place of confinement and escapes, or breaks the place of confinement although an escape is not actually made, is guilty of a felony."

2.   Facts

Fred Lamberlin is serving 15 to 20 years in the state penitentiary for armed robbery. While he is playing basketball in the prison courtyard one day during recreation period, he runs toward the prison wall in an attempt to escape, but he is stopped before he can scale the wall.

3.   Question

Is Lamberlin likely to be convicted of violating § 750.197c?

4.   *Analysis*

a.   "any person"

Unquestionably established.

b.   "lawfully imprisoned in a jail, other place of confinement established by law for any term, or lawfully imprisoned for any purpose at any other place"

Unquestionably established.

c.   "without being discharged from the place of confinement, or other lawful imprisonment by due process of law"

Unquestionably established.[3]

d.   "through the use of violence, threats of violence or dangerous weapons assaults an employee of the place of confinement or the custodian knowing the person to be an employee or custodian *or* breaks the place of confinement and escapes, or breaks the place of confinement although an escape is not actually made"

(1)   "through the use of violence, threats of violence or dangerous weapons assaults an employee of the place of confinement or the custodian knowing the person to be an employee or custodian"

(a)   "through the use of violence, threats of violence or dangerous weapons"

Clearly not established.

(b)   "assaults"

Clearly not established.

(c)   "an employee of the place of confinement or the custodian knowing the person to be an employee or custodian"

Clearly not established.

or   **(2)**   "breaks the place of confinement and escapes"

Clearly not established.

or   **(3)**   breaks the place of confinement although an escape is not actually made

Debatable; What exactly is meant by the "place of confinement"? Was it any of the area within the prison walls, or was it the particular area within the prison walls where he was supposed to be at that time? Did he "break" the place of confinement, or did he simply *attempt* to break it, and is that sufficient? Research is needed.

5. *Conclusion*

Whether Lamberlin is likely to be convicted of § 750.197c depends upon the court's interpretation of the terms "breaking" and "place of confinement." Research should yield some answers to these questions.

REVIEW QUESTIONS

The following questions are based on fictitious statutes and facts, and are used for instructional purposes only.

1. The police are summoned to Harry's property on the basis of a reported trespass. As the police pull up, Harry's property is on fire, and Ann is seen on the property with a gasoline can in her possession. The police charge her with violating STATE STATUTE § 321.5, which states that "any person willfully and maliciously burning the dwelling house of another shall be punished by a period of incarceration not greater than five years and/or a fine of not more than $5,000."

   Please write an interoffice memorandum on the subject of whether Ann is or is not likely to be convicted of violating STATE STATUTE § 321.5.

2. Bob, who is in his apartment on the second floor of the building, gets into an oral argument with his neighbor, who is on the sidewalk 100 yards from his window. Both of them are using obscene language. Bob threatens to throw a potted plant at his neighbor, and Bob actually picks it up, making gestures that indicate that he is about to throw it (although he never does). Bob is arrested for violating STATE STATUTE § 975.31, which states that an assault is "an intentional threat by word or act to do violence to another, coupled with an apparent ability to do so, and doing some act which creates a well-founded fear in such other person that such violence is imminent."

   Please write an interoffice memorandum on the subject of whether Bob is or is not likely to be convicted of violating STATE STATUTE § 975.31.

3. John decides to burglarize Mary's condominium by entering through some sliding glass doors. When he breaks the glass around the door handle and sticks his finger through the hole to undo the latch, an alarm goes off and John flees. He is arrested several blocks away and charged with violating STATE STATUTE § 123.678, which states that "any person breaking and entering the dwelling house of another during the nighttime shall be punished by a period of not greater than five years and/or a fine of not more than $5,000."

Please write an interoffice memorandum on the subject of whether John is or is not likely to be convicted of violating STATE STATUTE § 123.678.

4. Lucy was recently on a fishing trip to the Bahamas. When she docked back at Port Everglades, she found that she had accidentally picked up an eel in her nets along with a catch of more than 800 fish. She ended up throwing out the eel into the Intercoastal Waterway. She was charged with violating STATE STATUTE § 987.65, which states that it is unlawful "to either import for sale or use, or release within the state, any fish of any species without first obtaining a permit from the Fish and Game Commission."

   Lucy had no permit, and your law office represents her on the charge. Please write an interoffice memorandum on the subject of whether she is or is not likely to be convicted of violating STATE STATUTE § 987.65.

5. Harry is hunting in the Everglades. He shoots at what he believes to be a quail, but instead, he hits and kills a Florida panther. Quail hunting is permissible in the Everglades. Harry is arrested and charged with violating STATE STATUTE § 14.82, which states that it is unlawful "for any person to intentionally injure or kill any animal native to Florida in a state-designated game preserve area."

   Please write an interoffice memorandum on the subject of whether Harry, who has retained the law office where you are employed, is or is not likely to be convicted of violating STATE STATUTE § 14.82.

6. Saunders and Sons, a business that is involved in the purification of sulfur products, owns a factory next door to the Paxton water processing plant. The purification factory routinely emits small amounts of zinc oxide into the atmosphere, and it is cited for violating STATE STATUTE § 135.79, which states that it is unlawful "for any person or corporation to dump hazardous waste materials within 250 feet of a municipal water processing plant. Those in violation of this statute shall be punishable by a fine not exceeding an amount of $1,000."

   Please write an interoffice memorandum on the subject of whether Saunders and Sons, whose representatives have retained the law office where you are employed, is likely to be convicted of violating STATE STATUTE § 135.79.

7. Bobby Randall is a professional stock car driver from Lancaster, Pennsylvania. He uses a picture of the Confederate flag with a giant "X" through it on the hood of his car in order to display his displeasure, in general, with the South and, in particular, with his two primary competitors, both of whom are Southerners. While in the South for the Mayville 400 stock car race, he is charged with violation of STATE STATUTE § 864.20. The statute states that "it is unlawful for any person or corporation to contemptuously abuse or defile a flag or emblem representing the state."

Please write an interoffice memorandum on the subject of whether the Randall racing group is or is not likely to be convicted of violating STATE STATUTE § 864.20.

FOOTNOTES

[1]Sometimes a statute includes terms that are defined in other related statutes. When this is the case, the person doing the legal analysis may find that some potential issues have already been settled. For the examples in this section, the author has intentionally ignored statutory definitions so that he can illustrate some of the issues that might otherwise arise.

[2]In both this example and the next one, some constitutional issues dealing with freedom of expression might be raised even though they might not be discerned through the usual analyses of the individual elements. The discernment of such issues would often be the responsibility of the attorney.

[3]Note that it is not necessary to research the meaning of the term "due process" under these circumstances, since there can be little doubt that he was lawfully imprisoned.

4 *Legal Research*

CHAPTER OVERVIEW

4. Updated with Pocket Parts

5. Special Volumes

   a. Table of Statutes

   b. Legal and Business Forms

   c. Table of Cases and Numeric Case Names

D. The State Digests

  1. Examples in Various States

  2. Never Cited

  3. Alphabetical Organization

  4. Updated with Pocket Parts

  5. Special Volumes

   a. The Table of Cases

   b. The Defendant/Plaintiff Table

   c. The Descriptive-Word Index

   d. Words and Phrases

4-4 Four Basic Federal Research Tools

A. The Federal Reporters

  1. Federal Supplement

  2. Federal Reporter

  3. The Three U.S. Supreme Court Reporters

   a. United States Reports

   b. The Supreme Court Reporter

   c. United States Supreme Court Reports, Lawyer's Edition

B. The Federal Statutes

  1. The United States Code

  2. The United States Code Annotated

  3. The United States Code Service

C. The National Encyclopedias

  1. American Jurisprudence

  2. Corpus Juris Secundum

D. The Federal Digests

4-5 The Organization of a Typical Law Library

A. The State Materials for the State in Which the Library Is Located

  1. The Cases

  2. The Statutes

  3. The Encyclopedias

  4. The Digests

B. The Federal Materials

  1. The Cases

  2. The Statutes

  3. The Encyclopedias

  4. The Digests

C. The Regional Reporters

D. The State Materials for States Other than the One in Which the Library Is Located

E. All Other Materials

4-6 Shepard's Citations

4-7 Sample Case with Exhibits Showing Connections Between Research Sets

4-8 Hints for Choosing Which Research Set to Use

A. Is the Issue Likely to Be Governed by Legislative Law?

B. Does the Issue Require a Legal Definition?

C. Does the Issue Deal with a Totally Unfamiliar Subject?

D. Does the Issue Require Further Case Law Under a Particular Key Number?

E. Does the Issue Require Exact Language from a Specifically Cited Case?

SEC. 4-1
INTRODUCTION

While it is possible to research an issue in many different ways through the use of a wide variety of research tools, this introductory text puts special emphasis on several sets of books central to an understanding of basic legal research. After the important distinction between primary and secondary authority is drawn, both state and federal materials will be analyzed in detail. The focus of this chapter is a study of the essential information necessary for legal research whether it is ultimately accomplished on the computer or in the more traditional law library.

SEC. 4-2
PRIMARY AND SECONDARY AUTHORITY

Before one begins legal research, it is important to understand the distinction between primary and secondary authority. *Primary authority* is the law itself as indicated in statutes, constitutions, administrative regulations, case law, and elsewhere. The sources of law discussed in detail in Chapter 1, Sec. 1-5 are principal examples of primary authority. Courts routinely rely on this kind of authority when rendering decisions. Furthermore, primary authority may itself be subdivided into mandatory and persuasive authority. Mandatory authority, such as a court ruling from a higher court within the same court system, must be followed by the court currently considering the case. This kind of authority takes precedence over persuasive authority. The court may follow persuasive authority, but it is not required to do so. An example of persuasive authority would be a state court decision from another state.

While *secondary authority* is not the law itself, it includes the many kinds of materials that refer the researcher to primary authority. Examples of secondary authorities would be law review articles and scholarly books about general subject areas of the law. While these kinds of publications are not generally cited for the courts in appellate briefs and memoranda of law, they may include references to cases, statutes, and other primary authorities that are themselves cited. Courts rely on secondary authority only when adequate primary authorities are not available. Courts routinely regard primary authority as having precedence over secondary authority.

SEC. 4-3
FOUR BASIC STATE RESEARCH TOOLS

The four sets to be analyzed are:

A. the state and regional reporters,
B. the state statutes annotated,
C. the state encyclopedias, and
D. the state digests.

A.   *The State and Regional Reporters*

Reporters in this context refers to sets of books that contain written court decisions in the order in which those decisions were rendered. While a very small number of states have reporters for state trial court cases, most state reporters contain written opinions from state appellate courts only. They do not usually include state trial cases. While the detailed disposition of trial court cases can easily be found by consulting the original court file in the county in which the case was heard, the judge will not in most cases provide a detailed explanation of his or her opinion in the Final Judgment found in that file. Since the decisions of the state appellate courts within the same court system are mandatory authority and therefore binding on the trial courts, the law from state trial courts is seldom cited in appellate briefs or memoranda of law.

The state reporters also do not contain any of the decisions of the federal courts. Those opinions can be found in an entirely different series of volumes discussed in Sec. 4-4, subsection A.

In addition to the state reporters, there is also a series of regional reporters of state cases published by West Publishing Company. These reporters, which are tan with red labels, contain the written decisions of the appellate court justices in all cases that have been appealed in state courts. They do not include either federal court decisions or state trial court decisions. West has divided the country into seven regions and created a separate reporter for each area.

1. Division of the Reporter System by Region

   a. *Atlantic Reporter, Second Series* (A.2d) includes state court appellate decisions in Connecticut, Delaware, Maine, Maryland, New Hampshire, New Jersey, Pennsylvania, Rhode Island, Vermont, and the District of Columbia.

   b. *North Eastern Reporter, Second Series* (N.E.2d) includes state court appellate decisions in Illinois, Indiana, Massachusetts, New York, and Ohio.

   c. *North Western Reporter, Second Series* (N.W.2d) includes state court appellate decisions in Iowa, Michigan, Minnesota, Nebraska, North Dakota, South Dakota, and Wisconsin.

   d. *Pacific Reporter, Second Series* (P.2d) includes state court appellate decisions in Alaska, Arizona, California, Colorado, Hawaii, Idaho, Kansas, Montana, Nevada, New Mexico, Oklahoma, Oregon, Utah, Washington, and Wyoming.

   e. *South Eastern Reporter, Second Series* (S.E.2d) includes state court appellate decisions in Georgia, North Carolina, South Carolina, Virginia, and West Virginia.

   f. *South Western Reporter, Second Series* (S.W.2d) includes state court appellate decisions in Arkansas, Missouri, Tennessee, Kentucky, and Texas.

   g. *Southern Reporter, Second Series* (So.2d) includes state court appellate decisions in Florida, Alabama, Louisiana, and Mississippi.

For a reproduction of a case decision found in a regional reporter, see the case of *The Florida Bar v. Furman,* shown in Figures 2-1a through 2-1e.

2. Manner of Citation

References to any appellate court decisions will usually include a series of numbers and abbreviations known collectively as a *citation*. The purpose of a citation is to help the reader locate the written decision in the law library and provide other information, such as the name of the court hearing the case and the year in which the case was heard. Standard abbreviations for the regional reporters can be found in Sec. 4-3, subsection A.1 immediately above.

Citations appear in many different forms, but one example will be examined to show the nature of information given in a citation. An example of a citation is *City of Miami v. Thomas,* 657 So.2d 927 (Fla. 1st DCA 1995). The key elements of this citation are as follows:

a. Case name.   When referring to individual parties, first names are not used, a "v." rather than a "vs." is utilized, and the entire case name always appears in either italics or underlined form.

b. Volume number.   The first number indicates in what volume the case can be found within the set of books (in this example, volume 657)

c. Identification of the set of books containing the case.   This example shows that the case can be located in the set of books known as *Southern Reporter, Second Series.*

d. Page number.   In this example, the case can be found on page 927 of volume 657.

e. Information in parentheses.   This may vary from state to state, but it may include the following:

1. The state in which the case was heard (in this example, Florida).
2. The court that heard the case (in this example, the First District Court of Appeals). Whenever the citation does not refer to a specific court, there is a presumption that it was heard in the highest court in the state.
3. The year the decision was rendered (in this example, 1995).

Sometimes, there are *parallel citations* for a case, because the court's decision can be found verbatim in more than one set of books. For example, the citation for the case of *Townes v. State* is 314 Md. 71, 548 A.2d 832 (1988). The parallel citations show that the decision can be found in volume 314, page 71 of the set of books known as *Maryland Reports* as well as in volume 548, page 832 of *Atlantic Reporter, Second Series.* The state name is not generally included within the parentheses of the citation when the reference to the state reporter clearly confirms where the case was heard.

Many but not all of the states have separate state reporters, and citations of cases in such states should contain references to both the state and regional reporters, with the reference to the state reporter appearing first. In states in which there are no state reporters, the citation of a state appellate case will refer only to the regional reporter.

The publication entitled *A Uniform System of Citation* (also known as "the blue book")[1] is regarded as a standard for determining correct citation form for all state and federal sources of authority. Furthermore, each state has its own rules governing correct citation form, and care should be taken to follow those rules precisely.

3.   Chronological Organization

The state and regional reporters are organized in chronological order. Consequently, the volumes with the highest numbers have the most recent cases.
Any decisions rendered prior to the first case published in volume 1 of the
current series can be found in the previous series of that reporter. For example, volume 1 of *Southern Reporter, Second Series* begins with cases reported in
1940; all state court appellate decisions in that region issued prior to that time
are found in the first series of *Southern Reporter,* which is referred to simply as
Southern Reporter (as opposed to *Southern Reporter, First Series*). The first and
second series of a regional set will be next to each other in most law libraries;
care should therefore be taken to avoid mistaking one set for the other. The
bindings of each book in each set clearly indicate where particular volumes
belong.

4.   Updated with Advance Sheets

The regional reporters are updated every few weeks with *advance sheets,* which
are paperback books containing the latest decisions. They will be found on the
shelf after the highest numbered bound volume in the set and will contain
cases that have been rendered since the publication of the last bound volume.
The owner of the set must pay a fee to the publisher to receive the advance
sheets as they are issued. Approximately every month, any owner of the set
who subscribes to the updating service will receive a bound volume of the
cases included in several of the advance sheets. The advance sheets containing the material covered in the new volume can then be discarded. The pages
in the bound volumes will be literally identical to those found in the advance
sheets. If the advance sheets were not routinely replaced by bound volumes,
however, the set would rapidly accumulate dozens and perhaps even hundreds of the paperbacks that could easily be lost or reshelved in the wrong
order.

5.   Special State Editions of the Regional Reporters

The publisher of the regional reporter series also makes available special editions that contain only the cases from one particular state, such as *Southern Reporter, Second Series, Florida cases.* These editions have the same general appearance as the regional reporters, but they have the state name prominently
displayed on the binding. They are identical to the regional reporters, except
that the pages containing cases from states other than the specifically designated one have been deleted. For example, in a particular state volume of the

regional reporter, page numbers may go directly from page 92 to 518, since the missing pages represent cases decided in other states within that region. In order to minimize confusion with regard to the citation of cases, the page numbers are not renumbered for the state editions.

B.   *The State Statutes Annotated*

These sets, which are known in some states as the state *code* annotated when they are organized by subject matter, contain all the legislative acts currently in force in a particular state.

Each individual statute printed in the set is followed by *annotations*, which are brief summaries of cases that have interpreted the statute, and they are generally only one or two sentences in length. The purpose of these summaries is to allow the reader to make a quick judgment as to whether the case is relevant to the research issue and, if so, to provide the reader with a citation for further research. A reproduction of a page from a set of state statutes can be seen in Figure 4-9.

If the set does not include annotations, it is known simply as the state statutes or the state code.

1.   *Examples in Various States*

The set in the state of Illinois is *West's Smith Hurd Illinois Compiled Statutes Annotated*; for Arizona, it is *Arizona Revised Statutes Annotated*.

2.   *Manner of Citation*

References to state statutes are made by the statute number rather than the page number in the state statutes annotated volumes. Even the index volumes within the state statutes annotated usually refer to statutes by the number assigned to the legislative act. For the exact citation form appropriate for the statutes or code of a particular state, one should consult the local citation rules for the state or *A Uniform System of Citation*.[2]

3.   *Numerical Organization*

State statutes annotated volumes are organized by statute number. One common numbering system starts with Statute § 1.000 in volume one and goes through several dozen volumes to the highest numbered statutes. Therefore, unless one already has a statute number, it will be necessary to utilize the index at the end of the set. That index, which may be several volumes in length, is organized alphabetically by topic. For example, someone wanting to find the statute dealing with arson would have to look under "A" in the index. The statute number next to the word "arson" could then be located, which would direct the researcher to the main part of the set.

4.   Updated with Pocket Parts

This set is updated annually with *pocket parts,* which are paperback books that slide into the back cover of each book in the set. This system of updating is unlike the one used with reporters in which all of the new material appears in paperback books at the end of the entire set. Each year's pocket parts are cumulative so that they contain all of the material in the previous year's pocket parts as well as the material added for the past year. Once the pocket parts become very large, a newly bound volume is prepared by the publisher, and the old volume and its pocket parts are thrown out.

In addition, subscribers to the updating service generally receive the session laws, which are paperback books containing the legislative acts in chronological order according to the date on which they were passed. The session laws are normally placed at the end of the entire set of books. Once these laws are organized in a manner consistent with that of the main volumes, they will be included in the next year's pocket parts.

The pocket parts and the session laws should always be checked by the reader before using the main volumes so that it can be verified that the statute being researched has not been repealed, altered, or affected by late-breaking developments in the law.

5.   Special Volumes

There are several special volumes at the end of the state statutes annotated volumes that are worthy of particular mention. These volumes, which contain annotations like the main volumes in the set, have been added to the state statutes annotated even though they do not contain statutory material. These special kinds of volumes may include:

a. Rules of procedure.   These rules govern the procedure to be followed by courts of various jurisdictions, and they may encompass several volumes. They often include rules of civil procedure, criminal procedure, summary procedure, traffic procedure, appellate procedure, and probate and guardianship procedure.

b. The state constitution with annotations.

c. The State Bar and Judiciary Rules. This volume may include the various rules pertaining to such matters as ethics, standards of conduct for attorneys and judges, and state bar admission requirements.

C. The State Encyclopedias

This is a multivolume encyclopedia of the law for a single state. In states in which no state encyclopedia exists, the researcher will need to use one of the national encyclopedias such as *American Jurisprudence 2d* or *Corpus Juris Secundum* (see Sec. 4-4, subsection C of this chapter). These volumes are particularly useful to one who is attempting to gain general background information about a particular subject matter. Just as in the case of the reporters, the researcher should be careful to use the most current series available. A reproduction of a page from a state jurisprudence volume can be seen in Figure 4-10.

1. Examples in Various States

The set for the state of Georgia is *Georgia Jurisprudence*; for New York, it is *New York Jurisprudence 2d* (the second series of the New York Jurisprudence set); for Texas, it is *Texas Jurisprudence 3d* (the third series of the Texas Jurisprudence set).

2. Never Cited

While state jurisprudence volumes refer to primary authority, the analyses found in these books are not primary authority themselves. Consequently, researchers do not quote directly from these encyclopedias in appellate briefs or memoranda of law. If one finds case law by using these encyclopedias, the cases themselves would be cited rather than the encyclopedic references. Other types of primary authority found in these volumes would also be directly cited.

3. Alphabetical Organization

State jurisprudence volumes are set up alphabetically by legal topic. Although there are comprehensive index volumes at the end of the sets, it is not generally necessary to use them any more than it would be to use an index to any encyclopedia. One wishing to read about the general topic of Burglary would, for example, immediately turn to the "B" volume.[3] The index can, nevertheless, be useful if one is unable to immediately locate a particular topic.

4. *Updated with Pocket Parts*

This set is updated annually with pocket parts in exactly the same manner as that for the state statutes annotated (see above).

5. *Special Volumes*

a. *Table of Statutes.*   This book lists the state statutes counting from the lowest number to the highest and then indicates next to each statute every section in the encyclopedia that refers to that statute.[4] For example, one wishing to find out which sections of Fla Jur 2d (*Florida Jurisprudence, Second Series*) refer to § 455.011 of the *Florida Statutes* will turn to the *Table of Statutes* and find that Bus & Org § 27 is listed next to that statute number. The researcher turns to the "B" volume[5] and looks up Businesses and Organizations,[6] and then turns to section 27 of that topic, and will find an allusion to that statute. References to the jurisprudence volumes are by section number rather than page number. To find all the references in the encyclopedia to a particular statute, check both the pocket part and the main volume.

b. *Legal and Business Forms.*   These volumes contain forms that attorneys find helpful when drafting documents. They help ensure that all necessary elements are included. Forms may be included for the preparation of documents relating to such areas as business enterprises, real and personal property, leases and consumer protection, estate planning, and contracts.

c. *Table of Cases and Numeric Case Names.*   These volumes list in alphabetical order the names of every case referred to in the state's jurisprudence volumes. Each case name is followed by a citation so that the researcher can find the court's written decision. As an additional feature, it is also followed by a list of the sections in the state jurisprudence volumes in which the case is cited. For example, suppose one needed to locate *Peden v. State Board of Funeral Directors and Embalmers* but had no citation and therefore no initial way of finding the case. By checking in the Table of Cases volume under the letter "P," one could find the following notation: "*Peden v. State Board of Funeral Directors & Embalmers* (1966, Fla App D3) 189 So.2d 526—Adm. L. §§165, 173, 175; Bus & Occ §60." This indicates that:

1. it is a 1966 case that was heard in the Florida Appellate Court, Third District;

2. the written decision of the court can be found in volume 189 of Southern Reporter, Second Series at page 526; and

3. this case is referred to in the main volumes of Fla Jur 2d dealing with the subject of Administrative Law in sections 165, 173, and 175; it is also referred to in section 60 of the subject of Businesses and Occupations.

Anyone who is not sure what an abbreviation such as "Adm.L." means can simply check the front of the volume for the chart that defines all abbreviations used in that volume.

Cases that have names that begin with numbers, such as *163rd Street Bank v. Smith,* are listed separately in a table of numeric case names at the end of the volume. If the number is usually spelled out, it will be listed in both the alphabetical and the numeric tables.

D. *The State Digests*

The purpose of this set is to provide a method whereby the researcher can use one case to find other cases dealing with similar issues. The digests can also serve as a starting point for legal research when the initial focus of the research effort is to obtain relevant case law (as opposed to other kinds of primary authority such as statutory law).

The digests serve as a kind of index to the "key number" system created by the West Publishing Company. With this system, the publisher has divided the entire body of law into several hundred legal topics. Each topic has then been divided into numerous subtopics. For example, the publisher happens to have subdivided the topic of "Homicide" into 354 subtopics such as "Deliberation and premeditation" and "Solicitation of murder." Every one of the subtopics of "Homicide" has then been arbitrarily assigned a "key number" from 1 to 354. The subtopic of "Deliberation and premeditation" has been assigned Homicide key number 14. "Solicitation of murder" has been assigned Homicide key number 26. Each topic (such as "Homicide") that appears in the digest begins with a table of contents showing what each key number represents.

To find case law concerning the issue of deliberation and premeditation as it pertains to homicide, turn to the "Homicide" section of the state digest, look under key number 14 within that topic, and find one-sentence summaries or "annotations" (along with citations) of all state court appellate cases within that state that pertain to that topic.

West Publishing Company, which publishes all the regional reporters as well as the digests, has analyzed every appellate court case in the United States (as well as federal trial court cases and other materials) and has determined what key issues are raised in each one. The key numbers relevant to any particular case have been placed at the top of each printed appellate decision. For example, see the case of *The Florida Bar v. Furman,* which has been reproduced from *Southern Reporter, Second Series* in Figures 2-1a through 2-1e. This case has two headnotes. The first contains one key number (Injunction key number 131). The second contains four key numbers [Attorney and Client key number 11(3), Constitutional Law key numbers 90.1(1) and 230.3(9), and Injunction key number 89(5)]. If one reading the case of *The Florida Bar v. Furman* finds that the paragraph within the second headnote is on point with regard to the issues being researched, the researcher can look in the digest under the topic of "Attorney and Client," look under key number 11(3) within that topic, and then find annotations along with corresponding citations for all cases dealing with the same legal issue as the one addressed in the second headnote of *The Florida Bar v. Furman*. The researcher can also find cases related to that headnote from a constitutional law perspective by looking in the digest under the topic of "Constitutional Law" and then examining key numbers 90.1(1) and 230.3(9) within that topic. Cases related to the second headnote can also be found under the topic of "Injunctions" key number 11(3) if the researcher is interested in the legal point made in that headnote with regard to injunctions.

A reproduction of a page from a state digest volume can be found in Figure 4-3.

1.   Examples in Various States

The set for the state of Oregon is known as *West's Oregon Digest 2d*; for Indiana, it is known as *West's Indiana Digest 2d*.

2.   Never Cited

While state digests refer to case law, which is regarded as primary authority, the analyses found in these books are not primary authority themselves. Consequently, researchers do not quote directly from the digests in appellate briefs or memoranda of law. If one finds case law by using the digests, the cases themselves would be cited rather than references from the digest.

3.   Alphabetical Organization

The state digests are set up alphabetically by legal topic, and a general index is therefore not required to locate specific subjects. For example, to read about the general topic of "Adoption," turn directly to the "A" volume.[7] Nevertheless, there is a *Descriptive-Word Index* at the end of the set that may be helpful (a) if one is unable to locate a topic, (b) if the topic being researched has been disbursed under many different subtopics, or (c) if one wishes to begin the research process by looking for case law using a key word as a starting point. To illustrate, when looking up "Probate" in the main volumes of the digest, the researcher may be surprised to find that probate is not listed as a separate topic. On the other hand, if the researcher looks up "Probate" in the Descriptive-Word Index, many references with their corresponding key numbers will be found under other topics such as "Executors and Administrators," "Wills," and "Courts." For further information concerning the *Descriptive-Word Index*, see subsection 5.d immediately following.

4.   *Updated with Pocket Parts*

5.   *Special Volumes*

The digests generally contain several special research tools, including:

a. The Table of Cases.   These are one or two volumes at the end of the set that contains all the cases listed alphabetically by the name of the plaintiff. It could be referred to as the *Plaintiff/Defendant Table*. The case of *Smith v. Jones* would, therefore, be listed in the "S" section as *Smith v. Jones*, and it would be followed by its citation. This table provides a means of locating a case if the researcher recalls the name of the plaintiff but cannot recall the name of the defendant. If the researcher finds more than one case under the same name for the plaintiff, the correct one can be found by examining the year in the citation or by reading the decision in the reporter. This volume is updated annually with pocket parts. See Figure 4-9 for a sample page from the Table of Cases.

b. The Defendant/Plaintiff Table.   These are one or two volumes at the end of the set that contain all the cases listed alphabetically by the name of the defendant. For example, the case of *Smith v. Jones* would be listed with its title in the "J" section as "*Jones, Smith v.*" Each case is followed by its corresponding citation. This gives researchers the opportunity to locate a case if they recall only the name of the defendant, but cannot to recall the name of the plaintiff. If the researcher finds more than one case under the same name for the defendant, the correct one can be found by examining the year in the citation or by reading the decision in the reporter. This volume is updated annually with pocket parts. See Figure 4-1 for a sample page from the Defendant/Plaintiff Table.

c. The Descriptive-Word Index.   This index includes one or more volumes at the end of the set that indicate under which topics and key numbers each of the words can be found in the state digest series. The descriptive words are listed in this index in alphabetical order. Some researchers who are specifically looking for case law find this index to be an excellent starting point for their research. See Figure 4-8 for a sample page from the Descriptive Word Index.

To illustrate how the index can be used, suppose that one wished to locate cases pertaining to grounded vessels. Looking in the *Descriptive-Word Index* under "grounded vessels," one can find the following reference: "Grounded Vessels, collision with. Collision 75(6)." This shows that one-sentence summaries of cases that pertain to collisions with grounded vessels can be found under key number 75(6) within the topic of "Collisions." Since the digests are organized alphabetically, one could find the topic of "Collisions" in the "C" book, and then look at the annotations under key number 75(6).

d. Words and Phrases.   This special section, which is often combined with the *Defendant/Plaintiff Table,* lists words and phrases that are defined in cases included in the digest series. They appear in alphabetical order and each one is followed by the name and citation of the case that defines it.

SEC. 4-4
FOUR BASIC FEDERAL RESEARCH TOOLS

A.   The Federal Reporters

These books contain the written decisions of the federal courts, and they include the following sets:

1.   Federal Supplement

This set includes the decisions of the U.S. District Courts and the United States Court of International Trade. The fact that the case can be found in this set establishes that it emanates from one of these two courts. *Federal Supplement* is organized chronologically and updated with advance sheets. A citation of a case that appears in this set, such as *Richmond Boro Gun Club, Inc. v. City of New York,* 896 F.Supp. 276 (E.D. N.Y. 1995), shows that the case can be found in volume 896, page 276 of *Federal Supplement,* and that this was a 1995 case coming from the Eastern District of New York.

2.   Federal Reporter

This set contains the decisions of the U.S. Circuit Courts of Appeal. Any case with a citation to the *Federal Reporter* is by definition from these courts. *Federal Reporter 3d,* the third series of this set, is organized chronologically and updated with advance sheets. A citation of a case that appears in this set, such as *Safeco Life Insurance Co. v. Musser,* 65 F.3d 647 (7th Cir. 1995), shows that the case can be found in volume 65, page 647 of *Federal Reporter 3d,* and that it was a 1995 case coming from the Seventh Circuit.

3. ***The Three U.S. Supreme Court Reporters***

Any Supreme Court decision can be found in one of the three following sets:

a. United States Reports (abbreviated "U.S.") is the official reporter of Supreme Court decisions.

b. The Supreme Court Reporter (abbreviated "S.Ct.") is the West Publishing Company reporter. This is the only set of the three that contains the key numbers, since the key number system is the exclusive property of West Publishing Company.

c. United States Supreme Court Reports, Lawyer's Edition (abbreviated "L.Ed." for the first series or "L.Ed.2d" for the second series) is the Lawyers Cooperative Publishing Company reporter of these cases.

While there is some debate as to whether all three of the Supreme Court reporters should be included in a U.S. Supreme Court citation, the trend is to include all of them. A citation of a case from this court, such as *Renne v. Geary,* 501 U.S. 312, 111 S.Ct. 2331, 115 L.Ed.2d 288 (1991) shows that the case can be found in volume 501, page 312 of *United States Reports.* It can also be found in volume 111, page 2331 of *The Supreme Court Reporter* and in volume 115, page 288 of *United States Supreme Court Reports, Lawyer's Edition, Second Series.* It further shows that the decision was rendered in 1991.

B. ***The Federal Statutes***

The federal statutes can be found in any one of three different sets published by different publishers:

1. *The United States Code,* which is published by the United States Government Printing Office,

2. *The United States Code Annotated,* which is published by West Publishing Company, and

3. *The United States Code Service,* which is published by Lawyer's Cooperative Publishing Company.

C. ***The National Encyclopedias***

There are two commonly used national encyclopedias of the law, and both of them are usually found in any complete law library. They each contain references to both federal and state materials.

1. *American Jurisprudence* is published by Lawyer's Cooperative Publishing Company, and

2. *Corpus Juris Secundum* is published by West Publishing Company.

D. The Federal Digests

Like the state digests (see Sec. 4-3, subsection D), these books serve as an index to the key number system, but they are designed for federal research and therefore refer to cases in the U.S. District Courts, the U.S. Circuit Courts of Appeal, and the U.S. Supreme Court. The federal digests (all published by West Publishing Company) include *Federal Digest* (for cases before 1939), *Modern Federal Practice Digest* (1939 to 1961), *West's Federal Practice Digest 2d* (1961 to 1975), and *West's Federal Practice Digest 3d* (1975 until its supplementation by *West's Federal Practice Digest 4th* in the early 1990s).

SEC. 4-5
THE ORGANIZATION OF A TYPICAL LAW LIBRARY

Law libraries are generally organized on the following basis:

A. The State Materials for the State in Which the Library Is Located

All of the following state sets would normally be located in one section of the library.

1. *The cases:* The state reporter (if any) and the regional reporter.

2. *The statutes:* The state statutes or code annotated and/or the state statutes.

3. *The encyclopedias:* The state jurisprudence volumes; if there is no state encyclopedia, then one or more nation encyclopedias.

4. *The digests*

For example, in the state of New Hampshire, this section would at least include:

The cases: New Hampshire Reports (since a state reporter exists in this state) and *Atlantic Reporter, Second Series* (the applicable regional reporter).

The statutes: The New Hampshire Revised Statutes Annotated, and the session laws (as found in the Laws of the State of New Hampshire).

The encyclopedias: American Jurisprudence 2d or *Corpus Juris Secundum* (since there is no New Hampshire jurisprudence set).

The digests: West's New Hampshire Digest

Other materials: It might also include other materials such as the New Hampshire Code of Administrative Rules, which contains the administrative regulations for the state.

In the state of Rhode Island, this section would at least include:

The cases: Rhode Island Reports (for cases prior to 1980) and *Atlantic Reporter, Second Series* (the applicable regional reporter).

The statutes: The General Laws of Rhode Island and the session laws (as found in the Public Laws of Rhode Island and Providence Plantations, and the Acts and Resolves of Rhode Island and Providence Plantations).[8]

The encyclopedias: American Jurisprudence 2d or *Corpus Juris Secundum* (since there is no Rhode Island jurisprudence set).

The digests: West's Rhode Island Digest.

B. *The Federal Materials*

All of the following federal sets would normally be located in one section of the library.

1. *The cases: Federal Supplement, Federal Reporter,* and one or all of the following sets: *United States Reports, The Supreme Court Reporter,* and/or the *United States Supreme Court Reports, Lawyer's Edition.*

2. *The statutes:* The *United States Code Annotated,* the *United States Code,* and/or the *United States Code Service.*

3. *The encyclopedias:* One or both of the following: *American Jurisprudence, Second Series* and *Corpus Juris Secundum.*

4. *The digests: Federal Digest* (for cases before 1939), *Modern Federal Practice Digest* (1939–1961), *West's Federal Practice Digest 2d* (1961–1975), and *West's Federal Practice Digest 3d* (1975 until its supplementation by *West's Federal Practice Digest 4th* in the early 1990s).

C. *The Regional Reporters*

This area of the library includes all volumes (both first and second series) of *Atlantic Reporter, North Eastern Reporter, North Western Reporter, Pacific Reporter,*

South Eastern Reporter, South Western Reporter, and *Southern Reporter.* A second set of the regional reporter that includes the state in which the library is located would normally be placed with the section of the library devoted to state materials.

D. *The State Materials for States Other Than the One in Which the Library Is Located*

These shelves are generally organized alphabetically beginning with the materials for the state of Alabama and ending with those for Wyoming. The materials for each state will usually include the state statutes, the state reporters (if they exist for that particular state), the state jurisprudence volumes (if they exist for that particular state), and the state digests.

E. *All Other Materials*

This section would include law review articles, treatises (which are books dealing with various subject areas of the law), periodicals, and other library acquisitions.

SEC. 4-6
SHEPARD'S CITATIONS

The purpose of the sets of books known as *Shepard's Citations* is to verify the current status of a known case, rule, or law. These sets are often simply referred to as "citators." If, for example, the citation for a known case is researched in *Shepard's Citations,* one can find out among many other things whether the case has been reversed, modified, or upheld on appeal, overruled in subsequent cases, or simply referred to in other cases. If a statute is checked in *Shepard's Citations,* one can discover such information as whether the statute has been repealed or modified. Materials that can be "shepardized" include state and federal statutes, cases, constitutional provisions, administrative regulations, rules of procedure, and many other sources of law. Many different sets of *Shepard's Citations* (usually several volumes in length) can be found throughout the library. For example, one can be found at the end of *Atlantic Reporter,* another at the end of *North Eastern Reporter,* another at the end of the local state's statutes, another at the end of *Federal Supplement,* and at the ends of numerous other sets. For a sample page from a set of *Shepard's Citations,* see Figure 4-13.

SEC 4-7
SAMPLE CASE WITH EXHIBITS SHOWING CONNECTIONS BETWEEN RESEARCH SETS[9]

Suppose one wanted to research the Florida case of *Alexander v. State* but faced the following obstacles: (1) No citation for the case was given. (2) No relevant statutes or constitutional provisions were given. (3) The research assignment was in connection with a case in which the client of the firm was to plead insanity, but the firm did not know the procedure to be followed in court to raise the issue. This researcher could begin by using several possible approaches.

To research the case of *Alexander v. State* when you do not already have a citation for the case, look under the letter "A" for Alexander in the *Table of Cases* or the letter "S" in the *Defendant/Plaintiff Table* of *Florida Digest 2d*. Figure 4-1[10] shows a copy of the appropriate page from the Defendant/Plaintiff Table. The reference on that page shows the entry of "STATE-Alexander, Fla. 477 So.2d 557." Since listings are by the name of the defendant first, the allusion is to the case of *Alexander v. State* (rather than *State v. Alexander*). A copy of the court's decision can therefore be found by turning to volume 477, page 557 of *Southern Reporter, Second Series*.

The court's decision, as found in *Southern Reporter, Second Series*, is reproduced in Figures 4-2a through 4-2d.[11] One can find in Figure 4-2a below the name and docket number of the case at the bottom of the first column that it is a 1985 case from the Supreme Court of Florida. The complete citation for the case is *Alexander v. State*, 477 So.2d 557 (Fla. 1985).

The second headnote of the case is entitled "Weapons key number 10." By looking in the *Florida Digest* under the topic of "Weapons" and then under key number 10 within that topic, the researcher can find the page reproduced in Figure 4-3.[12] This page shows one-sentence summaries or "annotations" for all of the state court cases that have made the same legal point with regard to weapons as the one made in the second headnote of *Alexander v. State*. Note that the *Alexander* case itself is also located in this section, and it can be found as the second annotation under Weapons key number 10. Every case under this key number in the digest should have a headnote with Weapons key number 10 at the top of the case in *Southern Reporter, Second Series*. For example, the fourth annotation under Weapons key number 10 refers to the case of *Boren v. State*, 576 So.2d 798 (Fla. 1st DCA 1991). Look up this case in volume 576, page 798 of *Southern Reporter, Second Series* to find the *Boren* case. The first page of the case is reproduced in Figure 4-4.[13] Note that the first of the three headnotes in that case is entitled Weapons key number 10.

Consult Plaintiff Table for Key Number Digest Classification and Case History

STATE—Aguilera, FlaApp 1 Dist, 606 So2d 1194.
STATE—A.H., FlaApp 2 Dist, 499 So2d 27.
STATE—A.H., FlaApp 3 Dist, 577 So2d 699.
STATE—Ahedo, FlaApp 2 Dist, 603 So2d 80.
STATE—Ahlberg, FlaApp 3 Dist, 541 So2d 775.
STATE—Ahnen, FlaApp 2 Dist, 565 So2d 855.
STATE—Aikens, FlaApp 1 Dist, 488 So2d 543.
STATE—Aira, FlaApp 5 Dist, 583 So2d 419.
STATE—A.J., FlaApp 3 Dist, 561 So2d 1198.
STATE—Akbar, FlaApp 1 Dist, 570 So2d 1047.
STATE—Alba, FlaApp 3 Dist, 541 So2d 747.
STATE—Alberty, FlaApp 3 Dist, 536 So2d 283.
STATE—Albo, FlaApp 3 Dist, 477 So2d 1071.
STATE—Albritton, Fla, 476 So2d 158.
STATE—Albritton, FlaApp 2 Dist, 502 So2d 954.
STATE—Albritton, FlaApp 2 Dist, 500 So2d 639.
STATE—Albritton, FlaApp 5 Dist, 561 So2d 19.
STATE—Albritton, FlaApp 5 Dist, 458 So2d 320.
STATE—Albury, FlaApp 3 Dist, 541 So2d 1262.
STATE—Aldazabal, FlaApp 3 Dist, 471 So2d 639.
STATE—Aldret, FlaApp 1 Dist, 592 So2d 264.
STATE—Aldridge, Fla, 503 So2d 1257.
STATE—Aldridge, Fla, 351 So2d 942.
STATE—Alejo, FlaApp 2 Dist, 483 So2d 117.
STATE—Aleman, FlaApp 2 Dist, 535 So2d 342.
STATE—Aleman, FlaApp 2 Dist, 498 So2d 967.
STATE—Aleman, FlaApp 3 Dist, 536 So2d 384.
STATE—Alen, FlaApp 3 Dist, 596 So2d 1083.
STATE—Alexander, Fla, 477 So2d 557.
STATE—Alexander, FlaApp 1 Dist, 553 So2d 312.
STATE—Alexander, FlaApp 1 Dist, 470 So2d 856.
STATE—Alexander, FlaApp 2 Dist, 513 So2d 1117.
STATE—Alexander, FlaApp 3 Dist, 603 So2d 658.
STATE—Alexander, FlaApp 4 Dist, 575 So2d 1370.
STATE—Alexander, FlaApp 4 Dist, 450 So2d 1212.
STATE—Alexander, FlaApp 5 Dist, 576 So2d 350.
STATE—Alfaro, FlaApp 4 Dist, 471 So2d 1345.
STATE—Alfonso, FlaApp 3 Dist, 561 So2d 1207.
STATE—Alfonso, FlaApp 3 Dist, 528 So2d 383.
STATE—Alford, FlaApp 1 Dist, 460 So2d 1000.
STATE—Ali, FlaApp 2 Dist, 476 So2d 308.
STATE—Al Johnson Const. Co., FlaApp 1 Dist, 473 So2d 209.
STATE—Al Johnson Const. Co., FlaApp 1 Dist, 473 So2d 206.
STATE—Allah, FlaApp 3 Dist, 471 So2d 121.
STATE—Allen, Fla, 599 So2d 996.
STATE—Allen, Fla, 526 So2d 69.

STATE—Allen, FlaApp 1 Dist, 529 So2d 789.
STATE—Allen, FlaApp 1 Dist, 515 So2d 256.
STATE—Allen, FlaApp 1 Dist, 506 So2d 1149.
STATE—Allen, FlaApp 1 Dist, 493 So2d 1080.
STATE—Allen, FlaApp 1 Dist, 492 So2d 802.
STATE—Allen, FlaApp 1 Dist, 482 So2d 529.
STATE—Allen, FlaApp 2 Dist, 598 So2d 240.
STATE—Allen, FlaApp 2 Dist, 585 So2d 366.
STATE—Allen, FlaApp 2 Dist, 579 So2d 200.
STATE—Allen, FlaApp 2 Dist, 561 So2d 1339.
STATE—Allen, FlaApp 2 Dist, 560 So2d 294.
STATE—Allen, FlaApp 2 Dist, 529 So2d 321.
STATE—Allen, FlaApp 2 Dist, 510 So2d 654.
STATE—Allen, FlaApp 2 Dist, 508 So2d 360.
STATE—Allen, FlaApp 2 Dist, 479 So2d 257.
STATE—Allen, FlaApp 2 Dist, 476 So2d 309.
STATE—Allen, FlaApp 4 Dist, 584 So2d 1126.
STATE—Allen, FlaApp 4 Dist, 566 So2d 892.
STATE—Allen, FlaApp 4 Dist, 522 So2d 850.
STATE—Allen, FlaApp 4 Dist, 487 So2d 410.
STATE—Allen, FlaApp 4 Dist, 474 So2d 261.
STATE—Allen, FlaApp 5 Dist, 604 So2d 23.
STATE—Allen, FlaApp 5 Dist, 580 So2d 339.
STATE—Allen, FlaApp 5 Dist, 560 So2d 1329.
STATE—Allen, FlaApp 5 Dist, 543 So2d 347.
STATE—Alley, FlaApp 4 Dist, 553 So2d 354.
STATE—Allied Fidelity Ins. Co., FlaApp 1 Dist, 499 So2d 932.
STATE—Alloway, FlaApp 1 Dist, 593 So2d 1193.
STATE—Alpern, FlaApp 3 Dist, 605 So2d 1291.
STATE—Alphonse, FlaApp 2 Dist, 593 So2d 612.
STATE—Alvarado, FlaApp 2 Dist, 466 So2d 335.
STATE—Alvarado, FlaApp 3 Dist, 574 So2d 274.
STATE—Alvarado, FlaApp 3 Dist, 521 So2d 180.
STATE—Alvarez, FlaApp 2 Dist, 593 So2d 289.
STATE—Alvarez, FlaApp 2 Dist, 535 So2d 341.
STATE—Alvarez, FlaApp 3 Dist, 592 So2d 1213.
STATE—Alvarez, FlaApp 3 Dist, 574 So2d 1119.
STATE—Alvarez, FlaApp 3 Dist, 573 So2d 400.
STATE—Alvarez, FlaApp 3 Dist, 561 So2d 5.
STATE—Alvarez, FlaApp 3 Dist, 527 So2d 913.
STATE—Alvarez, FlaApp 3 Dist, 485 So2d 470.
STATE—Alvarez, FlaApp 3 Dist, 467 So2d 455.
STATE—Alvarez, FlaApp 4 Dist, 525 So2d 946.

STATE—Alvarez, FlaApp 4 Dist, 515 So2d 286.
STATE—Alvarez, FlaApp 5 Dist, 600 So2d 559.
STATE—Alvarez–Botero, FlaApp 5 Dist, 562 So2d 783.
STATE—Alvin, Fla, 548 So2d 1112.
STATE—Alvin, FlaApp 5 Dist, 573 So2d 418.
STATE—Alvord, Fla, 459 So2d 316.
STATE—A.M., FlaApp 3 Dist, 574 So2d 1185.
STATE—A.M., FlaApp 3 Dist, 561 So2d 1301.
STATE—A.M., FlaApp 4 Dist, 593 So2d 316.
STATE—Amado, Fla, 585 So2d 282.
STATE—Amado, FlaApp 2 Dist, 563 So2d 736.
STATE—Amaker, FlaApp 1 Dist, 492 So2d 419.
STATE—Aman, FlaApp 4 Dist, 486 So2d 15.
STATE—Amann, FlaApp, 403 So2d 1006.
STATE—Amaya, FlaApp 2 Dist, 580 So2d 885.
STATE—Amazon, Fla, 487 So2d 8.
STATE—Amazon, FlaApp 2 Dist, 537 So2d 170.
STATE—Amell, FlaApp 2 Dist, 438 So2d 42.
STATE—Ames, FlaApp 1 Dist, 518 So2d 465.
STATE—Ames, FlaApp 5 Dist, 470 So2d 94.
STATE—Amicarelli, FlaApp 1 Dist, 547 So2d 712.
STATE—Amison, FlaApp 2 Dist, 504 So2d 473.
STATE—Ammons, FlaApp 1 Dist, 606 So2d 1210.
STATE—Amoros, Fla, 531 So2d 1256.
STATE—Amoroso, FlaApp 4 Dist, 487 So2d 415.
STATE—Amoss, FlaApp 1 Dist, 547 So2d 716.
STATE—Amoss, FlaApp 1 Dist, 529 So2d 789.
STATE—A.M.R., Fla, 604 So2d 813.
STATE—Amrein, FlaApp 1 Dist, 504 So2d 783.
STATE—Anderson, Fla, 574 So2d 87.
STATE—Anderson, FlaApp 1 Dist, 592 So2d 1119.
STATE—Anderson, FlaApp 1 Dist, 579 So2d 344.
STATE—Anderson, FlaApp 1 Dist, 570 So2d 1101.
STATE—Anderson, FlaApp 1 Dist, 504 So2d 1270.
STATE—Anderson, FlaApp 1 Dist, 489 So2d 855.
STATE—Anderson, FlaApp 1 Dist, 471 So2d 661.
STATE—Anderson, FlaApp 2 Dist, 576 So2d 319.
STATE—Anderson, FlaApp 2 Dist, 532 So2d 4.
STATE—Anderson, FlaApp 2 Dist, 503 So2d 388.
STATE—Anderson, FlaApp 2 Dist, 502 So2d 1288.
STATE—Anderson, FlaApp 2 Dist, 487 So2d 85.
STATE—Anderson, FlaApp 3 Dist, 557 So2d 136.
STATE—Anderson, FlaApp 3 Dist, 530 So2d 1104.
STATE—Anderson, FlaApp 3 Dist, 507 So2d 775.
STATE—Anderson, FlaApp 3 Dist, 467 So2d 781.
STATE—Anderson, FlaApp 3 Dist, 463 So2d 276.
STATE—Anderson, FlaApp 4 Dist, 602 So2d 585.

FIGURE 4-1

sulted in harmful error requiring reversal of each of appellant's convictions. *Teffeteller v. State,* 439 So.2d 840, 845 (Fla.1983), *cert. denied,* 465 U.S. 1074, 104 S.Ct. 1430, 79 L.Ed.2d 754 (1984). We again caution prosecutors to note that repeated failure to curb this misconduct adds fuel to the flame of those who advocate the adoption of a per se rule of reversal for such misconduct.

We find that none of the alleged trial court errors asserted by appellant affected his convictions. Accordingly, we affirm appellant's convictions and sentences with the exception of the death sentence. For the reasons expressed, we vacate the sentence of death and remand for a new sentencing proceeding before a new jury.

It is so ordered.

BOYD, C.J., and OVERTON, McDONALD, EHRLICH and SHAW, JJ., concur.

ADKINS, J., concurs in the convictions, but dissents from the sentences.

Jimmie Lee ALEXANDER, Petitioner,

v.

STATE of Florida, Respondent.

No. 65666.

Supreme Court of Florida.

Oct. 10, 1985.

Defendant pleaded nolo contendere to charge of carrying concealed firearm, reserving for appeal the denial of his motion to dismiss. The Circuit Court, Broward County, Harry G. Hinckley, Jr., J., withheld adjudication and placed defendant on probation, and defendant appealed. The District Court of Appeal, 450 So.2d 1212, affirmed. Upon defendant's application for review on the basis of statutory validity, the Supreme Court, Adkins, J., held that: (1) statutory prohibitions against carrying a concealed weapon that is readily accessible for immediate use did not violate due process and were not unconstitutionally vague, and (2) firearm, found in defendant's zippered hand purse with wallet, driver's license, and other forms of identification, was encased in a "gun case," precluding prosecution of defendant for carrying a concealed weapon.

Reversed and remanded with directions.

McDonald, J., dissented.

1. Weapons ⟋2

Promoting firearms safety and crime prevention are permissible legislative objectives. West's F.S.A. § 790.25(1).

2. Weapons ⟋10

Primary requirement of Florida statute, § 790.25(5), permitting a person to carry a concealed weapon in a private conveyance if weapon is securely encased or not otherwise readily accessible for immediate use, is that firearm not be readily accessible for immediate use. West's F.S.A. § 790.25(5).

3. Constitutional Law ⟋258(3)
   Weapons ⟋3

Prohibition of Florida statutes, §§ 790.01(2), 790.25(5), proscribing the carrying of a concealed weapon on or about the person that is readily accessible for immediate use, is reasonably related to the permissible legislative purposes of promoting firearms safety and preventing use of firearms in crimes and, thus, does not violate the due process clauses of the State and Federal Constitutions. West's F.S.A. §§ 790.001(15, 16), 790.01(2), 790.25(5); West's F.S.A. Const. Art. 1, § 9; U.S.C.A. Const.Amends. 5, 14.

4. Weapons ⟋3

Prohibitions of Florida statutes, §§ 790.01(2), 790.25(5), proscribing the carrying of a concealed weapon on or about

FIGURE 4-2a

103

the person that is readily accessible for immediate use, are not unconstitutionally vague due to lack of statutory definition for term "gun case" used in definition of phrase "securely encased" set forth in § 790.25(5); term "gun case" means any type of receptacle for carrying a gun that makes the gun not readily accessible for immediate use. West's F.S.A. §§ 790.01(2), 790.25(5).

> See publication Words and Phrases for other judicial constructions and definitions.

5. Weapons ⊫10

Firearm, found in defendant's zippered hand purse with wallet, driver's license, and other forms of identification, was encased in a "gun case," so that defendant could not be prosecuted for carrying a concealed weapon that was not securely encased or that was readily accessible for immediate use. West's F.S.A. §§ 790.001(16), 790.01(2), 790.25(5).

———

Richard L. Jorandby, Public Defender, and Gary Caldwell and Dean Willbur, Asst. Public Defenders, Fifteenth Judicial Circuit, West Palm Beach, for petitioner.

Jim Smith, Atty. Gen., and Marlyn J. Altman and Sarah B. Mayer, Asst. Attys. Gen., West Palm Beach, for respondent.

Robert Dowlut, Washington, D.C., for National Rifle Association, amicus curiae.

ADKINS, Justice.

Petitioner appeals the Fourth District Court of Appeal's affirmance of the trial court's denial of his motion to dismiss. The district also held section 790.01(2), Florida Statutes (1981), to be constitutional. *Alexander v. State*, 450 So.2d 1212 (Fla. 4th DCA 1984). We have jurisdiction. Art. V, § 3(b)(3), Fla. Const.

We hold that section 790.01(2), Florida Statutes (1981), as modified by sections 790.25(5) and 790.001(15) & (16), Florida Statutes (Supp.1982), is not unconstitutional. However, on the facts of this case, we hold that the trial court erred in denying petitioner's motion to dismiss.

Petitioner was charged by information with carrying a concealed weapon in violation of section 790.01(2), Florida Statutes (1981). He moved to dismiss the charge, citing an exception to the prohibition against carrying a concealed weapon found in section 790.25(5), Florida Statutes (Supp. 1982). That section provides:

(5) POSSESSION IN PRIVATE CONVEYANCE.—Notwithstanding subsection (2), it is lawful and is not a violation of s. 790.01 to possess a concealed firearm or other weapon for self-defense or other lawful purpose within the interior of a private conveyance, without a license, if the firearm is securely encased or is otherwise not readily accessible for immediate use. Nothing herein contained prohibits the carrying of a legal firearm other than a handgun anywhere in a private conveyance when such firearm is being carried for lawful use. Nothing herein contained shall be construed to authorize the carrying of a concealed firearm or other weapon on the person. This subsection shall be liberally construed in favor of the lawful use, ownership, and possession of firearms and other weapons, including lawful self-defense as provided in s. 776.012.

Petitioner presents the following version of the facts leading up to his arrest. On September 7, 1982, petitioner, an employee of Wags, was sitting in the driver's seat of his car which was parked in the Wags parking lot. Police Officer Lerman asked petitioner for identification. In his sworn motion to dismiss petitioner asserted that when asked for the identification, petitioner opened his zippered pouch, looked inside it and was unable to find his identification, then zippered the pouch shut. On appeal to this Court, however, petitioner accepts the state's version of the facts as set forth in its traverse to the motion to dismiss as follows: When asked for identification petitioner said he had identification and began to unzip his black leather hand purse. He then stopped unzipping it, zipped it back up, and said he did not have his wallet or identification on his person at that time.

FIGURE 4-2b

The resolution of the issues in this case do not turn on this particular aspect of the facts, however. What occurred afterward is agreed upon by both parties. Lerman became suspicious of a bulky object in the pouch. He took the pouch from petitioner, opened it, found a firearm inside and arrested petitioner for possession of a concealed firearm. Petitioner's wallet, driver's license, and other forms of identification were found in the purse.

In the trial court petitioner argued that his gun was in a zippered gun case and thus was "securely encased" within the meaning of 790.001(16), Florida Statutes (Supp.1982). "Securely encased" is defined in that section as follows:

(16) "Securely encased" means encased in a glove compartment, whether or not locked; in a snapped holster; in a gun case, whether or not locked; in a zippered gun case; or in a closed box or container which requires a lid or cover to be opened for access.

The state argued that the object was a man's black leather hand purse and not a zippered gun case, pointing out that defendant's wallet, driver's license, and other forms of identification were later found inside.

The trial court denied petitioner's motion to dismiss, ruling that the bag was neither a zippered gun case nor a container that requires opening a cover or a lid for access and therefore was not securely encased. Petitioner pled nolo contendre, reserving the right to appeal the denial of his motion to dismiss. The trial court withheld adjudication and placed him on probation.

On appeal, petitioner argued that the trial court erred in denying his motion to dismiss and that section 790.01(2), Florida Statutes (1981), as refined in sections 790.-25(5), Florida Statutes (Supp.1982), and 790.001(15), Florida Statutes (Supp.1982), is unconstitutional. The district court affirmed the denial of the motion to dismiss. Regarding the constitutional issue, the court held that the facial invalidity of a statute could be raised for the first time on appeal citing *Trushin v. State*, 425 So.2d

1126 (Fla.1983). It concluded, however, that the statutes in question are not void for vagueness.

Petitioner argues that this statutory scheme violates the due process clause of the state and federal constitutions because it is not rationally related to a legitimate state purpose and because it is so vague that it does not give persons of ordinary intelligence fair notice of what is proscribed.

[1] We have held that a statute is constitutional if it bears a reasonable relation to a permissible legislative objective and is not discriminatory, arbitrary, or oppressive. *Lasky v. State Farm Insurance Co.*, 296 So.2d 9 (Fla.1974). The legislature has declared that the objectives of Chapter 790 are "to promote firearms safety and to curb and prevent the use of firearms and other weapons in crime and by incompetent persons without prohibiting the lawful use in defense of life, home, and property, and the use by United States or state military organizations, and as otherwise now authorized by law, including the right to use and own firearms for target practice and markmanship on target practice ranges or other lawful places, and lawful hunting and other lawful purposes." § 790.25(1), Fla.Stat. (Supp.1982). Certainly promoting firearms safety and crime prevention are permissible legislative objectives.

[2, 3] Next, we must determine if the means chosen in the statutes bear a reasonable relationship to those objectives. Section 790.01, Florida Statutes (1981), proscribes carrying a concealed weapon. An exception to that proscription is provided in section 790.25(5), Florida Statutes (Supp. 1982), which allows for carrying a concealed weapon in a private conveyance, if "the firearm is securely encased or not otherwise readily accessible for immediate use." "Securely encased" and "readily accessible for immediate use" are defined in the statutory scheme. *See* §§ 790.001(15), (16), Fla.Stat. (Supp.1982). We agree with the state that by using the *"or is otherwise"* phrase the legislature clearly indi-

FIGURE 4-2c

cated that the primary requirement is that the firearm not be "readily accessible for immediate use." The prohibition against carrying a concealed weapon that is readily accessible for immediate use is reasonably related to the legislative purposes of promoting firearms safety and preventing the use of firearms in crimes.

[4] We likewise do not find that these statutes are void for vagueness.

The test of a statute insofar as vagueness is concerned is whether the language conveys sufficiently definite warning as to the proscribed conduct when measured by common understanding and practice.... "The constitutional requirement of definiteness is violated by a criminal statute that fails to give a person of ordinary intelligence fair notice that his contemplated conduct is forbidden by the statute. The underlying principle is that no man shall be held criminally responsible for conduct which he could not reasonably understand to be proscribed."

Zachary v. State, 269 So.2d 669, 670 (Fla. 1972) (citations and footnote omitted). The proscribed conduct in this statutory scheme is carrying a concealed weapon that is not securely encased or is readily accessible for immediate use. § 790.25(5), Fla.Stat. (Supp.1982). Petitioner argues that section 790.001(16), Florida Statutes (Supp.1982), is unconstitutionally vague because the term "gun case" is undefined. We do not agree.

As we point out below, a gun case can be of any type of receptacle for carrying a gun that makes the gun not readily accessible for immediate use. As long as the purposes of the statute are fulfilled, any further definitions are unnecessary.

[5] We do agree with petitioner that his motion to dismiss should have been granted. His argument is that the firearm was in a zippered gun case, and therefore his carrying of it in his automobile was not in violation of the statute. The state counters that the pouch was not a zippered gun case, because it contained additional objects inside other than the gun. However, as the National Rifle Association points out in

its *amicus curiae* brief, zippered gun cases are manufactured with room for carrying objects additional to the gun. Therefore, under the facts of this case, we hold that there was no dispute of fact, and as a matter of law, petitioner's pouch was a zippered gun case. This interpretation of the statute is consistent with its purposes, i.e., to promote firearms safety and to prevent crime. It would frustrate the intent of the legislature if we were to hold that the carrying of a firearm in a zippered pouch like petitioner's was proscribed by the statute, since it is no less readily accessible for immediate use.

In summary, section 790.01(2), Florida Statutes (1981), as well as sections 790.25(5), 790.001(15), (16), is constitutional. Petitioner's motion to dismiss should be granted. We remand to the district court with directions to further remand to the trial court for proceedings consistent with this opinion.

It is so ordered.

BOYD, C.J., and OVERTON, EHRLICH and SHAW, JJ., concur.

McDONALD, J., dissents.

THE FLORIDA BAR, Complainant,

v.

Raymond E. LaPORTE, Respondent.

Nos. 63527, 64092, 65817 and 66083.

Supreme Court of Florida.

Oct. 10, 1985.

Attorney disciplinary proceedings were brought. The Supreme Court held that neglect of legal matter due to lack of communication with an employee warrants

FIGURE 4-2d

C.A.11 (Fla.) 1989. Offense of possession with intent to distribute constitutes a "drug trafficking crime" within meaning of statute prohibiting carrying a firearm during and in relation to a drug trafficking crime. 18 U.S.C.A. § 924(c)(1, 2).—U.S. v. Rivera, 889 F.2d 1029, certiorari denied 110 S.Ct. 2191, 495 U.S. 939, 109 L.Ed.2d 519, certiorari denied Santiago v. U.S., 110 S.Ct. 3244, 497 U.S. 1006, 111 L.Ed.2d 754, certiorari denied Sud v. U.S., 111 S.Ct. 93, 498 U.S. 831, 112 L.Ed.2d 65.

C.A.11 (Fla.) 1986. In order to be convicted of carrying a firearm unlawfully during the commission of a felony, the defendant's act of carrying the firearm must, in and of itself, have violated federal, state, or local law. 18 U.S.C.(1982 Ed.) § 924(c)(2).—U.S. v. Machado, 804 F.2d 1537.

C.A.11 (Fla.) 1985. Under 18 U.S.C. (1982 Ed.) § 924 an offense can only be made out if the carrying of the firearm is in violation of federal, state, or local law.—U.S. v. Rouco, 765 F.2d 983, rehearing denied 772 F.2d 918, certiorari denied 106 S.Ct. 1646, 475 U.S. 1124, 90 L.Ed.2d 190.

&⚬**7. —— Intent or purpose.**

U.S.Fla. 1993. Phrase "in relation to," within meaning of statute requiring imposition of specified penalties if defendant, during and in relation to drug trafficking crime, uses or carries firearm, while expansive, clarifies, at minimum, that firearm must have some purpose or effect with respect to drug trafficking crime; its presence or involvement cannot be result of accident or coincidence. 18 U.S.C.A. § 924(c)(1).—Smith v. U.S., 113 S.Ct. 2050, 124 L.Ed.2d 138, rehearing denied 114 S.Ct. 13, 125 L.Ed.2d 765.

Fla.App. 5 Dist. 1990. Whether defendant convicted of carrying concealed weapon intended to violate prohibition against concealment was immaterial, as was his belief that he had valid permit to carry firearm; knowledgeable possession of concealed firearm was enough to constitute violation. West's F.S.A. § 790.01(1).—Wolfram v. State, 568 So.2d 992.

To convict person of crime of carrying concealed weapon, it must be shown, at minimum, that person charged knew he possessed weapon, that he had it "on or about" his person; knowledge of possession can be inferred from act of actual possession. West's F.S.A. § 790.01(1).—Id.

&⚬**8. —— Weapons prohibited.**

C.A.11 (Fla.) 1985. Under Florida law, operability is not a determinative factor in defining a firearm. West's F.S.A. § 790.001(6).—U.S. v. Rouco, 765 F.2d 983, rehearing denied 772 F.2d 918, certiorari denied 106 S.Ct. 1646, 475 U.S. 1124, 90 L.Ed.2d 190.

Fla.App. 1 Dist. 1991. A starter pistol is not designed to fire projectile, so that State had the burden of proving that it could either expel a projectile or be readily converted to do so in order to show that it was a firearm which it was illegal for defendant to carry in a concealed manner. West's F.S.A. §§ 790.001(6), 790.01(2).—Charley v. State, 590 So.2d 5.

Starter pistol whose barrel was substantially blocked by a metal plug, and each of whose chambers was blocked by a circular piece of metal formed inside the cylinder was not shown to be capable of expelling a projectile or readily converted to do so, and thus was not a "firearm" which was illegal to carry in a concealed manner. West's F.S.A. §§ 790.001(6), 790.01(2).—Id.

Fla.App. 5 Dist. 1993. Defendant could not be properly convicted for carrying concealed firearm where uncontroverted evidence was presented that firearm in defendant's automobile was unloaded and thus not readily accessible for immediate use. West's F.S.A. § 790.25(5).—Smith v. State, 617 So.2d 444, review dismissed 623 So.2d 496.

Fla.App. 5 Dist. 1989. A "deadly weapon" within meaning of statutory definition relating to concealed weapons is any instrument which will likely cause death or great bodily harm when used in the ordinary and usual manner contemplated by its design and construction. West's F.S.A. § 790.001(3)(a).—Robinson v. State, 547 So.2d 321.

An object can become a "deadly weapon" if its sole modern use is to cause great bodily harm. West's F.S.A. § 790.001(3)(a).—Id.

An object can be construed as a "deadly weapon" because of its use or threatened use during an alleged crime. West's F.S.A. § 790.001(3)(a).—Id.

A razor blade, like a nail file, keys or hatpin, is a common household item which when carried on or about a person, such as in a lady's pocketbook, is not a "concealed weapon" unless it is used in a threatening manner so that it might be considered deadly. West's F.S.A. § 790.001(3)(a).—Id.

Ordinary one-edged razor blade found in defendant's jacket pocket was not a "concealed weapon," in absence of evidence that defendant used the razor in a threatening manner. West's F.S.A. § 790.001(3)(a).—Id.

&⚬**10. —— Manner of carrying or concealment.**

Fla. 1993. Firearm was "readily accessible for immediate use," within meaning of statute setting forth offense of carrying concealed weapon, where firearm was found under driver's seat of stopped vehicle and ammunition for firearm and fully loaded clip were found under passenger's seat. West's F.S.A. § 790.01(2).—Ridley v. State, 621 So.2d 409.

Fla. 1985. Primary requirement of Florida statute, § 790.25(5), permitting a person to carry a concealed weapon in a private conveyance if weapon is securely encased or not otherwise readily accessible for immediate use, is that firearm not be readily accessible for immediate use. West's F.S.A. § 790.25(5).—Alexander v. State, 477 So.2d 557.

Firearm, found in defendant's zippered hand purse with wallet, driver's license, and other forms of identification, was encased in a "gun case," so that defendant could not be prosecuted for carrying a concealed weapon that was not securely encased or that was readily accessible for immediate use. West's F.S.A. §§ 790.001(16), 790.01(2), 790.25(5).—Id.

Fla. 1985. Firearm carried by occupant of motor vehicle having tinted window glass which prevents firearm from being visible within ordinary sight of persons outside the vehicle, although firearm was otherwise in clear view and unconcealed, was not a "concealed firearm" within meaning of West's F.S.A. § 790.001(2) defining a concealed firearm as one carried in such a manner as to conceal it from ordinary sight of another person.—State v. Teague, 475 So.2d 213.

Fla.App. 1 Dist. 1991. Firearm is "concealed," for purpose of crime of carrying concealed firearm, when it is on or about person and hidden from ordinary sight of another person; that is, firearm must be physically on person or readily accessible to him, and it must be hidden from casual and ordinary observation of another in normal associations of life. West's F.S.A. § 790.01(2).—Boren v. State, 576 So.2d 798.

Fla.App. 2 Dist. 1994. Rifle and shotgun that were partially enclosed in professionally made gun case attached to back of truck's seat cover were not "readily accessible," and thus their possession was not carrying concealed weapon in violation of statute; because of length of weapons and their position behind driver's seat, defendant could only retrieve guns by opening door and awkwardly reaching behind seat, such that guns could not be retrieved "as easily and quickly as if carried on the

FIGURE 4-3

Israel ROBAINA, etc., et al.,
Petitioners,

v.

ROYAL MARINE, INC., et al.,
Respondents.

No. 91–00325.

District Court of Appeal of Florida,
Third District.

March 8, 1991.

Following review of this petition for writ of certiorari, it is ordered that said petition is hereby denied. See *Venus Lab., Inc. v. Katz*, 573 So.2d 993 (Fla.3rd DCA 1991).

HUBBART, JORGENSON and
GODERICH, JJ., concur.

Herbert Allan BOREN, Appellant,

v.

STATE of Florida, Appellee.

No. 90–462.

District Court of Appeal of Florida,
First District.

March 11, 1991.

Rehearing Denied April 11, 1991.

Defendant was convicted of carrying concealed firearm, in the Circuit Court, Leon County, Kevin Davey, J., and defendant appealed. The District Court of Appeal held that evidence did not require finding as matter of law that firearm was not concealed.

Affirmed.

1. Weapons ⟋10

Firearm is "concealed," for purpose of crime of carrying concealed firearm, when it is on or about person and hidden from ordinary sight of another person; that is, firearm must be physically on person or readily accessible to him, and it must be hidden from casual and ordinary observation of another in normal associations of life. West's F.S.A. § 790.01(2).

See publication Words and Phrases for other judicial constructions and definitions.

2. Weapons ⟋17(5)

Whether firearm is concealed is to be determined by trier of fact under circumstances of each case.

3. Weapons ⟋17(5)

Evidence in trial for carrying concealed firearm did not establish as matter of law that firearm was not concealed, where firearm was placed beneath portable ventilation cushion next to door on driver's side of pickup truck, butt of firearm was facing outward and seat cushion was slightly raised, and officer saw firearm after defendant opened locked truck door. West's F.S.A. § 790.01(2).

Charles A. McMurry, Tallahassee, for appellant.

Robert A. Butterworth, Atty. Gen., Carolyn J. Mosley, Asst. Atty. Gen., Tallahassee, for appellee.

PER CURIAM.

Appellant challenges his conviction for carrying a concealed firearm contrary to section 790.01(2), Florida Statutes (1989). We affirm.

Appellant argues, among other things, that the firearm at issue was not concealed as a matter of law. It was the uncontroverted testimony of the arresting officer that the firearm was placed underneath a portable ventilation cushion next to the door on the driver's side of a pick-up truck; the butt of the gun was facing outward and the seat cushion was slightly raised.

FIGURE 4-4

To determine the general subject matter of Weapons key number 10, turn to the topic of "Weapons" in the "W" volume of *Florida Digest 2d* and find a table of contents at the beginning of that topic. The table of contents breaks down the topic of "Weapons" into subtopics and the key numbers that have been assigned to each one. The first page of the Weapons table of contents in the digest can be found in Figure 4-5.[14] This page shows that the general subject matter of Weapons key number 10 is "Manner of carrying or concealment."

From the first page of the *Alexander* case found in Figure 4-2a, one can see a reference in the second headnote to Florida statute § 790.25(5). To research the exact language of the statute, find it in the *Florida Statutes Annotated* under that number. A copy of the statute from this set is reproduced in Figure 4-6.[15] This exhibit came from the pocket part of the volume in *Florida Statutes Annotated* that includes § 790.25. Note that § 790.25(1), (2), part of (3), and (4) can be found in the main volume. The actual language of Florida statute § 790.25(5), which is the one we are concerned with, appears on this page reproduced from the pocket part. Several annotations appear at the bottom of the page where the title "Notes of Decisions" appears.

From the first page of the *Alexander* case found in Figure 4-2a, one can see a reference in the third headnote to Article I, § 9 of the Florida Constitution. To find the exact language of this constitutional provision, look at the end of the *Florida Statutes Annotated* to find the volumes pertaining to the Florida Constitution. By turning to Article I, § 9 of the constitution, the researcher finds the page reproduced in Figure 4-7.[16] This page from *Florida Statutes Annotated* shows the constitutional provision entitled "Due Process." The entire text of this section is only one sentence long. The annotations that interpret the meaning of this portion of the state constitution can be found on the page that immediately follows this page in the research set.

If one had not been given the case of *Alexander v. State* as a starting point but did know that the issue to be researched dealt with the topic of carrying and concealing weapons, the researcher could use the *Descriptive-Word Index* at the end of *Florida Digest 2d*. One could locate the topic of "Weapons" in this volume and find the page reproduced in Figure 4-8.[17] This page shows that the topic of "Weapons" has a subtopic of "Carrying—Baggage. Weap. 10." This means that this subject area can be found under Weapons key number 10. By turning to this topic and key number, one could find the page reproduced in Figure 4-3, which would lead to the *Alexander* case and other relevant cases.

Another possible strategy for beginning research in this case is to use *Florida Jurisprudence, Second Series,* the legal encyclopedia for the state of Florida. Begin by going to the volume referred to as the *Table of Cases* at the end of the set. The cases in this volume are in alphabetical order, and the page containing the *Alexander* case has been reproduced in Figure 4-19.[18] Under the

WEAPONS

SUBJECTS INCLUDED

Right to bear arms in self-defense or in defense of the state

Regulation of manufacture, dealing in, and use of weapons

Liabilities for injuries therefrom caused by negligence

Offenses of having or carrying weapons concealed or in any other manner prohibited, pointing or shooting firearms, etc., not constituting any other distinct offense

SUBJECTS EXCLUDED AND COVERED BY OTHER TOPICS

Militia, matters relating to, see MILITIA

Specific injuries or crimes committed by use of weapons, see ASSAULT AND BATTERY, HOMICIDE, and other specific topics

For detailed references to other topics, see Descriptive-Word Index

---

Analysis

1. Right to bear arms.
2. Power to make regulations.
3. Constitutional and statutory provisions.
4. Manufacture, sale, gift, loan, possession, or use.
5. Carrying weapons.
6. —— Nature and elements of offenses in general.
7. —— Intent or purpose.
8. —— Weapons prohibited.
9. —— Places prohibited.
10. —— Manner of carrying or concealment.
11. —— Persons and occasions exempted or privileged.
    (1). Officers and persons aiding them.
    (2). Travelers.
    (3). Mail carriers.
12. —— Licenses or permits.
13. —— Justification or excuse.
14. Pointing or exhibiting weapon.
15. Shooting firearms.
16. Penalties and forfeitures.
17. Criminal prosecutions.
    (1). Indictment and information.
    (2). Presumptions and burden of proof.
    (3). Admissibility of evidence.
    (4). Weight and sufficiency of evidence.
    (5). Questions for jury.
    (6). Instructions.

FIGURE 4-5

convicted felon. Creamer v. State, App. 1 Dist., 605 So.2d 541 (1992).

32. Double jeopardy

Three separate convictions of possession of firearm by convicted felon for three separate weapons discovered at same time in defendant's home constituted double jeopardy violation. Plowman v. State, App. 2 Dist., 622 So.2d 91 (1993).

Conviction for possession of firearm in commission of felony as well as convictions for sexual

battery with firearm and burglary with assault and while armed violated double jeopardy. Gauthier v. State, App. 1 Dist., 605 So.2d 1284 (1992).

33. Expungement of records

When circuit court has expunged all of individual's criminal records, individual is placed in same position he occupied prior to arrest and, therefore, such individual would have no impediments to possessing firearm. Op.Atty.Gen. 91–63, Aug. 27, 1991.

790.25. Lawful ownership, possession, and use of firearms and other weapons

[See main volume for (1) and (2)]

(3) Lawful uses.—The provisions of ss. 790.053 and 790.06 do not apply in the following instances, and, despite such sections, it is lawful for the following persons to own, possess, and lawfully use firearms and other weapons, ammunition, and supplies for lawful purposes:

(a) Members of the Militia, National Guard, Florida State Defense Force, Army, Navy, Air Force, Marine Corps, Coast Guard, organized reserves, and other armed forces of the state and of the United States, when on duty, when training or preparing themselves for military duty, or while subject to recall or mobilization;

Amended by Laws 1993, c. 93–269, § 1, eff. June 3, 1993.

[See main volume for (b) to (p); (4)]

(5) Possession in private conveyance.—Notwithstanding subsection (2), it is lawful and is not a violation of s. 790.01 for a person 18 years of age or older to possess a concealed firearm or other weapon for self-defense or other lawful purpose within the interior of a private conveyance, without a license, if the firearm or other weapon is securely encased or is otherwise not readily accessible for immediate use. Nothing herein contained prohibits the carrying of a legal firearm other than a handgun anywhere in a private conveyance when such firearm is being carried for a lawful use. Nothing herein contained shall be construed to authorize the carrying of a concealed firearm or other weapon on the person. This subsection shall be liberally construed in favor of the lawful use, ownership, and possession of firearms and other weapons, including lawful self-defense as provided in s. 776.012.

Amended by Laws 1993, c. 93–416, § 7, eff. Jan. 1, 1994.

Historical and Statutory Notes

Laws 1993, c. 93–269, § 1, eff. June 3, 1993, in subsec. (3)(a), substituted "Florida State Defense Force" for "Florida State Guard".

Laws 1993, c. 93–416, § 7, eff. Jan. 1, 1994, in subsec. (5), in the first sentence, inserted "for a person 18 years of age or older".

Notes of Decisions

2. Construction and application

Statutory authority for carrying concealed firearm, without license, that is securely encased or is otherwise not readily accessible for immediate use was limited to possession within interior of private conveyance, and did not extend to firearm being carried in zippered leather pouch on defendant's person while defendant was in shopping mall. Dima v. State, App. 4 Dist., 621 So.2d 480 (1993).

Defendant could not be properly convicted for carrying concealed firearm where uncontroverted evidence was presented that firearm in defendant's automobile was unloaded and thus not readily accessible for immediate use. Smith v. State, App. 5 Dist., 617 So.2d 444 (1993) review dismissed 623 So.2d 496.

6. Place of business

State v. Commons, App. 3 Dist., 592 So.2d 317 (1991) [main volume] review dismissed 599 So.2d 658.

9. Secure encasement

Firearm possessed by defendant while committing felony was "securely encased" and thus defendant could not be convicted of possession of a firearm during commission of a felony, where revolver was found in center console of vehicle, lid of console was closed, and revolver was underneath papers and other objects in console. Bell v. State, App. 2 Dist., 636 So.2d 80 (1994).

10. Readily accessible for immediate use

Rifle and shotgun that were partially enclosed in professionally made gun case attached to back of

137

FIGURE 4-6

111

Cross References

Aggravated assault, see F.S.A. § 784.021.
Arrested person, taking from, etc., see F.S.A. § 790.08.
Burglary, possession of weapons while committing, see F.S.A. § 810.02.
Concealed weapons, see F.S.A. § 790.01 et seq.
Discharging firearms, see F.S.A. §§ 790.15, 790.19.
Exhibiting dangerous weapons, see F.S.A. § 790.10.
Furnishing to minors, insane persons, etc., penalty, see F.S.A. § 790.17.
License to carry pistol or repeating rifle, see F.S.A. § 790.06.
Public arms, safe keeping of, see Art. 10, § 2.

Law Review Commentaries

Right to bear arms. Roger J. Waybright, 13
Fla.L.J. 253 (July 1939).

Library References

Constitutional Law ⟐82.
Weapons ⟐1.
WESTLAW Topic Nos. 92, 406.

C.J.S. Constitutional Law §§ 444, 445, 460,
619 to 648.
C.J.S. Weapons § 2.

Notes of Decisions

Construction and application 1
Statutes regulating carrying of weapons 2

1. Construction and application

Legislature may prohibit possession of weapons which are ordinarily used for criminal and improper purposes and which are not among those which are legitimate weapons of defense and protection. Rinzler v. Carson, 262 So.2d 661 (1972).

Although legislature may not entirely prohibit the right of the people to keep and bear arms, it can determine that certain arms or weapons may not be kept or borne by the citizen. Id.

Adding of word "keep" to constitutional provision concerning right of people to bear arms did not render inapplicable prior decisions concerning power of legislature to regulate manner of bearing arms. Id.

Constitutional guarantee of right of people to bear arms in their own defense was intended to secure to people right to carry weapons for their protection, but was also designed to protect people from bearing of weapons by the unskilled, irresponsible, and lawless. Davis v. State, 146 So.2d 892 (1963).

2. Statutes regulating carrying of weapons

In regulating the manner of bearing arms, state may require that one obtain and possess a license in order to carry a handgun and may criminally punish those who do not. Robarge v. State, App. 5 Dist., 432 So.2d 669 (1983) review denied 450 So.2d 855.

State may make it illegal to carry certain types of weapons such as concealed weapons or those ordinarily used for criminal purposes such as machine guns and short-barreled shotguns. Id.

Statutory prohibition of possession of pistol by convicted felon whose civil rights have not been restored was reasonable public safeguard, and F.S.A. § 790.23 was not unconstitutional. Nelson v. State, 195 So.2d 853 (1967).

F.S.A. § 790.05 [repealed; see,now, § 790.06] prohibiting carrying of pistols and repeating rifles without license was not unconstitutional infringement of right of people to bear arms in their own defense or invalid exercise of police power. Davis v. State, 146 So.2d 892 (1963).

The statutes against carrying weapons have no connection with this section, preserving to people the right to bear arms. Carlton v. State, 63 Fla. 1, 58 So. 486 (1912).

§ 9. Due process

No person shall be deprived of life, liberty or property without due process of law, or be twice put in jeopardy for the same offense, or be compelled in any criminal matter to be a witness against himself.

111

FIGURE 4-7

WAIVER—Cont'd
FRAUDS, statute of, see also, Statute of frauds, post
IMMUNITY—
   Eleventh Amendment, see Eleventh Amendment, ante
SPOUSAL privilege. Witn 219(2)

WAR AND NATIONAL EMERGENCY
FEDERAL preemption—
   State laws or regulations. States 18.89
PENALTIES. War 120
POWERS—
   State courts. War 35
PRISONERS—
   Criminal prosecution. War 32
   Transfer. War 11
PRISONERS' rights. War 11

WARRANTS
ARREST—
   On criminal charge—
      See also, this index Preliminary Warrants or Other
         Process
FORFEITURES. Forfeit 5
HOSPITALS—
   Sterilization—
      Requirement that warranty be in writing. Hosp 7

WARRANTY
BAILMENT—
   Condition of and defects in property. Bailm 9
PRINCIPAL and agent—
   Breach of warranty, action against agent. Princ & A
     136(2)

WARSAW CONVENTION
CAUSE of action—
   Injuries. Carr 307(6)
EXCLUSIVE causes of action—
   Air disasters. Carr 310
INJURY to passengers—
   Mental suffering—
      Compensability of mental anguish alone. Damag 50
PREEMPTION—
   Of state cause of action. Treaties 11
RIGHTS of action—
   Personal injuries. Carr 311

WASTE
DANGEROUS waste disposal—
   Environmental protection, see Environmental protection
     regulations, post
ENVIRONMENTAL protection regulations—
   Waste disposal—
     Hazardous, dangerous, or toxic waste. Health & E
      25.5(5.5)
GARBAGE, see this index Garbage
HAZARDOUS waste disposal—
   Environmental protection, see Environmental protection
     regulations, ante
RUBBISH, see this index Rubbish
SOLID waste—
   Disposal—
     Environmental protection regulations. Health & E
      25.5(5)
TOXIC waste disposal—
   Environmental protection, see Environmental protection
     regulations, ante

WASTE DISPOSAL SERVICE
PRICE-FIXING—
   Flow of commerce. Monop 31(1.3)

WATER POLLUTION
JUDICIAL review of regulations or intervention. Health & E
   25.15
Scope or inquiry or review. Health & E 25.15(8)

WATER UTILITIES
Generally, see this index Public Water Supply

WATER WELLS
ORDINANCE prohibiting within city limits. Monop
   12(15.5)

WATERS AND WATER COURSES
ENVIRONMENTAL protection regulations—
   Impact statement—
     Content, sufficiency, and accuracy. Health & E
      25.10(6.5)
     Necessity for. Health & E 25.10(2–5)
FEDERAL preemption—
   State laws or regulations. States 18.91
IMPACT development fees—
   Establishment. Waters 203(6)
INDIANS—
   Water rights and management. Indians 16.5
TAKING of property—
   Acts and regulations constituting a taking without just
     compensation. Em Dom 2(10)

WAYS OF NECESSITY
IMPLIED easements—
   Unity of title requirement. Ease 18(4)

WEAPONS
CARRYING—
   Baggage. Weap 10
DIFFERENT offenses in same transaction. Crim Law
   29(15)
DOUBLE jeopardy, weapons offenses and other offenses.
   Double J 140
EVIDENCE—
   Expert testimony. Crim Law 476.1
FIREMEN'S rule. Weap 18(1)
HANDGUN sale regulation, county preemption. Mun Corp
   55
INMATES possession. Convicts 5
NUNCHAKU—
   As "deadly weapons." Weap 4
SEARCHES and seizures. Searches 67–71
   Traffic arrest or stop, search or seizure consequent to.
     Autos 349.5(10)
SENTENCE and criminal prosecution—
   Enhancement factor, see this index Criminal Law

WEARING APPAREL
PRISONERS—
   Maintenance and care of. Prisons 17(3)

WHARTON'S RULE
CONSPIRACY, criminal liability. Consp 28(1)

WHEELS
CONSPIRACIES. Crim Law 24(3)

WHISTLE–BLOWER ACT
COUNTIES—
   Discharged officers—
     Actions. Counties 67

WHISTLEBLOWING
DISCHARGE of employee. Mast & S 30(6.35)

FIGURE 4-8

Alexander v State (1991, Fla App D5) 576 So 2d 350, 16 FLW D 586—Contpt § 62

Alexander v State (1992, Fla App D3) 603 So 2d 656, 17 FLW D 1885—Evid § 633

Alexander v State (1993, Fla App D1) 616 So 2d 540, 18 FLW D 845—Crim L § 864

Alexander v State (1993, Fla App D1) 627 So 2d 35, 18 FLW D 2414—Evid § 239

Alexander v State (1993, Fla App D3) 615 So 2d 239, 18 FLW D 690—Crim L § 1764

Alexander v State (1985, Fla) 477 So 2d 557, 10 FLW 546—Crim L § 4773

Cited in:

43 ALR2d 492 (Offense of carrying concealed weapon as affected by manner of carrying or place of concealment)

Alexander v United States (1993, US) 125 L Ed 2d 441, 113 S Ct 2766, 21 Media L R 1609, 93 CDOS 4813, 93 Daily Journal DAR 8156, 7 FLW Fed S 621, (US) RICO Bus Disp Guide (CCH)¶ 8328—Crim L § 874; Penalty § 4

Cited in:

4 L Ed 2d 1821 (Constitutionality of federal and state regulation of obscene literature, federal cases)

21 L Ed 2d 976 (The Supreme Court and the right of free speech and press)

33 L Ed 2d 932 (Federal constitutional guaranty against cruel and unusual punishment, Supreme Court cases)

45 L Ed 2d 725 (Supreme Court's views as to overbreadth of legislation in connection with First Amendment rights)

Alfonso v Department of Envtl. Regulation (1993, Fla) 616 So 2d 44, 18 FLW S 194—App Rev § 33

Alfonso v State (1929) 97 Fla 255, 120 So 361—Crim L § 1915, 3843

Alfonso v State (1983, Fla App D3) 443 So 2d 176—Crim L § 1697

Alfonso v State (1988, Fla App D3) 528 So 2d 383, 13 FLW 275—Crim L § 1767, 1768, 3380

Cited in:

82 ALR3d 245 (Antagonistic defenses

as ground for separate trials of codefendants in criminal cases)

Alford v Alford (1992, Fla App D5) 594 So 2d 443, 17 FLW D 586—Fam L § 732

Alford v Blake (1967, CA5 Fla) 385 F2d 1010—Auto § 608, 609

Cited in:

40 ALR3d 9 (Automobiles: liability of owner or operator of motor vehicle for injury, death, or property damage resulting from defective brakes)

80 ALR2d 5 (Instructions on sudden emergency in motor vehicle cases)

Alford v Cornelius (1980, Fla App D5) 380 So 2d 1183—Crim L § 3150

Alford v G. Pierce Woods Memorial Hosp. (1993, Fla App D1) 621 So 2d 1380, 18 FLW D 1579—Work Comp § 218

Alford v Parker's Mechanical Constructors, Inc. (1970, Fla App D1) 241 So 2d 759—Auto § 686

Cited in:

51 ALR2d 120 (Employee's operation of employer's vehicle outside regular working hours as within scope of employment)

Alford v State (1889) 25 Fla 852, 6 So 857—Crim L § 3189

Alford v State (1918) 76 Fla 122, 79 So 437—Crim L § 3278-3280

Alford v State (1938) 132 Fla 624, 181 So 839—Crim L § 3797

Alford v State (1973, Fla App D3) 280 So 2d 479—Crim L § 1969

Alford v State (1975, Fla) 307 So 2d 433—Crim L § 3622

Cited in:

38 ALR4th 378 (Admissibility or use in criminal trial of testimony given at preliminary proceeding by witness not available at trial)

73 ALR2d 769 (Admissibility of photograph of corpse in prosecution for homicide or civil action for causing death)

77 ALR2d 841 (Admissibility, in prosecution for sexual offense, of evidence of other similar offenses)

Cited in refers to annotation's main text and supplement

FIGURE 4-9

name of the case, there is a reference to "Crim L § 4773." This means that the *Alexander* case is referred to under the topic of "Criminal Law" in § 4773 of that topic. Turning to that topic and section, the researcher finds that a reference to the case appears in footnote 61 on that page (see Figure 4-10).[19]

On the first page of the *Alexander* case (see Figure 4-2a), one can find a reference in the second headnote to Florida statute § 790.25(5). If one wanted to find each and every section of the *Florida Jurisprudence, Second Series* that referred to that statute, the researcher would be able to find the exact places in this encyclopedia that would be relevant. This can be accomplished by consulting the *Table of Statutes* at the end of the *Florida Jurisprudence 2d* set. Since the statute numbers are listed in numerical order, it should be easy to locate the statutory reference. Turning to the page that lists Florida statute 790.25(5) (see Figure 4-11),[20] one can see the following listing: "Crim L § 4768, 4773, 4773." This means that Florida statute § 790.25(5) is specifically referred to under the topic of Criminal Law in sections 4768 once and 4773 twice. Figure 4-10 discussed in the previous paragraph clearly demonstrates that a reference to this statute is in fact in § 4773.[21]

The issue that needs to be researched with regard to the procedure for raising the subject of incompetence can be found in the *Rules of Criminal Procedure*. These rules are located at the end of the Florida Statutes Annotated. Since this volume of rules of procedure has its own table of contents and its own index, one can look in the index of that volume under the subject of "Incompetence" and find a reference to Rule 3.210. A reproduction of the rule entitled "Incompetence to Proceed: Procedure for Raising the Issue" can be seen in Figures 4-12a and 4-12b,[22] as it appears in the *Rules of Criminal Procedure*.

To verify that the materials researched have been checked for up-to-date developments in the law, all references should be shepardized (see Sec. 4-6).[23] For example, to shepardize the *Alexander* case, look for the *Shepard's Citations* at the end of *Southern Reporter, Second Series*. It will be necessary for several of the citators in this set to be examined in order to check thoroughly for late breaking developments in the law. Figure 4-13[24] shows a page from a citator for *Southern Reporter, Second Series* that includes the reference to the *Alexander* case. Note:

1. Since the *Alexander* case comes from *Southern Reporter, Second Series*, we are using the *Shepard's Citations* associated with that set. The name of that regional reporter can be seen in the top center of the page.

2. The volume number (477) of the *Alexander* case appears in the upper right-hand corner of the page.

3. The page numbers within that volume appear in bold face type in the body of the citator page.

and it could not have been put to use by the defendant without opening the lid of the pouch.[59] Another individual carrying an unloaded gun in an unlatched case in the back seat of his truck was held not in violation of FS § 790.15(5) for carrying a concealed weapon, on the ground that the gun was "securely encased" as defined by FS § 790.01(15) and was not "readily accessible for immediate use" as defined by FS § 790.01(16).[60] Similarly, a zippered pouch was held to be the equivalent of a zippered gun case so that the weapon at issue was securely encased and, therefore, the offense of carrying a concealed weapon was not committed.[61] And where the firearm was contained in a console compartment of an automobile with the lid closed, the offense of carrying of a concealed weapon was not committed.[62] By contrast, a defendant was properly convicted of the offense of carrying a concealed weapon where he was riding a motorcycle with the firearm in his jacket pocket.[63]

The statutory prohibition against carrying a concealed weapon on or about the person[64] in a private conveyance, that is not securely encased or is readily accessible for immediate use,[65] has been upheld as constitutional on the grounds that it is reasonably related to the legitimate governmental goal of promoting firearm safety and preventing the use of firearms in crimes, and conveys sufficient warning of the proscribed conduct when measured by common understanding and practice.[66]

A finding of false arrest and damages of $50,000 was upheld where the defendant was arrested for the offense of carrying a concealed weapon, but the weapon at issue, .25 caliber revolver, was found at the time of arrest in the closed console compartment of the defendant's automobile.[67]

59. Urquiola v State (1991, Fla App D3) 590 So 2d 497, 16 FLW D 2992.

60. State v Williams (1991, 9th Cir Ct) 45 Fla Supp 2d 190.

61. Alexander v State (1985, Fla) 477 So 2d 557, 10 FLW 546.

62. Miami v Swift (1985, Fla App D3) 481 So 2d 26, 10 FLW 2718, review den (Fla) 491 So 2d 278.

63. State v Miller (1982, Fla App D5) 413 So 2d 1295.

64. FS § 790.001.

65. FS § 790.25(5).

66. Alexander v State (1985, Fla) 477 So 2d 557, 10 FLW 546.

67. Miami v Swift (1985,Fla App

FIGURE 4-10

FLORIDA STATUTES—Continued

FS §§	Fla Jur 2d	FS §§	Fla Jur 2d
790.161(1)	Crim L § 4786	790.23(1)	Crim L § 4751; Evid § 122
790.161(2)	Crim L § 4786		
790.161(3)	Crim L § 4786	790.23(2)	Crim L § 4755
790.161(4)	Crim L § 4786	790.23(3)	Crim L § 4751
790.1612	Explos § 10; Weapons § 2	790.24	Crim L § 4779
		790.25(1)	Crim L § 4741
790.1615(1)	Crim L § 4787	790.25(2)(b)(1)	Crim L § 4766
790.1615(2)	Crim L § 4787	790.25(2)(b)(2)	Crim L § 4766
790.1615(3)	Crim L § 4787	790.25(2)(b)(3)	Crim L § 4766
790.162	Crim L § 4788	790.25(3)	Police § 6
790.163	Crim L § 4790	790.25(3)(a)	Crim L § 4766
790.165(1)	Crim L § 4791	790.25(3)(b)	Crim L § 4766
790.165(2)	Crim L § 4791	790.25(3)(c)	Crim L § 4766
790.165(3)	Crim L § 4791	790.25(3)(d)	Crim L § 4766
790.165(4)	Crim L § 4791	790.25(3)(e)	Crim L § 4766
790.17	Negl § 51; Weapons § 11	790.25(3)(f)	Bus & O § 274; Crim L § 4766
790.17(1)	Crim L § 4782	790.25(3)(h)	Crim L § 4766
790.17(2)	Crim L § 4782	790.25(3)(n)	Crim L § 4767
790.173(2)	Crim L § 4741, 4742	790.25(4)	Crim L § 4742, 4743
790.174(1)	Crim L § 4783	790.25(5)	Crim L § 4768, 4773, 4773
790.174(2)	Crim L § 4783	790.27	Crim L § 4778
790.174(3)	Crim L § 4783	790.27(1)(a)	Crim L § 4778
790.175	Crim L § 4783	790.27(1)(b)	Crim L § 4778
790.18	Crim L § 4782	790.27(2)(a)	Crim L § 4778
790.19	Crim L § 4794; Fam L § 258	790.27(2)(b)	Crim L § 4778
		790.28	Crim L § 4741, 4799
790.22	Crim L § 4784	790.29(3)(a)	Crim L § 4780
790.22(3)	Crim L § 4784	790.29(3)(b)	Crim L § 4780
790.22(4)	Crim L § 4784	790.29(4)	Crim L § 4780
790.221	Crim L § 4767, 4793; Evid § 14	790.31(2)(a)	Crim L § 4792
790.221(1)	Crim L § 4793, 4796	790.31(2)(b)	Crim L § 4792
		790.31(2)(c)	Crim L § 4792
		790.31(3)	Crim L § 4792
790.221(2)	Crim L § 328, 2166, 4796	790.33(1)	Crim L § 4743
790.221(3)	Crim L § 4793, 4796	791	Explos § 15
		791.001	Explos § 15
790.222(5)	Crim L § 4784	791.01	Explos § 15
790.225(1)	Crim L § 4795	791.013	Explos § 15
790.225(2)	Crim L § 4795	791.04	Explos § 19
790.225(3)	Crim L § 4795	791.055	Explos § 15
790.23	Crim L § 4751; Evid § 122; Statutes § 185	Ch 794	Records § 18, 20, 25
		794	Crim § 2359

FIGURE 4-11

For an excellent article on notice of alibi statutes, court decisions thereunder, and some empirical data on the practical effect of the rules, see David M. Epstein, "Advance Notice of Alibi," 55 J.Crim. Law & Criminology 29 (1964).

1972 Amendment. Same as prior rule.

1992 Amendment. The purpose of the amendments is to gender neutralize the wording of the rule.

Notes of Decisions

4. Witness list

Trial court reversibly erred in refusing to allow defendant's alibi witness to testify because of misspelling of witness' name in notice of intent to claim alibi where court made no finding as to whether State was actually prejudiced by misspelling and considered no alternatives for rectifying any prejudice State suffered short of excluding testimony of witness. Pelham v. State, App. 2 Dist., 567 So.2d 537 (1990).

6. Time of notice

Defendant offering alibi witness is required to furnish prosecuting attorney notice of intent to call witnesses and witness' name and address at least ten days before trial. Small v. State, App. 3 Dist., 608 So.2d 829 (1992) approved, remanded 630 So.2d 1087.

15. Waiver

Trial court was not required to conduct good cause hearing inquiring into circumstances surrounding defendant's failure to timely provide prosecuting attorney with notice of intent to offer alibi witness before determining whether good cause existed to waive requirement that notice be provided ten days before trial; defense learned of alibi witness during first trial and failed to notify state in timely manner, and defense again violated notice of alibi rule at defendant's second trial by failing to provide name and address of alibi witness. Small v. State, 630 So.2d 1087 (1994).

Trial court's failure to conduct good cause hearing regarding compliance with notice of alibi rule should be reviewed to determine whether defendant was harmed by such failure. Small v. State, 630 So.2d 1087 (1994).

Hearing inquiring into circumstances surrounding defendant's failure to timely provide prosecuting attorney with notice of intent to offer alibi witness was required to determine whether good cause existed to waive requirement that notice be provided ten days before trial. Small v. State, App. 3 Dist., 608 So.2d 829 (1992) approved, remanded 630 So.2d 1087.

Rule 3.201. Battered–Spouse Syndrome [1]

(a) Battered-Spouse Syndrome. When in any criminal case it shall be the intention of the defendant to rely on the defense of battered-spouse syndrome at trial, no evidence offered by the defendant for the purpose of establishing that defense shall be admitted in the case unless advance notice in writing of the defense shall have been given by the defendant as hereinafter provided.

(b) Time for Filing Notice. The defendant shall give notice of intent to rely on the defense of battered-spouse syndrome no later than 30 days prior to trial. The notice shall contain a statement of particulars showing the nature of the defense the defendant expects to prove and the names and addresses of the witnesses by whom the defendant expects to show battered-spouse syndrome, insofar as possible.

Adopted Oct. 21, 1993 (630 So.2d 172).

[1] Name line supplied by the Publisher.

Historical Notes

The Florida Supreme Court, in the case of Florida v. Hickson 630 So.2d 172, Oct. 21, 1993, adopted emergency Rule 3.201. The court stated, in part,

"... the Court will reconsider any appropriate changes to the emergency rule sixty days after the filing of this opinion".

Rule 3.210. Incompetence to Proceed: Procedure for Raising the Issue

(a) Proceedings Barred during Incompetency. A person accused of an offense or a violation of probation or community control who is mentally incompetent to proceed at any material stage of a criminal proceeding shall not be proceeded against while incompetent.

(1) A "material stage of a criminal proceeding" shall include the trial of the case, pretrial hearings involving questions of fact on which the defendant might be expected to testify, entry of a plea, violation of probation or violation of community control proceedings, sentencing, hearings on issues regarding a defendant's failure to comply with court orders

FIGURE 4-12a

or conditions, or other matters where the mental competence of the defendant is necessary for a just resolution of the issues being considered. The terms "competent," "competence," "incompetent," and "incompetence," as used in rules 3.210–3.219, shall refer to mental competence or incompetence to proceed at a material stage of a criminal proceeding.

(2) The incompetence of the defendant shall not preclude such judicial action, hearings on motions of the parties, discovery proceedings, or other procedures that do not require the personal participation of the defendant.

(b) Motion for Examination. If, at any material stage of a criminal proceeding, the court of its own motion, or on motion of counsel for the defendant or for the state, has reasonable ground to believe that the defendant is not mentally competent to proceed, the court shall immediately enter its order setting a time for a hearing to determine the defendant's mental condition, which shall be held no later than 20 days after the date of the filing of the motion, and shall order the defendant to be examined by no more than 3, nor fewer than 2, experts prior to the date of the hearing. Attorneys for the state and the defendant may be present at the examination.

(1) A written motion for the examination made by counsel for the defendant shall contain a certificate of counsel that the motion is made in good faith and on reasonable grounds to believe that the defendant is incompetent to proceed. To the extent that it does not invade the lawyer-client privilege, the motion shall contain a recital of the specific observations of and conversations with the defendant that have formed the basis for the motion.

(2) A written motion for the examination made by counsel for the state shall contain a certificate of counsel that the motion is made in good faith and on reasonable grounds to believe the defendant is incompetent to proceed and shall include a recital of the specific facts that have formed the basis for the motion, including a recitation of the observations of and statements of the defendant that have caused the state to file the motion.

(3) If the defendant has been released on bail or other release provision, the court may order the defendant to appear at a designated place for evaluation at a specific time as a condition of such release. If the court determines that the defendant will not submit to the evaluation or that the defendant is not likely to appear for the scheduled evaluation, the court may order the defendant taken into custody until the determination of the defendant's competency to proceed. A motion made for evaluation under this subdivision shall not otherwise affect the defendant's right to release.

(4) The order appointing experts shall:

(A) identify the purpose or purposes of the evaluation, including the nature of the material proceeding, and specify the area or areas of inquiry that should be addressed by the evaluator;

(B) specify the legal criteria to be applied; and

(C) specify the date by which the report should be submitted and to whom the report should be submitted.

Amended Sept. 24, 1992, effective Jan. 1, 1993 (606 So.2d 227).

Committee Notes

1968 Adoption. (a) Same as section 917.01, Florida Statutes, except it was felt that court cannot by rule direct institution officials. Thus words, "he shall report this fact to the court which conducted the hearing. If the officer so reports" and concluding sentence, "No defendant committed by a court to an institution, by reason of the examination referred to in this paragraph, shall be released therefrom, without the consent of the court committing him," should be omitted from the rule but retained by statute.

(b) Same as section 909.17, Florida Statutes.

(c) Same as section 917.02, Florida Statutes.

1972 Amendment. Subdivision (a)(3) refers to Jackson v. Indiana, 406 U.S. 715, 730, 92 S.Ct. 1845, 32 L.Ed.2d 435 (1972); also, United States v. Curry, 410 F.2d 1372 (4th Cir.1969). Subdivision (d) is added to give the court authority to confine an insane person who is likely to cause harm to others even if the person is otherwise entitled to bail. The amendment does not apply unless the defendant contends that he or she is insane at the time of trial or at the time the offense was committed. The purpose of the amendment is to prevent admittedly insane persons from being at large when there is a likelihood they may injure themselves or others.

95

FIGURE 4-12b

559So2d²203
63A⁴621n

—542—
In re Florida
Rules of
Practice and
Procedure for
Traffic Courts
1985

—544—
Winfield v
Division of
Pari-Mutuel
Wagering,
Department
of Business
Regulation
1985

s443So2d455
e500So2d¹535
508So2d⁴465
e521So2d110
f529So2d²715
529So2d⁴715
529So2d⁷715
531So2d³120
j536So2d1021
541So2d⁴102
543So2d⁴267
544So2d¹222
544So2d²222
544So2d³222
551So2d1191
f551So2d¹1192
551So2d⁴1192
551So2d⁵1192
e551So2d¹1197
f553So2d1151
e553So2d⁴153
e553So2d⁶153
553So2d²1187
559So2d¹382
562So2d¹741
565So2d¹393
568So2d10
570So2d³1260
j570So2d264
576So2d865
j590So2d418
j603So2d547
619So2d⁴420
Cir. 11
669FS⁵407
e 810FS¹1574
e 810FS³1574
Idaho
745P2d1096
Kan
850P2d825
Wyo
846P2d648

—548—
Houser v
Florida
1985
s453So2d484

—551—
Florida Bar
v Toothaker
1985

—553—
Hill v Florida
1985
US cert den
in 485US993
in 108SC1302
s515So2d176
cc556So2d1385
487So2d1042
487So2d³1120
490So2d⁶202
497So2d972
f501So2d⁶43
505So2d⁸614
506So2d³1072
j507So2d1
508So2d3
514So2d³427
516So2d⁶44
525So2d³872
525So2d⁵872
525So2d⁶873
f527So2d⁶924
j527So2d925
f534So2d⁶1233
538So2d³489
540So2d³202
542So2d⁵967
j542So2d972
543So2d²879
543So2d⁶1300
f545So2d383
f545So2d⁶384
f546So2d⁵734
547So2d295
547So2d³632
f547So2d⁸682
547So2d971
e553So2d202
f553So2d⁶202
f557So2d1367
f560So2d⁸329
563So2d1113
564So2d⁶1244
565So2d³307
566So2d⁶878
567So2d³928
569So2d²1230
569So2d³1230
569So2d⁶1230
570So2d⁶1083
571So2d⁶552

d574So2d1081
576So2d⁶693
e583So2d733
586So2d⁵378
586So2d⁶378
597So2d⁶929
601So2d³532
h606So2d⁶1200
611So2d⁵14
Conn
613A2d250
Idaho
808P2d1318
W Va
382SE325

—557—
Alexander
v Florida
1985
s450So2d1212
481So2d⁵27
f484So2d⁴1281
508So2d²786
526So2d105
d540So2d²221
590So2d⁵498
f601So2d³1231
619So2d²296
d621So2d²480
621So2d⁵480

—560—
Florida Bar
v LaPorte
1985

—562—
Florida Bar v
Diaz-Silveira
1985
cc557So2d570

—563—
Florida Bar
v Barenz
1985

—564—
Chatman
v Florida
1985
s458So2d86

—565—
Florida v Davis
1985
s458So2d42

486So2d¹62
488So2d676
490So2d¹182
490So2d¹1027
492So2d411
492So2d1172
492So2d¹1390
493So2d¹1095
501So2d¹753
509So2d284
509So2d¹1301
510So2d314
510So2d1114
j510So2d1116
559So2d608

—566—
Jones v Florida
1985
s433So2d564
j478So2d816
e483So2d¹24
486So2d¹589
e487So2d1124
j488So2d529
488So2d¹644
f488So2d877
f489So2d¹783
e490So2d¹164
f490So2d¹1077
f490So2d¹1270
e491So2d¹1310
493So2d552
d494So2d¹529
495So2d¹1170
496So2d120
f496So2d¹121
499So2d¹849
f501So2d¹40
502So2d¹1274
502So2d³1275
e503So2d343
508So2d¹1248
516So2d¹327
518So2d918
520So2d¹251
L520So2d¹253
520So2d¹255
j520So2d256
520So2d567
520So2d571
530So2d925
540So2d¹843
577So2d⁶690
583So2d¹703
591So2d¹594
606So2d1220
621So2d¹743

—569—
Florida Bar
re Berzner
1985
cc423So2d365

—570—
Florida v
Williams
1985
s462So2d23
482So2d471
484So2d¹80
486So2d¹62
488So2d143
498So2d¹577

—571—
Florida Bar
v Wilson
1985

—572—
Hall v Florida
1985
r509So2d1093
f476So2d220
f476So2d749
477So2d³612
483So2d³763
j500So2d130
500So2d234

—576—
Health Quest
Realty v
Department of
Health and
Rehabilitative
Services
1985
489So2d792
N C
390SE452

—579—
NCNB
National Bank
of Florida v
Aetna Casualty
and Surety Co.
1985
j590So2d1065

—584—
Ferguson
v Florida
1985

—585—
Bystrom v
Union Land
Investments
Inc.
1985
s488So2d69
501So2d²695
559So2d1187
564So2d¹1136
582So2d176
583So2d768

—591—
Anderson
v S & S
Diversified Inc.
1985
s486So2d597
477So2d²654
490So2d1353
543So2d860
544So2d266
549So2d³1389
555So2d⁴423
f555So2d³949
560So2d⁴376
576So2d406
578So2d⁴462
579So2d⁴159
f599So2d709
600So2d515

—596—
Ron Burton
Inc. v Villwock
1985
s488So2d69
501So2d¹1347
Cir. 11
804FS309
Mo
839SW25

—600—
Conley v Boyle
Drug Co.
1985
r570So2d275
495So2d1231
Cir. 11
723FS³1457
e 723FS¹1459
744FS¹1126
744FS³1127
754FS¹195
Haw
823P2d727
Ill
527NE342

FIGURE 4-13

Each of the letters in front of the references under *Alexander v. State* has a special meaning. For a list of the abbreviations and their respective meanings, see Figure 4-18. For example, an "f" appears in front of the citation under *Alexander* for 484 So.2d 1281. Using Figure 4-14,[25] the researcher can discover that the case located in volume 484, page 1281 of the *Southern Reporter, Second Series* followed the decision in the *Alexander* case.

SEC. 4-8
HINTS FOR CHOOSING WHICH RESEARCH SET TO USE

To determine which one of the sets discussed in this chapter would be most helpful in finding the answer to an issue, the researcher must ask several important questions. One of the first is to determine whether he or she is seeking state or federal law. A second is to determine the nature of the issue itself.

A. Is the Issue Likely to Be Governed by Legislative Law?

If so, then the statutes annotated should be consulted first. For example, if one is trying to ascertain the maximum or minimum penalty for violation of a criminal law (such as the drunk driving statute), it would be reasonable to assume that this subject would be one determined by statute.

B. Does the Issue Require a Legal Definition?

If so, the state jurisprudence volumes might be the best place to begin.

C. Does the Issue Deal with a Totally Unfamiliar Subject?

If so, the jurisprudence volumes, which are really legal encyclopedias, might be consulted.

D. Does the Issue Require Further Case Law Under a Particular Key Number?

If so, consult the digests.

E. Does the Issue Require Exact Language from a Specifically Cited Case?

If so, the appropriate reporter should be consulted.

ABBREVIATIONS—ANALYSIS

History of Case

a	(affirmed)	Same case affirmed on appeal.
cc	(connected case)	Different case from case cited but arising out of same subject matter or intimately connected therewith.
D	(dismissed)	Appeal from same case dismissed.
m	(modified)	Same case modified on appeal.
r	(reversed)	Same case reversed on appeal.
s	(same case)	Same case as case cited.
S	(superseded)	Substitution for former opinion.
v	(vacated)	Same case vacated.
US cert den		Certiorari denied by U. S. Supreme Court.
US cert dis		Certiorari dismissed by U. S. Supreme Court.
US reh den		Rehearing denied by U. S. Supreme Court.
US reh dis		Rehearing dismissed by U. S. Supreme Court.

Treatment of Case

c	(criticised)	Soundness of decision or reasoning in cited case criticised for reasons given.
d	(distinguished)	Case at bar different either in law or fact from case cited for reasons given.
e	(explained)	Statement of import of decision in cited case. Not merely a restatement of the facts.
f	(followed)	Cited as controlling.
h	(harmonized)	Apparent inconsistency explained and shown not to exist.
j	(dissenting opinion)	Citation in dissenting opinion.
L	(limited)	Refusal to extend decision of cited case beyond precise issues involved.
o	(overruled)	Ruling in cited case expressly overruled.
p	(parallel)	Citing case substantially alike or on all fours with cited case in its law or facts.
q	(questioned)	Soundness of decision or reasoning in cited case questioned.

ABBREVIATIONS—COURTS

Cir. DC.–U.S. Court of Appeals, District of Columbia Circuit
Cir. (number)–U.S. Court of Appeals Circuit (number)
Cir. Fed.–U.S. Court of Appeals, Federal Circuit
CCPA–Court of Customs and Patent Appeals
CIT–United States Court of International Trade
ClCt–Claims Court (U.S.)
CtCl–Court of Claims Reports (U.S.)
CuCt–Customs Court
ECA–Temporary Emergency Court of Appeals
ML–Judicial Panel on Multidistrict Litigation
RRR–Special Court Regional Rail Reorganization Act of 1973

FIGURE 4-14

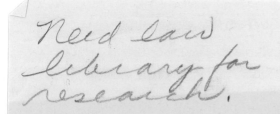

...ure to Be Followed by the Court?

...rocedural, one should consult the volumes of ...atutes or code annotated.

...ation When the Name of at Least One of the

...*Cases* or the *Defendant/Plaintiff Table* in the digests.

...*ackground Information?*

...nes should be consulted.

IMPORTANCE OF A CLEARLY DEFINED ISSUE

The greatest difficulty encountered in research is a failure to specifically define the issue. Every researcher should begin by first writing down on a piece of paper the exact issue involved. This cannot be emphasized strongly enough. Problems in reducing an issue to written form may be an indication that the researcher has not yet clearly formulated the issue. Until this has been done, effective legal research is impossible.

SEC. 4-10
SAMPLE RESEARCH QUESTIONS

The following is a series of sample research issues that can be used to gain practical experience in applying the information learned in this chapter. The first ten questions are answered with a step-by-step analysis. It should be understood that the approach used may be only one of several possible ways in which to solve the problem.

The remainder of the questions are for the reader to use in practicing research skills. Some questions are considerably more difficult than others. For those that the reader attempts to do on his or her own, the key words in any given question may sometimes give a clue as to where to look. For example, if one is asked to locate information concerning credit card fraud, he or she might begin by looking in the appropriate set under "C" for credit or credit cards or under "F" for fraud. All of the answers can be found with the aid of the four basic state and federal sets discussed in detail above. Advance sheets and pocket parts should be consulted first.

REVIEW QUESTIONS

1. What is the name of the case that can be found at 515 A.2d 439?

    Answer—*Coleman v. United States.* This case was located by going to volume 515 of Atlantic Reporter, Second Series and turning to page 439.

2. What general subject matter is discussed in Article V, § 10A of the Oklahoma Constitution?

    Answer—"House of Representatives—Number of members—Formula—Tenure." The Oklahoma Constitution can be found in the final volumes of *Oklahoma Statutes Annotated.*

3. What is the number of the statute in Alabama that prohibits the discharging of a firearm into an airplane?

    Answer—§ 13A-11-61. Since it is known that a statute number from the state of Alabama is being sought, it is logical to look at the statutes for that state, which are known collectively as the Code of Alabama. The only way to answer the question is to consult the index volumes that accompany the set. In order to effectively utilize the index, one has to identify the key words in the question. If one looks up the word "Firearms," the index directs the reader to the heading of "Weapons" in the index. Under "Weapons," there is a subcategory of "Aviation," and under that, a division entitled "Discharging firearm into aircraft, §13A-11-61." In doing research, one should always check the pocket part first for statutory language and annotations.

4. What is the name of the case that can be found at 168 N.E. 612?

    Answer—*Kaminski v. State.* The answer is not *Thomas Foods, Inc. v. Pennsylvania Railroad,* which is the case that can be found at 168 N.E.2d 612.

5. Give the names and citations for three Wyoming cases that have Wills key number 100.

    Answer—*Kerper v. Kerper,* 780 P.2d 923 (appeal after remand 819 P.2d 407 (1989)); *Shook v. Bell,* 599 P.2d 1320(1979); and *In re: Stringer's Estate,* 80 Wyo. 389, 343 P.2d 508 (1959) [rehearing denied at 80 Wyo. 426, 345 P.2d 786 (1959)]. *West's Wyoming Digest* would be the primary resource tool for solving this problem. The researcher should examine the pocket part as well as the main volume containing the subject of "Wills." Once the section has been found, look under key number 100 to find the cases listed above. Wills key number 100 pertains to the subtopic of joint and mutual wills. Therefore, any cases under Wills key number 100, including those listed above, will pertain to that topic. To verify this, look up any of the cases cited above to find that Wills key number 100 appears at the top of the case.

6. What is the main statute in Iowa that deals with the care of animals in commercial establishments?

    Answer—IOWA CODE § 162.1 *et seq.* Look under "Animals" in the index of the *Iowa Code Annotated* to find the subtopic of "Commercial Establishments, 162.1 *et seq.*" This means Iowa Statute § 162.1 and the ones that immediately follow it.

7. Give the name and citation of a Missouri state court case that has the same key number as the one that appears in *State v. Dole*, 684 S.W.2d 69 (Mo. Ct. App. 1984).

    Answer—*State v. Wise*, 879 S.W.2d 494 (MO. 1994). To answer this question, first find what key number appears in *State v. Dole*, 684 S.W.2d 69 (Mo. Ct. App. 1984). After locating the case in *South Western Reporter, Second Series*, note that it has only one key number, which is Criminal Law key number 414. From this point forward, follow the same approach used in the previous question. By looking in *West's Missouri Digest 2d* at the "Criminal Law" volume and pocket part, the researcher will find key number 414 and see the *Wise* case cited.

8. Give the name and citation of a Vermont state court case that has the same key number as the one that appears in *State v. Dole*, 684 S.W.2d 69 (Mo. Ct. App. 1984).

    Answer—*State v. Keith*, 160 Vt. 257, 628 A.2d 1247 (1993). Like the previous question, first find what key number appears in *State v. Dole*, 684 S.W.2d 69 (Mo. Ct. App. 1984). After locating the case in *South Western Reporter, Second Series*, note that it has only one key number, which is Criminal Law key number 414. To find a Vermont case with this key number, look in the *Vermont Key Number Digest* in the "Criminal Law" volume and pocket part, and then look under 414 within that topic to find the *Keith* case.

9. What procedural court rule in the state of Minnesota pertains to the record of proceedings in grand juries?

    Answer—Rule 18.05. Since the question is asking for a court rule of procedure, go to the court rules volume at the end of *Minnesota Statutes Annotated.* It is not appropriate to go to the index since the index will generally refer one to the statutes rather than to the rules of procedure. The volume or volumes that contain the various kinds of rules of procedure have individual indexes for each set of rules.

    The next problem to resolve is which set of rules is applicable. Since grand juries pertain to criminal matters, turn to the *Rules of Criminal Procedure.* The answer can then be found in one of several ways:

a. Turn to the index at the back of the single volume of the *Rules of Criminal Procedure* and look first under the topic of "Grand Juries" and then under the subtopic of "Record of proceedings."

b. Turn to the index at the back of the single volume of the *Rules of Criminal Procedure* and look first under the topic of "Records and Recordation" and then under the subtopic of "Grand juries."

c. Scan the table of contents in the front of the single volume of the *Rules of Criminal Procedure* to readily find a rule specifically pertaining to grand juries.

10. What is the name of the judge or justice who wrote the decision in the Tennessee case of *Huffine v. Riadon?*

   Answer—Justice Brock. To find this information, it is necessary to locate the written decision itself. In this case, however, no citation is given. All that is known is that it is a Tennessee case. Therefore, with a case name but no citation, the *Table of Cases* volume in *West's Tennessee Digest 2d* should be consulted. The case is listed alphabetically under "H," and a citation of 541 S.W.2d 414 is given. When one looks up that case, he or she will find that Justice Brock was the author of the decision. The justice's name will appear after the headnotes but before the body of the decision.

11. What is in Article II, §1 of the Illinois Constitution?

12. What are the main elements of a trust?

13. What is the name of the case that can be found at 127 N.W.2d 400? What is the name of the case that can be found at 188 So. 446?

14. What happens at an arraignment in a criminal case in your state?

15. Is there a rule of civil procedure in your state that indicates how long a plaintiff can fail to prosecute a case before the case is dismissed for lack of activity? Is the case automatically dismissed after that time period, or does someone have to request that the case be dismissed? If a request is necessary, who can make that request?

16. What is the maximum penalty for arson in your state?

17. What is the procedure to be followed in traffic court in your state if the defendant is an out-of-state resident and fails to appear in court on the date set for the hearing?

18. There is a Florida case in which the name of one of the parties is Culpepper, and the name of the other is something like Wint or White. The plaintiff in that case is a motorcyclist. Find the decision.

19. What is the number of the Arkansas statute that indicates under what circumstances a dance hall can constitute a public nuisance?

20. Give the names and citations for two Arizona cases that have Contracts key number 168.

21. Give the name and citation for a Connecticut case that has the same key number as the one found in *Unemployment Compensation Board of Review v. Brown*, 23 Pa. Commw. 100, 350 A.2d 445 (1976).

22. What is the citation in *South Eastern Reporter, Second Series* for the South Carolina case of *Kreke v. Ohio Gear-Wallace Murray Corp.*?

23. Give the name and citation of a Wisconsin case that has the same key number as the one found in the Wisconsin case of *Coffee-Rich, Inc. v. McDowell.*

24. What rule of appellate procedure in Connecticut pertains to the time and place to file briefs?

25. What is the meaning of the term "mistake" as it pertains to contract law?

FOOTNOTES

[1]The publisher of *A Uniform System of Citation* is The Harvard Law Review Association, Gannett House, 1511 Massachusetts Avenue, Cambridge, MA 02138.

[2]See the previous footnote.

[3]In reality, there is no volume per se in this set listed under a particular letter. The bindings of the books will demonstrate, however, that the books are organized alphabetically. The volume that contains the topic of "Burglary," for example, might be labeled in a manner such as "Building and Construction Contracts to Carriers."

[4]The *American Jurisprudence 2d,* the national encyclopedia, has a Table of Statutes, Rules, and Regulations Cited, but the references are to federal statutes, rules, and regulations only.

[5]See footnote 3.

[6]If it is unclear what the abbreviation "Bus & Org" or any other abbreviations represent, a chart in the front of the Table of Statutes identifies them.

[7]See footnote 3.

[8]Even though the statutes for the state of Rhode Island have a rather unusual name, it would be reasonable for anyone seeing the "Public Laws ..." to assume that the set contained the state's legislative acts.

[9]The case analyzed and the exhibits used are from the state of Florida, but the same kind of analysis can be made using the state research sets for any state in the United States. To understand which state materials would be applicable in another state, see Sec. 4-5, subsection A.

[10]Reprinted with permission from the *Defendant/Plaintiff Table* of *West's Florida Digest 2d,* page 196 of the 1995 pocket part, copyright © 1995 by West Publishing Company.

[11]Reprinted with permission from 477 *Southern Reporter, Second Series,* page 557 *et seq.,* copyright © 1985 by West Publishing Company.

[12]Reprinted with permission from volume 32 of *West's Florida Digest 2d,* page 32 of the 1995 pocket part, copyright © 1995 by West Publishing Company.

[13]Reprinted with permission from 576 *Southern Reporter, Second Series,* page 798 *et seq.,* copyright © 1991 by West Publishing Company.

[14]Reprinted with permission from volume 32 of *West's Florida Digest 2d*, page 158, copyright © 1985 by West Publishing Company.

[15]Reprinted with permission from Section 790.25(5) of the *Florida Statutes Annotated*, page 137 of the 1995 pocket part, copyright © 1995 by West Publishing Company.

[16]Reprinted with permission from Article 1, Section 9 of the Florida Constitution in *Florida Statutes Annotated*, page 111 of the main volume, copyright © 1995 by West Publishing Company.

[17]Reprinted with permission from the *Descriptive-Word Index*, volume 36 of *West's Florida Digest 2d*, page 39 of the 1995 pocket part, copyright © 1995 by West Publishing Company.

[18]Reprinted with permission from the *Table of Cases* of the *Florida Jurisprudence, Second Series*, page 24 of the 1995 pocket part, copyright © 1995 by Lawyer's Cooperative Publishing Company, a division of Thomson Legal Publishing, Inc.

[19]Reprinted with permission from volume 16 of the *Florida Jurisprudence, Second Series*, Criminal Law Section 4773 in the main volume, copyright © 1995 by Lawyer's Cooperative Publishing Company, a division of Thomson Legal Publishing, Inc.

[20]Reprinted with permission from the *Table of Statutes* of the *Florida Jurisprudence, Second Series*, page 334 of the 1995 pocket part, copyright © 1995 by Lawyer's Cooperative Publishing Company, a division of Thomson Legal Publishing, Inc.

[21]See footnote 19.

[22]Reprinted with permission from Rule 3.200 of the *Florida Rules of Criminal Procedure* in the *Florida Statutes Annotated*, page 94 of the 1995 pocket part, copyright © 1995 by West Publishing Company.

[23]To be able to shepardize this case, one must, of course, have a correct citation first.

[24]Reproduced by permission of Shephard's, a subsidiary of The McGraw-Hill Companies. Further reproduction of any kind is strictly prohibited.

[25]Reproduced by permission of Shephard's, a subsidiary of The McGraw-Hill Companies. Further reproduction of any kind is strictly prohibited.

5 *Writing Skills*

This chapter is designed to help the reader develop technical writing skills that can be used either on the job or in school settings where writing is required on essay exams, homework assignments, and term papers. Use of these techniques should help one to create a considerably better product even when the writer has no more knowledge of the subject matter than he or she had before the application of these skills. For the purpose of illustration, the following discussion of writing techniques will examine the manner in which answers might be written to essay test questions.

SEC. 5-1
ORGANIZATION

The organization of an essay has a substantial influence on how it is perceived. The reader of the essay must invariably believe, at least subconsciously, that if it is well organized, the essay was written by a knowledgeable person.

A.   Format

While there are many different ways to organize an essay answer to any particular question, all answers can fall within the basic essay format described in the following list:

1. The first paragraph establishes the organizational pattern that will be followed in the essay. Most answers will be broken down into three or four categories. For this particular example, it will be assumed that there are three categories.
2. Paragraph two contains a discussion of the first category.
3. Paragraph three contains a discussion of the second category.
4. Paragraph four contains a discussion of the third category.
5. The final paragraph contains either a summarization of the points made or a series of conclusions that may be drawn from an analysis of the previous paragraphs.

B.   Example 1

Question: Discuss how the federal government of the United States is organized.
   Note: The numbers are included only to show how the original pattern of this essay parallels the one immediately above. In practice, giving an answer in outline form when an essay is requested is not acceptable.

1. The federal government is divided into three main branches: the executive, the legislative, and the judicial.

2. The executive branch is composed of the President and his advisors such as the White House staff and the Cabinet. Each member of the Cabinet is in charge of a specific department of the government such as Defense, Housing and Urban Development, or Veterans' Affairs.

3. The legislative branch is divided into two main parts: the Senate and the House of Representatives. Each state has two senators regardless of state size or population while the number of U.S. representatives from any state depends upon the population of that state.

4. The judicial branch includes all three levels of the federal court system. Starting with the lowest court, those three levels are the U.S. District Court, the U.S. Circuit Court of Appeals, and the U.S. Supreme Court.

5. The federal government is, therefore, composed of three separate and distinct branches, each with a well-defined structure and identifiable function of its own.

C.   *Example 2*

Question: What are the absolutely essential elements of all contracts? (Again, paragraph numbers would be deleted.)

1. Five basic elements must be shown in order to establish the existence of a valid contract. Those elements are an agreement, mutuality of assent, competent parties, consideration, and a lawful subject matter.

2. First, an agreement must be shown between the offeror (the party making the offer) and the offeree (the party to whom the offer is made). Any agreement is composed of two main parts, which are the offer and the acceptance.

3. Second, there must be mutuality of assent. This means that both parties must be in a position to comprehend the terms of the contract without constraint or coercion. Examples in which mutuality of assent may not exist include fraud, concealment, misrepresentation, duress, and undue influence.

4. Third, the parties must be competent to enter into a contract. In this context, the term "competent" refers to the mental status of the contracting parties. Everyone is presumed competent to enter into a contract unless reason is shown to rebut that presumption. Two examples of parties who may not be deemed to be fully capable are small children and people declared insane by a court of law.

5. Fourth, there must be consideration on both sides of the contract. This means that both parties must be giving up or receiving something of value. If, for example, A agrees to pay B $20 in return for B's promise to mow A's lawn, both the promise to pay $20 and the promise to mow the lawn are of value, and the consideration requirement would therefore be met.

6. Fifth, the subject matter must be lawful. As an example, agreements based on gambling debts are not honored in many states, and those based upon such obligations would be unenforceable in a court of law.

7. A contract is not valid unless all five of these elements (an agreement, mutuality of assent, competent parties, consideration, and a lawful subject matter) are present.

D. Example 3

Question: Sue invites Ron into her apartment for a cocktail. After he has been there only a short while, she falls asleep on the sofa, so Ron decides to leave. As he starts to go, Ron decides to take the speakers from Sue's stereo system with him. He sells them one hour later at a pawn shop. Assuming that the facts given can be proven, is Ron likely to be convicted of the crime of burglary under STATE STATUTE § 123.45?

1. In order to be convicted of burglary under STATE STATUTE § 123.45, the following elements must be established: (a) a breaking and entering; (b) of the building or structure; (c) of another; (d) with the intent to commit a crime therein.[1]

2. A breaking sufficient to justify a charge of burglary in this state requires a forcible entry into the premises by the defendant. While the facts clearly show that Ron entered the premises, he was "invited," so it appears that the required breaking did not occur.

3. Since the facts state that Sue invited Ron into "her" apartment, it is clear that it was a building or structure "of another."

4. The facts do not indicate that there was intent to commit a crime at the time that Ron entered, even though he ultimately decided to take the speakers.

5. Since it is unlikely that the prosecution could establish that there was a breaking, or that at the time of the entry there was an intent to commit a crime therein, it would appear that key elements of the crime are missing and conviction would be unlikely.

E. Example 4

Question: Discuss the various methods used for amending the U.S. Constitution.

1. There are four primary means of amending the U.S. Constitution. They include (a) the passage and ratification of express amendments, (b) constitutional convention, (c) executive action, and (d) court interpretation.

2. Express amendments can be added to the U.S. Constitution if the wording of the proposed amendment is passed by two-thirds of the Senate, two-thirds of the House of Representatives, and three-fourths of the state legislatures. The first ten amendments, known as the Bill of Rights, were passed shortly after the approval of the Constitution. In the 200-year period that has followed, only 17 other amendments have been added to the original 10.

3. The Constitution could also be amended if three-fourths of the states' legislatures passed a resolution calling for a constitutional convention to consider a constitutional amendment. No such convention has been convened in two hundred years, and it is unclear not only who would represent each state, but also whether the convention would be limited in scope to a discussion of the particular amendment referred to in the state resolutions.

4. Another way to amend the Constitution is by executive action. The Constitution indicates, for example, that the president may make treaties with the advice and consent of the Senate. President Washington assumed this provision only required him to submit treaties that had already been negotiated to the Senate for ratification. This created a precedent that has been followed since that time.

5. Whenever the Constitution is subjected to interpretation by the courts, the resulting court precedent may have the effect of "amending" the Constitution. If, for example, the court rules that the death penalty is not "cruel and unusual punishment" within the meaning of the Constitution, it has considered the general phrase in the Constitution and applied it to a specific set of circumstances. Each time this is done, it could be said that the Constitution has been amended or, more specifically, defined. The process of amendment by court interpretation is a never-ending process, and it has occurred constantly throughout the history of our country.

6. While amendment through court interpretation has provided the greatest change in the way we understand the Constitution, the document has also been effectively amended by executive action as well as

express amendment as a result of passage and ratification of the constitutional language. Constitutional conventions have not been utilized in the past 200 years for amendment purposes.

SEC. 5-2
THE ORGANIZATIONAL FORMAT AND THE WRITING PROCESS

A.   Preparation of Outline

If one has the time to prepare a written outline before actually writing the composition itself, the quality of the essay is likely to be vastly improved. This will not only organize the essay, but it will also ensure that it has substance. Once the outline is prepared, the writer should follow it without deviation.

The likelihood of creating a successful outline largely depends on an intelligent determination of the organizational format (see Section B immediately following).

B.   Determination of Organizational Format

The organization of the answer may be self-evident, such as in Sec. 5-1, subsection B, because the question is asking for a series of categories.

If the question is not asking for a series of specific categories, then a clue to the organization may be found in an examination of the key words of the question. For example, if a particular set of facts is given and the student is asked, "Is the defendant likely to be found liable for negligence?", one might begin by discussing what must be shown in order to establish a case of negligence. The writer could then proceed to analyze those elements to determine which ones must be discussed in order to render a complete answer. Even for a longer paper, the organization should be based on the same basic format.

C.   Amplification of Paragraph Categories

On longer tests, homework assignments in essay form, and term papers, the paper could be greatly expanded even though the original pattern would be identical. The opening and closing paragraphs would be the same, but the middle portion might be pages in length. In the main body of the essay the writer can elaborate on a broader knowledge of the categories themselves. For example, note that in Sec. 5-1, subsection B, the writer shows not only an awareness of the existence of the legislative branch, but also that it is divided into two sub-categories, which are the Senate and the House of Representatives. It further demonstrates that the writer is aware of the manner in which the numbers of senators and congressmen representing each state are determined. In Sec. 5-1, subsection E, note that the writer has shown not only that the Constitution can be expressly amended, but exactly what is required in order to enact an express amendment, how many total amendments there are, and what the collective name is for the first ten amendments. In still another example, note that in Sec. 5 1, subsection C, the writer demonstrates familiarity not only with the element known as the "agreement," but also with the fact that the agreement is itself divided into two parts, which are the offer and the acceptance.

When writing a lengthier essay, the writer will improve the end product only if the portions added have substance and content. A number of strategies can be used to expand a composition and at the same time increase its overall quality. They include:

1.   *Use of Examples*

Both the quality and the length of the essay can be increased by using specific applications or examples to demonstrate one's knowledge of the subject matter. Abstract definitions should always be clarified by the inclusion of examples.

2.   *Efficient Use of the Time Allotted*

Since almost any answer can be endlessly expanded depending on the amount of time given for writing the essay, every effort should be made to include as much information as time permits. The answers found in Sec. 5-1, subsections B–E would be adequate if one were given just a few minutes to respond, but obviously they would be totally inadequate if an hour had been allotted, or if the question had been the subject of a homework assignment or a term paper.

3.   *Definition of All Technical Terms*

In essay test situations, if the answer uses any terms with which the writer was unfamiliar prior to a study of the subject matter, then definitions of such terms should be included in the test answer. For example, if one refers to what is known as the felony murder rule, one should automatically define that rule in the answer. If the writer refers to the contributory negligence doctrine, the definition of that doctrine should be an automatic part of the answer. Note, for example, that in Sec. 5-1, subsection C, the writer has not only mentioned the terms "offeror" and "offeree," but has also given a short definition of each one of them. By simply defining all the terms being used, the student can greatly expand an answer and, at the same time, demonstrate knowledge of the subject matter.

D.   *Avoidance of Unjustified Assumptions*

One of the most common errors an essay writer makes is to assume that the reader has a substantial knowledge of the subject matter. This is especially true with regard to essay answers to test questions. While the assumption is presumably correct when a teacher is the reader, the teacher is the one who is attempting to ascertain how much the student knows. When students make such assumptions (often subconsciously), it is left to the teacher to speculate whether the student has left out material because the student considered it to be obvious or because the student did not know it. A student who knows 10 percent of the material and writes down 95 percent of it will invariably do better than one who knows 90 percent of the material and writes down only 2 percent of it.

Below is an example of a question with both a poor answer and a better answer. The section following the answers attempts to explain some of the features of the second answer that make it a better one.

1.   *Example*

Question: On January 4, John says to Mary, "You can have my sailboat if you agree to pay me $500." On January 9, Mary responds by saying, "I'll give you $500 for the boat and your green trailer." On February 2, John says, "I don't like your offer, but I guess I will go along with it." On the basis of the information given, is there a contract?

a. Poor answer.   Yes, because John accepted Mary's new offer within a reasonable period of time.

b. Better answer.   In order to establish a contract, five elements must be shown. Those elements are an agreement, mutuality of assent, competent parties, consideration, and lawful subject matter. In order for there to be a contract, all five elements must be present. The question in this case deals primarily with whether there was an agreement between the parties.

In order for there to be an agreement, there must be both a valid offer and an acceptance. John's statement of January 4 was a valid offer. Mary's response of January 9 was a counteroffer rather than an acceptance since her response significantly changed the terms of the original offer. Once John accepted the counteroffer on February 2, which was within a reasonable time of the counteroffer, a valid contract existed.

Since there was a valid offer and a valid acceptance within a reasonable period of time, there was an agreement. Since the other elements of a contract also seem to be present, there is a binding contract.

c. Analysis of both answers.   There are several very specific reasons why the second answer is the better one.

(1) The writer of the better answer started with the most general and proceeded toward the more specific. Since the question dealt with whether a contract existed, the writer began by telling what is necessary in order to establish the existence of a contract. The writer then determined which issues were truly under discussion. The one who wrote the poor answer may have gone through the same mental process, but the reader has no way of knowing it.

(2) Once the writer of the better answer determined what was at issue, the key issue was itself subdivided into two categories, which were the offer and the acceptance. The writer of the poor answer gambled that the reader knew of the writer's knowledge of this material.

(3) The writer of the better answer has expressly stated that Mary's first statement is a counteroffer, and has implicitly defined what is meant by a counteroffer. In the poor answer, there is no indication that the writer is aware of the meaning or nature of a counteroffer, and there is, therefore, no explanation of why John, rather than Mary, is accepting an offer.

(4) The writer of the poor answer is obviously aware of some "reasonableness" test, but the answer does not clearly state what that test is. Furthermore, it does not even refer to the existence of a counteroffer, so any reference to a reasonable time requirement would be innately confusing. The writer of the better answer has expressly referred to the existence of a counteroffer and implicitly indicated that the acceptance of a counteroffer must be made within a reasonable time of the counteroffer.

FOOTNOTE

[1]At common law, it also had to be demonstrated that the breaking and entering occurred "during the nighttime," that the structure entered was a "dwelling house," and that the defendant intended to commit a "felony" therein.

6 *Ethics*

CHAPTER OVERVIEW

SEC. 6-1
INTRODUCTION

The subject of ethics deals with principles of conduct that are deemed to be correct based on moral judgment. The ethical guidelines governing the paralegal come from a variety of potential sources including codes of ethics, statutes, and case law. The ultimate purpose of these rules is to help protect the public and to give the paralegal guidance in determining the kinds of activities that are or are not appropriate for the paralegal.

As long as the definition of a paralegal remains imprecise, the regulation of paralegals is going to be difficult. There is no licensing of paralegals in any state at the present time. This is primarily due to the fact that paralegals are generally working for attorneys who themselves must have licenses and who are accountable for the activities of their paralegal employees. In spite of the absence of a licensing requirement, the kind of conduct that has been deemed appropriate for paralegals has been governed by various sources.

First, legal assistants are obviously responsible for any criminal law violations. This is true even when the crimes are committed within the scope of the legal assistant's authority. When illegal activity by the paralegal is directed or even condoned by the attorney, both parties may bear responsibility for the paralegal's act. Included in this category are activities that would be regarded as the unauthorized practice of law by the legal assistant.

Second, legal assistants are personally responsible for any torts that they commit. *Torts* are civil wrongs (as opposed to crimes) other than suits for breach of contract, and they include such causes of action as negligence, libel, slander, fraud, invasion of privacy, and trespass. The commission of torts by the legal assistant may subject both the legal assistant and the attorney to civil liability. This includes actions constituting malpractice. Since the illegal, tortious, or unethical actions of the paralegal can create significant difficulties with the courts or with the bar for the supervising attorney, one of the serious consequences of such actions by the paralegal can be his or her dismissal by the attorney.

Third, each of the professional associations of paralegals in the United States has codes of ethics to govern their members. The National Federation of Paralegal Associations (NFPA) published a newly revised Model Code of Ethics and Professional Responsibility in 1993, and a copy of it has been reprinted in Sec. 6-2. The National Association of Legal Assistants (NALA) first issued its Code of Ethics and Professional Responsibility in 1975, and the code has been revised several times since then. A copy of this organization's code is reprinted in Sec. 6-3. Both codes provide the paralegal with guidelines for working in the field of paralegal assisting and can give the paralegal a clearer idea of the kinds of activities that paralegals can engage in.

Documents showing how attorneys can properly utilize paralegals can assist the paralegals in determining what appropriate and ethical conduct is in the profession. About one-half of the states have guidelines that address ethical problems that arise when paralegals are used. The rules may emanate from the bar or from the state's highest court. It should be noted, however, that since paralegals are not licensed by state or local bars, they are not subject to the same disciplinary rules that govern attorneys. Nevertheless, it is possible that proceedings can be initiated against an attorney who employs a paralegal and then provides insufficient supervision.

NALA has issued Model Standards and Guidelines for the Utilization of Legal Assistants Annotated. These standards and guidelines go into somewhat greater detail concerning underlying issues, and they give some of the case law in which these matters have been considered. The NALA Model Standards and Guidelines have been reprinted in Sec. 6-4.

In the final section of this chapter (Sec. 6-5), specific comments by the author of this book are made concerning various ethical issues. The National Association of Legal Assistant's Code of Ethics is used as a framework for that analysis. In the discussion, reference is made to two codes of ethics that have been promulgated by the American Bar Association. While both of these documents are directed at attorneys, there are a number of sections that have a bearing on paralegals, such as Model Rule 5.3 which deals with the attorney's responsibilities regarding nonlawyer assistants.

The first of these codes is the 1969 Code of Professional Responsibility. It is composed of nine canons of ethics, each of which is supplemented by Ethical Considerations and Disciplinary Rules. Ethical Considerations only indicate the kind of conduct that an attorney should endeavor to follow. Failure of an attorney to abide by a Disciplinary Rule, on the other hand, can result in disciplinary action. The second code is the Model Rules of Professional Conduct, which was issued in 1983 to revise the Code of Professional Responsibility. Even though the Model Rules is the more recent of the codes issued by the American Bar Association, knowledge of the previous one is necessary because many of the state bar associations have not yet chosen to adopt some or all of the provisions of the new code.

SEC. 6-2
NFPA MODEL CODE OF ETHICS AND PROFESSIONAL RESPONSIBILITY[1]

Preamble

The National Federation of Paralegal Associations, Inc. ("NFPA") is a professional organization comprised of paralegal associations and individual paralegals throughout the United States. Members of NFPA have varying types of backgrounds, experience, education, and job responsibilities which reflect the diversity of the paralegal profession. NFPA promotes the growth, development and recognition of the paralegal profession as an integral partner in the delivery of legal services.

NFPA recognizes that the creation of guidelines and standards for professional conduct are important for the development and expansion of the paralegal profession. In May 1993, NFPA adopted this Model Code of Ethics and Professional Responsibility ("Model Code") to delineate the principles for ethics and conduct to which every paralegal should aspire. The Model Code expresses NFPA's commitment to increasing the quality and efficiency of legal services and recognizes the profession's responsibilities to the public, the legal community, and colleagues.

Paralegals perform many different functions, and these functions differ greatly among practice areas. In addition, each jurisdiction has its own unique legal authority and practices governing ethical conduct and professional responsibilities.

It is essential that each paralegal strive for personal and professional excellence and encourage the professional development of other paralegals as well as those entering the profession. Participation in professional associations intended to advance the quality and standards of the legal profession is of particular importance. Paralegals should possess integrity, professional skill and dedication to the improvement of the legal system and should strive to expand the paralegal role in the delivery of legal services.

Canon 1

A paralegal[2] shall achieve and maintain a high level of competence.
EC-1.1 A paralegal shall achieve competency through education, training, and work experience.
EC-1.2 A paralegal shall participate in continuing education to keep informed of current legal, technical and general developments.
EC-1.3 A paralegal shall perform all assignments promptly and efficiently.

Canon 2

A paralegal shall maintain a high level of personal and professional integrity.
EC-2.1 A paralegal shall not engage in any ex parte[3] communications involving the courts or any other adjudicatory body in an attempt to exert undue influence or to obtain advantage for the benefit of only one party.
EC-2.2 A paralegal shall not communicate, or cause another to communicate, with a party the paralegal knows to be represented by a lawyer in a pending matter without the prior consent of the lawyer representing such other party.
EC-2.3 A paralegal shall ensure that all timekeeping and billing records prepared by the paralegal are thorough, accurate, and honest.
EC-2.4 A paralegal shall be scrupulous, thorough and honest in the identification and maintenance of all funds, securities, and other assets of a client and shall provide accurate accountings as appropriate.
EC-2.5 A paralegal shall advise the proper authority of any dishonest or fraudulent acts by any person pertaining to the handling of the funds, securities or other assets of a client.

Canon 3

A paralegal shall maintain a high standard of professional conduct.

EC-3.1 A paralegal shall refrain from engaging in any conduct that offends the dignity and decorum of proceedings before a court or other adjudicatory body and shall be respectful of all rules and procedures.

EC-3.2 A paralegal shall advise the proper authority of any action of another legal professional which clearly demonstrates fraud, deceit, dishonesty, or misrepresentation.

EC-3.3 A paralegal shall avoid impropriety and the appearance of impropriety.

Canon 4

A paralegal shall serve the public interest by contributing to the delivery of quality legal services and the improvement of the legal system.

EC-4.1 A paralegal shall be sensitive to the legal needs of the public and shall promote the development and implementation of programs that address those needs.

EC-4.2 A paralegal shall support bona fide efforts to meet the need for legal services by those unable to pay reasonable or customary fees; for example, participation in pro bono projects and volunteer work.

EC-4.3 A paralegal shall support efforts to improve the legal system and shall assist in making changes.

Canon 5

A paralegal shall preserve all confidential information[4] provided by the client or acquired from other sources before, during, and after the course of the professional relationship.

EC-5.1 A paralegal shall be aware of and abide by all legal authority governing confidential information.

EC-5.2 A paralegal shall not use confidential information to the disadvantage of the client.

EC-5.3 A paralegal shall not use confidential information to the advantage of the paralegal or of a third person.

EC-5.4 A paralegal may reveal confidential information only after full disclosure and with the client's written consent; or, when required by law or court order; or, when necessary to prevent the client from committing an act which could result in death or serious bodily harm.

EC-5.5 A paralegal shall keep those individuals responsible for the legal representation of a client fully informed of any confidential information the paralegal may have pertaining to that client.

EC-5.6 A paralegal shall not engage in any indiscreet communications concerning clients.

Canon 6

A paralegal's title shall be fully disclosed.[5]

EC-6.1 A paralegal's title shall clearly indicate the individual's status and shall be disclosed in all business and professional communications to avoid misunderstandings and misconceptions about the paralegal's role and responsibilities.

EC-6.2 A paralegal's title shall be included if the paralegal's name appears on business cards, letterhead, brochures, directories, and advertisements.

Canon 7

A paralegal shall not engage in the unauthorized practice of law.

EC-7.1 A paralegal shall comply with the applicable legal authority governing the unauthorized practice of law.

Canon 8

A paralegal shall avoid conflicts of interest and shall disclose any possible conflict to the employer or client, as well as to the prospective employers or clients.

EC-8.1 A paralegal shall act within the bounds of the law, solely for the benefit of the client, and shall be free of compromising influences and loyalties. Neither the paralegal's personal or business interest, nor those of other clients or third persons, should compromise the paralegal's professional judgment and loyalty to the client.

EC-8.2 A paralegal shall avoid conflicts of interest which may arise from previous assignments whether for a present or past employer or client.

EC-8.3 A paralegal shall avoid conflicts of interest which may arise from family relationships and from personal and business interests.

EC-8.4 A paralegal shall create and maintain an effective recordkeeping system that identifies clients, matters, and parties with which the paralegal has worked, to be able to determine whether an actual or potential conflict of interest exists.

EC-8.5 A paralegal shall reveal sufficient non-confidential information about a client or former client to reasonably ascertain if an actual or potential conflict of interest exists.

EC-8.6 A paralegal shall not participate in or conduct work on any matter where a conflict of interest has been identified.

EC-8.7 In matters where a conflict of interest has been identified and the client consents to continued representation, a paralegal shall comply fully with the implementation and maintenance of an Ethical Wall.[6]

> National Federation of Paralegal Associations, Inc.
> P.O. Box 33108
> Kansas City, MO 64114-1018
> (816) 941-4000 ★ (816) 941-2725 fax

SEC. 6-3
NALA CODE OF ETHICS AND PROFESSIONAL RESPONSIBILITY[7]

A legal assistant must adhere strictly to the accepted standards of legal ethics and to the general principles of proper conduct. The performance of the duties of the legal assistant shall be governed by specific canons as defined herein so that justice will be served and goals of the profession attained. (See NALA Model Standards and Guidelines for Utilization of Legal Assistants, Section II.)

The canons of ethics set forth hereafter are adopted by the National Association of Legal Assistants, Inc., as a general guide intended to aid legal assistants and attorneys. The enumeration of these rules does not mean there are not others of equal importance although not specifically mentioned. Court rules, agency rules and statutes must be taken into consideration when interpreting the canons.

Definition: Legal assistants, also known as paralegals, are a distinguishable group of persons who assist attorneys in the delivery of legal services. Through formal education, training, and experience, legal assistants have knowledge and expertise regarding the legal system and substantive and procedural law which qualify them to do work of a legal nature under the supervision of an attorney.

Canon 1

A legal assistant must not perform any of the duties that attorneys only may perform nor take any actions that attorneys may not take.

Canon 2

A legal assistant may perform any task which is properly delegated and supervised by an attorney, as long as the attorney is ultimately responsible to the client, maintains a direct relationship with the client, and assumes professional responsibility for the work product. (See NALA Model Standards and Guidelines for Utilization of Legal Assistants, Sections IV and VII.)

Canon 3

A legal assistant must not (See NALA Model Standards and Guidelines for Utilization of Legal Assistants, Section VI.):

a. engage in, encourage, or contribute to any act which could constitute the unauthorized practice of law; and

b. establish attorney-client relationships, set fees, give legal opinions or advice or represent a client before a court or agency unless so authorized by that court or agency; and

c. engage in conduct or take any action which would assist or involve the attorney in a violation of professional ethics or give the appearance of professional impropriety.

Canon 4

A legal assistant must use discretion and professional judgment commensurate with knowledge and experience but must not render independent legal judgment in place of an attorney. The services of an attorney are essential in the public interest whenever such legal judgment is required. (See NALA Model Standards and Guidelines for Utilization of Legal Assistants, Section VII.)

Canon 5

A legal assistant must disclose his or her status as a legal assistant at the outset of any professional relationship with a client, attorney, a court or administrative agency or personnel thereof, or a member of the general public. A legal assistant must act prudently in determining the extent to which a client may be assisted without the presence of an attorney. (See NALA Model Standards and Guidelines for Utilization of Legal Assistants, Section V.)

Canon 6

A legal assistant must strive to maintain integrity and a high degree of competency through education and training with respect to professional responsibility, local rules and practice, and through continuing education in substantive areas of law to better assist the legal profession in fulfilling its duty to provide legal service.

Canon 7

A legal assistant must protect the confidences of a client and must not violate any rule or statute now in effect or hereafter enacted controlling the doctrine of privileged communications between a client and an attorney. (See Model Standards and Guidelines for Utilization of Legal Assistants, Section V.)

Canon 8

A legal assistant must do all other things incidental, necessary, or expedient for the attainment of the ethics and responsibilities as defined by statute or rule of court.

Canon 9

A legal assistant's conduct is guided by bar associations' codes of professional responsibility and rules of professional conduct.

SEC. 6-4
MODEL STANDARDS AND GUIDELINES FOR
UTILIZATION OF LEGAL ASSISTANTS ANNOTATED[8]

Introduction

The purpose of this annotated version of the National Association of Legal Assistants, Inc. (NALA) Model Standards and Guidelines for the Utilization of Legal Assistants is to provide references to the existing case law and other authorities where the underlying issues have been considered. The authorities cited will serve as a basis upon which conduct of a legal assistant may be analyzed as proper or improper.

The Guidelines represent a statement of how the legal assistant may function in the law office. The Guidelines are not intended to be a comprehensive or exhaustive list of the proper duties of a legal assistant. Rather, they are designed as guides to what may or may not be proper conduct for the legal assistant. In formulating the Guidelines, the reasoning and rules of law in many reported decisions of disciplinary cases and unauthorized practice of law cases have been analyzed and considered. In addition, the provisions of the American Bar Association's Model Code of Professional Responsibility and the Model Rules of Professional Conduct, as well as the ethical promulgations of various state courts and bar associations have been considered in development of the Guidelines.

While the Guidelines may not have universal application, they do form a sound basis for the legal assistant and the supervising attorney to follow in the operation of a law office. The Model will serve as a definitive and well-reasoned guide to those considering voluntary standards and guidelines for legal assistants. If regulation is to be imposed in a given jurisdiction the Model may serve as a comprehensive resource document.

I.   Preamble

Proper utilization of the services of legal assistants affects the efficient delivery of legal services. Legal assistants and the legal profession should be assured that some measures exist for identifying legal assistants and their role in assisting attorneys in the delivery of legal services. Therefore, the National Association of Legal Assistants, Inc., hereby adopts these Model Standards and Guidelines as an educational document for the benefit of legal assistants and the legal profession.

Comment

The three most frequently raised questions concerning legal assistants are (1) How do you define a legal assistant; (2) Who is qualified to be identified as a legal assistant; and (3) What duties may a legal assistant perform? The definition adopted answers the first question insofar as legal assistants serving attorneys are concerned. The Model sets forth minimum education, training, and experience through standards which will assure that one denominated as a legal assistant has the qualifications to be held out to the public in that capacity. The Guidelines identify those acts which the reported cases hold to be proscribed and give examples of services which the legal assistant may perform under the supervision of an attorney.

The three fundamental issues in the preceding paragraph have been raised in various cases for the pasty fifty years. In *Ferris v. Snively,* 19 P.2d 942 (Wash. 1933), the Court stated work performed by a law clerk to be proper and not the unauthorized practice of law requiring supervision by the employing attorney. The Court stated:

> We realize that law clerks have their place in a law office, and we recognize the fact that the nature of their work approaches in a degree that of their employers. The line of demarcation as to where their work begins and where it ends cannot always be drawn with absolute distinction or accuracy. Probably as nearly as it can be fixed, and it is sufficient to say that it is work of a preparatory nature, such as research, investigation of details,

the assemblage of data and other necessary information, and such other work as will assist the employing attorney in carrying the matter to a completed product, either by his personal examination and approval thereof or by additional effort on his part. The work must be such, however, as loses its separate identify and becomes either the product, or else merged in the product, of the attorney himself. (19 P.2d at pp. 945–46) (*See* Florida EC 3-6, *infra* at, Section IV.)

The NALA Guidelines constitute a statement relating to services performed by non-lawyer employees as approved by court decisions and other sources of authority. The purpose of the Guidelines is not to place limitations or restrictions on the legal profession. Rather, the Guidelines are intended to outline for the legal profession an acceptable course of conduct. By voluntary recognition and utilization of the Model Standards and Guidelines the legal profession will avoid many problems.

II. Definition

Legal assistants[9] are a distinguishable group of persons who assist attorneys in the delivery of legal services. Through formal education, training, and experience, legal assistants have knowledge and expertise regarding the legal system and substantive and procedural law which qualify them to do work of a legal nature under the supervision of an attorney.

Comment

This definition has been used to foster a distinction between a legal assistant as one working under the direct supervision of an attorney and a broader class of paralegals who perform tasks of a similar nature, but not necessarily under the supervision of an attorney. In applying the standards and guidelines it is important to remember that they in turn were developed to apply to the legal assistant as defined therein.

III. Standards

A legal assistant should meet certain minimum qualifications. The following standards may be used to determine an individual's qualifications as a legal assistant:

1. Successful completion of the Certified Legal Assistant ("CLA") examination of the National Association of Legal Assistants, Inc.;

2. Graduation from an ABA approved program of study for legal assistants;

3. Graduation from a course of study for legal assistants which is institutionally accredited but not ABA approved, and which requires not less than the equivalent of 60 hours of classroom study;

4. Graduation from a course of study for legal assistants, other than those set forth in (2) and (3) above, plus not less than six months of in-house training as a legal assistant;

5. A baccalaureate degree in any field, plus not less than six months in-house training as a legal assistant;

6. A minimum of three years of law-related experience under the supervision of an attorney, including at least six months of in-house training as a legal assistant; or

7. Two years of in-house training as a legal assistant.

For purposes of these Standards, "in-house training as a legal assistant" means attorney education of the employee concerning legal assistant duties and these Guidelines. In addition to review and analysis of assignments, the legal assistant should receive a reasonable amount of instruction directly related to the duties and obligations of the legal assistant.

Comment

The Standards set forth suggested minimum qualifications for a legal assistant. These minimum qualifications as adopted recognize legal related work backgrounds and formal educational backgrounds, both of which should provide the legal assistant with a broad base in exposure to and knowledge of the legal profession. This background is necessary to assure the public and the profession that the one being identified as a legal assistant is qualified.

The Certified Legal Assistant (CLA) examination offered by NALA is the only voluntary nationwide certification program for legal assistants. The CLA designation is a statement to the legal profession and the public that the legal assistant has met the high levels of knowledge and professionalism required by NALA's certification program. Continuing education requirements, which all certified legal assistants must meet, assure that high standards are maintained. Certification through NALA is available to any legal assistant meeting the educational and experience requirements.

IV. Guidelines

These guidelines relating to standards of performance and professional responsibility are intended to aid legal assistants and attorneys. The responsibility rests with an attorney who employs legal assistants to educate them with respect to the duties they are assigned and to supervise the manner in which such duties are accomplished.

Comment

In general, a legal assistant is allowed to perform any task which is properly delegated and supervised by an attorney, so long as **the attorney is ultimately responsible to the client and assumes complete professional responsibility for the work product.**

The Code of Professional Responsibility of the American Bar Association, EC 3-6 states:

> A lawyer often delegates tasks to clerks, secretaries, and other lay persons. Such delegation is proper if the lawyer maintains a direct relationship with his clients, supervises the delegated work, and has complete professional responsibility for the work product. This delegation enables a lawyer to render legal services more economically and efficiently.[10]

ABA Model Rules of Professional Conduct, Rule 5.3 provides:

> With respect to a non-lawyer employed or retained by or associated with a lawyer:
>
> **(a)** a partner in a law firm shall make reasonable efforts to ensure that the firm has in effect measures giving reasonable assurance that the person's conduct is compatible with the professional obligations of the lawyer;
>
> **(b)** a lawyer having direct supervisory authority over the non-lawyer shall make reasonable efforts to ensure that the person's conduct is compatible with the professional obligations of the lawyer; and
>
> **(c)** a lawyer shall be responsible for conduct of such a person that would be a violation of the rules of professional conduct if engaged in by a lawyer if:
>
> **(1)** the lawyer orders or, with the knowledge of the specific conduct ratifies the conduct involved; or
>
> **(2)** the lawyer is a partner in the law firm in which the person is employed, or has direct supervisory authority over the person, and knows of the conduct at a time when its consequences can be avoided or mitigated but fails to take reasonable remedial action.[11]

The Florida version of EC 3-6 provides:

A lawyer or law firm may employ nonlawyers such as secretaries, law clerks, investigators, researchers, legal assistants, accountants, draftsmen, office administrators, and other lay personnel to assist the lawyer in the delivery of legal services. A lawyer often delegates tasks to such persons. Such delegation is proper if a lawyer retains a direct relationship with his client, supervises the delegated work, and has complete professional responsibility for the work product.

The work which is delegated is such that it will assist the employing attorney in carrying the matter to a completed product either by the lawyer's personal examination and approval thereof or by additional effort on the lawyer's part. The delegated work must be such, however, as loses its separate identity and becomes either the product or else merged in the product of the attorney himself.

The Kentucky Paralegal Code defines a legal assistant as:

… a person under the supervision and direction of a licensed lawyer, who may apply knowledge of law and legal procedures in rendering direct assistance to lawyers engaged in legal research; design; develop or plan modifications or new procedures, techniques, services, processes or applications; prepare or interpret legal documents and write detailed procedure for practicing in certain fields of law; select, compile and use technical information from such references as digests, encyclopedias or practice manuals; and analyze and follow procedural problems that involve independent decisions.

Kentucky became the first state to adopt a Paralegal Code, which sets forth certain exclusions to the unauthorized practice law:

For purpose of this rule, the unauthorized practice of law shall not include any service rendered involving legal knowledge or advice, whether representation, counsel or advocacy, in or out of court, rendered in respect to the acts, duties, obligations, liabilities or business relations of the one requiring services where:

A. The client understands that the paralegal is not a lawyer;

B. The lawyer supervises the paralegal in the performance of his duties; and

C. The lawyer remains fully responsible for such representation, including all actions taken or not taken in connection therewith by the paralegal to the same extent as if such representation had been furnished entirely by the lawyer and all such actions had been taken or not taken directly by the attorney. Paralegal Code, Ky. S.Ct.R. 3.700, Sub-Rule 2.

While the Kentucky rule is an exception, it does provide a basis for expanding services which may be performed by legal assistants.

There are many interesting and complex issues involving the use of legal assistants. One issue which is not addressed in the Guidelines is whether a legal assistant, as defined herein, may make appearances before administrative agencies. This issue is discussed in *Remmer, Representation of Clients Before Administrative Agencies: Authorized or Unauthorized Practice of Law?* 15 VALPARAISO UNIV. L.REV. 567 (1981). The State Bar of California Standing Committee on Professional Responsibility and Conduct, in opinion 1988-103 (2/8/89) has stated a law firm can delegate authority to a legal assistant employee to file petitions or motions and make other appearances before the Worker's Compensation Appeals Board, provided adequate supervision is maintained by the attorney and the client is informed and has consented to the use of the legal assistant in such fashion.

In any discussion of the proper role of a legal assistant attention must be directed to what constitutes the practice of law. The proper delegation of work and duties to legal assistants is further complicated and confused by the lack of adequate definition of the practice of law and the unauthorized practice of law.

In *Davies v. Unauthorized Practice Committee*, 431 S.W.2d 590 (Texas, 1968), the Court found that the defendant was properly enjoined from the unauthorized practice of law. The Court, in defining the "practice of law," stated:

> According to the generally understood definition of the practice of law, it embraces the preparation of pleadings and other papers incident to actions of special proceedings, and the management of such actions in proceedings on behalf of clients before judges in courts. However, the practice of law is not confined to cases conducted in court. In fact, the major portion of the practice of any capable lawyer consists of work done outside of the courts. The practice of law involves not only appearance in court in connection with litigation, but also services rendered out of court, and includes the giving of advice or the rendering of any service requiring the use of legal skill or knowledge, such as preparing a will, contract or other instrument, the legal effect of which under the facts and conclusions involved must be carefully determined.

The important distinguishing fact between the defendant in *Davies* and the legal assistant is that the acts of the legal assistant are performed under the supervision of an attorney.

EC 3-5 of the Code of Professional Responsibility states:

> It is neither necessary nor desirable to attempt the formulation of a single, specific definition of what constitutes the practice of law. Functionally, the

practice of law relates to the rendition of services for others that call for the professional judgment of a lawyer. The essence of the professional judgment of the lawyer is his educated ability to relate the general body and philosophy of law to a specific legal problem of a client; and thus, the public interest will be better served if only lawyers are permitted to act in matters involving professional judgment. Where this professional judgment is not involved, non-lawyers, such as court clerks, police officers, abstracters, and many governmental employees, may engage in occupations that require a special knowledge of law in certain areas. But the services of a lawyer are essential in the public interest whenever the exercise of professional legal judgment is required.[12]

There are many cases relating to the unauthorized practice of law, but the most troublesome ones in attempting to define what would or would not form the unauthorized practice of law for acts performed by a legal assistant are those such as *Crawford v. State Bar of California*, 355 P.2d 490 (Calif. 1960), which states that any act performed in a law office is the practice of law because the clients have sought the attorney to perform the work because of the training and judgment exercised by attorneys.

See also, Annot. "Layman's Assistance to Parties in Divorce Proceedings as Unauthorized Practice of Law," 12 ALR4 656; Annot. "Activities of Law Clerks as Illegal Practice of Law," 13 ALR3 1137; Annot. "Sale of Books or Forms Designed to Enable Layman to Achieve Legal Results Without Assistance of Attorney as Unauthorized Practice of Law," 71 ALR3 1000; Annot. "Nature of Legal Services or Law-Related Services Which May Be Performed for Others By Disbarred or Suspended Attorney," 87 ALR3 272. See also, Karen B. Judd, CLA, "Beyond the Bar: Legal Assistants and the Unauthorized Practice of Law," *Facts & Findings*, Vol. VIII, Issue 6, National Association of Legal Assistants, May–June, 1982.

V

Legal assistants should:

1. Disclose their status as legal assistants at the outset of any professional relationship with a client, other attorneys, a court or administrative agency or personnel thereof, or members of the general public;

2. Preserve the confidences and secrets of all clients; and

3. Understand the attorney's Code of Professional Responsibility and these guidelines in order to avoid any action which would involve the attorney in a violation of that Code, or give the appearance of professional impropriety.

Comment

Routine early disclosure of the legal assistant's status when dealing with persons outside the attorney's office is necessary to assure that there will be no misunderstanding as to the responsibilities and role of the legal assistant. Disclosure may be made in any way that avoids confusion. If the person dealing with the legal assistant already knows of his or her status, further disclosure is unnecessary. If at any time in written or in oral communication the legal assistant becomes aware that the other person may believe the legal assistant is an attorney, it should be made clear that the legal assistant is not an attorney.

The attorney should exercise care that the legal assistant preserves and refrains from using any confidence or secrets of a client, and should instruct the legal assistant not to disclose or use any such confidences or secrets.

DR 4-101(D), ABA Code of Professional Responsibility, provides in part that:

> A lawyer shall exercise reasonable care to prevent his employees, associates, and others whose services are utilized by him from disclosing or using confidences or secrets of a client ...[13]

This obligation is emphasized in EC 4-2:

> It is a matter of common knowledge that the normal operation of a law office exposes confidential professional information to non-lawyer employees of the office, particularly secretaries and those having access to the files; and this obligates the lawyer to exercise care in selecting and training his employees so that the sanctity of all confidences and secrets of his clients may be preserved.[14]

The ultimate responsibility for compliance with approved standards of professional conduct rests with the supervising attorney. *See In the Matter of Martinez*, 107 N.M. 171, 754 P.2d 842 (N.M. 1988). However, the legal assistant should understand what he may or may not do. The burden rests upon the attorney who employs a legal assistant to educate the latter with respect to the duties which may be assigned and then to supervise the manner in which the legal assistant carries out such duties. However, this does not relieve the legal assistant from an independent obligation to refrain from illegal conduct. Additionally, and notwithstanding that the Code is not binding upon non-lawyers, the very nature of a legal assistant's employment imposes an obligation not to engage in conduct which would involve the supervising attorney in a violation of the Code. NALA has adopted the ABA Code as a part of its Code of Ethics.

VI

Legal assistants should not:

1. Establish attorney-client relationships; set legal fees; give legal opinions or advice; or represent a client before a court; nor

2. Engage in, encourage, or contribute to any act which would constitute the unauthorized practice of law.

Comment

Reported cases holding which acts can and cannot be performed by a legal assistant are few.

The legal assistant cannot create the attorney-client relationship. *De-Vaux v. American Home Assur. Co.,* 444 N.E.2d 355 (Mass., 1983).

The legal assistant cannot make court appearances. The question of what constitutes a court appearance is also somewhat vague. See, for example, *People v. Alexander,* 53, Ill. App.2d 299, 202 N.E.2d 841 (1964), where preparation of a court order and transmitting information to court was not the unauthorized practice of law, and *People v. Belfor,* 611 P.2d 979 (Colo. 1980), where the trial court found that the acts of a disbarred attorney did not constitute an appearance and the Supreme Court of Colorado held that only the Supreme Court could make the determination of what acts constituted an appearance and the unauthorized practice of law.

The following cases have identified certain areas in which an attorney has a duty to act, but it is interesting to note that none of these cases state that it is improper for an attorney to have the initial work performed by a legal assistant. This again points out the importance of adequate supervision by the employing attorney.

Courts have found that attorneys have the duty to check bank statements, preserve a client's property, review and sign all pleadings, insure that all communications are opened and answered, and make inquiry when items of dictation are not received. *Attorney Grievance Commission of Maryland v. Goldberg,* 441 A.2d 338, 292 Md. 650 (1982). See also *Vaughn v. State Bar of California,* 100 Cal.Rptr. 713, 494 P.2d 1257 (1972).

The legal assistant cannot exercise professional legal judgment or give legal advice. In *Louisiana State Bar v. Edwins,* 540 So.2d 294 (La. 1989), the court held a paralegal was engaged in activities constituting the unauthorized practice of law, which included evaluation of claims and giving advice on settlements. The attorney who delegated the exercise of these acts aided in the unauthorized practice of law. See also *People of the State of Co. v. Gelker,* 770 P.2d 402 (Col. 1989).

Attorneys have the responsibility to supervise the work of associates and clerical staff. *Moore v. State Bar Association,* 41 Cal.Rptr. 161, 396 P.2d 577 (1964); *Attorney Grievance Committee of Maryland v. Goldberg,* supra.

An attorney must exercise sufficient supervision to ensure that all monies received are properly deposited and disbursed. *Black v. State Bar of California,* 103 Cal.Rptr. 288, 499 P.2d 968 (1972); *Fitzpatrick v. State Bar of California,* 141 Cal.Rptr. 169, 569 P.2d 763 (1977).

The attorney must ensure that his staff is competent and effective to perform the work delegated. *In Re: Reinmiller,* 325 P.2d 773 (Oregon, 1958). See also *State of Kansas v. Barrett,* 483 P.2d 1106 (Kansas, 1971); *Attorney Grievance Committee of Maryland v. Goldberg,* supra.

The attorney must make sufficient background investigation of the prior activities and character and integrity of his employees to insure that legal assistants have not previously been involved in unethical, illegal, or other nefarious schemes which demonstrate such person unfit to be associated with the practice of law. See *In the Matter of Shaw,* 88 N.J. 433, A.2d 678 (1982), wherein the Court announced that while it had no disciplinary jurisdiction over legal assistants, it directed that disciplinary hearings make specific findings of fact concerning paralegals' collaboration in nefarious schemes in order that the court might properly discipline any attorney establishing an office relationship with one who had been implicated previously in unscrupulous schemes.

VII

Legal assistants may perform services for an attorney in the representation of a client, provided:

1. The services performed by the legal assistant do not require the exercise of independent professional legal judgment;

2. The attorney maintains a direct relationship with the client and maintains control of all client matters;

3. The attorney supervises the legal assistant;

4. The attorney remains professionally responsible for all work on behalf of the client, including any actions taken or not taken by the legal assistant in connection therewith; and

5. The services performed supplement, merge with and become the attorney's work product.

Comment

EC 3-6, ABA Code of Professional Responsibility, recognizes the value of utilizing the services of legal assistants, but provides certain conditions to such employment:

> A lawyer often delegates tasks to clerks, secretaries, and other lay persons. Such delegation is proper if the lawyer maintains a direct relationship with his client, supervises the delegated work, and has complete professional responsibility for the work product. This delegation enables a lawyer to render legal services more economically and efficiently.[15]

VIII

In the supervision of a legal assistant, consideration should be given to:

1. Designating work assignments that correspond to the legal assistants' abilities, knowledge, training and experience;

2. Educating and training the legal assistant with respect to professional responsibility, local rules and practices, and firm policies;

3. Monitoring the work and professional conduct of the legal assistant to ensure that the work is substantively correct and timely performed;

4. Providing continuing education for the legal assistant in substantive matters through courses, institutes, workshops, seminars and in-house training; and

5. Encouraging and supporting membership and active participation in professional organizations.

Comment

Attorneys are responsible for the actions of their employees in both malpractice and disciplinary proceedings. The attorney cannot delegate work to a legal assistant which involves activities constituting the unauthorized practice of law. See *Louisiana State Bar v. Edwins*, 540 So.2d 294 (La. 1989), and *People of the State of Colorado v. Felker*, 770 P.2d 402 (Col. 1989). In the vast majority of the cases, the courts have not censured attorneys for the particular act delegated to the legal assistant, but rather, have been critical of and imposed sanctions against attorneys for failure to adequately supervise the legal assistants. *See e.g., Attorney Grievance Commission of Maryland v. Goldberg*, supra.

The attorney's responsibility for supervision of legal assistants must be more than a willingness to accept responsibility and liability for the legal assistant's work. The attorney must monitor the work product and conduct of the legal assistant to insure that the work performed is substantively correct and completely performed in a professional manner. This duty includes the responsibility to provide continuing legal education for the legal assistant.

Supervision of legal assistants must be offered in both the procedural and substantive legal areas in the law office.

In *Spindell v. State Bar of California*, 118 Cal.Rptr. 480, 530 P.2d 168 (1975), the attorney was suspended from practice because of the improper legal advice given by a secretary. The case illustrates that it is important that both attorneys and legal assistants confirm all telephonic advice by letter.

In all instances where the legal assistant relays information to a client in response to an inquiry from the client, the advice related telephonically by the legal assistant should be confirmed in writing by the attorney. This will eliminate claims if the client acts contrary to the advice given. It will establish that the legal advice given is in fact that of the attorney, not the legal assistant, and obviate any confusion resulting from transmission of the advice through the legal assistant.

The *Spindell* case is an example of an attorney's failure to supervise and educate his staff. Not only was the secretary uneducated as to the substantive provisions of the law, but more importantly, was uneducated as to an employee's duty and authority as an employee of the attorney.

IX

Except as otherwise provided by statute, court rule or decision, administrative rule or regulation, or the attorney's Code of Professional Responsibility; and within the preceding parameters and proscriptions, a legal assistant may perform any function delegated by an attorney, including, but not limited to the following:

1. Conduct client interviews and maintain general contact with the client after the establishment of the attorney-client relationship, so long as the client is aware of the status and function of the legal assistant, and the client is under the supervision of the attorney.

2. Locate and interview witnesses, so long as the witnesses are aware of the status and function of the legal assistant.

3. Conduct investigations and statistical and documentary research for review by the attorney.

4. Conduct legal research for review by the attorney.

5. Draft legal documents for review by the attorney.

6. Draft correspondence and pleadings for review by and signature of the attorney.

7. Summarize depositions, interrogatories, and testimony for review by the attorney.

8. Attend executions of wills, real estate closings, depositions, court or administrative hearings and trials with the attorney.

9. Author and sign letters provided the legal assistant status is clearly indicated and correspondence does not contain independent legal opinions or legal advice.

Comment

The U.S. Supreme Court has recognized the variety of tasks being performed by legal assistants and has noted that use of legal assistants encourages cost effective delivery of legal services, *Missouri v. Jenkins,* 491 U.S. 274, 109 S.Ct. 2463, 2471, n.10 (1989). In Jenkins, the court further held that legal assistant time should be included in compensation for attorney fee awards at the prevailing practice in the relevant community to bill legal assistant time.

Except for the specific proscription contained in Section VI, the reported cases, such as *Attorney Grievance Commission of Maryland v. Goldberg,* supra, do not limit the duties which may be performed by a legal assistant under the supervision of the attorney. The Guidelines were developed from generally accepted practices. Each supervising attorney must be aware of the specific rules, decisions and statutes applicable to legal assistants within the attorney's own jurisdiction.

SEC. 6-6
ANALYSIS USING THE CODE OF ETHICS FOR THE
NATIONAL ASSOCIATION OF LEGAL ASSISTANTS, INC.

The following is a summary of some of the ethical standards that should be considered when dealing with specific situations. While the canons promulgated by the National Association of Legal Assistants, Inc. are used as a framework for this analysis, all comments following each canon are not part of any document issued by that organization, and they are solely those of the author of this book.

Canon 1

A legal assistant shall not perform any of the duties that lawyers only may perform nor do things that lawyers themselves may not do.

In order to comply with the dictates of Canon 1, it is necessary to determine first what kinds of duties may only be performed by attorneys.

The case of *Florida Bar v. Furman*[16] demonstrates how difficult it is sometimes to draw the line between the kinds of activities that only attorneys may perform and those that may be performed by nonlawyers. In this case, Furman established a business known as Northside Secretarial Service for the alleged purpose of assisting people with the preparation of pleadings designed to meet the desires of the clients. She denied giving any of her clients legal advice and argued that she was assisting her clients in representing themselves. She further maintained that because of the relatively modest fee she was charging, indigent clients were assisted in obtaining access that they might not otherwise have to the state's domestic relations courts. It was maintained by the Florida Bar that Furman was selling "do-it-yourself divorce kits," and that she held herself out to the general public as having legal expertise. The Bar did not, however, suggest that she ever claimed to be an attorney, that her customers did not receive the services that were advertised, or that any of her customers were harmed by her assistance. Even though Furman maintained that she gave no legal advice and that her sole purpose was to assist people in helping themselves, the Bar objected to her activities as constituting the unauthorized practice of law, and it asked the court to enjoin her from all such future actions.

The Florida Supreme Court ruled in favor of the Florida Bar Association and issued an injunction against Rosemary Furman. In its ruling, the court relied upon a previous case[17] involving similar facts in which the court held that the respondent could sell legal forms and printed material purporting to explain legal practice and procedure to the public in general. It was permissible for her to type the forms for her clients as long as she only used the written information given to her and did not correct errors or omissions. She could not advise her clients as to remedies available to them, answer questions concerning which forms were necessary, help them in filling out the forms, help them in filing the forms, or assist them in preparing for their hearings.

Furman continued her business in spite of the court decision and was subsequently held in contempt of court, fined court costs, and sentenced to four months in jail. Three months of the sentence was to be suspended if she agreed to abide by the requirements of the court's injunction. After she agreed to shut down her business, the governor of Florida suspended her entire sentence and reduced her fine.

The ethical questions surrounding the preparation of documents have been particularly difficult for paralegals, since nonlawyers in some states have been permitted to prepare business documents involving only the filling in of blanks on standard forms. Real estate brokers, for example, may in some states prepare sales contracts. The paralegal has to be familiar with the rules that govern in his or her particular state of operations.

The signing of pleadings poses difficulties inherently different from the ethical problems associated with other kinds of document preparation. Since the signing and submission of pleadings to a court of law would be tantamount to appearing before that court, such actions would be regarded as the unauthorized practice of law and would be strictly prohibited.

The second part of this canon prohibits the legal assistant from performing any duties that attorneys themselves may not engage in. Such activities would at the very least include torts[18] and crimes. Rule 1.8 of the ABA Model Rules of Professional Conduct indicates some of the kinds of transactions that attorneys may not engage in. They include entering into certain kinds of business transactions with clients, using information relating to the client's representation to the client's disadvantage, preparing documents for the client's representation to the client's disadvantage, preparing documents for the client that make substantial gifts to the attorney or an immediate family member of the attorney, providing financial assistance in connection with pending or contemplated litigation, and obtaining an aggregate settlement without each client's consent in a case in which more than one client is represented. Other kinds of prohibited conduct include limiting the attorney's liability for malpractice prospectively, handling the case of a client who has an interest adverse to a party represented by one of the attorney's close relatives, or acquiring a proprietary interest in the cause of action. Many of these kinds of conduct are subject to exception, so the paralegal should become familiar with the details of the rule.[19]

Rule 4.2 of the ABA Model Rules of Professional Conduct addresses the basic prohibition that exists against communications with individuals already represented by counsel. It states that:

> In representing a client, a lawyer shall not communicate about the subject of the representation with a party the lawyer knows to be represented by another lawyer in the matter, unless the lawyer has the consent of the other lawyer or is authorized by law to do so.[20]

Furthermore, an employer as well as a paralegal can be held responsible for the acts of the paralegal done within the scope of employment.

Neither the attorney nor the paralegal may tape conversations without the permission of the other party.

Canon 2

> *A legal assistant may perform any task delegated and supervised by a lawyer so long as the lawyer is responsible to the client, maintains a direct relationship with the client, and assumes full professional responsibility for the work product.*

Canon 2 approves conduct that is "delegated and supervised" by the attorney under specified conditions. Questions may arise in specific situations as to what constitutes supervision by an attorney.

As a general rule, the drafting of legal documents in the absence of the attorney is not per se a violation of ethical standards. The drafting process is not considered unsupervised as long as the attorney gives the work a stamp of approval before the client sees it. However, if the paralegal turns the documents over to the client without the prior examination of the attorney, the paralegal has violated the dictates of this canon. As the canon itself states, it is the lawyer who must be responsible to the client and assume full professional responsibility for the work product. This is true even if that work product was originally the creation of the paralegal.

Similarly, it is generally permissible for a paralegal to send out to a client letters on behalf of the attorney and on the attorney's stationery as long as no legal advice is rendered or other ethical canons are violated. Such correspondence should, however, clearly indicate that the sender is not an attorney. A notation under the sender's signature indicating paralegal status is sufficient.

Questions have also arisen concerning the appropriateness of a paralegal conducting a real estate closing in the absence of a supervising attorney. Some states prohibit paralegals from doing so on the theory that they will be placed in a position requiring the rendering of legal advice. Other states allow this practice provided that certain specific restrictions are followed. Those restrictions generally include at least client consent and attorney availability during the closing.

The acceptability of a paralegal's handling of will executions poses similar problems. State laws must be followed precisely with regard to who may sign as witnesses, how many witnesses are needed, and many other issues. As with real estate closings, there is a split of opinion as to whether legal assistants may conduct them outside the presence of a supervising attorney. Some states discourage the practice, while others allow it.

While a paralegal may not ask questions at a deposition, the requirement of supervision by an attorney does not prevent the paralegal from preparing possible deposition questions for the attorney to ask, since the attorney would not use the questions unless they were implicitly approved. (For a definition of the term "deposition," see the "Discovery" chapter of this text.)

No problem is created with regard to the requirement of attorney supervision when legal assistants are hired on a freelance basis since any given task performed by the legal assistant is performed under the supervision of an attorney for that task. Because the contractual relationship for legal representation is between the attorney and the client, a contact by the paralegal with the attorney's clients can raise ethical questions. Whenever the paralegal deals with a client of the attorney, the paralegal should inform that client of the paralegal's status at the earliest possible time during the initial contact with the client.

In addition, this holds true for telephone conversations between the client and the paralegal, as well as for correspondence signed by the paralegal that is coming from the law office. It may be necessary for the paralegal to remind the client if the client ever does or says anything that suggests a misunderstanding of the paralegal's status. The reason for these rules is to avoid any possibility that members of the public will assume that legal assistants are in fact attorneys.

The attorneys, in addition to the legal assistants, have an obligation toward the public to verify that nonlawyer personnel are not being mistaken for attorneys. As Canon 2 indicates, attorneys also accept ultimate responsibility for the work product emanating from the office. If the employer fails to adequately supervise the paralegal's actions, the employer can be held responsible for the acts of the paralegal, both ethically and legally. Rule 5.3(c) of the ABA Model Rules of Professional Conduct states that:

> With respect to a nonlawyer employed or retained by or associated with a lawyer: ...
>
> **(c)** a lawyer shall be responsible for conduct of such a person that would be a violation of the Rules of Professional Conduct if engaged in by a lawyer if:
>
> **(1)** the lawyer orders or, with the knowledge of the specific conduct, ratifies the conduct involved; or
>
> **(2)** the lawyer is a partner in the law firm in which the person is employed, or has direct supervisory authority over the person, and knows of the conduct at a time when its consequences can be avoided or mitigated but fails to take reasonable remedial action.[21]

Canon 3

A legal assistant shall not engage in the practice of law by accepting cases, setting fees, giving legal advice or appearing in court unless otherwise authorized by court or agency rules.

This canon defines four specifically prohibited activities. Paralegals may not accept cases for their employers or even suggest whether they feel their employers are likely to accept them. There are several reasons for this restriction. First of all, the case might be rejected because the attorney feels that it lacks merit, and the decision to reject the case would involve the exercise of legal judgment. Second, the attorney might feel compelled to reject an apparently substantial case because of a potential conflict of interest. Third, the matter might be outside the firm's area of expertise. The prohibitions against accepting cases applies to a paralegal's oral statements as well as to written representations.

All fee arrangements are to be determined exclusively by the attorney and the client. The reason for this is that it is the attorney, rather than the paralegal, who has the contractual relationship with the client. Furthermore, the fees may be dependent upon the complexity of the legal issues involved, and an examination of those issues requires the exercise of legal judgment.

The prohibition against the giving of legal advice by a paralegal does not prevent that person from simply conveying in oral or written form the opinion of the attorney. In such situations, however, the person transmitting the information must make the paralegal status clear and must identify the opinion as that of the attorney. In some states, a distinction is made between a paralegal giving legal advice to individual "clients" as opposed to information given to the general public. An example of the latter might include information in a book written for the public by a paralegal. Those states that permit such writings stress the absence of a direct contractual relationship between the "client" and the paralegal, the lack of any communication between those parties, and the assumption that people buying a publication dispensing general legal advice are implicitly assuming the risk that the advice may not apply to their particular situation. Not all states, however, make the distinction between personal advice and public information.

As a general rule, paralegals are restricted from making appearances in virtually all courts. Nevertheless, a very limited number of states are now allowing appearances in justice of the peace or other lower courts, and others are permitting paralegals to appear in routine matters such as uncontested continuances or requests for hearing dates. These are, however, relatively rare exceptions to the generally enforced rule.

The restrictions pertaining to appearances by legal assistants in administrative courts differ from those that pertain to ordinary courts of law. Administrative courts operate in administrative agencies, which are agencies created by legislatures and given the power to promulgate rules and regulations governing particularly defined subject matters. Examples of administrative agencies are the Environmental Protection Agency and the Federal Communications Commission. Procedures in federal administrative agencies are governed by the Administrative Procedure Act, 5 U.S.C. § 555 (1967). This act specifically provides that when one is forced to appear before an administrative agency, that person may be "accompanied, represented, and advised by counsel or, if permitted by the agency, by another qualified representative."

This allows the agency itself to determine when to allow nonlawyer practice (whether by paralegals or other individuals). Some agencies are much more lenient in this regard than others.

Rules governing state administrative agencies vary widely, and appearances by legal assistants before administrative courts even for limited purposes may or may not be permitted.

Canon 4

A legal assistant shall not act in matters involving professional legal judgment as the services of a lawyer are essential in the public interest whenever the exercise of such judgment is required.

This canon is designed to prohibit conduct by the paralegal that directly provides legal services from the paralegal to the client. For example, since the acceptance of a settlement offer in a case would involve the use of professional judgment directly on behalf of a law office client, such an acceptance by a paralegal would be regarded as unethical. Settlements are ultimately the responsibility of the attorney. On the other hand, various kinds of permissible activities require the paralegal to use legal judgment, such as the drafting of legal documents. As long as the attorney reviews and approves the documents prior to sending them out to the general public, the attorney is taking responsibility for the final product, and the dictates of this canon are not violated.

The witnessing of legal documents does not in any event involve the exercise of legal knowledge, judgment, or abilities and is therefore generally permissible.

Canon 5

A legal assistant must act prudently in determining the extent to which a client may be assisted without the presence of a lawyer.

The best way for a paralegal to determine the boundaries of ethical conduct is by becoming thoroughly familiar with the codes, rules, and case law that govern the profession. As a general rule, if the paralegal is unsure whether a particular activity is ethical, it is best to refrain from engaging in it.

Neither this canon nor any other prohibits a paralegal from talking with opposing counsel as long as the paralegal is not violating any other ethical canons, and status as a paralegal is clearly indicated.

Canon 6

A legal assistant shall not engage in the unauthorized practice of law.

This canon poses some of the greatest difficulties for paralegals in the area of ethics, because the "unauthorized practice of law" has never really been clearly defined in any jurisdiction. Restrictions on the unauthorized practice of law traditionally have been justified on the grounds of protecting the public from those who have not demonstrated competence to practice by fulfilling stringent educational requirements and passing the bar examination. Some critics of such restrictions have more cynically suggested that regulations against the unauthorized practice of law have been used by attorneys to protect their own businesses from competition.

In determining whether an activity constitutes the unauthorized practice of law, several factors should be considered. One is whether the activity involves the use of legal knowledge, judgment, and abilities. This is far from being a determinative test, however, since nonlawyers use their legal knowledge, judgment, and abilities in their jobs on a daily basis. Real estate brokers, bankers, insurance representatives and those in many other occupations fall within this category. Furthermore, as noted in the discussion of Canon 4, paralegals routinely use their legal judgment in performing tasks that must ultimately be reviewed by the attorney who is to take responsibility for the final work product.

Another factor to be considered in determining whether a particular activity constitutes the unauthorized practice of law is whether the action has been traditionally handled by attorneys. Many courts have emphasized that any attempt to create an all-encompassing abstract definition of the unauthorized practice of law may not be helpful in addressing specific unauthorized practice violations.

Virtually all states have criminal law statutes prohibiting the unauthorized practice of law. Violations of unauthorized practice rules are generally handled either through criminal prosecutions or suits for injunctive relief against the wrongdoer.

Failure to abide by the dictates of Canon 6 can result in trouble for the supervising attorney. Rule 5.5(b) of the ABA Model Rules of Professional Conduct indicates that "A lawyer shall not: ... (c) assist a person who is not a member of the bar in the performance of any activity that constitutes the unauthorized practice of law."[22]

Canon 7

> *A legal assistant must protect the confidences of a client, and it shall be unethical for a legal assistant to violate any statute now in effect or hereafter to be enacted controlling privileged communications.*

Confidentiality is crucial if law office clients are to be assured that they can speak freely. The paralegal is bound just as the attorney by the same rules of confidentiality. Cases involving this issue arise not only from the general rules of ethics, but also from the areas of attorney-client privilege and "work product."

The attorney–client privilege is the right of clients to refuse to divulge (or allow their attorneys to divulge) information given to the attorneys in confidence. As a general rule, the privilege can be waived only by the client. The privilege does not normally extend to protecting the client's identity, although there are exceptional cases ruling to the contrary.

The "work product" of the law office, which includes notes and other materials prepared in anticipation of trial, is also a matter of confidentiality. It is not subject to discovery. In other words, a law office need not turn such material over to the opposing party or counsel. Federal Rule of Civil Procedure 26(b) (3) states that one may obtain such information

> ... only upon a showing that the party seeking discovery has substantial need of the materials in the preparation of the party's case and that the party is unable without undue hardship to obtain the substantial equivalent of the materials by other means.

Rule 1.6 of the ABA Model Rules of Professional Conduct gives some specific guidelines with regard to the issue of confidentiality.

> **(a)** A lawyer shall not reveal information relating to representation of a client unless the client consents after consultation, except for disclosures that are impliedly authorized in order to carry out the representation, and except as stated in paragraph (b).
>
> **(b)** A lawyer may reveal such information to the extent the lawyer reasonably believes necessary:
>
> **1)** to prevent the client from committing a criminal act that the lawyer believes is likely to result in imminent death or substantial bodily harm; or
>
> **2)** to establish a claim or defense on behalf of the lawyer in a controversy between the lawyer and the client, to establish a defense to a criminal charge or civil claim against the lawyer based upon conduct in which the client was involved, or to respond to allegations in any proceeding concerning the lawyer's representation of the client.[23]

Canon 8

> *It is the obligation of the legal assistant to avoid conduct which would cause the lawyer to be unethical or even appear to be unethical, and loyalty to the employer is incumbent upon the legal assistant.*

While it may be self-evident that a paralegal should avoid the kind of conduct prohibited by this canon, it may be much more difficult to define the exact boundaries of this canon in specific situations.

It is unethical for paralegals to enter into partnerships, associations, or corporations with attorneys in a business involving the practice of law. Circumstances in which a paralegal agrees to split a fee with an attorney are similarly regarded as unethical, because such situations necessarily imply that the paralegal is a business partner or associate of the attorney. Nevertheless, it has been held that a paralegal may benefit from a law firm's retirement program even though the program is founded partially on the basis of profit sharing.

The question has arisen as to whether the paralegal's name may appear on the letterhead of a law firm's stationery. There now seems to be a clear trend in favor of permitting it in light of the rulings of the Supreme Court pertaining to the right of advertising in the legal profession. The few states that prohibit the inclusion of the paralegal's name on the letterhead, such as Kansas, Michigan, New Hampshire, New Mexico, and North Carolina, generally do so on the basis of an ABA Informal Opinion that has subsequently been withdrawn since the Supreme Court's decision on legal advertising.

The use of business cards by the paralegal also raises similar issues pertaining to advertising. Those who object to their use contend that it is an undignified advertisement of a firm's legal services. Most states, however, allow paralegals to use business cards with the name of the law firm on them as long as the individual's nonlawyer status is clearly indicated.

Any conflicts of interest that a paralegal has with regard to a particular case can give the attorney the appearance of impropriety and, therefore, place the paralegal in direct violation of this ethical canon as well as Canon 7. The paralegal should notify the attorney at the earliest possible time of any such potential conflict. Furthermore, the paralegal should be aware of some of the basic conflict of laws rules that govern the conduct of attorneys. While the applicable ABA Model Rules of Professional Conduct are too numerous to individually quote in their entirety, a few merit special mention. Rule 1.7(a) provides that:

> **(a)** A lawyer shall not represent a client if the representation of that client will be adverse to another client, unless:
>> **(1)** the lawyer reasonably believes the representation will not adversely affect the relationship with the other client; and
>> **(2)** each client consents after consultation.[24]

Any attorney who has represented one client is specifically prohibited under Rule 1.9 from representing another client in a substantially related matter if the two clients' interests are adverse unless the former client consents.[25] Rule 1.10(a) indicates that "While lawyers are associated in a firm, none of them shall knowingly represent a client when any one of them practicing alone would be prohibited from doing so ..."[26]

While there is nothing improper about paralegals responding to questions concerning their place of employment, the solicitation of business for the law firm from those not seeking legal advice is prohibited. Rule 7.3 of the Model Rules of Professional Conduct provides guidance to the attorney with regard to advertising and the solicitation of business from prospective clients.[27]

Because the conduct of the paralegal has the potential for reflecting either positively or negatively on the ethical reputation of the supervising attorney, it is essential that the paralegal become familiar with Rule 3.4 of the ABA Rules of Professional Conduct. That rule, dealing with fairness to the opposing party and counsel, states the following:

> A lawyer shall not:
>
> **(a)** unlawfully obstruct another party's access to evidence or unlawfully alter, destroy or conceal a document or other material having potential evidentiary value. A lawyer shall not counsel or assist another person to do any such act;
>
> **(b)** falsify evidence, counsel or assist a witness to testify falsely, or offer an inducement to a witness that is prohibited by law;
>
> **(c)** knowingly disobey an obligation under the rules of a tribunal except for an open refusal based on an assertion that no valid obligation exists;
>
> **(d)** in pretrial procedure, make a frivolous discovery request or fail to make reasonably diligent effort to comply with a legally proper discovery request by an opposing party;
>
> **(e)** in trial, allude to any matter that the lawyer does not reasonably believe is relevant or that will not be supported by admissible evidence, assert personal knowledge of facts in issue except when testifying as a witness, or state a personal opinion as to the justness of a cause, the credibility of a witness, the culpability of a civil litigant or the guilt or innocence of an accused; or
>
> **(f)** request a person other than a client to refrain from voluntarily giving relevant information to another party unless:
>
> > **(1)** the person is a relative or an employee or other agent of a client; and
> >
> > **(2)** the lawyer reasonably believes that the person's interest will not be adversely affected by refraining from giving such information.[28]

Closely related to Rule 3.4 is Rule 4.4 which prohibits an attorney who is representing a client from using "means that have no substantial purpose other than to embarrass, delay, or burden a third person, or use methods of obtaining evidence that violate the legal rights of such a person."[29]

Sometimes potential conflict of interest problems occur when a legal assistant leaves one law office and seeks employment at another. If the first firm is representing one party in a particular case and the second firm is representing the other, the employment of the paralegal at the new firm could place that firm in jeopardy of disqualification from the case. For that reason, it may be necessary to establish procedures at the new firm whereby the legal assistant has no access to materials pertaining to the case. These procedures may include restrictions on the paralegal's access to computer or physical files, notes to all office employees that materials from the case are not to get into the hands of the paralegal, and other restrictions. Such blocks are referred to as *screens* or *Chinese walls*. If a firm is considering the hiring of a paralegal and it perceives that the creation of such Chinese walls could be cumbersome, such a situation can impede the employment of the paralegal.

Canon 9

> *A legal assistant shall work continually to maintain integrity and a high degree of competency throughout the legal profession.*

This canon imposes upon paralegals the responsibility not only to maintain the highest standards of integrity and competence, but also to do whatever they can to encourage others to strive toward these goals.

The mandate of integrity makes it improper for paralegals to misrepresent their identity as paralegals. A paralegal may not, for example, fraudulently represent to a debtor that the paralegal works for a collection agency.

Canon 10

> *A legal assistant shall strive for perfection through education in order to better assist the legal profession in fulfilling its duty of making legal services available to clients and the public.*

There are opportunities in all states to obtain an education in many different kinds of educational institutions. Several hundred across the country have received an "approval" from the American Bar Association. While no program must obtain such an approval, it demonstrates a standard of excellence in the legal community. Nevertheless, because the approval process is voluntary and cumbersome, many schools have chosen not to obtain it.

In addition to the courses available through institutions of higher learning, there are always seminars and publications that can keep paralegals abreast of late-breaking developments in the law.

Canon 11

> *A legal assistant shall do all other things incidental, necessary, or expedient for the attainment of the ethics and responsibilities imposed by statutes or rule of court.*

This canon is designed as a "catchall" provision, and it is intended to stress the responsibility of the paralegal to follow rules emanating from legislatures or courts with regard to ethical issues.

There are various ethical situations that have not yet been addressed under any of the previous canons that give rise to commonly asked questions. Paralegals cannot pay witnesses for their testimony other than the ordinary witness fees that may be specifically provided by law. It is considered improper to threaten people with criminal prosecution for failure to pay an outstanding debt even though other nonlawyers may possibly be able to do so under certain circumstances. In some states, it is even impermissible for paralegals to threaten debtors with the filing of a civil suit.

Canon 12

> *A legal assistant is governed by the American Bar Association Code of Professional Responsibility.*

As indicated previously in this chapter, the American Bar Association Code of Professional Responsibility has been largely replaced by the 1983 Model Rules of Professional Conduct. Familiarity with the Code of Professional Responsibility is still necessary, however, because many state bar associations have not chosen to use the Model Rules of Professional Conduct as a format for their own canons of ethics.

REVIEW QUESTIONS

1. Next to each of the lines below mark an "E" if the act would generally be regarded as ethical, or a "U" if the act would generally be regarded as unethical.

   a. preparing questions for interrogatories _____

   b. disclosing a client's name to a person outside of the law office _____

   c. arguing cases in court for your law firm's clients after being given specific authority to do so by your employer _____

    d. drafting questions to be used by the attorney at deposition _____

    e. witnessing signatures on real estate documents _____

2. Bonnie is working as a paralegal for the law firm of Smith and Wesson. One day, Bonnie's employer comes into her office and tells her that he has to leave the office on an emergency, but that he would like her to get some statistical information from the client before the client leaves. He tells her to go into his office, introduce herself, and proceed with the interview. She follows his instructions. When Bonnie finishes the discussion with the client, the client asks her whether the case looks good, and she says that it does indeed look promising. She says that the firm will probably take the case. Bonnie's only further contact with the client is that she later mails back to the client some of his original documents along with a cover letter from herself.

    Discuss the ethical implications of each and every one of the activities that Bonnie did, considered doing, or was requested to do in this case.

3. Since Paul, a recently hired paralegal at Jones, Jones, and Jones, had prepared all of the documents for the Smith/Peters real estate closing, his employer asked him to come along to the closing with him. Paul never gave any specific legal advice at the closing, but he did sign as a witness on some of the documents. As per his agreement with Mr. Jones, he received one third of the attorney fee paid at closing. When he was back at the cafeteria in his office building later on in the day, he mentioned to one of the nurses who worked in the doctor's office next door that he did all of the paperwork for Mrs. Smith. He did not, however, disclose any of the details of the transaction. At the end of the day, he sent out some copies to Mrs. Smith and signed the letter, "Paul Hess, Paralegal."

    Discuss the ethical implications of each and every one of the activities that Paul did, considered doing, or was requested to do in this case.

4. Next to each of the lines below, mark an "E" if the act would generally be regarded as ethical, or a "U" if the act would generally be regarded as unethical.

    a. signing as a witness on a client's will _____

    b. asking questions at a deposition _____

    c. preparing a warranty deed _____

    d. splitting a contingency fee with an attorney _____

    e. attending a real estate closing _____

    f. accepting cases for the law firm that employs you _____

5. Why are the limitations of permissible conduct so difficult to ascertain when it comes to determining whether one is engaged in the unauthorized practice of law?

6. John, Susan's employer, asks her to do two things. The first is to draw up a will and send a copy of it along with a cover letter to the client. The second is to draft questions for his deposition that afternoon and then meet him at the location for the deposition at 3:30 P.M. When Susan gets there, she is given a message that John has been detained. She knows that he is not likely to alter any questions, and she feels certain that he would want her to go ahead and begin asking the questions in order to save everyone's time.

   Discuss the ethical implications of each and every one of the activities that Susan did, considered doing, or was requested to do in this case.

7. Ben, a paralegal at the law firm of Stein and Lord, picks up an incoming phone call one day when the secretary is out to lunch. The caller, Belinda Handler, asks Ben how much the law firm would charge for a breach of contract case, and she explains the details of the case to him. He says that he will have to check with one of the attorneys and call her back. He informs Mr. Lord of the details of the conversation, and Lord instructs him to tell Handler that the law firm would charge $600. The law suit is subsequently filed. Three months later, Handler calls the office and tells Ben that she thinks that a settlement can be reached in the case with the adverse party, Sharon Nickerson, if someone from the law office will contact Nickerson. Ben makes the phone call to Nickerson and manages to settle the case for an amount that is close to the total originally demanded by Handler.

   Discuss the ethical implications of each and every one of the activities that Ben did, considered doing, or was requested to do in this case.

FOOTNOTES

[1]Reprinted with permission of the National Federation of Paralegal Associations, P.O. Box 33108, Kansas City, MO 64114. © 1993.

[2]"Paralegal" is synonymous with "Legal Assistant" and is defined as a person qualified through education, training, or work experience to perform substantive legal work that requires knowledge of legal concepts and is customarily, but not exclusively, performed by a lawyer. This person may be retained or employed by a lawyer, law office, governmental agency or other entity or may be authorized by administrative, statutory or court authority to perform this work.

[3]"Ex Parte" denotes actions or communications conducted at the instance and for the benefit of one party only, and without notice to, or contestation by, any person adversely interested.

[4]"Confidential Information" denotes information relating to a client, whatever its source, which is not public knowledge nor available to the public ("Non-Confidential Information" would generally include the name of the client and the identity of the matter for which the paralegal provided services).

[5]"Disclose" denotes communication of information reasonably sufficient to permit identification of the significance of the matter in question.

[6]"Ethical Wall" refers to the screening method implemented in order to protect a client from a conflict of interest. An Ethical Wall generally includes, but is not limited to, the following elements: (1) prohibit the paralegal from having any connection with the matter; (2) ban discussions with or the transfer of documents to or from the paralegal; (3) restrict access to files; and (4) educate all members

of the firm, corporation or entity as to the separation of the paralegal (both organizationally and physically) from the pending matter. For more information regarding the Ethical Wall, see the NFPA publication entitled "The Ethical Wall—Its Application to Paralegals."

[7]Reprinted with permission of the National Association of Legal Assistants, Inc., 1516 S. Boston, Suite 200, Tulsa, OK 74119. Copyright 1975, revised 1979, 1988, 1995.

[8]Reprinted with permission of the National Association of Legal Assistants, Inc., 1516 S. Boston, Suite 200, Tulsa, OK 74119. Copyright 1984, revised 1991.

[9]Within this occupational category some individuals are known as paralegals.

[10]Model Code of Professional Responsibility, copyright © 1981 by American Bar Association. All rights reserved. Reprinted by permission of the American Bar Association.

[11]Model Rules of Professional Conduct, copyright © 1995 by American Bar Association. All rights reserved. Reprinted by permission of the American Bar Association.

[12]Model Code of Professional Responsibility, copyright © 1981 by American Bar Association. All rights reserved. Reprinted by permission of the American Bar Association.

[13]Model Code of Professional Responsibility, copyright © 1981 by American Bar Association. All rights reserved. Reprinted by permission of the American Bar Association.

[14]Model Code of Professional Responsibility, copyright © 1981 by American Bar Association. All rights reserved. Reprinted by permission of the American Bar Association.

[15]Model Code of Professional Responsibility, copyright © 1981 by American Bar Association. All rights reserved. Reprinted by permission of the American Bar Association.

[16]*See* 376 So.2d 378 (Fla. 1979) with further proceedings at 451 So.2d 808 (Fla. 1984).

[17]*Florida Bar v. Brumbaugh,* 355 So.2d 1186 (Fla. 1978).

[18]A *tort* is a civil wrong other than a breach of contract action. Examples of torts include fraud and libel.

[19]Model Rules of Professional Conduct, copyright © 1995 by American Bar Association. All rights reserved. Reprinted by permission of the American Bar Association.

[20]Model Rules of Professional Conduct, copyright © 1995 by American Bar Association. All rights reserved. Reprinted by permission of the American Bar Association.

[21]Model Rules of Professional Conduct, copyright © 1995 by American Bar Association. All rights reserved. Reprinted by permission of the American Bar Association.

[22]Model Rules of Professional Conduct, copyright © 1995 by American Bar Association. All rights reserved. Reprinted by permission of the American Bar Association.

[23]Model Rules of Professional Conduct, copyright © 1995 by American Bar Association. All rights reserved. Reprinted by permission of the American Bar Association.

[24]Model Rules of Professional Conduct, copyright © 1995 by American Bar Association. All rights reserved. Reprinted by permission of the American Bar Association.

[25]Model Rules of Professional Conduct, copyright © 1995 by American Bar Association. All rights reserved. Reprinted by permission of the American Bar Association.

[26]Model Rules of Professional Conduct, copyright © 1995 by American Bar Association. All rights reserved. Reprinted by permission of the American Bar Association.

[27]Model Rules of Professional Conduct, copyright © 1995 by American Bar Association. All rights reserved. Reprinted by permission of the American Bar Association.

[28]Model Rules of Professional Conduct, copyright © 1995 by American Bar Association. All rights reserved. Reprinted by permission of the American Bar Association.

[29]Model Rules of Professional Conduct, copyright © 1995 by American Bar Association. All rights reserved. Reprinted by permission of the American Bar Association.

7

Substantive Civil Law and Procedure

CHAPTER OVERVIEW

3. Nominal Damages

7-3 The Basics of Civil Litigation and Procedure

A. In General

B. The Basic Format of Pleadings
   1. The Introductory Material at the Top
      a. The upper right-hand corner or the top center
      b. The upper left-hand corner
      c. The title
   2. The Main Body of the Pleading
   3. The Conclusion

C. Documents Commonly Involved in a Simple Civil Action
   1. The Summons
      a. Who may serve summonses
      b. The content of a summons
      c. The requirement of a separate summons for each defendant
      d. The service of subsequent pleadings
      e. Alias and pluries summonses
      f. Service of process on corporations
   2. The Complaint or Original Petition
      a. Statement of jurisdiction
      b. Statement of the facts
      c. Possibility of multiple counts
      d. Performance of conditions precedent
      e. Attachment of documents
      f. Statutory references
      g. Demand for jury trial
      h. Amendment of complaints
   3. The Answer
      a. Responses to specific allegations in the complaint
      b. Sham and frivolous answers
      c. The time within which to respond
         (1) The use of tickler files
      d. Default
         (1) The necessity of a final judgment from the court
         (2) The expiration of the period for responsive pleadings
      e. Demand for a jury trial
      f. Affirmative defenses
         (1) Res judicata
         (2) Release
         (3) Contributory negligence
         (4) Comparative negligence
         (5) Statute of limitations
      g. Amendment of answers
      h. Counterclaims
         (1) Compulsory counterclaims
         (2) Permissive counterclaims
      i. Cross-claims
      j. Third-party complaints
   4. Motions
   5. Subpoenas
      a. Issuance by the clerk
      b. Service of subpoenas
      c. Fees
      d. Failure to obey a subpoena
      e. Return of proof of service
      f. Use of the subpoena duces tecum
   6. Dismissals
      a. Voluntary dismissals
      b. Involuntary dismissals

SEC. 7-1
INTRODUCTION

Civil suits involve the adjudication of private rights between two or more parties. In civil matters, one party is making a claim against another party either for money or for a court order. This is fundamentally different from a prosecution for a criminal law violation in which the government is attempting to punish a party for conduct that violates the rights of society as a whole. When plaintiffs sue and prevail in a civil case, they are entitled to a recovery from the defendant. On the other hand, when parties are prosecuted and convicted of a crime, they may face punishment in the form of imprisonment, a fine payable to the government, execution, or some other penalty. The purpose of a criminal prosecution is to punish defendants rather than to compensate victims for their losses, although criminal courts always have the option to make restitution to defendants as a part of the sentence.

Both substantive civil law and procedural civil law are examined in this chapter. *Substantive law* defines the actual rights and liabilities of the parties. An example of a substantive law is the law of fraud, including the various elements that must be shown in order to establish such a case. In contrast, *procedural laws* bear on the process that must be followed to enforce the rights one has under substantive law. For example, all jurisdictions have a rule of civil procedure that indicates the number of days that the defendant has to respond to the written complaint of the plaintiff. Section 7-2 addresses substantive civil law issues, while Sec. 7-3 concentrates on procedural matters.

SEC. 7-2
THE BASICS OF SUBSTANTIVE CIVIL LAW

The body of substantive civil law can be subdivided into several categories, such as breach of contract and tort cases. A *tort* is a civil wrong other than a breach of contract action, although a tort may be based on an underlying contract. For example, if one party defrauds another on a contract, the fraud would constitute a tort even though the breach of contract would not. In such a case, a plaintiff could sue the defendant on both claims. Since each claim requires the establishment of different elements, the plaintiff might prevail on one cause of action but not the other.

An important distinction between tort and breach of contract cases is that torts are based on the violation of a duty imposed by law whereas breach of contract cases are based on the violation of a duty imposed by the parties' agreement. In the case of the tort of negligence, for example, the plaintiff's claim for money damages is not based on the agreement of the parties, but rather on the legally recognized right to sue when the defendant's carelessness results in injury to the plaintiff.

Torts may be either intentional or unintentional, and sections A and B below provide several examples.

A.   Examples of Intentional Torts

1.   Fraud

Fraud requires the showing of a misstatement of a past or present fact with knowledge of its falsity or reckless disregard for the truth. To prove a case of fraud, one must also show that it was the defendant's intent to have the plaintiff rely on the misrepresentation and that the plaintiff did in fact rely on it. Finally the plaintiff must demonstrate that he or she sustained damages as a result of the misrepresentation. For example, if one party sells swampland to another after tricking the latter into believing that the property is suitable for construction, the party making the misrepresentation can be liable for damages.

2. *False Imprisonment*

False imprisonment is the intentional and unprivileged detention of another person without that person's consent. The term "unprivileged" means that the defendant does not fall into the category of individuals, such as police officers and security guards, who have the right to detain others. The term detention does not require that a person be physically imprisoned. Leaving someone in a position with no means of escape is sufficient. False imprisonment should be distinguished from kidnapping, which is a crime for which a person can be arrested, as opposed to a tort for which a person can be sued.

3. *Battery*

A battery is committed in civil law when there is an intentional, offensive bodily "touching" of another person without provocation or consent. Such a contact can be direct, as when one party strikes another, or by the use of a weapon, as when one party shoots or stabs the other person.

4. *Assault*

A civil assault occurs when one party places another in reasonable apprehension of a battery. When a person demands money at gunpoint from the cashier at a convenience store, an assault is committed even though the gun is never fired. This would be an example in which the plaintiff has a claim of assault against the defendant without an accompanying claim for battery. When one is hit from behind, the victim may have a claim for battery without an accompanying claim for assault. When a party is physically threatened and subsequently physically injured by the wrongdoer, the victim may have a claim for both assault and battery.

In a case of assault, courts will generally require a showing by the plaintiff that the defendant took actual steps toward the commission of the battery before recovery will be allowed.

B. *The Unintentional Tort of Negligence*

A right of recovery is recognized by law even when the harm caused is not intentional. There are various unintentional torts, but the most common of all is negligence.

Negligence exists when a person harms another after failure to exercise the degree of care that would be shown by a reasonable person. For example, a person who injures another by driving after drinking excessively would be responsible for the tort of negligence. When determining whether the defendant has failed to act as a reasonable person, the defendant's conduct is compared to that of the reasonable person acting under the same circumstances. To illustrate, if the plaintiff is knocked over on the sidewalk by a blind man who is using a cane, the blind man is held to the same standard of care that a reasonable blind person would exhibit under the circumstances. It would obviously be patently unfair to expect a blind person to be aware of all of the dangers that could be anticipated by a sighted person.

In any negligence case, the plaintiff must clearly establish that there is a causal connection between the wrongful act of the defendant and the injury sustained by the plaintiff. This is referred to as "actual causation." The plaintiff must also establish that the act of the defendant was not such a remote cause of the injury that it would be unfair to hold the defendant responsible. Courts have determined that injuries to the plaintiff that were not "foreseeable" at the time of the defendant's actions may be too remote. Proof of "proximate causation" or foreseeability as well as actual causation must be established in any negligence case.

Various defenses are commonly raised in negligence actions. One is the defense of contributory negligence, which is applicable only in negligence cases and only in some states. It releases the defendant from liability if the defendant can prove any negligence on the part of the plaintiff. Assume, for example, that the plaintiff and the defendant were involved in an automobile accident and that the plaintiff is claiming that the defendant's negligence and carelessness is directly responsible for the plaintiff's injuries. In states that apply the contributory negligence rule, if the defendant can prove that the plaintiff was at least partially responsible for the plaintiff's own injuries, the plaintiff will be entitled to nothing even if it can be shown that the defendant was also negligent.

Because the contributory negligence rule can sometimes lead to unjust results, a large number of states now apply the rule of comparative negligence instead. This rule can be best understood by example. If it can be shown in a case that the total damages to the plaintiff were $100,000, that the defendant was 70 percent responsible, and that the plaintiff was 30 percent responsible, courts in states applying the comparative negligence rule should award the plaintiff $70,000. Those in states that recognize the contributory negligence rule would award the plaintiff nothing under these circumstances since the plaintiff was responsible to at least some degree.

Another common defense in negligence cases is assumption of risk. In cases involving this defense, the defendant is arguing that recovery by the plaintiff should be barred or reduced because the plaintiff voluntarily accepted being exposed to a known risk. This defense has been abolished with regard to workers' compensation claims (see Sec. C, subsection 1.b below).

C. *The General Rule that Fault Must Be Proven*

As a general rule in any civil case, plaintiffs must not only establish that they suffered damages or harm, but also prove fault on the part of the defendant. The fact that plaintiffs have been injured or harmed in some way is not alone a basis for recovery.

1. *The Exception of Absolute Liability*

There are a few exceptional circumstances where the defendant can be held "absolutely liable" without a proof of fault. In such cases, proof of neither intent nor carelessness is necessary because the particular activities are regarded as inherently dangerous to society. While the activities in question are not prohibited, those who engage in them face a higher risk of liability in the event that anyone is harmed. Examples of these kinds of activities include the following:

a. Ultrahazardous activities.   An example of conduct that falls within this category would be the handling of explosives. If a contractor is using dynamite in a downtown construction site and someone is ultimately injured by flying debris, the contractor can be held responsible. This is true even if it can be shown that the contractor exercised the greatest degree of care possible. All that a potential plaintiff would have to establish is that the plaintiff was injured by the debris and that the debris came from the contractor's construction site. Proof of fault would not be necessary.

b. Workers' compensation.   On the basis of statute, workers can be compensated without proving responsibility on the part of the employer when they sustain work-related injuries. Those subject to workers' compensation statutes cannot, however, choose to seek redress in the regular court system beyond the scope of the statute even if they believe that by doing so they might obtain a larger recovery.

c. Food and drug contamination.   When food and drug products are distributed to the general public in a contaminated state, the producers may be held liable even without proof that the contamination was either intentional or negligent. The justification for this rule lies in the tremendous number of people potentially harmed when such products are distributed to the general public.

D. *Historical Immunities from Tort Liability*

Traditionally, certain parties were not held responsible even if it could be proven that they had committed a wrongful act that would otherwise be a tort. All of these immunities have been criticized by legal commentators, and the strong trend is toward their partial or complete abolition.

1.   Government (Sovereign Immunity)

Historically, governmental entities were immune from tort liability, but many exceptions have been created in recent years. Some of the exceptions have been created by statute, such as in the case of the Federal Tort Claims Act that sharply limits the federal government's liability in tort cases. Sovereign immunity has also been significantly curtailed as a result of court decisions on both the state and federal levels.

2.   Very Small Children

Most states refuse to hold very small children responsible for the commission of acts that would otherwise constitute torts if they had been committed by adults. While the age limitations may vary from state to state, it is common for states to regard those seven years of age and under as immune.

3.   Charities

Charities were historically held immune from tort liability on the grounds that large judgments against charities would have a negative effect on charitable giving. It was argued that people would be less likely to donate if they felt that their money would be used to pay off a judgment rather than support a charitable cause. In spite of this argument, a large number of states have abolished charitable immunity altogether.

4.   Spouses and Immediate Family Members

The right of parties to claim immunity from liability for torts committed against immediate family members is a rapidly disappearing defense. One of the reasons for the trend toward abolition of this immunity is the serious problem of domestic violence. In the past, it had been argued that allowing one spouse to sue the other would not promote "domestic harmony." On the other hand, commentators have noted that there is little domestic harmony to preserve when one spouse desires to file a tort action against the other.

E.   Vicarious Liability

While a person is not normally responsible for the wrongful acts of others, there are circumstances in which one party is accountable for such acts on the basis of *vicarious liability*. An example of vicarious liability is when an employer is found to be liable for the fraudulent acts of an employee acting within the scope of the employee's authority and with the employer's full knowledge and consent. Under current law, it is possible that one party may be vicariously liable for the acts of another in cases of both intentional and unintentional torts. The mere fact, however, that the act was committed on the job does not per se impose liability on the employer.

The rule that employers or principals can be held responsible for the torts of their employees or agents acting within their scope of authority is known not only as vicarious liability, but also as the rule of *respondeat superior.*

As a general rule parents are not vicariously liable for the torts of their minor children, although there are exceptions to this rule as a result of both statutes and case law.

F.   Damages

A suit for damages is a suit asking for money. Three kinds of damages may be obtained in a civil suit.

1.   Compensatory Damages

An award of compensatory damages is designed to place the plaintiff in the financial position that existed prior to the commission of the tort. In a suit for compensatory damages, one is seeking reimbursement for four possible kinds of losses sustained. They include:

   a.   Medical bills,

   b.   Lost wages,

   c.   Property damage, and

   d.   Pain and suffering.

2.   Punitive Damages

Sometimes plaintiffs demand monetary damages for the sole purpose of punishing the defendant for the harm inflicted on them. This kind of a damage claim for "punitive damages" would be for amounts above and beyond those claimed for compensatory damages. Punitive damages will be awarded only upon proof that the defendant acted intentionally and maliciously to harm the plaintiff, or the defendant acted in such a grossly negligent manner that the actions were the equivalent of an intentional act. Punitive damages will not be awarded in cases involving ordinary negligence or carelessness. As an example, if the plaintiff is suing a defendant who inflicted great bodily harm by intentionally and maliciously beating him, the plaintiff might ask the court for

$10,000 in compensatory damages plus an additional $30,000 in punitive damages. Since the purpose of such a punitive damages award would be to punish the defendant rather than compensate the plaintiff for any specific loss, an award of the $30,000 would amount to a windfall for the plaintiff.

When the amount of punitive damages awarded by a jury is grossly disproportionate to the amount of compensatory damages, higher courts may reduce the total damages award on appeal.

3.   Nominal Damages

If a court, after hearing evidence in a case, holds that the plaintiff should win, but that the plaintiff has not established a right to any significant actual or compensatory damages, it may award the plaintiff one dollar, $10, or some other minimal amount. This would be an example of a *nominal damages* award, because the failure of the plaintiff to establish an actual loss resulted in a victory in name only.

SEC. 7-3
THE BASICS OF CIVIL LITIGATION AND PROCEDURE

A.   In General

This section focuses on the procedural rules that govern most actions of a civil nature. The rules applicable in state courts are usually promulgated by the highest state court or the legislature. Most civil actions in the federal courts are governed by the Federal Rules of Civil Procedure. They cover a wide variety of topics including such matters as the acceptable format for pleadings, the service of legal papers, the various forms of discovery, and some of the requirements pertaining to the drafting of pleadings.

The subject of discovery, which pertains to such matters as depositions and interrogatories, is included in the Rules of Civil Procedure, but it covers such a wide scope of material that it is addressed in the next chapter ("Civil Discovery").

Some civil matters are not generally governed by civil procedure rules include:

> Probate, which concerns matters pertaining to decedents' estates,
>
> Guardianship, which pertains to situations in which a party is appointed to be responsible for the person or property of another, and
>
> Small claims actions.[1]

As in other areas of the law, the procedural rules for one state may differ from those of another. The material in this chapter is based on the Federal Rules of Civil Procedure (FED. R. CIV. P.), because many of the states' procedural rules are modeled after them. The federal rules are directly quoted only when the wording prior to a footnote appears with quotation marks. While a large percentage of the following information may be applicable in any given state, it is imperative that readers become familiar with the procedural rules of their own state.

B. The Basic Format of Pleadings

Under Federal Rule of Civil Procedure 10(a), "every pleading shall contain a caption setting forth the name of the court, the title of the action, the file number, ..." and the title of the pleading, such as "Complaint" or "Answer." While the precise organization of these elements may differ under state rules, the following is a common pattern used in numerous court systems.

1. The Introductory Material at the Top

a. The upper right-hand corner or the top center. In this location, the court hearing the case is identified. For example, one might see a phrase such as "In the Circuit Court of the 17th Judicial Circuit in and for Broward County, Florida." Notice that this statement identifies the exact court (Circuit), the judicial circuit (17th), and the geographical location (Broward County, Florida).

Below this statement will be the case number stamped by the clerk of the court when the case is filed. In preparing the pleadings that will initiate a cause of action, the secretary for the plaintiff's attorney will type in the words "Case Number" and leave a blank space after them, since at the time of preparation, the case number will be unknown. All subsequent pleadings pertaining to the cause of action, however, must include the case number that was stamped on the initial pleading at the clerk's office.

The schedules of some courts are divided into terms, and state rules of procedure may require the pleader to identify the term during which the case is filed. The attorney's bar identification number may also appear here.

b. The upper left-hand corner. In this portion of the pleading, there is a section, sometimes boxed, that identifies the case by the names of the parties involved. This is referred to as the "style" of the case. For example, the style of the case might appear as "Donald Jones, Plaintiff v. Ben Arthurs, Defendant." "In the complaint the title of the action shall include the names of all the parties, but in other pleadings it is sufficient to state the name of the first party on each side with an appropriate indication of other parties."[2]

c. The title.   The title of a pleading such as "Complaint," "Answer," or "Motion to Dismiss" appears to the right of the boxed area or is centered on the page below that area.

2.   *The Main Body of the Pleading*

Virtually all pleadings begin with an initial paragraph indicating the fundamental purpose of the document. This paragraph is then followed by numbered allegations or defenses. "All averments of claim or defense shall be made in numbered paragraphs, the contents of each of which shall be limited as far as practicable to a statement of a single set of circumstances ..."[3]

3.   *The Conclusion*

Pleadings are ordinarily signed by the attorney. The party's signature is generally necessary only if the party is unrepresented or if the party is required by law to sign the pleading or submit an affidavit with it. Unless a particular statute or court rule calls for a notarization, it is generally not required. A pleading must in any event be signed at the end, and it must include the address and telephone number of the signer.

All pleadings other than the complaint or original petition contain a certification signed by the attorney that makes a statement similar to the following: "I HEREBY CERTIFY THAT a copy hereof has been furnished to (here insert name or names) by (delivery) (mail) this _____ day of _____, 19 ____." This statement is known as a *certificate of service.* There is no need for such a representation in either a complaint or original petition since these pleadings are formally served with a summons (see Sec. 7-3, subsection C.1).

C.   *Documents Commonly Involved in a Simple Civil Action*

Courts do not, as a general rule, adjudicate civil matters unless those matters have been formally brought before them. For a court to have jurisdiction in any particular case, pleadings must be filed by one of the parties. The term "pleadings" normally includes complaints, answers, counterclaims, cross-claims, third-party complaints, and answers to any and all of these documents. In a more general sense, it refers to written documents that have been submitted to the court and that contain the claims and defenses of the parties. The purpose of pleadings is to help define the nature of the controversy for the court. While their format and drafting is extensively covered by rules of procedure in all fifty states, courts try to prevent a strict adherence to the technical procedural rules from hindering just results.

Below are some of the basic documents that could be involved in a simple civil action. Standard rules of procedure will be discussed in connection with each individual pleading. Samples of each pleading can be found throughout the chapter.

It should be recognized that there are many different kinds of civil actions and that the discussion below is not intended to encompass all possible situations. Its primary purpose is to familiarize the reader with the basic format of pleadings and the fundamental rules that govern a civil practice.

1. The Summons

It has long been established that in order to obtain a personal judgment against a party, the defendant or respondent must receive formal notice of the suit. This requirement, which is derived from the U.S. Constitution, is not fulfilled by the mailing of a copy of the complaint to the defendant. The complaint must be "served" on the defendant, and such service usually requires physical delivery of the papers to the party or parties being sued. The document designed to effectuate this purpose is known as a summons. (It is also possible that statutes may provide for service of process by newspaper publication or some other means in certain specific kinds of cases.)

The summons is prepared and filed with the complaint, and the parties named by the plaintiff in the summons should be the exact same parties named in the complaint. The clerk of the court issues the summons by signing it and stamping it with an official seal. Once this has been done, the summons can be left there for delivery to the office of the Sheriff's Office, Civil Division (if the plaintiff has chosen that division as the process server), or it can be taken to any other process server. The use of a process server other than the Sheriff's Office, Civil Division (or other similar governmental body) may require court approval. A specially appointed process server under these circumstances is referred to as an *elisor*.

Once service of process has been effected, the server signs a document called a *return of service* and files it with the court. It will include the place, date, and time of service. If the server was unsuccessful, the return of service will show the address where the unsuccessful attempt took place.

a. Who may serve summonses. The individual who serves the summons is generally one of the following: an employee of the Sheriff's Office, Civil Division or other similar legal entity that has the specific responsibility for serving legal papers; an employee of a private company that is in the business of service of process; or an individual who has been appointed by the court for this purpose in a specific case. A fee is charged by a process server for the delivery.

Once the summons has been served, it is the responsibility of the server to return to the clerk's office a signed statement that verifies the time and place of service.

b. The content of a summons. The summons is addressed to the one responsible for service of process, and it directs him or her to serve the papers on the person named in the summons. Since the defendant receives a copy of the summons with the complaint at the time of personal service, the language of the summons also informs the defendant of the maximum amount of time within which to file an answer or other responsive pleading. Failure of the defendant to file such a responsive pleading within the allotted time may result in the permanent waiver of the right to do so. (See subsection C.3.d entitled "Default.") The format for the top portion of the summons will be similar to that designated in Sec. 7-3, subsection B.1.

c. The requirement of a separate summons for each defendant. If there is more than one defendant, a separate summons must be prepared for each one. The only difference between the summonses for the individual parties will be the name and address of the person being served. If service of process is not ultimately obtained on all defendants, the plaintiff will be entitled to a judgment only against the defendants who are served. If service of process is not ultimately obtained on any given defendant, a judgment may not be entered against the defendant.

d. The service of subsequent pleadings. Pleadings filed after the initial one must also be "served," but such service can be accomplished by sending the documents to the attorney for the opposing party through the mail or by hand-delivery. All pleadings filed after the initial pleading must have a certification similar to the one in Sec. 7-3, subsection B.3.

e. Alias and pluries summonses. If the first summons is defective in form or manner of service, it may be necessary to have additional summonses issued. For example, if service is not possible at the location listed in the original summons, and the plaintiff has reason to believe that the defendant can be found elsewhere, a second or *alias summons* with a different address can be prepared. It will differ from the original summons in only two respects: the word "alias" will be typed above the word "summons" in the title of the document, and the information concerning the defendant or the defendant's address will be appropriately altered. It is important that the word "alias" be included in the title so that the process server does not assume that it is a second copy of the original summons. If both the original and alias summonses cannot be used, a third version called a *pluries summons* may be issued.

f. Service of process on corporations. When a corporation files papers with the state government that are necessary in order to establish the right to do business within the state, the corporation will be required to designate a *registered agent*. The registered agent is an individual who agrees to receive any legal documents, including summonses and subpoenas, on behalf of the corporation. While service of a summons on the registered agent constitutes legal notice to the corporation that it is being sued, the registered agent is not subject to personal liability

For an example of a summons designed for personal service on a natural person, see Figure 7-1.

2. The Complaint or Original Petition

A complaint is the pleading that most commonly initiates a law suit.[4] Unlike the summons, which is a generalized form that informs the defendant that he or she is being sued and that certain procedures must be followed in order to respond, the complaint contains the actual underlying facts that gave rise to the particular suit in question and a demand for relief. The plaintiff must show not only that a cause of action exists, but that the plaintiff is the party who has been harmed and is entitled to recovery. Similarly, it must be shown that the harm has been done to the plaintiff by the named defendants in the suit.[5]

a. Statement of jurisdiction. Rules of civil procedure also usually require that the complaint include a statement of jurisdiction justifying why the plaintiff has chosen to file in a particular court. For example, the complaint may contain an allegation similar to a statement that "[t]his is an action for damages in an amount greater than $15,000 and therefore falls within the jurisdiction of the Circuit Court." Failure to include a jurisdictional statement may result in the filing of a motion by the opposing party to dismiss the case.

b. Statement of the facts. The complaint must contain a clear statement of the facts that must be established for the plaintiff to recover on the cause of action. Whether the plaintiff's initial pleading is proper may depend on whether the facts alleged, if assumed to be true, state a substantive case entitling the plaintiff to recovery. The plaintiff should include dates, times, locations, and other information with as much specificity as possible.

c. Possibility of multiple counts. The plaintiff may have more than one theory upon which to base a claim, and the claim may therefore be in several counts. For example, if the plaintiff is suing the defendant because the defendant defrauded him or her on a contract, the plaintiff might sue the defendant both for fraud and breach of contract. Since the elements of each cause of action are

IN THE **CIRCUIT** COURT OF THE **17TH** JUDICIAL CIRCUIT
IN AND FOR **BROWARD** COUNTY, STATE OF **FLORIDA**

Case No:

WILLIE L. SANDERS,   )
)
       Plaintiff,   )
)
v.   )
)
JOHN M. MARINO and   )
DAVID R. ROBINSON,   )
)
       Defendants.   )
_____)

Fla. Bar #987654

This form is designed for
instruction, and not for use
in all jurisdictions.

Serve: **David R. Robinson**
            290 Carlton Place
            Donaldsville, Florida 33913

SUMMONS:

(PERSONAL SERVICE
ON A NATURAL PERSON)

A lawsuit has been filed against you. You have 20 calendar days after this summons is served on you to file a written response to the attached complaint with the clerk of this court. A phone call will not protect you. Your written response, including case number given above and the names of the parties, must be filed if you want the court to hear your side of the case. If you do not file your response on time, you may lose the case, and your wages, money, and property may thereafter be taken without further warning from the court. There are other legal requirements. You may want to call an attorney right away. If you do not know an attorney, you may call an attorney referral service or a legal aid office (listed in the phone book).

If you choose to file a written response yourself, at the same time you file your written response to the court you must also mail or take a copy of your written response to the "Plaintiff/Plaintiff's Attorney" named below.

Harold Bishop
Plaintiff's Attorney
Harold Bishop
Bishop and Zubin
4317 Weston Road
Fairwood, FL 33318
(999) 432-8612

STATE OF **Florida**

TO EACH SHERIFF OF THE STATE

You are commanded to serve this summons and a copy of the complaint in this law suit on the above-named Defendant.

DATED this   day of   , 19   .

                                 Clyde Clerk
             (Seal)   As Clerk of the Court

                               _____
                               As Deputy Clerk
                               My commission expires:

FIGURE 7-1

different and one may be easier to prove than another, the plaintiff's best course of action is usually to raise as many legitimate counts as possible against the defendant. There is no limitation on the number of counts that may be raised in a civil complaint, and the counts need not be consistent either in the federal courts[6] or in most state courts.

When more than one kind of cause of action is involved, the splitting of the allegations into separate counts may not only be desirable, but also necessary under many state rules. In fact, failure to include all possible grounds for suit may result in the waiver of those that are omitted. Each count must be sufficient without reliance upon the allegations of other counts. However, it is generally permissible to incorporate sections of one count into another provided that the incorporation references are clear and unequivocal.

d. Performance of conditions precedent.   Sometimes certain conditions must be met by the plaintiff before the cause of action "accrues." For example, suppose A and B enter into a contract that requires B to supply A with machine parts for A's tanks in the event of a formal declaration of war. Since the condition is part of the contract, any suit by A against B must include an averment that the condition has occurred. In some jurisdictions, a statement that "all conditions precedent have been met" may be sufficient.

e. Attachment of documents.   If the plaintiff's claim is based upon written documents such as contracts or promissory notes, copies of those documents should be attached to the complaint.

f. Statutory references.   Whenever a claim is based on a right conferred upon the plaintiff by statute, all the facts that bring the plaintiff within the provisions of that statute must be stated. When referring to statutes, many jurisdictions do not require use of the exact words of the statute, although direct quotations from the statute may be desirable. Simply stating the statute does not, however, make the complaint sufficient when no supporting facts are alleged. All claims based on statutory authority should refer to statute numbers specifically.

g. Demand for jury trial.   While the plaintiff in most civil actions has a right to trial by jury, that right normally exists only where it is conferred by a constitution or statute. Generally, the right to trial by jury does not exist in an equity suit. If the plaintiff desires a jury trial, it must be requested "… in writing at any time after commencement of the action and not later than ten days after the service of the last pleading directed to such issue."[7] The theory behind this rule is that preparation for a trial by jury may be very different from that necessary for a trial by judge. Fairness therefore dictates that each side should notify the other long before the matter actually comes to trial of its decision to have the case heard before a jury.

Demands for trial by jury are commonly found in complaints. They may also be found in the initial pleadings of the defendant or respondent (see the discussion in Sec. 7-3, subsection C.3.e that follows). Whether a party chooses to have a trial by jury, rather than a trial in which the judge is the sole finder of fact, is a decision that will be made after consultation between the client and the attorney. That determination may depend upon such factors as whether the plaintiff feels that the issues involved are so complicated and confusing that a jury verdict would be unpredictable, or whether a jury might be more sympathetic than the judge in a highly emotional case. If a party fails to serve and file a demand for a jury trial within the designated time period, the party is deemed to have waived the right to do so.[8]

h. Amendment of complaints.   As a general rule, the plaintiff has the automatic right to amend the complaint once at any time before an answer or other responsive pleading is served. After that time, any amendment of the complaint will require permission of the court or written consent of the adverse party.[9] For an example of a simplified complaint, see Figures 7-2a and b.

3.   The Answer

The document filed by the defendant which responds to each allegation of the complaint is known as the *answer.* For an example of a very simplified answer, see Figures 7-3a and b. The introductory paragraph indicates that the defendant is answering the plaintiff's allegations on the basis of the information that follows. That paragraph is followed by numbered statements that respond to each of the allegations of the complaint by number.

a. Responses to specific allegations in the complaint.   Other than allegations pertaining to the amount of damages, any allegations in the complaint that the defendant fails to deny are presumed to be admitted.[10] "When a pleader intends in good faith to deny only a part or a qualification of an averment, the pleader shall specify so much of it as is true and material and shall only deny the remainder."[11] For example, if one of the plaintiff's allegations is that "the defendant, while in an intoxicated state, caused his automobile to collide with that of the plaintiff," the defendant might respond in the answer with something similar to the following: "It is admitted that the defendant's automobile collided with the plaintiff's vehicle. It is denied, however, that the defendant caused the collision or that the defendant was intoxicated at that time."

"If a party is without knowledge or information sufficient to form a belief as to the truth of an averment, the party shall so state and this has the effect of a denial."[12]

IN THE CIRCUIT COURT OF THE 17TH JUDICIAL CIRCUIT
IN AND FOR BROWARD COUNTY, STATE OF FLORIDA

Case No:

Fla. Bar #987654

WILLIE L. SANDERS,)
)
    Plaintiff,)
)
v.   )
)
JOHN M. MARINO and)
DAVID R. ROBINSON,)
)
    Defendants.)
_____)

COMPLAINT

The plaintiff, WILLIE L SANDERS, sues the defendants, JOHN M. MARINO, and DAVID R.ROBINSON, and alleges:

1. This is an action for damages in excess of $15,000.

2. On or about November 22, 1996, defendant, JOHN M. MARINO, and defendant, DAVID R. ROBINSON owned and operated their respective motor vehicles at the intersection of Wildwood Drive and Chester Road in Fort Lauderdale, Florida.

3. The plaintiff, WILLIE L. SANDERS, was a passenger in the vehicle owned and operated by JOHN M. MARINO.

4. At the time and place mentioned in allegation #2 above defendants, or one of them, negligently operated or maintained their motor vehicles so that they collided.

5. As a result plaintiff suffered bodily injury and resulting pain and suffering, disability, disfigurement, mental anguish, loss of capacity for the enjoyment of life, expense of hospitalization, medical and nursing care and treatment, loss of earnings, loss of ability to earn money and aggravation of a previously existing condition. The losses are either permanent or continuing and plaintiff will suffer the losses in the future. The plaintiff's automobile was damaged and she lost the use of it during the period required for its repair or replacement.

FIGURE 7-2a

Demand for Jury Trial

6. The plaintiff hereby demands trial by jury as to all issues so triable.

WHEREFORE plaintiff demands judgment against defendants.

DATED this 8th day of July, 1997.

Harold Bishop
Harold Bishop
Plaintiff's Attorney
Bishop and Zubin
4317 Weston Road
Fairwood, FL 33318
(999) 432-8612

FIGURE 7-2b

IN THE CIRCUIT COURT OF THE 17TH JUDICIAL CIRCUIT
IN AND FOR BROWARD COUNTY, STATE OF FLORIDA

Case No: 97-582732

Fla. Bar #314151

WILLIE L. SANDERS,   )
)
    Plaintiff,   )
)
v.   )
)
JOHN M. MARINO and)
DAVID R. ROBINSON,)
)
    Defendants.)
_____)

ANSWER

COMES NOW the defendant, DAVID R. ROBINSON, by and through his undersigned attorney, and answers the allegations of the plaintiff's complaint as follows:

1. Allegation #1 of the plaintiff's complaint is admitted.

2. Allegation #2 of the plaintiff's complaint is admitted.

3. Allegation #3 of the plaintiff's complaint is denied.

4. As to allegation #4, DAVID R. ROBINSON admits that his vehicle collided with that of the co-defendant, JOHN M. MARINO, but denies that it was due to any negligence on his own part.

5. Allegation #5 of the plaintiff's complaint is denied.

Affirmative Defense

6. The plaintiff had a seat belt readily available to him that would have either significantly decreased or eliminated the chance of serious injury that the plaintiff claims to have suffered, and because of the fact that the plaintiff was negligent in failing to use the seat belt, his recovery should be reduced proportionately to reflect such negligence.

FIGURE 7-3a

Demand for Jury Trial

DAVID R. ROBINSON hereby demands trial by jury as to all issues so triable.

I HEREBY CERTIFY that a copy of the foregoing Answer has been mailed to Mr. Harold Bishop, Bishop and Zubin, 4317 Weston Road, Fairwood, Florida 33318 this 25th day of July, 1997.

William Benlow
William Benlow
Benlow and Sheen
Attorneys for defendant David
  R. Robinson
326 61st Avenue
Pleasantville, FL 33019
(999) 564-5000

FIGURE 7-3b

b. *Sham and frivolous answers.*   A sham answer is one that may appear on its face to be a valid and legitimate answer, but which is in fact based on falsehood. It is generally submitted in bad faith or for the purposes of delay. An answer is considered to be frivolous when the statements in the answer appear to be true but raise no actual defense even after a cursory examination by the court. The filing of a sham or frivolous pleading may not be effective in prohibiting the entry of a judgment against the party filing such pleading.

c. *The time within which to respond.*   Defendants are given only a limited time within which to respond to the complaint under the rules of all states. The rule applicable in the federal courts states that "a defendant shall serve his answer within 20 days after the service of the summons and complaint [upon that defendant]...."[13] (According to the federal rules and the rules of many states, one actually has three additional days beyond the 20-day period to respond in order to accommodate the built-in time delay involved with delivery by United States mail. Procedural rules governing state courts may provide for as many as five additional days.)[14]

The plaintiff can send a request to the defendant to have service of the complaint and summons waived under the federal rules. If the defendant agrees to such a waiver, the defendant must answer "within 60 days after the date when the request for waiver was sent ..." for defendants addressed within the United States.[15] By waiving service of the summons, defendants are not waiving their right to subsequently object to venue or jurisdiction issues.[16] If the defendants refuse to waive the service of the summons and the documents are subsequently served, they will bear the responsibility for the costs incurred.[17] In computing the 20-day period, the first day is the day after the date of service of process on the defendant. "The last day of the period so computed shall be included, unless it is a Saturday, Sunday or legal holiday, or, when ... the weather or other conditions have made the office of the clerk of the district court inaccessible, in which even the period runs until the end of the next day which is not one of the aforementioned days."[18] Any Saturdays, Sundays, and legal holidays that occur during the 20-day period are, however, counted.

If the defendant responds during the required time period by filing one of several different kinds of motions (such as a motion for more definite statement in which it is argued that the complaint is so vague or ambiguous that the defendant cannot reasonably respond), that filing has the effect of stopping the clock until the matter addressed in the motion is resolved.

(1) *The use of tickler files.* To keep track of deadlines, such as the number of days remaining for the attorney to respond to a complaint filed against an office client, all law offices have some form of "tickler file." Before computers were prevalent in law offices, tickler files were prepared with index cards. A typical system would be organized with dividers for each month and each day of the month. To illustrate how a tickler file might be used, suppose Jones was served with a summons on September 9, and she came into the law office on the 12th. After the client left, a white card would be placed in the file behind the tab for September 13 that would say something similar to "17 days left to answer the Jones complaint." The number 17 in this case came from the fact that the first day of the 20-day period was on the 10th, which was the day after the date of service. In the file behind the tab for the date of the 14th, a white card would be placed in the file that would say "16 days left to answer the Jones complaint." Cards for the remaining days of the 20-day period would also be placed in the card file immediately. For the last eight or ten days of the 20-day period, red cards might be used to signify that action on the matter should be taken soon. For the last two or three days of the period, orange cards might be used to indicate that an emergency exists and that action on the case must be taken immediately. Once an answer is filed in the case, all the current cards pertaining to that matter would be removed and replaced with cards for the next required action in the case.

When attorneys used the traditional system, cards for all the cases that were being handled by the attorney would be included in one tickler file so that the attorney could have a clear picture of which cases required immediate attention. One or more people within the law office would have the responsibility to check the tickler file immediately upon arrival at the office in the morning to identify the most important work that needed to be done that day.

Now that computers are common pieces of equipment in the modern law office, tickler files are set up electronically. Law offices have many different systems, but they all operate on the same principles employed in creating traditional tickler files. If a law office has established a workable computer system for keeping track of important dates and deadlines, the paralegal should come to the office expecting to adapt to the system that is already in place.

d. Default. If the defendant does not file a responsive pleading within the designated time period, the plaintiff can request that the clerk enter a *default* against the defendant. The entry of such a default precludes the defendant from arguing the case on the merits in the future and establishes the plaintiff's right to a favorable judgment. A default can never be entered by the clerk until the day after the time period for responding to the complaint has expired. If the suit is for damages, it is possible that there may be a further hearing or submission of evidence to the court with regard to the amount of damages, but the defendant will not be permitted to deny liability as alleged in the complaint.

The plaintiff's request to the clerk in this situation is known as a *motion for default,* and the clerk's signed statement granting the request is known simply as a *default.* If both the plaintiff's request for a default and the statement prepared for the clerk's signature are found on the same document, the document is referred to as a *motion for default, and default.* An example of such a document can be seen in Figure 7-4.

(1) *The necessity of a final judgment from the court.* The clerk has no power to enter a final judgment against the defendant even in the case of a default. Consequently, once the default is issued, the plaintiff must file a motion for a *default judgment* based upon the defendant's failure to respond. For an example of a default judgment, see Figure 7-5. The procedural rules do provide an opportunity for the defendant to contest the entering of a default judgment, but courts are hesitant to vacate a default without a showing of substantial cause. Furthermore, arguments by the defendant that pertain to the merits of the case will not generally be considered by the court at a hearing dealing with the entering of a default judgment.

(2) *The expiration of the period for responsive pleadings.* A default will not automatically occur unless the plaintiff files a request for it with the court. Therefore, if the defendant in a federal civil case files an answer on the 40th day and a default has not yet been entered, the court will proceed with the case as if the answer had been filed in a timely manner. If there has been no responsive pleading or motion for default and the time for filing a responsive pleading has expired, it is possible in many jurisdictions for the court to enter a default on its own initiative. The volume of cases handled by the courts, however, makes it unlikely that they will become aware of a potential default before a substantial period of time has elapsed.

e. Demand for a jury trial. If the defendant desires a trial by jury, the demand must generally be made in writing "not later than 10 days after the service of the last pleading directed to such issue."[19] *Demands for trial by jury* are commonly included in the answer itself. Failure to make such a demand may result in the waiver of that right. On the other hand, court rules or statutes may

IN THE CIRCUIT COURT OF THE 17TH JUDICIAL CIRCUIT
IN AND FOR BROWARD COUNTY, STATE OF FLORIDA

Case No. 97-58273

Fla. Bar #987654

WILLIE L. SANDERS,　　　)
　　　　　　　　　　　　　)
　　　　Plaintiff,　　　　)
　　　　　　　　　　　　　)
v.　　　　　　　　　　　　)
　　　　　　　　　　　　　)
JOHN M. MARINO and　　　)
DAVID R. ROBINSON,　　　)
　　　　　　　　　　　　　)
　　　　Defendants.　　　)
_____)

This form is designed for
instruction, and <u>not</u> for use
in all jurisdictions.

MOTION FOR DEFAULT

PLAINTIFF MOVES for an entry of a default by the clerk against
Defendant JOHN M. MARINO for failure to serve any paper on the
undersigned or file any paper as required by law.

I HEREBY CERTIFY that a copy of the foregoing Motion for Default,
and Default has been mailed to JOHN M. MARINO, 339 Calley Circle,
Davie, Florida 33123 on this the 4th day of August, 1997.

Harold Bishop
Harold Bishop
Plaintiff's Attorney
Bishop and Zubin
4317 Weston Road
Fairwood, FL 33318
(999) 432-8612

DEFAULT

A DEFAULT is entered in this action against the defendant named in
the foregoing motion for failure to serve or file any paper as
required by law.

DATED this 4th day of August, 1997.

Elizabeth Cody
As Clerk of the Court

By: *George Wall*
As Deputy Clerk

FIGURE 7-4

IN THE CIRCUIT COURT OF THE 17TH JUDICIAL CIRCUIT
IN AND FOR BROWARD COUNTY, STATE OF FLORIDA

Case No: 97-58273

WILLIE L. SANDERS,   )
)
        Plaintiff,   )
)
v.   )
)
DAVID R. ROBINSON,   )
)
        Defendants.   )
_____   )

FINAL JUDGMENT

THIS ACTION was heard after entry of default against defendant and

IT IS ADJUDGED that Plaintiff, WILLIE L. SANDERS, recover from defendant, JOHN M. MARINO, the sum of $29,000.00 with costs in the sum of $2,612.50, making a total of $31,612.50, that shall bear interest at the legal rate of interest, for which let execution issue.

ORDERED in Fort Lauderdale, Broward County, in the State of Florida on this, the 15th day of August, 1997.

Susan Mayer
Circuit Judge

cc: Harold Bishop
      Attorney for the Plaintiffs
      Bishop and Zubin
      4317 Weston Road
      Fairwood, FL 33318

      William Benlow
      Attorney for the Defendant
      David R. Robinson
      326 61st Avenue
      Pleasantville, FL 33019

      John M. Marino
      339 Calley Circle
      Davie, Florida 33123

FIGURE 7-5

provide that a demand for trial by jury may not be withdrawn without the consent of the other party or parties.

f. Affirmative defenses.   *Affirmative defenses* are defenses which, if accepted by the court, will relieve the defendant of liability even if the allegations of the complaint are shown to be true. In many states, if a defendant files an answer containing affirmative defenses and the plaintiff intends to avoid the defenses, the plaintiff is under an obligation to file a reply to them. The Federal Rules of Civil Procedure list 19 affirmative defenses, and the rules further allow for "any other matter constituting an avoidance or affirmative defense."[20] Examples of affirmative defenses include:

(1) *Res judicata.* When using the defense of *res judicata*, the defendant is arguing that, regardless of the truth of the allegations in the complaint, the matter has already been ruled upon by a court of law and the present case should, therefore, be dismissed.

(2) *Release.* With the defense of *release*, the defendant is contending that the plaintiff has already agreed to release the defendant from responsibility for the matters alleged in the complaint. Simple releases are commonly prepared on standard written forms obtainable at local office supply stores.

(3) *Contributory negligence.* The traditional defense of *contributory negligence* is applicable only in negligence cases and only in a minority of states. It releases the defendant from liability if the defendant can prove any negligence on the part of the plaintiff. Assume, for example, that the plaintiff and the defendant were involved in an automobile accident and that the plaintiff is claiming that the defendant's negligence and carelessness is directly responsible for the plaintiff's injuries. In applying this rule, if the defendant can prove that the plaintiff was at least partially responsible for the plaintiff's own injuries, the defendant will be entitled to a favorable judgment even if it can be shown that the defendant was also partly to blame or even more to blame than the plaintiff.

(4) *Comparative negligence.* Because of the fact that the contributory negligence rule can result in apparently unjust results, most states now apply the rule of *comparative negligence* instead. To illustrate, if it could be shown in the above example that total damages to the plaintiff were $100,000, that the defendant was 70 percent responsible, and that the plaintiff was 30 percent responsible, courts in states applying the comparative negligence rule should award the plaintiff $70,000. Courts in

states that recognize the contributory negligence rule would award the plaintiff nothing under these circumstances since the plaintiff was at least partially responsible for the accident.

(5) *Statute of limitations.* All states have statutes that nullify the rights of a party who waits an excessively long period of time before filing suit. The *statute of limitations* applies to the period of time from the date that the cause of action accrued to the date of filing. It has no relevance to the period of time required by either the parties or the court to resolve the case after it has been filed.

To illustrate, a court will deny a plaintiff's breach of contract claim if the breach took place 30 years ago and the plaintiff has not until the present time initiated a cause of action. Even if the plaintiff can now demonstrate a clear case of breach of contract, the claim will be defeated if the defendant raises the statute of limitations. The maximum time allowed for the filing of a case will differ for each type of cause of action.

g. Amendment of answers.   A party may amend an answer once as a matter of course at any time before a responsive pleading is served. Such a responsive pleading might be an answer by the plaintiff to the affirmative defenses of the defendant. Amendment of the answer after that time is only possible by permission of the court or by written consent of the adverse party.[21]

h. Counterclaims.   If the defendant has a claim against the plaintiff, the defendant may make a *counterclaim* against the plaintiff and request that both the original claim and the counterclaim be heard together. In some states, the counterclaim can be included in the answer and handled by the clerk's office under the same case number, while in others, it must be filed as a separate pleading. Any answer with a counterclaim may be served through ordinary mail or by hand delivery. Under such circumstances, a summons is not necessary since the plaintiff will already be subject to the jurisdiction of the court as a result of the filing of the initial complaint.

The term "counterclaim" may in some jurisdictions include claims that would be classified as cross-claims in others (see this subsection, item i).

(1) *Compulsory counterclaims.* These counterclaims must be raised by the defendant at the time of the plaintiff's lawsuit or be regarded as forever waived. Those that fall within this category arise "out of the transaction or occurrence that is the subject matter of the opposing party's claim...."[22]

Assume, for example, that the plaintiff and the defendant were in an automobile accident and that the plaintiff sued the defendant for injuries that were sustained in the collision. The defendant might include in the answer a counterclaim for damage to the defendant's car. Since both of the claims arose out of the same occurrence, the defendant's property damage claim would be regarded as a compulsory counterclaim, and it would be waived if it was not raised during the plaintiff's suit.

(2) *Permissive counterclaims.* While not required to do so, the defendant may state any existing claim against the plaintiff when the claim is "not arising out of the transaction or occurrence that is the subject matter of the opposing party's claim."[23] This kind of counterclaim is known as a *permissive counterclaim.*

As in the case above, assume that the plaintiff and the defendant were in an automobile accident and that the plaintiff sued the defendant for injuries sustained in the collision. The defendant might include in the answer a counterclaim for a breach of contract claim that the defendant happens to have against the plaintiff. Since the original claim and the counterclaim did not arise out of the same transaction, the defendant's claim with regard to the breach of contract would be regarded as a permissive counterclaim.

The court always retains the right to order separate trials for the original claim and the counterclaim if it determines that such a severance is desirable to further convenience or avoid prejudice and confusion.

i. Cross-claims. A *cross-claim* is appropriate when there is a claim "by one party against a co-party arising out of the transaction or occurrence that is the subject matter either of the original action or of a counterclaim therein or relating to any property that is the subject matter of the original action."[24] If, for example, the plaintiff has filed suit against two defendants, the first defendant may choose to file a cross-claim against the second defendant and argue that the other defendant is responsible for all or part of the claim. For an example of a cross-claim, see Figures 7-6a and b.

j. Third-party complaints. "At any time after commencement of the action a defending party, as a third-party plaintiff, may cause a summons and complaint to be served upon a person not a party to the action who is or may be liable to the third-party plaintiff for all or part of the plaintiff's claim against the third-party plaintiff."[25]

A third-party complaint would be appropriate if, for example, the plaintiff filed suit against a single defendant and the defendant claimed that a party not sued in the original action was responsible. Since any third-party complaint necessarily involves an attempt to bring a new party into the legal proceedings, service of a summons and the third-party complaint on the new party is required.

IN THE CIRCUIT COURT OF THE 17TH JUDICIAL CIRCUIT
IN AND FOR BROWARD COUNTY, STATE OF FLORIDA

Case No: 97-58273

Fla. Bar #314151

WILLIE L. SANDERS,)
)
     Plaintiff,   )
)
v.   )
)
JOHN M. MARINO and)
DAVID R. ROBINSON,)
)
     Defendants.)
_____)

CROSS-CLAIM

Defendant DAVID R. ROBINSON, by and through his undersigned
attorney, sues co-defendant JOHN M. MARINO in cross-claim and
alleges the following:

1. This is an action for damages in excess of $15,000.

2. On or about November 22, 1996, defendant, JOHN M. MARINO, owned
and operated a motor vehicle at the intersection of Wildwood Drive
and Chester Road in Fort Lauderdale, Florida.

3. At that time and place defendant JOHN M. MARINO negligently
operated or maintained the motor vehicle so that it collided with
the vehicle of DAVID R. ROBINSON.

4. As a result DAVID R. ROBINSON suffered bodily injury and
resulting pain and suffering, disability, disfigurement, mental
anguish, loss of capacity for the enjoyment of life, expense of
hospitalization, medical and nursing care and treatment, loss of
earnings, loss of ability to earn money and aggravation of a
previously existing condition. The losses are either permanent or
continuing and DAVID R. ROBINSON will suffer the losses in the
future. The plaintiff's automobile was damaged and he lost the use
of it during the period required for its repair or replacement.

Count II

5. This is an action for damages in excess of $15,000.

FIGURE 7-6a

6. On or about November 22, 1996, defendant JOHN M. MARINO owned and operated a motor vehicle at the intersection of Wildwood Drive and Chester Road in Fort Lauderdale, Florida.

7. At that time and place defendant JOHN M. MARINO negligently operated or maintained the motor vehicle so that it collided with the vehicle of DAVID R. ROBINSON.

8. WILLIE L. SANDERS was a passenger in the vehicle owned and operated by JOHN M. MARINO.

9. WILLIE L. SANDERS filed suit against both DAVID R. ROBINSON and JOHN M. MARINO in Broward County Circuit Court for damages sustained as a result of the collision.

10. Defendant JOHN M. MARINO was so negligent in the maintenance and operation of his automobile that such negligence was the sole legal cause of the damages demanded in the plaintiff's complaint, and DAVID R. ROBINSON is therefore entitled to indemnification for any amounts recoverable from DAVID R. ROBINSON by the plaintiff. Alternatively, JOHN M. MARINO was responsible for the plaintiff's damages to such a degree that any amounts recovered by the plaintiff against DAVID R. ROBINSON will entitle DAVID R. ROBINSON to contribution from JOHN M. MARINO in direct proportion to JOHN M. MARINO's negligence under the doctrine of comparative negligence.

Demand for Jury Trial

DAVID R. ROBINSON, by and through his undersigned attorney, hereby demands trial by jury as to all issues so triable.

WHEREFORE DAVID R.ROBINSON, by and through his undersigned attorney, demands judgment for damages against defendant JOHN M. MARINO.

I HEREBY CERTIFY that a copy of this cross-claim was mailed to Mr. Harold Bishop, Bishop and Zubin, attorneys for plaintiff, 4317 Weston Road, Fairwood, FL 33318 and Mr. John M. Marino,the co-defendant, 339 Calley Circle, Davie, FL 33123 this 25 day of July, 1997.

William Benlow
William Benlow
Benlow and Sheen
Attorneys for defendant
   David R. Robinson
326 61st Avenue
Pleasantville, FL 33019
(999) 564-5000

FIGURE 7-6b

The major difference between a cross-claim and a third-party complaint is that a cross-claim will be filed by one party against another party that has already been brought into the suit. As an illustration, the defendant in the example found in this section, subsection C.3.i was filing the cross-claim against the other defendant named in the original complaint. In contrast, the defendant in the example involving the third-party complaint was bringing in a new party who was not originally involved.

"When a counterclaim is asserted against a plaintiff, the plaintiff may cause a third party to be brought in under circumstances which ... would entitle a defendant to do so...."[26]

4. *Motions*

A number of different issues may be raised by motion rather than in a responsive pleading, including but not limited to "(1) lack of jurisdiction over the subject matter, (2) lack of jurisdiction over the person, (3) improper venue, (4) insufficiency of process, (5) insufficiency of service of process, (6) failure to state a claim upon which relief can be granted, [and] (7) failure to join [an indispensable] party."[27] Another common motion is a motion for judgment on the pleadings, in which the pleading party is asserting entitlement to a favorable judgment as a matter of law, assuming the allegations of the opposing party's pleading are assumed for the purposes of argument to be true. The defendant may, for example, raise such a motion if the allegations of the complaint, even if shown to be true, would not demonstrate liability on the part of the defendant. All the motions referred to in this paragraph are normally heard prior to trial unless the court orders otherwise.[28] Written motions will appear in the same format described in Sec. 7-3, subsection B.

A motion to strike may be appropriate if a pleading of an opposing party contains "... any insufficient defense or any redundant, immaterial, impertinent or scandalous matter."[29] The court also has the power to unilaterally strike such matter even in the absence of a motion from a party.[30]

A motion for a more definite statement is appropriate when the pleadings of the opposing party are so indefinite that a response to them is difficult or impossible. If the motion is granted, the court commonly provides the party with an opportunity to amend the pleadings during a specified period of time.

5. *Subpoenas*

A *subpoena* is used to compel the presence of an individual either at trial or deposition. (The subject area of depositions is addressed in the "Civil Discovery" chapter of this book.) In contrast, a summons is used to notify a party of the initiation of a legal action. A subpoena has to be formally served to be effective. The format for the top portion of the subpoena will be the one designated in Sec. 7-3, subsection B.

a. Issuance by the clerk.   As in the case of a summons, the clerk of the court issues the subpoena by signing it and stamping it with an official seal. Once this has been done, the subpoena can be left there for delivery to the office of the Sheriff's Office, Civil Division (if the plaintiff has chosen that division as the process server), or it can be taken by the individual filing the case to any other process server.

b. Service of subpoenas.   Those who are qualified to serve summonses are also generally qualified to serve subpoenas. They may include an employee of the Sheriff's Office, Civil Division, or other similar legal entity that has the specific responsibility for serving legal papers; an employee of a private company that is in the business of service or process; or an individual who has been appointed by the court for this purpose in a specific case.

c. Fees.   Checks will have to be prepared to compensate the process server, and in many states, the one who is being served. In those states that require that a check accompany the subpoena, the served party will not be bound by the subpoena if the check is missing. The amount of the check payable to the individual named in the subpoena will be based upon the mileage to the place of the trial, hearing, or deposition. Charts showing the correct amount to pay to those who are traveling from various locations are available at all offices that handle litigation in states where such fees are appropriate. When expert witnesses such as physicians are involved, there may be agreements between the legal community and professional representatives of those experts to pay a fee above and beyond mileage expenses that is commensurate with the witness's time and expertise.

d. Failure to obey a subpoena.   "Failure by any person without adequate excuse to obey a subpoena served upon that person may be deemed a contempt of the court from which the subpoena issued.[31]

e. Return of proof of service.   Once the subpoena has been served, it is the responsibility of the server to return to the clerk's office a signed statement that verifies the time and place of service, or if the witness was not served, the time and place of the unsuccessful attempt at service.

f. Use of the subpoena duces tecum.   A subpoena can be used not only to compel a witness to appear at the trial or hearing but also to force that witness to bring along certain specified documents or other kinds of tangible evidence. In order to accomplish this purpose, a form known as a *subpoena duces tecum,* rather than an ordinary subpoena, is appropriate. The format for a regular subpoena is generally the same as that for a subpoena duces tecum, except that the regular subpoena does not contain any language requiring the witness to bring documents or evidence. An example of a subpoena duces tecum for trial can be seen in Figure 7-7.

6. *Dismissals*

When an action is *dismissed*, it has come to an end even though there has been no trial of the issues. A *dismissal* may or may not constitute a decision on the merits. Furthermore, it may result from a voluntary decision on the part of one party, or it may be imposed upon a party by the court against the party's will.

a. Voluntary dismissals. Subject to several exceptions, a plaintiff has the opportunity to withdraw the cause of action "without prejudice," which means that the case can be refiled at a later time without affecting any right of recovery.[32] This can be done "… by filing a notice of dismissal at any time before service by the adverse party of an answer or of a motion for summary judgment, whichever first occurs, or … by filing a stipulation of dismissal signed by all parties who have appeared in the action …"[33] A motion for summary judgment is one in which a party is arguing that, based on the pleadings, affidavits of the parties and witnesses, and sworn answers in interrogatories and depositions alone, there is no significant disagreement of the facts and the party is therefore entitled to a judgment in its favor as a matter of law.

"If a counterclaim has been pleaded by a defendant prior to the service upon the defendant of the plaintiff's motion to dismiss, the action shall not be dismissed against the defendant's objection unless the counterclaim can remain pending for independent adjudication by the court."[34]

b. Involuntary dismissals. It is also possible for one party to ask the court to grant a dismissal of the opposing party's claim. For example, after the plaintiff's case has been presented in court but before the defendant has called the defense witnesses (if any), it is common for the defendant's attorney to move for a dismissal on the basis that the plaintiff has failed to establish either by facts or law a right to relief. In the event that the motion is denied, the defendant may proceed to present witnesses and evidence. The court has simply refused in this instance to rule in the defendant's favor prior to the presentation of the defendant's case.

If the court grants the motion, its order may be *with prejudice*, which means that unless the party adversely affected by the order can have it overturned, that party will be unable to bring the same matter again before the court on the merits. There are, however, exceptions to this rule. If a dismissal is, for ex-

IN THE **CIRCUIT** COURT OF THE **17TH** JUDICIAL CIRCUIT
IN AND FOR **BROWARD** COUNTY, STATE OF **FLORIDA**

Case No: 97-58273

Fla. Bar #987654

WILLIE L. SANDERS,   )
)
      Plaintiff,   )
)
v.   )
)
JOHN M. MARINO and   )
DAVID R. ROBINSON,   )
)
      Defendants.   )
_____)

This form is designed for
instruction, and <u>not</u> for use
in all jurisdictions.

TIME:

DATE:

SERVER:

SUBPOENA DUCES TECUM FOR TRIAL

THE STATE OF **FLORIDA**:

TO: **Susan Creswell**
      4900 18th Avenue S.W.
      Pierpoint, FL 33333

YOU ARE COMMANDED to appear before the Honorable **Susan Mayer**, Judge of the
Circuit Court, at the **Broward** County Courthouse in **Fort Lauderdale**, in the State
of Florida, on the **14th** day of **January, 1998**, at **9:00 A.M.** to testify in this
action and to have with you at that time and place the following:

the ledger books of the Creswell '
sole proprietorship for the
years 1994, 1995 and 1996.

If you fail to appear, you may be in contempt of court.

YOU ARE SUBPOENAED to appear by the following attorneys and unless excused from
this subpoena by these attorneys or the court, you shall respond to this subpoena
as directed.

Harold Bishop
Plaintiff's Attorney
Harold Bishop
Bishop and Zubin
4317 Weston Road
Fairwood, FL 33318
(999) 432-8612

DATED this **5th** day of **January, 1998**.

Kelly Rush
Clerk of the Court

By: *Kelly Rush*
As Deputy Clerk

FIGURE 7-7

ample, based upon lack of jurisdiction, improper venue, or lack of an indispensable party, the order to dismissal will be *without prejudice* unless the court otherwise orders, and the case can be refiled.[35]

c. Dismissal of counterclaims, cross-claims, or third-party claims. The rules that are applicable to the involuntary dismissal of the original complaint also govern the involuntary dismissal of counterclaims, cross-claims, and third-party claims.[36]

d. Failure to prosecute. If no pleadings or orders have been filed for an extensive period of time (generally one year) by the plaintiff, the rules of most states provide that the defendant can file a motion to have the case dismissed because of the plaintiff's failure to prosecute the matter.

D. Pretrial Conferences

Prior to trial, the court may require the attorneys to meet with the judge for one or more conferences to resolve various matters pertaining to the case. One of the ultimate purposes of such conferences is to avoid the unnecessary waste of time at trial. A few of the topics that might be addressed at a pretrial conference include:

1. the simplification of issues
2. the necessity or desirability of amendments to the pleadings
3. the avoidance of unnecessary proof
4. advance rulings on the admissibility of evidence
5. the identification of witnesses to testify and evidence to be submitted
6. the disposition of pending motions
7. the control and scheduling of discovery
8. an order for a separate trial ... with respect to any issue in the case
9. an order establishing a reasonable limit on the time allowed for presenting evidence, and
10. the possibility of settlement[37]

E. The Trial

Many cases will never reach the trial state. Information obtained during discovery will show the strengths and weaknesses of each party's position and may increase the likelihood of a settlement. In the event that the case does go to trial, the common sequence of events is as follows.

1. Jury Selection

Under the Seventh Amendment to the U.S. Constitution, "in suits at common law, where the value in controversy shall exceed twenty dollars, the right of trial by jury shall be preserved...." This right has been extended through both case law and the Federal Rules of Civil Procedure to include most kinds of federal civil cases. The right to a jury trial in state civil courts is governed by state laws and procedural rules. While states provide for jury trials in many different types of actions, the right to trial by jury may not exist in particular kinds of cases such as suits for dissolution of marriage.

The jury selection process is begun when a number of names are selected usually from the list of registered voters in the place where the case is being heard. While the rules of most states provide that those in certain categories such as parents with small children are exempt from jury duty, all others must appear on the date shown on the notice or they can be held in contempt of court.

On the date indicated in the notice, the members of the jury pool assemble at the courthouse and go with a bailiff to a courtroom when an individual judge is ready to proceed with jury selection. The choosing of a jury for a particular case, known as *voir dire*, will differ somewhat from state to state, but it is likely to begin with a series of questions by the judge. The questions may be directed at a number of people in the jury pool randomly selected to come forward and sit in the jury box, or the questions may be directed at all members of the jury pool. The judge's examination will focus on whether any of the jurors should be eliminated because of unfair prejudice in favor of one side or the other. Such a prejudice might exist, for example, if the juror knew one of the parties or attorneys personally. One might be disqualified from sitting on a jury for many reasons, including prior knowledge of the case or a personal interest in the outcome. An example of the latter situation would be that of a person who owned stock in a company and who had the duty to decide whether dividends had been lawfully issued by the management of that corporation.

A number of states have a procedural rule that is similar to Rule 47(a) of the Federal Rules of Civil Procedure. That rule provides that "[t]he court may permit the parties or their attorneys to conduct the examination of prospective jurors or may itself conduct the examination." In the latter situation, the judge may either allow the attorneys to ask questions after the judge is through, or the judge may ask questions that have been submitted by the attorneys.

If the attorney can convince the court that a potential juror is likely to be biased, the court will dismiss that person for cause. The attorney may also request that a limited number of individual jurors be dismissed without any explanation by the attorney for the rejection. Such a dismissal is known as a *peremptory challenge.* The number of people who can be rejected for cause is unlimited. In contrast, the number of peremptory challenges available will be limited by the procedural rules.

While a jury at common law contained twelve people, the U.S. Constitution does not require a specific number of jurors, and juries composed of six people are used in certain cases in both state and federal courts.

2. *Opening Statements*

Before any evidence is presented, the attorneys for each side have the opportunity to present some of the salient points that they expect to establish during the course of the trial. The attorneys may also choose to address some of the negative aspects of their cases during their opening remarks so that they can minimize any potential damage that may be done by the adverse party during the trial. The plaintiff's attorney has the opportunity to make the first opening statement. The defense attorney then has the option of following the plaintiff with an opening statement or deferring it until after the plaintiff's case has been presented.

3. *Testimony of the Witnesses and the Introduction of Evidence*

Each side will have the chance to present its own witnesses and raise objections to the testimony and evidence presented by opposing counsel. Witnesses who are hesitant to testify at the trial can be compelled to do so by the use of subpoenas.

Objections to testimony may be made on various technical grounds. If the court rules that a statement of a witness should be stricken, the objection will be *sustained,* and the jury will be instructed to ignore the remark. While it may be difficult for the jury to totally ignore a statement that it has heard, the ruling on the objection may be important in the event that the case is subsequently reviewed on appeal. The court may also choose to *overrule* an objection and thereby allow the evidence to be admitted.

Two of the most common objections are relevancy and hearsay. If the argument of *relevancy* is raised, the objecting party is maintaining that the testimony given or evidence presented has no bearing on the determinative issues of the case. The *hearsay* rule prohibits the introduction into court of out-of-court statements used to prove the truth of any matter asserted. To illustrate, John cannot testify in court, for example, that Mary told him that she saw Peter hit David. The primary theory behind prohibiting hearsay evidence in such a case is that Mary, rather than John, should be the appropriate party to testify about what she saw. Even though hearsay evidence is generally inadmissible, there are many exceptions that are recognized by the courts.

Objections are also commonly raised in court when a lay witness attempts to testify as to matters that require an expert opinion or a legal conclusion. In order for one to qualify as an *expert witness*, it need only be shown that the witness has more knowledge in the relevant subject area than that of the average person. Although lay witnesses can in some situations give their opinions in court, the general rule is that they are only to relate the facts as they perceived them. They are prohibited from rendering *legal conclusions* based upon those facts. For example, it would be permissible for a witness to testify that he or she saw the defendant's boat collide with one belonging to the plaintiff, but it would be inappropriate to testify that the defendant was driving the boat "negligently."

Tangible evidence may also be introduced by counsel for either the plaintiff or the defendant. In order to admit such evidence, however, it must be shown to be both relevant and authenticated. *Authentication* requires the attorney to establish that there was an unbroken chain of possession and control of the evidence from when it was first retrieved until the time it was introduced into court, that an accurate record of all those who handled the evidence during that period was kept, and that it was marked during that time for identification. When the evidence to be admitted is a document, rules of evidence generally require that the original must be introduced into court, although there are some exceptions to the rule. Before any tangible evidence can be admitted, a witness must be called to lay a proper foundation for its introduction.

In any civil trial, the plaintiff has the burden of proving that the defendant is responsible. It is not the responsibility of the defendant to prove the absence of liability. Nevertheless the defense often chooses to introduce affirmative evidence to refute the case presented by the plaintiff. The plaintiff has the obligation to prove the case by a *preponderance of the evidence,* which means that the plaintiff must prove that it is at least somewhat more likely that the defendant is responsible than that the defendant is not responsible. This burden of proof is a significantly lower burden than the one imposed in criminal cases, in which the prosecutor must prove the government's case beyond a reasonable doubt.

While trials will differ from state to state, the following is a typical sequence of events.

a. The questioning of each of the plaintiff's witnesses.

(1) *Direct examination.* After the jury is empaneled, the plaintiff's attorney will have the first opportunity to present testimony and evidence.

When the first witness is sworn in, the plaintiff's attorney will begin *direct examination,* which means that the attorney will have the opportunity to question the plaintiff's own witness. During direct examination, it is improper for the attorney to ask *leading questions* of those who are neither hostile nor expert witnesses. Leading questions are those which have been phrased to elicit a particular response. For example, it would be improper to ask a question such as "Isn't it true that Bill was standing about 75 feet from the accident?"

(2) *Cross-examination.* Following direct examination, the defense attorney has the opportunity to question the plaintiff's witness by *cross-examination.* During cross-examination, leading questions are generally regarded as permissible. One of the primary purposes of cross-examination is to *impeach* the witness by questioning the truthfulness of the witness's statements. This may involve questioning the witness's intent to tell the truth or the witness's ability to give accurate information based upon personal knowledge. Questions asked by the defense attorney during cross-examination must remain within the scope of the subjects brought up by the plaintiff's attorney on the direct examination.

(3) *Redirect examination.* During *redirect examination,* the plaintiff's attorney has an opportunity to ask questions after cross-examination in order to reestablish the credibility of the witness. Such an inquiry is limited in scope to the subject matter brought up by the defense attorney on cross-examination.

(4) *Recross examination.* The defense attorney will have the opportunity to follow the redirect examination by the plaintiff's attorney by asking further questions of the witness, but the attorney will generally be limited in scope to the subject matters previously addressed.

The sequence of events just described will be followed for each of the plaintiff's subsequent witnesses.

b. A motion for directed verdict by the defense attorney. When all the plaintiff's witnesses have testified, it is customary for the defense attorney to move for a directed verdict in favor of the defendant. This motion requests the court to rule in favor of the defendant on the grounds that the opposing party has failed to present at least some evidence to support every element of the cause of action. The purpose of the motion is to test the sufficiency of evidence as viewed in a light most favorable to the plaintiff. The granting of such a motion has the effect of taking the case away from the jury (when the case is being heard by a jury), so often the motion will be denied and the defense will be directed to proceed with its witnesses and evidence. This is because of the policy of the law favoring the resolution of a case only after a full discussion of its merits.

c. *The questioning of each of the defendant's witnesses.*

(1) *Direct examination.* Assuming the motion for directed verdict is denied, the defense attorney may then present witnesses to refute the statements made by the plaintiff's witnesses. The defense attorney will begin with a direct examination of his or her own witness. Just as in the case of the plaintiff's direct examination when the plaintiff's attorney was questioning his or her own witnesses, leading questions are regarded as improper unless the one testifying is a hostile or expert witness.

(2) *Cross-examination.* The plaintiff's attorney will have the chance to cross-examine the defendant's witnesses just as the defendant's attorney had the opportunity to question the plaintiff's witnesses. Leading questions are permissible, but the plaintiff's counsel must stay within the scope of the defense attorney's direct examination.

(3) *Redirect examination.* Redirect examination follows the same basic format for that of redirect examination by the plaintiff's attorney of the plaintiff's own witnesses. Again, the scope of redirect examination will be limited to subjects covered during cross-examination.

(4) *Recross examination.* The plaintiff's attorney will have the opportunity to follow the redirect examination by the defendant's attorney by asking further questions of the witness, but the attorney will generally be limited in scope to the subject matters previously addressed.

The sequence of events described in subsection E.3.c of this section will be followed for each of the defendant's subsequent witnesses.

d. *Renewal of the defense's motion for a directed verdict.*   At the close of the defendant's case, the defendant's attorney may renew his or her motion for a directed verdict (see subsection E.3.b above). For the reasons previously discussed, the motion is often denied.

e. *Presentation of further witnesses.*

(1) *Rebuttal.* If new matters were presented during the defendant's case that the plaintiff's attorney did not have reason to anticipate or expect, the plaintiff may be permitted to either recall former witnesses or call new witnesses to rebut the arguments by the defense.

(2) *Surrebuttal.* If rebuttal witnesses have been presented by the plaintiff's attorney, the defendant's attorney may be provided with an opportunity, known as *surrebuttal,* to counter the arguments raised during the rebuttal. Any matters raised by the defense at this time will be limited to the scope of the rebuttal evidence.

4. Closing Arguments

During closing arguments, each attorney has the chance to address the finder of fact, who will be the jury in a jury trial or the judge in a nonjury trial. The plaintiff's attorney has the opportunity to speak first since the plaintiff has the burden of proof in every civil case. The defense attorney will then follow with the closing remarks.

5. Jury Instructions

After closing arguments, the court will instruct the jury as to the applicable law in the case. The judge usually reads from a standard list of jury instructions, although instructions can be added to the standard ones upon request of counsel.

6. Jury Deliberations, the Verdict, and the Judgment

Once the jury retires, its deliberations are held in absolute secrecy. The jury's first responsibility is to select a *foreperson.* The foreperson is the one who addresses the court on behalf of the jury and delivers the verdict to the court.

The jury's primary function in a civil case is to decide in favor of the plaintiff or the defendant. If the jury finds in favor of a party claiming damages, it will also have the responsibility of determining the amount of damages to be awarded. Some states provide for separate hearings on the questions of liability and the amount of damages. Verdicts in most states and in most kinds of cases must be unanimous.

Once the jury has rendered its verdict, the court must then enter a formal judgment. It is common for a judgment to include a recitation of the court's claim of jurisdiction over the parties and the subject matter. While it is signed by the judge, it is usually prepared by the office of the attorney for the prevailing party. If a judgment for damages is entered against a party, the claimant has several options after the judgment is issued, such as garnishment or attachment. *Garnishment* involves the right of a *judgment creditor*[38] to seize a portion of the debtor's paycheck to pay off the judgment. *Attachment* of a judgment debtor's bank account allows the judgment creditor to freeze amounts in the debtor's account and seize funds from it.

7. *Motions in Anticipation of Appeal*

After a verdict is rendered, it is customary for the losing party to automatically file two motions to preserve rights that the party may have on appeal. The first is known as a *motion for a new trial* and is usually based upon the premise that there has been a substantial error in procedure that has made the outcome unfair. The second is referred to as a *motion for a judgment notwithstanding the verdict, a motion for a judgment non obstante veredicto,* or a *motion for a judgment N.O.V.* This motion requests the court to overrule the verdict of the jury on the grounds that there was insufficient evidence as a matter of law to support that verdict.

REVIEW QUESTIONS

1. Lester sues Barber and Kendricks. Barber claims that Kendricks is responsible for the harm that Lester has suffered. How would you describe Barber's claim against Kendricks?

2. Brandy sues Fenwick, Piston, and Graves. Piston claims that Aldonmaker is responsible for the harm that Brandy has suffered. How would you describe Piston's claim against Aldonmaker?

3. If you were served today with a complaint governed by the rules of civil procedure for your state, what would be the last date that you would have to file an answer?

4. Reston sues Barney, Mendel, and Simms. How many different original summonses must be prepared by Reston?

5. Korden files a cause of action against Sabin in a case requiring personal service of process, but the process server is unable to serve the papers on the defendant at the listed address. What are the legal ramifications if service of process is never achieved? What is the appropriate procedure for Korden to follow if he learns of an alternative address where the defendant may be located?

6. Janeway and Packer become involved in a fist fight and both parties are injured. Janeway brings a cause of action against Packer for damages due to the injuries he sustained. If Packer wishes to file a claim against Janeway, is it permissible for him to do so in his answer to Janeway's complaint? If so, is it mandatory that he either raise the issue at this time or waive it?

7. Prepare a complaint, summons, and answer based upon the following fictitious information. Use the samples and form provided in the book. The complaint should claim damages and injuries similar to those claimed in

the sample. The answer should admit the fundamental facts surrounding the automobile collision, but is should deny any negligence on the part of the defendant and demand strict proof of all damages and injuries sustained. It should also include the seat belt defense. Assume that the case was filed in your state with its own court system and jurisdictional limits.

Harold Lane files suit against Phyllis Jenko on March 11, 1997, for injuries and damages sustained in an automobile collision that took place on December 8, 1996. Both Lane and Jenko were the operators as well as the owners of their own vehicles at the time of the accident. The collision took place on the corner of Simons Street and Collins Avenue in the city of Oakland in your state. Lane maintains that his injuries were due entirely to the negligence of the defendant and that the injuries are permanent in nature. The plaintiff demands that the case be heard before a jury, and the defendant also demands a jury trial in her answer. Lane's attorney, Matthew Cortez of 1324 35th Avenue, Turlington, [your state and zip code] is filing the case in the appropriate court in the judicial circuit, court, county, and state where you live. Cortez' telephone number is (205) 555-5555. Jenko is represented by Martha Blackwell, who has an address of 220 Wellington Park Blvd., Suite 245 in the city of Oakland, [your state and zip code] and a telephone number of (205) 555-4671. The correct court in which to file should be evident by the fact that the plaintiff intends to demand more than $100,000 in damages, although he is not sure of the amount. The Bar number for Cortez is #2538946, and the one for Blackwell is #4239065. Assume for the purposes of this assignment that the case number assigned to the case (97-88942) has already been included on the complaint, the summons, and the answer. The answer is filed by Blackwell on March 24, 1997. The defendant is to be served at her home located at 21 Begley Circle in the city of Oakland, [your state and zip code].

8. Prepare a motion for default, and default to be submitted to the clerk's office based on the following fictitious information. Use the form provided in the book.

Mary Utley has filed suit against Debra Wescot in the appropriate court in your judicial circuit, county, and state. The correct court in which to file should be evident by the fact that the plaintiff demanded more than $100,000 in damages in the original complaint. The plaintiff's attorney is Paul Hart of Hart and Hart, P.A., and he has an address of 44 Cypress Drive, Rollings, [your state and zip code] and a telephone number of (567) 555-1928. The defendant's attorney is Kelly Hathaway, who has an address of 512 24th Avenue, Fort Halverson, [your state and zip code] and a telephone number of (567) 555-4444. The case number is 98-77487. Hart's Bar number is #3721586 and Hathaway's Bar number is #9123567. When the motion is hand-delivered to the clerk's office on January 9, 1999, it is immediately signed by Deputy Clerk Karen Valish.

9. Prepare a final judgment to be submitted to the judge based on the following fictitious information. Use the form provided in the book.

> This order, which is dated March 17, 1999, and which is based on a default, pertains to a suit filed by Doris Hardy against Ronald Deal in the appropriate court in your judicial circuit, city, county, and state. The correct court in which to file should be evident by the fact that the plaintiff demanded more than $100,000 in damages in the original complaint. The plaintiff's attorney is Steven Young, who has an address of 1984 Lakeview Drive, Mount Pleasant, [your state and zip code]. The defendant's attorney is Mary Thorison, who has an address of 481 Downey Road, St. Stevens, [your state and zip code]. The case number is 99-58531. The judgment is in the amount of $8,766.54 plus an additional $892.36 in interest, $1,575 in attorneys fees, and costs in the amount of $347.75. All these amounts are to bear interest at the legal rate until paid in full.

10. Prepare a cross-claim based on the following fictitious information. Use the sample form provided in the book.

> Spencer Martz filed a suit against Patricia Hodgekin and Marla West on October 31, 1999. West then filed a cross-claim on November 12, 1999, against Hodgekin for damages and injuries. The cross-claim should claim damages and injuries similar to those claimed in the sample found in the text. The case number is 99-33192. The case, which asks for damages well over $100,000, is being heard in the appropriate court in your judicial circuit, county, and state. The vehicles owned and operated by the two defendants collided at the intersection of Grover Boulevard and 22nd Avenue in Talton, [your state and zip code] on January 14, 1999. Martz was a passenger in Hodgekin's car. A demand for jury trial is included in the cross-claim. Martz is represented by Louis Montoya, who has an address of 722 Military Road, Rockway, [your state and zip code] and a telephone number of (299) 555-4680. West is represented by Caroline Fister, who has an address of 37 Sofia Street, Rockway, [your state and zip code] and a telephone number of (299) 555-6300. Her Bar number is #718234. Assume that the rule of comparative negligence applies in your state.

11. Prepare a subpoena duces tecum for trial based on the following fictitious information. Use the form provided in the book.

> This involves a suit by Roger Wallace against Melissa DeRosa in the appropriate court, judicial circuit, county, and state where you live. The case number is 97-53525 and the matter is to be heard before Judge Susan Wilson. Wallace is represented by Julia Cox, who has an address of 41 Maplewood Lane, Windsor, [your state and zip code]. The subpoena is needed by Cox in order to compel John Carlisle, presently of 982 40th Way, Marketville, [your state and zip code] to appear in court on April 5, 1997, at 9:00 A.M. At the trial, Carlisle is to have with him the ledger books

showing all receipts and expenditures for the ABC sole proprietorship owned and operated by Carlisle for the year 1989. Cox's Bar number is #7173629 and her telephone number is (497) 555-8000. The subpoena Deputy Clerk Daniel Evers on March 28, 1997.

FOOTNOTES

nall claims actions are sometimes referred to as the Rules of Summary

itial document may also be referred to in different states as a petition, a demand. All future references in this chapter to the complaint should be erms.

[11]FED. R. CIV. P. 8(b)

[12]FED. R. CIV. P. 8(b)

[13]FED. R. CIV. P. 12(a)

[14]FED. R. CIV. P. 6(e)

[15]FED. R. CIV. P. 12(a)(1)(B)

[16]FED. R. CIV. P. 4(d)

[17]FED. R. CIV. P. 4(d)

[18]FED. R. CIV. P. 6(a)

[19]FED. R. CIV. P. 38(b)

[20]FED. R. CIV. P. 8(c)

[21]FED. R. CIV. P. 15(a)

[22]FED. R. CIV. P. 13(a) continues to make the qualification that such claims will be compulsory as long as they do "not require for [their] adjudication the presence of third parties of whom the court cannot acquire jurisdiction."

[23]FED. R. CIV. P. 13(b)

[24]FED. R. CIV. P. 13(g)

[25]FED. R. CIV. P. 14(a)

[26]FED. R. CIV. P. 14(b)

[27]FED. R. CIV. P. 12(b)

[28]FED. R. CIV. P. 12(d)

[29]FED. R. CIV. P. 12(f)

[30]Fed. R. Civ. P. 12(f)

[31]Fed. R. Civ. P. 45(f)

[32]According to Fed. R. Civ. P. 41(a)(1), the dismissal will not be without prejudice if the party has already dismissed the case once before in the past.

[33]Fed. R. Civ. P. 41(a)(1)

[34]Fed. R. Civ. P. 41(a)(2)

[35]Fed. R. Civ. P. 41(b)

[36]Fed. R. Civ. P. 41(c)

[37]This is only a partial list of the subjects for consideration at a pretrial conference under the federal rules. For a complete list of appropriate matters for discussion at these meetings in the federal courts, see Fed. R. Civ. P. 16(c). State rules of civil procedure may, of course, include different matters for consideration and discussion at these conferences.

[38]A judgment creditor is a party to whom money is owed as a result of judgment by a court.

8 *Civil Discovery*

CHAPTER OVERVIEW

(3) Any exhibits to be used

(4) The qualifications of the witness

(5) The compensation to be paid for the study and testimony

(6) A listing of all other cases in which the expert has testified

b. The time frame for filing the report

c. Experts not expected to testify

C. A Scheduling Conference Followed by the Entry of a Scheduling Order Setting Limitations as to Various Matters

1. The Time to Join Other Parties and to Amend the Pleadings

2. The Time to File Motions

3. The Time to Complete Discovery

D. Additional Required Disclosures

1. Names, Addresses, and Telephone Numbers of Potential Witnesses at Trial

2. Identification of the Testimony That Will Be Presented by the Use of Depositions

3. Identification of Potential Exhibits

8-5 Forms of Discovery

A. Depositions

1. Definition and Elements

a. Oral questioning

b. Opportunity for cross-examination

c. Before the trial or hearing

d. Party or witness

e. Under oath

f. Customarily in the presence of a court reporter

2. When Depositions May Be Taken

3. Documents and Other Requirements Necessary for Setting Depositions

a. Preparation of a notice of taking deposition

b. Preparation of a subpoena for deposition

(1) The consequences of failure to attend

(a) By the deponent

(b) By the one setting the deposition

(2) The necessity of a subpoena when the deponent is a party

(3) The use of a subpoena duces tecum for deposition

c. Preparation of a witness fee check

d. Preparation of a service of process check

e. Arranging for the presence of a court reporter

4. Procedure at Depositions

5. Transcription of Depositions

6. The Use of Depositions in Court

a. Purposes for using depositions in court

(1) Impeachment

(2) Death of a witness

(3) Excessive traveling distance for the witness

(4) Age, illness, infirmity, or imprisonment of the witness

(5) Exceptional circumstances

   b. Partial use of depositions

   c. Objections to admissibility

B. Interrogatories

  1. Definition and Elements

   a. Written questions

   b. To be answered under oath

   c. Written answers

   d. Usually restricted to opposing parties only

  2. When Interrogatories May Be Served

  3. How many Questions May Be Served

  4. Objections to Interrogatories

  5. The Maximum Time Allotted for a Response

  6. General Procedure

  7. Requests to Produce Business Records

  8. Use of Interrogatories in Court

C. Production of Documents and Things and Entry Upon Land for Inspection and Other Purposes

  1. When the Request May Be Served

  2. Time Within Which to Respond

  3. Information that Must Be Included in the Response

  4. Requests Possible on Nonparties

D. Physical and Mental Examinations

  1. Who Must Submit to Mental and Physical Examinations

  2. A Request by the Person Being Examined to See the Physician's Report

   a. The right of the person causing the examination to see similar reports

E. Requests for Admission

  1. Definition

  2. Applicable to Parties Only

  3. When Requests for Admission May Be Sent

  4. The Maximum Time Allotted for a Response

  5. Partial Admission or Denial

  6. Responses Indicating Lack of Knowledge

  7. Failure to Respond

  8. The Effect of an Admission

8-6 The Frequency with Which Discovery Tools May Be Used

8-7 The Duty to Supplement Discovery

8-8 Sanctions for Failure to Cooperate with Discovery

A. Certain Facts May Be Taken as Established

B. Certain Claims, Defenses, or Evidence May Be Disallowed

C. Pleadings May Be Stricken, Proceedings May Be Stayed, or There May Be a Dismissal or Default

D. An Order of Contempt of Court May Be Issued

E. Attorneys Fees and Costs May Be Incurred

SEC. 8-1
IN GENERAL

A variety of methods are available to attorneys for discovering facts and information prior to the trial or final hearing. These methods, which are collectively referred to as *discovery,* are usually addressed in the federal and state rules of civil procedure. Examples of discovery are the opportunities that a party has to question a witness or other party under oath prior to the trial or final hearing, or to obtain the production of evidence from the other party by motion.

Discovery procedures in federal civil actions are governed by the Federal Rules of Civil Procedure (FED. R. CIV. P.) regardless of the state in which the court is located, while state court discovery procedures are governed by state court rules and statutes and may therefore differ from state to state. The discussion in this chapter is based on the federal rules not only because they apply in the federal courts, but also because they serve as a model for the procedural rules of many states. The rules are quoted verbatim only when the wording appears with quotation marks. Because the rules of any particular state may differ somewhat from the federal ones, it is imperative that readers become familiar with the discovery procedures of their own states.

SEC. 8-2
THE PURPOSES OF DISCOVERY

The process of discovery serves three primary purposes.

A.   *To Determine the Existence and Location of Evidence*

An attorney may have difficulty knowing where to look for specific tangible evidence without compelling a witness to testify under oath with regard to the matter or divulge the information through some other form of discovery.

B.   *To Obtain Evidence*

When an attorney knows, for example, that the contents of a document are critical to the success of the case, the attorney may need to be able to force the other party to produce the document.

C.   *To Clarify the Primary Issues in the Case*

It is important for an attorney to know the nature of the opposition's case in order to adequately prepare a client's case. If issues can be narrowed and defined before the trial begins, both sides will have the opportunity to concentrate on matters that are truly contested. Furthermore, after each party sees the relative strengths and weaknesses of the other party's positions, the possibilities of settlement may be substantially increased.

SEC. 8-3
THE SCOPE OF DISCOVERY

As a general rule, "… parties may obtain discovery regarding any matter, not privileged, which is relevant to the subject matter involved in the pending action, whether it relates to the claim or defense of the party seeking discovery or to the claim or defense of any other party, including the existence, description, nature, custody, condition, and location of any books, documents, or other tangible things and the identity and location of persons having knowledge of any discoverable matter … The information sought need not be admissible at the trial if the information sought appears reasonably calculated to lead to the discovery of admissible evidence."[1] In light of this evidentiary rule, it can be seen that the scope of discovery is extremely broad, although there are some important exceptions. Anyone who claims that information is privileged and therefore not subject to discovery has the responsibility to prove the existence of that privilege.

A. Information Not Generally Subject to Discovery

1. Information Lacking in Relevance

Both federal and state procedural rules clearly indicate that the information sought must be relevant to the pending case. The one claiming that the evidence is irrelevant and therefore not subject to discovery has the burden of establishing that irrelevance. Since the scope of inquiry is so broad, an attorney might use discovery procedures to ask one witness for the names of other people who may have been witnesses, so that they might also be questioned. "The information sought need not be admissible at the trial if the information sought appears reasonably calculated to lead to the discovery of admissible evidence."[2]

2. "Work Product"

Documents and tangible things "prepared in anticipation of litigation or for trial by or by another party or by or for that other party's representative" are referred to as *work products,* and they cannot be obtained by the other side in the case without a showing of substantial need for the materials in the preparation of the case and an inability to obtain the materials or their equivalent by other means.[3] Even when the court is convinced that such materials must be turned over, "the court will protect against disclosure of the mental impressions, conclusions, opinions, or legal theories of an attorney or other representative of a party concerning the litigation."[4] Materials considered to be the work product of an attorney are generally protected to give the attorneys an opportunity to prepare their cases independently, and to do so without giving to the other side the automatic benefit of their work. Documents and tangible evidence falling within the work product category may include materials prepared not only by attorneys, but also by private investigators and other agents of an attorney, provided that the work was done in anticipation of the litigation.

3. *Testimony of Experts Who Will Not Be Called as Witnesses*

Some experts are employed by a party purely for assistance in trial preparation and are not expected to testify. The other party may not generally obtain the expert's opinions through interrogatories or depositions except upon a showing of extraordinary circumstances.[5] Even when the court can be convinced that such extraordinary circumstances exist (which is uncommon), the party seeking discovery will be required "to pay the other party a fair portion of the fees and expenses reasonably incurred by the latter party in obtaining facts and opinions from the expert."[6]

In addition to the preceding exemptions, the court has the option of protecting a person from "annoyance, embarrassment, oppression, or undue burden or expense...."[7] by issuing an order limiting the discovery.

SEC. 8-4
AN ORGANIZED PLAN OF DISCOVERY

The federal and state rules may each provide for different ways of using all of the discovery tools, including the five discussed in Sec. 8-5. The federal approach is fairly methodical, and it follows the general outline that follows.

A. *The Meeting of the Attorneys to Plan for Discovery*

Under the federal rules, the parties or their representatives are required to meet as soon as is practicable "to discuss the nature and basis of their claims and defenses and the possibilities for a prompt settlement or resolution of the case, to make or arrange for initial disclosures ..., and to develop a proposed discovery plan."[8] The plan must include among other things when initial information that each party is entitled to (see subsection B below) either has been turned over to the other side or when it will be turned over, and "the subjects on which discovery may be needed, when discovery should be completed, and whether discovery should be conducted in phases or be limited to or focused upon particular issues."[9] A written copy of the proposed discovery plan must be submitted to the court within 10 days after the meeting.[10]

The attorneys may not generally seek discovery before this meeting takes place.[11]

B. *Information That Must Be Disclosed Without Request*

In the federal system, there is specific information that must be disclosed to the other side within 10 days after the planning meeting even in the absence of a discovery request. It includes:

1. *In General*

a. Names, addresses, and telephone numbers of each individual likely to have discoverable information …

b. Copies of documents and tangible evidence or a description by category and location of, all documents, data compilations, and tangible things in the possession, custody, or control of the party …

c. A computation of any category of damages claimed by the disclosing party, making available for inspection and copying … the documents or other evidentiary material, not privileged or protected from disclosure, on which such computation is based, including materials bearing on the nature and extent of injuries suffered; and

d. Insurance agreements for inspection and copying under which any person carrying on an insurance business may be liable to satisfy part or all of a judgment …[12]

2. *Expert Testimony*

In addition to these disclosure requirements, any party who may be calling an expert witness must reveal the expert's identity and submit a report concerning the expert to the opposing attorney.

a. Contents of the report when experts may testify.   With some qualifications, the report must include:

(1) *A complete statement of the expert's opinions,*

(2) *The information considered by the witness,*

(3) *Any exhibits to be used,*

(4) *The qualifications of the witness,*

(5) *The compensation to be paid for the study and testimony,* and

(6) *A listing of all other cases in which the expert has testified.*[13]

Depositions of experts are not generally permitted until after the report is provided.[14]

b. The time frame for filing the report.   The preceding disclosures must be made "at least 90 days before the trial date or the date the case is to be ready for trial or, if the evidence is intended solely to contradict or rebut evidence on the same subject matter identified by another party … within 30 days after the disclosure made by the other party."[15]

c. Experts not expected to testify.   When an expert is not expected to testify and has been employed by a party purely for trial preparation, the other party may not generally obtain the expert's opinions through interrogatories or depositions except upon a showing of extraordinary circumstances.[16] Even when the court can be convinced that such extraordinary circumstances exist (which is uncommon), the party seeking discovery will be required "to pay the other party a fair portion of the fees and expenses reasonably incurred by the latter party in obtaining facts and opinions from the expert."[17]

C. *A Scheduling Conference Followed by the Entry of a Scheduling Order[18] Setting Limitations as to Various Matters*

Once the court has received the discovery plan submitted by the parties, the court issues an order "that limits:

1. *The Time to Join Other Parties and to Amend the Pleadings*

2. *The Time to File Motions*

3. *The Time to Complete Discovery"[19]*

The order may also address other issues such as the date or dates for conferences before trial, a final pretrial conference, and trial …"[20] The order has to be issued "within 90 days after the appearance of the defendant and within 120 days after the complaint has been served on a defendant."[21]

D. Additional Required Disclosures

At least 30 days before trial, each party has the obligation to provide the other with the following information that it may present at trial for other than impeachment[22] purposes:

1. *Names, Addresses, and Telephone Numbers of Potential Witnesses at Trial*

2. *Identification of the Testimony That Will Be Presented by the Use of Depositions*

3. *Identification of Potential Exhibits*[23]

SEC. 8-5
FORMS OF DISCOVERY

Under the federal rules, various discovery options are available, including: "… depositions upon oral examination or written questions; written interrogatories; production of documents or things or permission to enter upon land or other property … for inspection and other purposes; physical and mental examinations; and requests for admission."[24]

A. Depositions

1. Definition and Elements

A *deposition* is the oral questioning (with an opportunity for cross-examination) before trial or hearing of a party or witness under oath and usually in the presence of a court reporter. The court reporter is in attendance both to administer the oath if qualified to do so in the jurisdiction and to take the testimony of the party or witness so that the testimony may be reduced to writing if requested.

If, for example, an attorney wishes to question a particular witness about the incident that forms the basis for the suit, the attorney may compel that witness to appear at a particular location (often an attorney's or court reporter's office) to answer questions under oath about the incident. The person giving the testimony is referred to as a *deponent.* The information obtained at that inquiry may be helpful not only in preparing for trial, but also in getting a clearer understanding of the other party's case.

There are several key elements to the definition of a deposition. Those elements are included in the following discussion.

a. Oral questioning. The term "deposition" usually refers to situations in which oral questions are being asked and oral answers are being given. The term, however, can also refer to situations in which written questions are read to the party or witness in order to obtain oral responses.

b. Opportunity for cross-examination. Attorneys representing each of the parties are normally given a chance to cross-examine the deponent.

c. Before the trial or hearing. While rules often provide for an opportunity to take the deposition of a person prior to the filing of an actual suit in order to perpetuate testimony, most depositions are taken after the commencement of the suit but before the actual trial or hearing.

d. Party or witness. Depositions can be taken from virtually anyone having information relevant to the case. Therefore, in federal and most state courts, each party has the opportunity to question opposing parties as well as witnesses.

e. Under oath. Generally, the oath is administered by "an officer authorized to administer oaths by the laws of the United States or of the place where the examination is held, or before a person appointed by the court in which the action is pending."[25] State statutes may provide that depositions may be taken before other kinds of individuals such as clerks of the court and notary publics. It is not uncommon for a court reporter to become a notary public in those jurisdictions in which depositions can be taken before notaries. In any event, the one before whom the deposition is taken must generally have an impartial status with regard to the case.

f. Customarily in the presence of a court reporter. Since depositions are taken to assist in case preparation, a court reporter is usually present to record the testimony, although procedural rules often provide for the possibility of recordation of testimony by other means. The attorney arranging for the deposition will have to contact the court reporter's office and verify that a court reporter will be available on the chosen date.

2. When Depositions May Be Taken

Permission to take a deposition is not generally required, although there are exceptions to the rule such as when (1) the person to be deposed is in prison, (2) it would result in more than 10 depositions being taken by the plaintiffs, by the defendants, or by third-party defendants, (3) the person has already been deposed, or (4) the party is attempting to take the deposition prior to the scheduling conference among the attorneys unless the person to be questioned is expected to leave the country.[26]

3. *Documents and Other Requirements Necessary for Setting Depositions*

a. Preparation of a notice of taking deposition.   The purpose of a *notice of taking deposition* is for one party to notify all other parties to the action that a deposition has been scheduled. "The notice shall state the time and place for taking the deposition and the name and address of each person to be examined ... If a subpoena duces tecum is to be served on the person to be examined, the designation of the materials to be produced as set forth in the subpoena shall be attached to or included in the notice."[27] (For a definition of the term "subpoena duces tecum for deposition," please see subsection 3.b.3 below.)

Blank forms for a Notice of Taking Deposition are available in all law offices that handle civil matters. The notice is generally addressed to the opposing counsel and will have the same format as all other civil pleadings. An example of a notice of taking deposition can be seen in Figure 8-1. The notice must usually be sent to every other party to the action.

b. Preparation of a subpoena for deposition.   A *subpoena for deposition* is required to compel the attendance of a witness. Like a notice of taking deposition, it has the same format of ordinary civil pleadings. When preparing a subpoena for deposition, it is imperative that a "Subpoena for Deposition" form be used rather than one labeled only as "Subpoena." A subpoena that does not include the words "for Deposition" in its title is used to compel the attendance of witnesses at trial or hearing rather than at a deposition.

(1) *The consequences of failure to attend.*

    (a) By the deponent. If a subpoena is served on a witness who fails to appear, the witness can face disciplinary action such as a contempt citation by the court. See Sec. 8-8 for a more detailed discussion of some of the options available to the court. On the other hand, if the witness agrees to attend without service of a subpoena, and the attorney therefore does not have the subpoena issued, the attorney may have little recourse against the witness who did not show up for the deposition.

    (b) By the one setting the deposition. "If the party giving the notice of the taking of a deposition fails to attend and proceed therewith and another party attends in person or by attorney pursuant to the notice, the court may order the party giving the notice to pay to such other party the reasonable expenses incurred by that party and that party's attorney in attending, including reasonable attorney's fees."[28]

(2) *The necessity of a subpoena when the deponent is a party.* A subpoena may not be required in some jurisdictions if an opposing party, rather than

IN THE **CIRCUIT** COURT OF THE **17TH** JUDICIAL CIRCUIT
IN AND FOR **BROWARD** COUNTY, STATE OF **FLORIDA**

Case No: 97-58273

Fla. Bar #987654

WILLIE L. SANDERS,   )
)
     Plaintiff,   )
)
v.   )
)
JOHN M. MARINO and   )
DAVID R. ROBINSON,   )
)
     Defendants.   )

This form is designed for
instruction, and not for use
in all jurisdictions.

NOTICE OF TAKING DEPOSITION

TO: Mr. William Benlow
      Benlow and Sheen
      326 61st Avenue
      Pleasantville, FL 33019

YOU, AS ATTORNEY for **defendant DAVID R. ROBINSON**, are hereby notified that **starting at 2:00 P.M.** on the 12th day of **December**, 1997, at **the Law offices of Bishop and Zubin, 4317 Weston Road, Fairwood**, in the County of **Broward** and the State of **Florida**, the plaintiff's attorney, in the above-styled cause will take the deposition by oral examination for purposes of discovery and for use as evidence in said cause, or both, of

          2:00 Karl O'Shea
          2:45 Linda Goldstein

SAID DEPOSITION will be taken before **Carla Norris**, a Notary Public, or any officer authorized to administer oaths by the laws of the jurisdiction, and a person who is neither a relative, nor employee, nor attorney, nor counsel of any of the parties and who is neither a relative nor employee of such attorney or counsel, and who is not financially interested in the action.

Said deposition to be taken pursuant to the State Rules of Civil Procedure in such cases. The said oral examination will continue from hour to hour and from day to day until completed.

I HEREBY CERTIFY that a copy of the above notice was furnished to the above-named addressee(s) by mail on this, the **29th** day of **November**, 1997.

                Harold Bishop
                Plaintiff's Attorney
                Harold Bishop
                Bishop and Zubin
                4317 Weston Road
                Fairwood, FL 33318
                (999) 432-8612

FIGURE 8-1

234

a witness, is to be deposed. It is often customary to arrange for the deposition of an opposing party by contacting the party's attorney and setting a time that is convenient for the attorneys and the deponent.

(3) *The use of a subpoena duces tecum for deposition.* A form known as a *subpoena duces tecum for deposition* must be used if the witness is to bring documents and tangible things to the deposition. It is similar in format to a regular subpoena for deposition except that it includes a command to bring specified documents or tangible evidence to the deposition. This special subpoena would be appropriate, for example, if the deponent is a bookkeeper and is expected to answer detailed questions requiring referral to corporate financial records.

Examples of a subpoena for deposition and a subpoena duces tecum for deposition can be seen in Figures 8-2 and 8-3.

c. Preparation of a witness fee check.   Most state rules provide that a subpoena must be accompanied by a check that compensates the witnesses for the mileage traveled to the deposition. The amount of the check will depend upon the distance traveled. Charts indicating the amount that must be paid to witnesses traveling from various locations to other locations are available at law offices handling civil litigation. While the check amounts are usually very small, the witness may not be compelled to attend the deposition in the states that provide for this fee unless the check has been included.

d. Preparation of a service of process check.   Subpoenas are served in a manner similar to that for summonses, and a check must therefore be prepared to compensate the process server for services rendered.

e. Arranging for the presence of a court reporter.   The court reporter's office will have to be contacted to verify that the date and time chosen for the deposition is one that is available for a court reporter from that office.

4.   Procedure at Depositions

At a deposition, the deponent is first sworn in. The attorney who arranged for the deposition then asks questions of the deponent as would be asked at trial. It is permissible for a deponent to respond to a question by indicating a lack of knowledge of the matter as long as the response is made in good faith. Opposing counsel have the opportunity to both raise objections and cross-examine the deponent. Any objections raised during the deposition must be noted by the officer, but since a judge is not usually present at a deposition, all objections must be dealt with at subsequent court hearings.

IN THE **CIRCUIT** COURT OF THE **17TH** JUDICIAL CIRCUIT
IN AND FOR **BROWARD** COUNTY, STATE OF **FLORIDA**

Case No: 97-58273

Fla. Bar #987654

WILLIE L. SANDERS,   )
)
         Plaintiff,   )
)   *This form is designed for*
v.   )   *instruction, and* <u>*not*</u> *for use*
)   *in all jurisdictions.*
JOHN M. MARINO and   )
DAVID R. ROBINSON,   )   TIME:
)
         Defendants.   )   DATE:
_____   )
                                                 SERVER:

SUBPOENA FOR DEPOSITION

THE STATE OF FLORIDA;

TO: **Mr. Karl O'Shea**
    1118 Lakeshore Drive
    Fort Lauderdale, FL 33318

YOU ARE COMMANDED to appear before a person authorized by law to take depositions at **the Law offices of Bishop and Zubin, 4317 Weston Road, Fairwood**, in the County of **Broward** and the State of **Florida**, on the **12th** day of **December, 1997**, at **2:00 P.M.** for the taking of your deposition in this action. If you fail to appear, you may be in contempt of court.

You are subpoenaed to appear by the following attorneys, and unless excused from this subpoena by these attorneys or the court, you shall respond to this subpoena as directed.

Harold Bishop
Plaintiff's Attorney
Harold Bishop
Bishop and Zubin
4317 Weston Road
Fairwood, FL 33318
(999) 432-8612

DATED this **29th** day of **November, 1997**.

                                        Clyde Clerk
                        (Seal)   As Clerk of the Court

                                        By: *Sandra Siegel*
                                        As Deputy Clerk

FIGURE 8-2

IN THE **CIRCUIT** COURT OF THE **17TH** JUDICIAL CIRCUIT
IN AND FOR **BROWARD** COUNTY, STATE OF **FLORIDA**

Case No: 97-58273

Fla. Bar #987654

WILLIE L. SANDERS,)
)
    Plaintiff,)
)
v.   )
)
JOHN M. MARINO and)
DAVID R. ROBINSON,)
)
    Defendants.)
_____)

This form is designed for instruction, and <u>not</u> for use in all jurisdictions.

TIME:

DATE:

SERVER:

SUBPOENA DUCES TECUM FOR DEPOSITION

THE STATE OF FLORIDA:

TO: Linda Goldstein
    15 Parson Lane
    Plantation, FL 33033

YOU ARE COMMANDED to appear before a person authorized by law to take depositions at **the Law offices of Bishop and Zubin, 4317 Weston Road, Fairwood,** in the County of **Broward** and the State of **Florida** on the 12th day of **December, 1997,** at **2:45 P.M.** for the taking of your deposition in this action and to have with you at the time and place the following:

             the ledger books of the Armcon
             sole proprietorship for 1995.

If you fail to appear, you may be in contempt of court.

YOU ARE SUBPOENAED to appear by the following attorneys, and unless excused from this subpoena by these attorneys or the court, you shall respond to this subpoena as directed.

Harold Bishop
Plaintiff's Attorney
Harold Bishop
Bishop and Zubin
4317 Weston Road
Fairwood, FL 33318
(999) 432-8612

    DATED this **29th** day of **November, 1997.**

                                  Clyde Clerk
                (Seal)   As Clerk of the Court

                                  By: *Douglas Linden*
                                  As Deputy Clerk

FIGURE 8-3

At the conclusion of the deposition, the deponent is generally given the option to "read or waive." By this, the person is being given a choice of either reading the transcription of the deposition testimony before it is filed with the court or waiving that right. If the deponent chooses not to waive that right and does read the transcription, then the deponent will have to sign a statement indicating any changes in the transcript and the reasons for those changes. This statement will then be submitted to the court file along with the transcript of the deposition. The right to read the transcription does not, however, give witnesses a second opportunity to consider the questions and alter their testimony. It only gives them a chance to verify that the transcription accurately reports the statements that were made.

5. Transcription of Depositions

Not all depositions are reduced to a typewritten form from court reporters' notes. This is not only because transcription of depositions can be expensive, but also because some depositions may not yield important information. If, however, one of the parties does request that the testimony be transcribed, it is at the expense of the requesting party.

"Documents and things produced for inspection during the examination of the witness, shall, upon the request of a party, be marked for identification and annexed to the deposition ..."[29] Under certain circumstances, copies as opposed to the originals may suffice.

6. The Use of Depositions in Court

a. *Purposes for using depositions in court.*   Depositions can be used in court in a number of ways including, but not limited to, the following:

(1) *Impeachment.* "Any deposition may be used by any party for the purpose of contradicting or impeaching the testimony of a deponent as a witness ..."[30] The term *impeach* means to question the veracity of a witness's statements. If, for example, a man declares on the witness stand that he saw a particular automobile accident but stated in deposition that he did not, his deposition testimony can be used in court to question the truthfulness of his testimony in court.

(2) *Death of a witness.* If a witness who has already given deposition testimony dies before the final hearing, the deposition can be introduced in the court proceedings.[31]

(3) *Excessive traveling distance for the witness.* State rules commonly provide that a witness's deposition can be used if the witness is an excessive distance from the location of the trial. Under the federal rules, a witness's deposition can be used in court if the witness "is at a greater distance than 100 miles from the place of trial or hearing, or is out of the United States, unless it appears that the absence of the witness was procured by the party offering the deposition ..."[32] or "that the party offering the deposition has been unable to procure the attendance of the witness by subpoena..."[33]

(4) *Age, illness, infirmity, or imprisonment of the witness.* A deposition of a witness may be used under these circumstances because the deponent may be physically incapable of giving live testimony in court.[34]

(5) *Exceptional circumstances.* A witness's deposition can be used in court if it can be shown that there exist such exceptional circumstances "... as to make it desirable, and in the interest of justice and with due regard to the importance of presenting the testimony of witnesses orally and in open court, to allow the deposition to be used."[35]

b. Partial use of depositions.   "If only part of a deposition is offered in evidence by a party, an adverse party may require the offeror to introduce any other part which ought in fairness to be considered with the part introduced, and any party may introduce any other parts."[36]

c. Objections to admissibility.   Subject to some qualifications, an attorney may generally object to the admission of deposition testimony into evidence under circumstances where the remarks would have been stricken if made during the course of a trial or hearing.[37]

B.   Interrogatories

1.   Definition and Elements

Interrogatories are written questions that are to be answered under oath and in writing. Under the federal rules, as well as those of many states, interrogatories can only be submitted to adverse parties.

There are several key elements to the definition of interrogatories. They are as follows:

a. Written questions.   The questions, unlike those in depositions, must be in writing.

b. To be answered under oath.   The party responding must swear to the truth of all answers. This is done by signing the answers to the interrogatories in the presence of a notary public or other appropriate official.

c. Written answers.   The person to whom the questions are sent must answer the questions in writing. As in the case of depositions, if the respondent has no knowledge of the information requested, it is generally permissible to respond by indicating a lack of knowledge with regard to the matter. If the answer to an interrogatory may be determined only by reference to the business records of the party being questioned, and it is just as easy for the questioner to obtain the answer by an examination of those records as it is for the respondent, the respondent may answer the question by simply indicating the availability of the records for inspection, copying, etc. by the other party.[38]

d. Usually restricted to opposing parties only.   Under the federal rules[39] and the rules of many of the states, interrogatories may only be served by a party on another party. If interrogatories are restricted to parties only, other forms of discovery such as depositions are appropriate for obtaining testimony or evidence from witnesses who are not parties to the action.

2.   *When Interrogatories May Be Served*

Under the federal rules, interrogatories may not be served on the opposing party prior to the conference held by the attorneys to schedule discovery unless a special court order is obtained.[40] The earliest time that interrogatories may be served under state rules will vary greatly from state to state.

3.   *How Many Questions May Be Served*

While state rules may differ, the federal rules provide that a party may serve on the other party a number of questions "… not exceeding 25 in number including all discrete subparts…."[41]

4.   *Objections to Interrogatories*

The person receiving the interrogatories who objects to any of the questions posed "shall state the reasons for objection and shall answer to the extent the interrogatory is not objectionable."[42] As a general rule, any ground for objection that is not stated in a timely fashion is waived.[43] As in the case of other forms of discovery, the scope of permissible inquiry is relatively broad, although there are exceptions (see Sec. 8-3, subsection A). Interrogatory questions are also subject to objection if the answering of the questions requires an inordinate effort or burden. For example, if the answer requires an examination of thousands of pages of financial data, courts would regard the question as unreasonable, although the statutes or rules might provide the proponent of the interrogatories with an opportunity to sort through the material.

5. *The Maximum Time Allotted for a Response*

Under the federal rules, a party responding to interrogatories has 30 days after the interrogatories have been sent to serve the answers (and objections if any) to the opposing side.[44] A shorter or longer time may be provided for by the court or by stipulation of the parties. The maximum time permitted for a response may differ in the state court system; so any time limitations should be carefully checked under the state rules for state court cases.

6. *General Procedure*

While the procedure for preparing and sending out interrogatories varies from state to state, the following example is typical.

The attorney preparing the interrogatories arranges the questions so that there is sufficient blank space underneath each question to allow for a complete answer. The questions are preceded by a cover page with the usual civil pleading format. The cover page must, however, contain a statement certifying the sending of the interrogatories by hand or by mail on a specified date. The original and a copy of the interrogatories are sent or delivered to the party to whom the interrogatories are directed, and copies are sent to every other party in the action.

Once the answers are prepared, they must be signed by the responding party and notarized since the party is swearing to the truth of the matters contained therein. Attorneys cannot swear to the answers in the interrogatories in the place of their clients.

7. *Requests to Produce Business Records*

"Where the answer to an interrogatory may be derived or ascertained from ... business records of the party upon whom the interrogatory has been served ... and the burden of deriving or ascertaining the answer is substantially the same [for both parties]," it is sufficient to answer the question by specifying the records from which the answer may be obtained and providing the other party with the opportunity to examine them.[45]

8. *Use of Interrogatories in Court*

Like depositions, interrogatories can be used in court proceedings. One of their primary uses is in the impeachment of testimony. This occurs when one's testimony in court directly contradicts the answers given in the interrogatories. Whenever the answer to an interrogatory is admitted into evidence in court, the other parties are generally given the right to request that the court enter into evidence any other interrogatories that should be considered with it. As a general rule, interrogatories can be used in court under the same circumstances as depositions can (see subsection A.6 above).

An example of a set of interrogatories can be seen in Figures 8-4a through e.

C. Production of Documents and Things and Entry Upon Land for Inspection and Other Purposes

"Any party may serve on any other party a request (1) to produce and permit the party making the request or someone acting on the requester's behalf, to inspect and copy, any designated documents (including writings, drawings, graphs, charts, photographs, phonorecords, and other data compilations from which information can be obtained, translated, if necessary, by the respondent through detection devices into reasonably usable form) or to inspect and copy, test, or sample any tangible things ... which are in the possession, custody, or control of the party upon whom the request is served; or (2) to permit entry upon designated land or other property in the possession or control of the party upon whom the request is served for the purpose of inspection and measuring, surveying, photographing, testing, or sampling the property or any designated object or operation ..."[46] Both kinds of requests must of course be seeking information that is within the normally permissible scope of discovery under governing procedural rules.[47]

1. When the Request May Be Served

As in the case of interrogatories, the federal rules provide that the request may not be served on the opposing party prior to the conference held by the attorneys to schedule discovery unless one obtains a special court order.[48] The earliest time that such requests may be served under state rules will vary from state to state.

2. Time Within Which to Respond

The federal rules provide that requests to produce documents and things or to enter land for inspection and other purposes must be answered within 30 days after the request has been sent.[49] A shorter or longer time may be provided by the court or by stipulation of the parties. The maximum time permitted for a response may differ in the state court system, so any time limitations should be carefully checked under the state rules.

IN THE CIRCUIT COURT OF THE 17TH JUDICIAL CIRCUIT
IN AND FOR BROWARD COUNTY, STATE OF FLORIDA

Case No: 97-58273

Fla. Bar #314151

WILLIE L. SANDERS,)
)
     Plaintiff,   )
)
v.   )
)
JOHN M. MARINO and)
DAVID R. ROBINSON,)
)
     Defendants.)
)

This is designed for instruction, and not for use in all jurisdictions.

INTERROGATORIES

The defendant, DAVID R. ROBINSON, propounds unto the plaintiff, WILLIE L. SANDERS, the attached Interrogatories to be answered by said party in writing under oath not later than October 27, 1997.

I HEREBY CERTIFY that a true and correct copy of these Interrogatories was mailed to Mr. Harold Bishop, Bishop and Zubin, 4317 Weston Road, Fairwood, FL 33318 on the 25th day of September, 1997.

William Benlow
William Benlow
Benlow and Sheen
Attorneys for defendant David
  R. Robinson
326 61st Avenue
Pleasantville, FL 33019
(999) 564-5000

FIGURE 8-4a

01. What is your name, address and, if you are answering for someone else, your official position?

02. Describe in detail, each act or omission on the part of the defendant you contend constituted negligence that was a contributing legal cause of the accident in question.

03. List the names and address of all persons who are believed or known by you, your agents or attorneys to have any knowledge concerning any of the issues raised by the pleadings and specify the subject matter about which the witness has knowledge.

04. List the name, residence address, business address and telephone number of each person believed or known by you, your agents or attorneys to have heard or who is purported to have heard the defendant make any statement, remark or comment concerning the accident described in the complaint and the substance of each statement, remark or comment.

05. Did any mechanical defect in the motor vehicle you were driving at the time of the accident contribute to the occurrence of the accident? If so, what was the nature of the defect?

06. Were you suffering from physical infirmity, disability, or sickness at the time of the occurrence of the accident described in the complaint? If so, what was the nature of the infirmity, disability, or sickness?

FIGURE 8-4b

07. Did you consume any alcoholic beverages or take any drugs or medications within 12 hours before the occurrence of the accident described in the complaint? If so, what type and amount of alcoholic beverages, drugs or medication were consumed and where did you consume them?

08. Have you ever been convicted of a crime? If so, what was the date and place of conviction?

09. Do you wear glasses or contact lenses? If so, who prescribed them, when were they prescribed, when were your eyes last examined and by whom?

10. Do you wear a hearing aid? If so, who last examined your ears?

11. Describe in detail how the accident happened, including all actions taken by you to prevent the accident.

12. List each item of expense that you claim to have incurred as a result of the injuries sued on in this action, giving for each item the date incurred, and to whom owed or paid the goods or services for which each was incurred.

FIGURE 8-4c

13. Do you contend that you have lost any form of compensation as a result of the injuries sued on in this action? If so, what was the amount lost, the period during which it was lost, the nature of the compensation and the method that you used in computing the amount?

14. Have any benefits been paid or any payable for the expenses listed in your answers to interrogatories 11 and 12 above? If so, which expenses are covered by insurance, what type of insurance, and who paid the premium for the insurance?

15. Describe each injury for which you are claiming damages specifying the part of your body that was injured; the nature of the injury; and, as to any injuries you contend are permanent, the effects on you that you claim are permanent.

16. List each physician who has treated you and each medical facility where you have received any treatment for the injuries for which you seek damages in this case, giving the dates that the treatment was received and stating which of the injuries described in you answer to interrogatory 15 the treatment was rendered for.

17. Do you intend to call any non-medical expert witnesses at the trial of this case? If so, identify each witness; describe his qualifications as an expert; state the subject matter upon which he is expected to testify; state the substance of the facts and opinions to which he is expected to testify; and give a summary of the grounds for each opinion.

FIGURE 8-4d

18. List the names, business addresses and business telephone numbers of all medical doctors by whom, and all hospitals at which, you have been examined and/or treated in the past 5 years.

19. List the names, addresses, phone numbers and rate of pay for all employers for whom you have worked in the past 5 years.

_____
Willie L. Sanders

STATE OF FLORIDA:
COUNTY OF BROWARD: SS:

Willie L. Sanders, being duly sworn, deposes and says that the attached answers to interrogatories are true to the best of his knowledge, information and belief.

Sworn to and subscribed before me this _____ day of _____, 19__.

_____
                                  Notary Public, State of Florida
(place seal here)   My commission expires:

Certificate of Service

The undersigned, counsel for the plaintiff, certifies that the foregoing original answers to interrogatories have been filed in accordance with the Florida Rules of Civil Procedure and a copy mailed to Mr. William Benlow, Benlow and Sheen, attorneys for defendant David R. Robinson, 326 61st Avenue, Pleasantville, FL 33019 this _____ day of _____, 19_____.

_____
                                  Harold Bishop
                                  Plaintiff's Attorney
                                  Bishop and Zubin
                                  4317 Weston Road
                                  Fairwood, FL 33318
                                  (999) 432-8612

FIGURE 8-4e

3. Information that Must Be Included in the Response

"The response shall state, with respect to each item or category, that inspection and related activities will be permitted as requested, unless the request is objected to, in which event the reasons for the objection shall be stated. If objection is made to part of an item or category, the part shall be specified..."[50]

4. Requests Possible on Nonparties

The federal rules make it clear that nonparties as well as parties "may be compelled to produce documents and things or to submit to an inspection...."[51]

D. Physical and Mental Examinations

"When the mental or physical condition (including the blood group) of a party, or of a person in the custody or under the legal control of a party, is in controversy, the court in which the action is pending may order the party to submit to a physical or mental examination by a suitably licensed or certified examiner or to produce for examination the person in the party's custody or legal control. The order may be made only on motion for good cause shown and upon notice to the person to be examined and to all parties and shall specify the time, place, manner, conditions, and scope of the examination and the person or persons by whom it is to be made."[52]

1. Who Must Submit to Mental and Physical Examinations

The federal rule clearly restricts such examinations to either parties or those under the custody or legal control of parties. This would include, for example, the physical examination of a minor child when the parent is suing to recover damages for injuries to the child.

2. A Request by the Person Being Examined to See the Physician's Report

"If requested by the party against whom an order is made ... or the person examined, the party causing the examination to be made shall deliver to the requesting party a copy of the detailed written report of the examiner setting out the examiner's findings, including results of all tests made, diagnoses and conclusions, together with the reports of all earlier examinations of the same condition."[53]

a. The right of the person causing the examination to see similar reports. If the physician's report is delivered to the person examined or the person against whom the order for the examination was made, "... the party causing the examination shall be entitled upon request to receive from the party against whom the order is made a like report of any examination, previously or thereafter made, of the same condition, unless, in the case of a report of examination of a person not a party, the party shows that such party is unable to obtain it...."[54]

E. Requests for Admission

1. Definition

A request for admission is a written request addressed to a party to the action to admit or deny certain matters pertaining to the case. The questions may relate to "... statements or opinions of fact or of the application of law to fact, including the genuineness of any documents described in the request."[55] Requests for admission, while usually classified as discovery tools, are not generally used to obtain information from a person or to determine a person's knowledge with regard to certain facts. Rather, the purpose of such requests is to clearly define the issues and avoid a waste of the court's time in establishing matters that are undisputed. As in interrogatories, blank spaces are provided for a response below each request.

2. Applicable to Parties Only

Since the very purpose of sending requests for admission is to determine which matters are admitted by a party and therefore do not require proof in court, such requests are applicable only to parties (as opposed to witnesses).[56]

3. When Requests for Admission May Be Sent

Federal rules restrict the service of requests for admission under normal circumstances until after the attorneys' meeting for scheduling discovery.[57] Any similar restrictions in state court matters will be governed by state procedural rules.

4. The Maximum Time Allotted for a Response

Under the federal rules, requests for admission must be answered within 30 days after they are sent.[58] A shorter or longer time may be provided by the court or by stipulation of the parties. State court rules should be checked carefully for time limitations in state court proceedings.

5.   *Partial Admission or Denial*

It is possible for a party to admit or deny in part any aspect of a particular request for admission as long as all portions of the question are addressed and the response is made in good faith.[59]

6.   *Responses Indicating Lack of Knowledge*

Unlike the case of responses to deposition questions or interrogatories, "an answering party may not give lack of information or knowledge as a reason for failure to admit or deny unless the party states that the party has made reasonable inquiry and that the information known or readily obtainable by the party is insufficient to enable the party to admit or deny."[60]

7.   *Failure to Respond*

If a response to a request for admission is not sent within the required time period, the matter addressed in the request is regarded as admitted.[61]

8.   *The Effect of an Admission*

As a general rule, any matter admitted in response to a request for admission is conclusively established. The admission only applies to the proceeding at hand, however, and cannot be used against the responding party in other proceedings.[62]

SEC. 8-6
THE FREQUENCY WITH WHICH DISCOVERY TOOLS MAY BE USED

"The frequency or extent of use of the discovery methods ... shall be limited by the court if it determines that: (i) the discovery sought is unreasonably cumulative or duplicative, or is obtainable from some other source that is more convenient, less burdensome, or less expensive; (ii) the party seeking discovery has had ample opportunity by discovery in the action to obtain the information sought; or (iii) the burden or expense of the proposed discovery outweighs its likely benefit, taking into account the needs of the case, the amount in controversy, the parties' resources, the importance of the issues at stake in the litigation, and the importance of the proposed discovery in resolving the issues.[63] The court can limit the extent and frequency of the discovery either upon the motion of a party or person from whom the discovery is sought, or upon its own motion.

Once a pretrial conference has taken place or the party has filed papers with the court indicating readiness for trial, the court may exercise its authority to limit further discovery.

SEC. 8-7
THE DUTY TO SUPPLEMENT DISCOVERY

A party who has provided information through interrogatories, requests for production, requests for admission, or other forms of discovery has a duty to notify the other side if it becomes clear that the answers provided were incomplete, incorrect, or in need of supplementation. This duty exists, however, only if "the additional or corrective information has not been made known to the other parties during the discovery process or in writing."[64] While this is a federal rule, state court rules often contain similar provisions.

For example, suppose that a party involved in an automobile negligence case truthfully states at deposition that the party has never been involved in any other automobile accidents in the past. Two weeks after the deposition, the same person is involved in a serious automobile accident and is clearly at fault. That person in many states would have an obligation to notify the deposing attorney that the answer to the deposition question would now be different.

Many states have a rule that is a direct counterpart to this rule. Other states may provide that a party is obliged to supplement a discovery answer with new information obtained since the original questioning only upon the submission of supplementary questions or requests by the other party. The duty to disclose the name of a newly found witness, for example, may not exist in some jurisdictions in the absence of a request.

SEC. 8-8
SANCTIONS FOR FAILURE TO COOPERATE WITH DISCOVERY

The one failing to comply with demands for discovery or giving incomplete answers can face severe consequences, including the following court sanctions:

A.   *Certain Facts May Be Taken as Established*

The court may impose "an order that the matters regarding which the order was made or any other designated facts shall be taken to be established for the purposes of the action in accordance with the claim of the party obtaining the order ..."[65]

B. Certain Claims, Defenses, or Evidence May Be Disallowed

An order may be entered "refusing to allow the disobedient party to support or oppose designated claims or defenses, or prohibiting that party from introducing designated matters into evidence ..."[66]

C. Pleadings May Be Stricken, Proceedings May Be Stayed, or There May Be a Dismissal or Default

The court may issue "an order striking out pleadings or parts thereof, or staying further proceedings until the order is obeyed, or dismissing the action or proceeding or any part thereof, or rendering a judgment by default against the disobedient party ..."[67] If the court were to strike certain pleadings, it could have the effect of eliminating claims or defenses raised in those pleadings. To "stay the proceedings" means to halt all further record activity on the case until there is compliance with the discovery requests.

The applicable federal rule also provides for a dismissal or default as a possible sanction. A plaintiff's case might be dismissed if the plaintiff fails to cooperate with discovery procedures initiated by adverse parties. Similarly, a default might be entered against a defendant who, for example, either refused to answer interrogatories or simply failed to respond.

D. An Order of Contempt of Court May Be Issued

"In lieu of any of the foregoing orders or in addition thereto, [the court may issue] an order treating as a contempt of court the failure to obey any orders except an order to submit to a physical or mental examination ..."[68]

E. Attorneys Fees and Costs May Be Incurred

If one of the parties incurs attorneys fees and costs in connection with the good faith filing of a motion to compel discovery or the resisting of a bad faith motion, the court may award attorneys fees and costs to that party. If the party is the one filing the motion, the court will have to be convinced that the party made an honest and reasonable effort to obtain the disclosure or discovery without court action.[69]

REVIEW QUESTIONS

3 "Prepare" exercises

ing may be used only on adverse parties under the fed-
h may be used on either parties or nonparties?

)cuments

ntal examinations

iission

juired to bring documents to a deposition? If so, how?

interrogatories on Thursday, May 16. What is the last
e can serve a copy of the answers on the adverse party
tions?

h requests for admission on Tuesday, August 10. What
ate that he can serve a copy of the answers on the ad-
~~.~~~~ fear of sanctions?

5. What are the main advantages of using depositions rather than interrogatories in a civil case?

6. What procedures must be followed to schedule a deposition? What documents must be prepared?

7. Prepare a notice of taking deposition based on the following fictitious information. Use the form provided in the book as a model. Assume that the
   case involves a suit for $100,000 in damages and that it has been filed in the
   appropriate court and judicial circuit in the county and state where you
   live. All the information provided may or may not be necessary to prepare
   the form.

   > This document, dated February 13, 1997, gives formal notice to Michael
   > LaRoche, the attorney for the plaintiff in the case of *Edward Haddix v.
   > Thomas Conlon* (case number 96-52333), that the plaintiff will be re-
   > quired to testify at a deposition conducted by Bruce Lyden, attorney for
   > the defendant. The deposition will take place at Lyden's office, which is
   > located at 6868 23rd Place, Thomastown, [your state and zip code].
   > LaRoche's office is located at 520 Furth Avenue, Thomastown, (your
   > state and zip code). Lyden's telephone number is (833) 555-1354, and
   > his Bar number is #443425. LaRoche's telephone number is (833) 555-
   > 2700 and his Bar number is #993821. This is the first time that a depo-
   > sition of the plaintiff has been scheduled in this case. The deposition is
   > scheduled for 2:00 P.M. on March 1, 1997. The trial in this case is
   > presently set for September 28, 1997. Haddix's address is 234 Hoover

Street, Cloverton, [your state and zip code]. Conlon's address is 94 Crossley Way, Thomastown, [your state and zip code]. The oath will be administered by Barbara Croft, who will be serving as both the court reporter and the notary public.

8. Prepare a subpoena for deposition based on the following fictitious information. Use the form provided in the book as a model. Assume that the case involves a suit for $100,000 in damages and that it has been filed in the appropriate court and judicial circuit in the county and state where you live. All the information provided may or may not be necessary to prepare the form.

This involves the case of *Donald Reardon v. Juliet Sedlik* (case number 97-51798). Reardon is represented by Cynthia Hoffman, whose address is 2000 Birch Drive, Davis City, [your state and zip code]. Her telephone number is (335) 555-4993, and her Bar number is #82009. Sedlik is represented by Arthur Irving, whose address is 442 21st Terrace, Holdenville, [your state and zip code]. His telephone number is (335) 555-6442 and his Bar number is #83656. Hoffman is going to be taking Sedlik's deposition on June 9, 1998, at 9:00 A.M. in Hoffman's office. Reardon's address is 572 49th Street, Davis City, [your state and zip code]. Sedlik's address is 886 Chandler Avenue, Rockaway, [your state and zip code]. The subpoena is dated May 19, 1998. The subpoena has not yet been signed by the Deputy Clerk.

9. Prepare a subpoena duces tecum for deposition based on the following fictitious information. Use the form provided in the book as a model. Assume that the case involves a suit for $100,000 in damages and that it has been filed in the appropriate court and judicial circuit in the county and state where you live. All the information provided may or may not be necessary to prepare the form.

This document, dated February 20, 1998, pertains to the case of *Harold Jaeger v. Elizabeth Schwab* (case number 97-88241). Jaeger's attorney is Richard Oshiro, whose office is located at 766 Buckeye Court, Waldron, [your state and zip code]. His telephone number is (188) 555-9245 and his Bar number is #264729. Schwab is represented by Stuart Walsh, whose address is 668 72nd Avenue, Waldron, [your state and zip code]. Walsh's telephone number is (188) 555-8222 and his Bar number is #225273. Jaeger presently resides at 400 Hampton Way, Waldron, [your state and zip code]. Schwab resides at 143 Newport Road, Hackley, [your state and zip code]. Oshiro will be taking the deposition of Schwab at Oshiro's law offices on March 4, 1998, at 11:00 A.M. At that time, Schwab is to have receipts and expenditures for the XYZ sole proprietorship owned and operated by her for the year 1996. The subpoena has not yet been signed by the Deputy Clerk.

FOOTNOTES

[1]FED. R. CIV. P. 26(b)(1)

[2]FED. R. CIV. P. 26(b)(1)

[3]FED. R. CIV. P. 26(b)(3)

[4]FED. R. CIV. P. 26(b)(3)

[5]FED. R. CIV. P. 26(b)(4)(B)

[6]FED. R. CIV. P. 26(b)(4)(C)

[7]FED. R. CIV. P. 26(c)

[8]FED. R. CIV. P. 26(f)

[9]FED. R. CIV. P. 26(f)(2)

[10]FED. R. CIV. P. 26(f)

[11]FED. R. CIV. P. 26(d)

[12]FED. R. CIV. P. 26(a)(1). The headings and their numbering and punctuation are from the author rather than from the federal rule.

[13]FED. R. CIV. P. 26(a)(2)(B). The headings and the numbering of them are from the author rather than from the federal rule.

[14]FED. R. CIV. P. 26(b)(4)(A)

[15]FED. R. CIV. P. 26(a)(2)(C)

[16]FED. R. CIV. P. 26(b)(4)(B)

[17]FED. R. CIV. P. 26(b)(4)(C)

[18]FED. R. CIV. P. 16(b). In addition to holding a scheduling conference, the court has the option of conferring with the attorneys by "telephone, mail, or other suitable means …"

[19]FED. R. CIV. P. 16(b)

[20]FED. R. CIV. P. 16(b)

[21]FED. R. CIV. P. 16(b)

[22]*Impeachment* is defined as questioning the truthfulness of the witness.

[23]FED. R. CIV. P. 26(a)(3)

[24]FED. R. CIV. P. 26(a)(5)

[25]FED. R. CIV. P. 28(a)

[26]FED. R. CIV. P. 30(a)

[27]FED. R. CIV. P. 30(b)(1)

[28]FED. R. CIV. P. 30(g)(1)

[29]FED. R. CIV. P. 30(f)(1)

[30]FED. R. CIV. P. 32(a)(1)

[31]FED. R. CIV. P. 32(a)(3)(A)

[32]FED. R. CIV. P. 32(a)(3)(B)

[33]FED. R. CIV. P. 32(a)(3)(D)

[34]FED. R. CIV. P. 32(a)(3)(C)

[35]FED. R. CIV. P. 32(a)(3)(E)

[36]FED. R. CIV. P. 32(a)(4)

[37]FED. R. CIV. P. 32(b)

[38]FED. R. CIV. P. 33(d)

[39]FED. R. CIV. P. 33(a)

[40]FED. R. CIV. P. 33(a)

[41]FED. R. CIV. P. 33(a)

[42]FED. R. CIV. P. 33(b)(1)

[43]FED. R. CIV. P. 33(b)(4)

[44]FED. R. CIV. P. 33(b)(3)

[45]FED. R. CIV. P. 33(d)

[46]FED. R. CIV. P. 34(a)

[47]FED. R. CIV. P. 34(a)

[48]FED. R. CIV. P. 34(b)

[49]FED. R. CIV. P. 34(b)

[50]FED. R. CIV. P. 34(b)

[51]FED. R. CIV. P. 34(c)

[52]FED. R. CIV. P. 35(a)

[53]FED. R. CIV. P. 35(b)(1)

[54]FED. R. CIV. P. 35(b)(1)

[55]FED. R. CIV. P. 36(a)

[56]FED. R. CIV. P. 36(a)

[57]FED. R. CIV. P. 26(d)

[58]FED. R. CIV. P. 36(a)

[59]FED. R. CIV. P. 36(a)

[60]FED. R. CIV. P. 36(a)

[61]FED. R. CIV. P. 36(a)

[62]FED. R. CIV. P. 36(b)

[63]FED. R. CIV. P. 26(b)(1)

[64]FED. R. CIV. P. 26(e)

[65]FED. R. CIV. P. 37(b)(2)(A)

[66]FED. R. CIV. P. 37(b)(2)(B)

[67]FED. R. CIV. P. 37(b)(2)(C)

[68]FED. R. CIV. P. 37(b)(2)(D)

[69]FED. R. CIV. P. 37(a)(4)

9

Criminal Law, Discovery, and Procedure

CHAPTER OVERVIEW

SEC. 9-1
BASIC BACKGROUND INFORMATION

A. In General

Our society punishes those who engage in certain kinds of behavior that unreasonably interferes with the rights of others or of society as a whole. For example, all states have passed laws prohibiting the theft of personal property. Such laws are required in order to guarantee an orderly society. One may be arrested for violating a criminal law, and the sentence for the commission of such an act may be imprisonment, fine, execution, or other punishment such as restitution to the victim. Examples of crimes are murder, rape, robbery, larceny, and burglary. (Note that the victim of a crime may also have a civil cause of action against the defendant. The prohibitions against double jeopardy in the U.S. Constitution do not prevent one from filing a civil suit when the defendant has already been charged or prosecuted for a violation of a criminal law.)

Since the rights of society, rather than the individual victim, are being protected in criminal cases, the victim does not necessarily benefit if the one committing the crime is convicted. In recent times, however, judges in criminal law cases have been more likely to include in a final sentence a requirement that the defendant make some form of restitution to the victim or to society as a whole.

When victims are asked by the police whether they wish to "press charges" against a particular individual, it is not because they are required to do so, since it is actually the state that will be pressing charges in a state criminal case. It is rather that the police wish to verify that the victim wants the perpetrator to be prosecuted and that the victim will cooperate in any future prosecution of that person.

Since a criminal case involves prosecution for an act committed against society, it is the government, either state or federal, that will be one of the two primary parties in a criminal action. Therefore, the names of criminal cases will be in the form of *State v. Smith, Florida v. Smith, U.S. v. Smith*, or some similar variation. (Case names may also appear as *Smith v. State* since the names are sometimes reversed on appeal.)

The fact that the state is one of the parties in the case does not necessarily mean that the case is criminal rather than civil. For example, if a dispute arose with a contractor over an agreement with the state of Montana to build a parking garage for a state building, the contractor might be sued in a civil action by the state. The state in this example would be in essentially the same position that it would be in if it were not a governmental entity.

B. Classification of Crimes

Crimes can be categorized according to the severity or the nature of the offense.

1. Felonies as Opposed to Misdemeanors

Crimes with more severe penalties are referred to as felonies while those with lesser penalties are referred to as misdemeanors. Whether a crime is classified as a felony or a misdemeanor may vary from state to state since each legislature determines the definition of and penalties for state criminal law violations. The U.S. Congress designates which acts shall constitute federal crimes and what maximum and minimum penalties shall be applicable to them. Examples of crimes that are felonies in most states are murder, arson, burglary, and robbery, while examples of misdemeanors are jaywalking, riding a motorcycle without a helmet, and prostitution.

An act that is a misdemeanor under one set of circumstances may be a felony under another. For example, possession of less than one ounce of marijuana is a misdemeanor while possession of 17 tons of marijuana is a felony. Stealing a can of hairspray from a department store is generally a misdemeanor, but stealing a television set may be a felony.[1]

The difference between the possible penalties for felonies and misdemeanors may be substantial. If, for example, one is convicted in Florida of petty larceny for stealing an item worth less than $300, the act would be classified as a second degree misdemeanor and the maximum penalty would be 60 days in jail and a possible fine of $500.[2] On the other hand, if an item worth more than $300 was taken, the act would be classified as a third degree felony, and the defendant could receive a maximum sentence of up to five years in the state penitentiary and a possible fine of $5,000.

2.   Mala in Se *as Opposed to* Mala Prohibita *Crimes*

Crimes may also be classified according to the nature of the offense. Many acts, known as *mala in se* offenses, have been designated as crimes because they are regarded as inherently evil. First degree murder, for example, has been designated everywhere as a crime because it is universally recognized as an act that is innately wrong and contrary to the best interests of society. Other examples of mala in se offenses are larceny, robbery, burglary, and arson.

Other acts are designated as crimes by legislatures even though the acts are not inherently evil or immoral. For example, it is a crime in many states for a person to ride a motorcycle without a helmet in spite of the fact that there is nothing morally wrong in doing so. In this example, a state legislature may simply have decided to protect motorcyclists from their own poor judgment. Such offenses are referred to as *mala prohibita* crimes because the legislature has chosen to define them as crimes and not because of their inherently evil nature.

Many *mala prohibita* offenses, such as the laws requiring the closing of bars at a certain hour, are often based upon relatively arbitrary limitations. The legislature may have determined, for example, that bars may not stay open after 2:00 A.M., even though there is nothing inherently more wrongful about operating a bar at 2:05 A.M. than 1:55 A.M. Similarly, a legislature may have chosen to prohibit the sale of alcoholic beverages to those under 18 years of age in spite of the fact that there is nothing inherently more wrongful about selling alcohol to a person who is 17 years and 364 days old than one who is 18 years old. While it is not true in all cases, penalties for *mala prohibita* offenses tend to be less severe than those for *mala in se* offenses.

C. The Role of the Mental State of the Accused

1. Intent, Motive, and Knowledge of Guilt

Intent is an actual element of many different crimes and must, therefore, be established in such cases by the prosecutor in order to obtain a conviction. The severity of a crime and the potential penalty for it may depend upon the degree to which the defendant intended to cause harm. Compare, for example, a situation in which a reckless driver accidentally runs over and kills a pedestrian to one in which a man commits the premeditated and unprovoked killing of a business competitor. Both are examples of homicides, but the first is likely to be classified as a manslaughter. The killing of the business competitor will probably be labeled as murder, and it is likely to carry a heavier penalty since the harm done is the result of intentional rather than reckless behavior.

While intent is often an element of a crime, motive is generally not. The prosecutor may nevertheless wish to introduce evidence of motive into a court of law since the existence of motive may suggest the likelihood of intent. Similarly, it is not usually necessary for the prosecutor to establish that the defendant was aware of the fact that the acts constituted a violation of criminal laws. Instead, the focus of the prosecution's case will center upon whether the defendant had the required *mens rea* or criminal state of mind necessary to commit the offense and whether the defendant actually committed the prohibited act.

2. Insanity of the Defendant

As a general rule, a defendant is not responsible for acts committed while the defendant is insane. The underlying reason for this rule is that an insane defendant is incapable of forming the necessary mental state required for the commission of the crime. For a further analysis of the insanity defense, see subsection F.2 that follows.

D. Parties to a Crime

Parties to a crime can be classified as either principals of the first degree, principals of the second degree, accessories before the fact, or accessories after the fact. When the terms "before the fact" or "after the fact" are used, the "fact" referred to is the crime.

1. Principals of the First and Second Degree

A principal of the first degree is the party who is actually involved in the perpetration of the crime. In the robbery of a bank, for example, the principal of the first degree is the one who is at the scene committing the act. A principal of the second degree is a party who aids or abets at the scene of the crime. Being "at the scene" includes the immediate environment of the crime location as well as the location itself. The driver of a get-away car, for example, is generally regarded as being at the scene and is, therefore, classified as a second degree principal.

2.   Accessories Before and After the Fact

An accessory before the fact is one not present at the scene of the crime who aids the principals of the first or second degree prior to the commission of the crime. A typical example of an accessory before the fact is a person who assists in the commission of a bank robbery by supplying the floor plan of the bank for an "inside job." An accessory after the fact is one who renders aid to the other criminal parties after the crime has already been committed, such as one who hides the criminal from law enforcement authorities. One of the most famous accessories after the fact in American history is Dr. Mudd, the physician who rendered medical treatment and other kinds of aid to John Wilkes Booth after Booth shot Abraham Lincoln.

Legislatures may designate different maximum or minimum penalties for each kind of party, although it still remains the judge's responsibility to determine in each case where the punishment should fall within the legislature's guidelines. While accessories after the fact have often faced lesser penalties in the past, there is a trend toward abolishing the distinctions between these various parties for the purposes of punishment.

E.   Burden of Proof

In any criminal case, it is the obligation of the prosecutor to prove that the defendant is responsible. The defendant is under no legal obligation to prove the absence of guilt since that individual is "innocent until proven guilty." Therefore, if the prosecutor is unable to establish the key elements of the case against the defendant, the prosecutor should lose regardless of whether the defendant has introduced any evidence of innocence.

The burden of proof, or the degree to which the prosecutor must prove the case, is much greater in a criminal case than in a civil one because the potential repercussions on the life of the defendant are so much greater in criminal cases. While many civil actions deal with disputes over very substantial amounts of money and property, criminal conviction can result in years of incarceration or even execution. In a criminal case, the prosecutor is, therefore, said to have the burden of proving the case "beyond a reasonable doubt." This means that the jury's function is not just to determine guilt, but to decide whether there is any reasonable doubt as to the defendant's guilt.

F. *Parties Not Responsible for Their Crimes in Some or All States*

Some parties are not held responsible for acts that would be crimes if committed by others. The list of those who are immune from criminal responsibility may vary from state to state, but the following parties may be included.[3]

1. *Small Children*

Under common law, minors under the age of seven were presumed incapable of forming the state of mind necessary to commit a crime. Those 14 years of age or older were presumed capable of committing a crime regardless of their level of maturity. In the case of minors between the ages of seven and fourteen, there was a presumption that the minor would not be held responsible for crimes committed, although the prosecution was provided with the opportunity to rebut the presumption. Statutes have been enacted in some jurisdictions that have abolished these common law presumptions.

2. *The Insane*

For the defense of insanity to apply, the courts look to the state of mind of the defendant at the time of the offense rather than at the time of the trial.[4] If a defendant is found not guilty by reason of insanity, the laws of most states provide that the defendant will be turned over to the custody of a mental health facility. It should be noted, however, that under these circumstances, the court will retain jurisdiction over the defendant's release.

Various tests have traditionally been used to determine whether a defendant is criminally insane, but the one most widely applied is the M'Naghten rule.

a. The M'Naghten rule. This rule defines insanity in terms of whether the defendant's mental illness resulted in his or her inability to understand the nature and quality of the act or to distinguish between right and wrong. The application of this test has caused problems because of its inherent vagueness. Furthermore, it is often difficult to obtain expert testimony from examining psychiatrists as to the meaning of the terms "right" and "wrong." In spite of these difficulties, the M'Naghten rule is still the standard used in most states.

3.   Those with Diplomatic Immunity

It is possible that those from other countries who have diplomatic status may not be held responsible for the criminal acts they commit in the United States. The reasoning behind the granting of diplomatic immunity is that diplomats should be subject to the criminal laws of their own countries. When diplomats from other countries do commit serious violations of American law in the United States, the most common response by the United States it to deport the guilty party.

4.   Involuntary Intoxicants

The defense of involuntary intoxication, while seldom applied, has been recognized by some American courts. Involuntary intoxication could be a defense, for example, when one committed a crime after being drugged against his or her will. In contrast, voluntary intoxication is not a defense, since under such circumstances, the use of either drugs or alcohol has occurred when the defendant knew or should have known that there might be an impairment of faculties. On the other hand, it is possible that a defendant may be able to argue successfully that even though voluntary intoxication provides no defense to the charge, the intoxicated state of the defendant nevertheless prevented the defendant from forming the necessary intent to commit the crime.

SEC. 9-2
TYPICAL SEQUENCE OF EVENTS FROM THE CRIME TO THE DISPOSITION

A.   Different Possible Events that May Trigger the Initiation of a Criminal Case

A criminal case may begin in a number of different ways. The following are examples of possible scenarios:

1.   Indictment or Information, Arrest, Magistrate's Hearing, and Arraignment

Some of the more serious felony cases are initiated when a *grand jury,* which is usually composed of as few as 12 or as many as 23 members, meets to decide whether there is probable cause that a person or persons committed criminal acts. *Probable cause* means that the existing evidence of the defendant's guilt would convince a reasonably prudent individual that the party committed the crime. If the grand jury determines that such probable cause exists and an *indictment* is therefore appropriate, a warrant for the person's arrest will then be issued.

In less serious offenses, this process may also begin with the filing of an *information* by the prosecutors, which is a document charging the party with the offense.

Once arrested, a person is generally taken to the police station and *booked*. This process includes the recording of paperwork describing both the arrest and the incident that gave rise to it. Also, pictures and fingerprints will be taken. If the police plan to hold the accused, any personal property in the possession of the accused at the time of the arrest will be inventoried and stored.

If the arrest is for a misdemeanor or lesser crime, the accused can generally post *bail* by putting up cash as security guaranteeing the accused's appearance before the judge. If the accused does not appear before the judge on the appointed date, the money will be forfeited. If the arrest is for a felony, the accused will usually be held in custody pending the subsequent hearing.

The person arrested by the police will be brought to a *magistrate's hearing* within a short period after arrest. At that hearing, the party will be informed of the charge and notified of the right to counsel. The magistrate will indicate that an attorney will be provided in the event that the party is unable to afford one. Bail may also be established at this time, but it will have to be in conformity with the Eighth Amendment to the U.S. Constitution. That amendment prohibits "excessive bail." In other words, the amount established will have to be reasonable in relationship to the primary purpose of bail, which is to verify that the party will return to court for subsequent proceedings. Within a number of days after the magistrate's hearing, an *arraignment* will be held. At that time, the charges will be reread and the person will have an opportunity to enter a plea after consultation with an attorney.

2. *Complaint, Arrest, Preliminary Hearing, Information, and Arraignment*

Other serious felony cases are begun when a person is arrested based on a complaint that has been filed. Following arrest, the party is brought to a *preliminary hearing*. The primary purpose of such a hearing is for a judge to determine whether probable cause exists. The prosecutor will often have to conduct an abbreviated trial to convince the judge of this fact. If the judge is convinced, the prosecutor's office will file an *information*. This will be followed by the arraignment and an entry of a plea by the defendant.

3. *Complaint, Arrest, Magistrate's Hearing, and Arraignment*

Some less serious cases (classified as misdemeanors) are initiated after a complaint has been filed and a judge has determined that probable cause exists. On the basis of the judge's finding, the person is arrested and taken to a magistrate's hearing and notified of the pending charges, the right to counsel, and any potential adjustment of the amount set for bail. There is no need in this case for a preliminary hearing because a judge has already determined that probable cause exists. An arraignment and an entry of a plea will soon follow the magistrate's hearing.

4. *Arrest, Magistrate's Hearing, Preliminary Hearing, Indictment or Information, and Arraignment*

A case is sometimes begun by an arrest that was not the result of an arrest warrant. A police officer may arrest a suspect if the officer has probable cause to believe that a felony has been committed or if a criminal offense has been committed in the officer's presence. After such an arrest, a magistrate's hearing, a preliminary hearing, an indictment or information, and an arraignment may then follow.

B. *Developments Subsequent to the Arraignment and Before Trial*

1. *Discovery*

Unlike civil trials, most states do not permit the taking of depositions in criminal cases, although a handful of states do. Even in states prohibiting depositions, there is a constitutional requirement for the prosecution to disclose *exculpatory evidence,* which is evidence that tends to support the innocence of the defendant. There may be additional disclosure requirements that vary from state to state. Some states, for example, may require the release of virtually all evidence that does not fall within the work product rule,[5] while others may be considerably more restrictive. The information that is subject to disclosure may be substantially different from that required under the rules of procedure in civil cases, and it is therefore important to become familiar with the local procedural rules.

2. *Pretrial Motions*

At the same time that discovery is being conducted, a broad variety of matters may be handled by the filing of motions, which are simply requests to the court.

a. Motions attacking the charging documents. The most common motions in this category would include motions to dismiss the case altogether and motions to suppress evidence wrongfully obtained. To illustrate an example of the latter, consider a situation in which a defendant has been charged with the possession of narcotics. If the drugs were obtained as a result of an illegal search and seizure in violation of the Fourth Amendment to the U.S. Constitution, the defendant's attorney will undoubtedly move to prohibit the prosecutor from offering the evidence for admission or making any reference to it during trial. If the defense attorney succeeds, the case has essentially been won since it would be impossible for the prosecutor to convict a defendant of narcotics possession without being able to refer to the narcotics.

In states in which the rules compel the prosecution to disclose substantial information prior to trial, a reciprocal obligation of disclosure is generally imposed on the defense.

b. Motions raising competency and sanity issues. Because incompetency and insanity are both widely recognized defenses in criminal cases, motions to request the appointment of experts to verify the mental state of the accused may be appropriate. Incompetency and insanity are recognized criminal defenses only if they existed at the time of the commission of the crime.

3. Developments Relating to the Charges

Once the parties have taken advantage of the various discovery opportunities available to them and have filed any pretrial motions that they believe are appropriate, any one of several developments may occur, including the entry of a guilty plea or plea bargaining.

a. A change of plea to guilty. If the defense attorney concludes that the case against the defendant is very strong, the defendant can always change the plea from not guilty to guilty. In this event, a hearing must then be held for a formal entry of the change of plea. The court will make certain that the plea was entered freely and voluntarily, and it will either impose a sentence at that hearing or defer sentencing until a later time.

b. Plea bargaining. After both sides have had a chance to employ the discovery tools available to them, the strengths and weaknesses of each side's case should be more apparent. At this point, it may become evident to both parties that an agreement between the prosecution and the defense regarding the disposition of the case may be in the best interest of both sides. Any agreement reached is subject, of course, to approval by the court. It is a common misunderstanding that plea bargaining is a tool used by defense attorneys to obtain lenient sentences through agreement with the prosecution that could not otherwise be obtained through the normal trial process. Other people believe that prosecutors surrender the rights of society through plea bargaining because the prosecution is unable or unwilling to do its job. While these perceptions can be true in individual cases, plea bargaining serves a valuable purpose in the criminal justice system. It is not necessarily in society's best interest to compel the parties to take every case through an expensive and time-consuming trial when both the prosecution and the defense agree that a particular outcome is acceptable to all parties.

4. Pretrial or Status Conference

As in the case of civil trials, there may be a pretrial conference attended by the judge and the attorneys for each side to resolve outstanding motions and issues, and to explore the possibility of settlement. Unlike many pretrial conferences in civil trials, the judge may take a personal and active role in settlement negotiations. Most states do not require such conferences under their rules of criminal procedure, although they may be mandated either by the judges themselves or by local rules.

C. The Sequence of Events in a Basic Criminal Jury Trial

A criminal trial normally takes place in the legal jurisdiction where the offense was committed. The sequence of events in a criminal trial is similar but not identical to that of a civil trial, and the prosecutor, therefore, generally addresses the court and presents evidence at the time that the plaintiff's attorney would in a civil case.

1. Jury Selection

It is solely the defendant's prerogative as to whether the case will be tried before a jury. The right to trial by jury is specifically addressed in the U.S. Constitution. Article III, § 2 provides that the "trial of all Crimes, except in Cases of Impeachment, shall be by Jury ..." The Sixth Amendment to the Constitution further states that in all criminal prosecutions, "the accused shall enjoy the right to a speedy and public trial, by an impartial jury of the State and district wherein the crime shall have been committed." If the defendant chooses to waive the right to a jury trial and proceed with the trial, the judge will determine all questions of fact as well as questions of law.

The process of jury selection, otherwise known as *voir dire*, is designed to afford both sides the opportunity to choose a fair and impartial jury. In reality, each attorney will seek to have a panel of jurors that will be most likely to favor the attorney's own arguments. After the judge asks questions to eliminate those who would have inherent bias, specific jurors are called forward to sit in the jury box, and the attorneys are then given an opportunity to ask questions of them. An unlimited number of jurors can be eliminated *for cause* if the court is convinced that they cannot fairly judge the defendant in the trial proceedings. Each side will also have a limited number of *peremptory challenges,* which means that each side may reject a limited number of prospective jurors without having to justify the rejection on specific grounds. The number of challenges available will depend on individual state court rules and the nature and severity of the criminal offense.

2. *Opening Statements*

In criminal trials, the prosecutor has the first opening statement to the jury since it is the prosecutor's burden to prove the case beyond and to the exclusion of every reasonable doubt. The defendant's attorney then follows with an opening statement, although state rules often provide that the defense's opening statement may be reserved until after the presentation of the prosecution's case.

3. *The Prosecution's Case*

The prosecution normally has the opportunity to call its own witnesses before the defense calls any of its witnesses since the defendant is innocent until proven guilty. When the prosecution questions its own witness for the first time, this is known as *direct examination.* This is followed by *cross-examination* by the defense, *redirect examination* by the prosecution, *recross examination* by the defense, and so forth. This sequence of questioning occurs for each one of the prosecution's witnesses. When the last of the prosecution's witnesses is questioned, the prosecution rests its case.

4. *Defendant's Motion for a Judgment of Acquittal*

At the end of the prosecution's case, the defense attorney routinely raises a motion for judgment of acquittal. In this motion, the defense is contending that, even if the court believes all matters presented by the prosecution, the prosecution has failed to establish all of the elements of the crime and that, as a matter of law, a prima facie case has not been established. While the granting of the motion would result in the acquittal of the defendant, courts are very hesitant to grant such motions. On the other hand, the motion must be raised by the defense counsel to preserve issues on appeal.

To illustrate a situation in which this motion might be granted, consider a case in which the defendant has been charged with possession of marijuana. In the course of the state's case, the facts clearly demonstrate that three other people were in the room where the marijuana was located and the defendant was arrested. If the prosecution has presented its entire case, and it has been unable to establish that the drugs belonged to the defendant rather than to one of the other parties, the judge might grant a motion for judgment of acquittal.

5. The Defense's Case

If the motion for judgment of acquittal is not granted, then the defense will proceed with its case. The defense is not obligated to present any evidence since the burden of proof is solely on the prosecution. Furthermore, under the Fifth Amendment to the U.S. Constitution, the defendant is not required to testify even though the jury would undoubtedly like to know the defendant's version of the facts. Nevertheless, the defense may wish to present evidence that refutes the prosecution's case so that the jury is not left with a one-sided presentation of the evidence.

When the defense questions its own witness for the first time, this is known as *direct examination.* This is followed by *cross-examination* by the prosecution, *redirect examination* by the defense, *recross examination* by the prosecution, and so forth. This sequence of questioning occurs for each one of the defense's witnesses. When the last of the defense's witnesses is questioned, the defense rests its case.

6. The Defendant's Second Motion for a Judgment of Acquittal

After the defense has rested its case, it is common for the defense to renew its motion for a judgment of acquittal. The argument being raised at this time is slightly different than the one raised at the end of the prosecution's case. The defense at this point is asking that the judge order an acquittal of the defendant on the ground that there is insufficient evidence as a matter of law to prove the case beyond a reasonable doubt. For example, if the defense attorney has a valid self-defense argument that has been uncontroverted by the prosecution, the court might be inclined to grant the motion. It should be noted, however, that it is relatively uncommon for a judge to issue a judgment of acquittal.

7. The Charge Conference

At a charge conference, the attorneys meet with the judge to formulate potential instructions for the jury to hear before it commences deliberations. Many states have standard suggested jury instructions that are commonly used. The attorneys may also draft original instructions that the court may or may not agree to read to the jury.

8. *Closing Arguments*

The order of closing arguments varies somewhat from state to state. The most common sequence is one in which the prosecution speaks first. It is then first followed by the defense's argument, which in turn is followed by a final statement from the prosecution. In some states, if the defense presents no exhibits or oral testimony other than that of the defendant, the defense gets the first closing argument, the prosecution gets the second, and the defense has one final opportunity to speak again.

9. *Jury Instructions Are Read*

While jury instructions follow the closing arguments in most states, there are some states in which the instructions are given prior to the attorneys' statements.

10. *Jury Deliberations and the Verdict*

a. Acquittal. If the jury verdict is one of acquittal, the defendant cannot be tried again for the same crime, since the Fifth Amendment to the U.S. Constitution specifically states that no person shall "be subject for the same offense to be twice put in jeopardy of life or limb ..." The constitutional prohibition against double jeopardy does not, however, prohibit the state from appealing the dismissal of charges against the defendant on technical grounds.

b. Conviction. If there is a conviction, then the judge usually orders a presentence investigation of many factors such as the defendant's criminal record so that the court can be assisted in rendering a just sentence.

(1) *Appeal.* Whenever the defendant exercises the right of appeal, arguments not raised in the original trial proceedings are deemed waived on appeal unless they involve plain errors or defects that substantially affect the rights of the defendant. Appellate courts are not inclined to overturn lower court decisions on the basis of *harmless errors* that did not significantly affect the outcome of the case.

REVIEW QUESTIONS

1. Putnam has been charged with armed robbery and is facing criminal prosecution. The prosecuting attorney wishes to compel Putnam to give deposition testimony. Can this be done if Putnam objects?

2. Explain the difference between a preliminary hearing and an arraignment.

3. What is the purpose of a grand jury?

4. Admissions made by the defense attorney on a client's behalf at a pretrial conference cannot be used against the defendant. What is the probable underlying reason for this rule?

5. Indicate the various ways in which a criminal case may be initiated.

6. How do pretrial conferences in criminal courts differ from those in civil courts?

7. Findley runs over Harcourt, a pedestrian, and is sued by Harcourt for damages. Findley is also arrested for criminal negligence. Who will have the greater burden of proof—the prosecutor in the criminal case or the plaintiff in the civil case? What is the burden of proof in a criminal case, and why are the burdens in criminal and civil cases different when the factual situation is the same?

FOOTNOTES

[1]The crime of "larceny" at common law was the taking and carrying away of the personal property of another with intent to permanently deprive. If the property had a value of less than a certain amount (often $200 or $300), the act was known as *petty larceny*. If the property had a value of greater than the designated amount, the act was known as *grand larceny*.

[2]Simply because the maximum penalty for the offense is 60 days with a possible fine of $500, it should not be assumed that a first-time offender would receive such a sentence under ordinary circumstances. The judge generally has the responsibility for determining the sentence to be imposed within the limits established by statute.

[3]In addition to the parties listed, corporations have not historically been held responsible for certain kinds of criminal acts for a variety of reasons. First, the crime itself may be of such a nature that it can only be committed by a natural person. Second, the criminal statute may provide for a kind of punishment, such as incarceration, that is inapplicable to cases in which a corporation is a defendant. Third, one or more of the elements of the offense may be of such a nature that they may only be established if the defendant is a natural person. Courts are now refusing to recognize many of the immunities that corporations have had in the past.

[4]While insanity at the time of the trial may not be a defense, the attorney for the defendant may argue that his client should not have to face trial at a given time because the defendant is incapable of assisting in his or her own defense.

[5]See Chapter 8, Sec. 8-3, subsection A.2 for a discussion of the meaning of "work product."

10 *Real Estate*

CHAPTER OVERVIEW

B. Grantee

C. Deposit Receipt Contract

D. Warranty Deed

E. Quitclaim Deed

F. Bill of Sale

G. No Lien Affidavit

H. Assumption of Mortgage

I. Mortgage Payoff

J. Recording

K. Abstract

L. Name Search

M. Purchase Money Mortgage

N. Balloon Mortgage

O. Amortized Loan

P. Satisfaction of Mortgage

Q. Closing Statement

R. Title Insurance

S. Claim of Lien

T. Release of Lien

U. Satisfaction of Judgment

V. Fee Simple Estate

10-5   Steps in a Very Basic Standard Residential Closing

A. A Deposit Receipt Contract Is Signed

B. An Abstract Is Ordered

C. The Buyer Applies for Credit Approval

D. Roof, Pool, or Termite Inspections

E. The Abstract Is Examined

F. A Request Is Sent for Assumption or Payoff Information

G. Arrangement for the Transfer or Purchase of Insurance Policies

H. A Closing Date Is Set, and Documents Are Prepared

I. The Real Estate Closing Takes Place

J. All Appropriate Documents Are Recorded

K. The Title Insurance Policy Is Sent to the Buyer

SEC. 10-1
IN GENERAL

The general subject area of real estate includes three basic categories: A. land and the structures built upon the land; B. fixtures; and C. rights in the land of others.

A.   Land and All Structures Built upon the Land

When a piece of land is the subject of a sales transaction, it is implicit that, unless otherwise indicated, the sale includes such structures as houses, barns, and garages. It is also implied in many states that the purchaser of the real estate is entitled to the mineral rights associated with the property unless they are specifically reserved by the seller in the sales contract.

B.   Fixtures

These are pieces of property that are so closely associated with real estate that they should be regarded as real estate. For example, if an owner has built a china cabinet into one of the walls of the home, it would be assumed in any real estate transaction involving the subsequent sale of the house that, unless otherwise agreed by the parties, the cabinet would pass with the sale of the real property (which would include the land and the house). This would be true because of the fact that the cabinet was attached to or affixed to the building.

In order to determine whether a particular item is a fixture, other factors need to be considered. One is the intent of the parties. If the real estate is to be sold and there is some question as to whether a certain item is a fixture, it is not sufficient for the buyer of the property to simply assert that it was his or her understanding that a particular piece of property should be regarded as a fixture. Mutual intent can often be ascertained from an examination of the original contract that was signed at the time the buyer put down the initial deposit. Failure to clarify which items are or are not fixtures can result in conflicts that may possibly be resolved only after court action.

Another factor that may determine whether an item is a fixture is whether the item is specially adapted for use with the structure.

C.   Rights in the Land of Others

There are many situations in real estate law in which a party does not own a portion of real estate but rather has an interest in real property that is owned by other people. Two of these situations are covered in the following discussion.

1.   Mortgages

Few buyers in the real estate market are able to pay the full purchase price for homes when they buy them. Therefore, they must borrow money in order to close the transaction. At that time, they agree to make periodic (often monthly) payments to the lender for a considerable period of time, which is frequently as long as 15 or 30 years. A standard lender such as a bank will charge interest for making such a loan, and the interest rate charged will generally depend upon the prevailing economic conditions at the time.

a. Two primary documents involved.   When a mortgage is drawn up, at least two separate documents are involved. They are listed in the following discussion.

(1) *A mortgage note.* This document is the actual instrument signed by the borrower, indicating that the borrower unconditionally promises to pay to the order of the lender a certain specified sum of money at a designated rate of interest over a stated period of time. It will generally include such information as the amount of the total loan, the amount of the monthly payment, the date that the first payment is due, the place where the payments should be sent, the interest rate, the loan period, and other information. An example of a mortgage note can be found in Figure 10-1, page 293.

(2) *A mortgage deed.* This document indicates, among many other things, that if the borrower fails to make prompt periodic payments to the lender, then the lender will have the right to take the real estate. This is called the right of *foreclosure.* If there is a foreclosure, the lender may then sell the property to recover the losses. If the amount received is in excess of the total amount due to the lender (including foreclosure costs, attorneys fees, and so on), then the owner who lost the property due to foreclosure is entitled to the difference. If, on the other hand, the property in foreclosure is sold for an amount that is less than the amount that the lender is entitled to, the owner who lost the property due to foreclosure will remain obligated to the lender for the balance. An example of a mortgage deed can be found in Figures 10-2a, 10-2b, and 10-2c, pages 294–296.

b. Second and subsequent mortgages.   Even if there is already a mortgage on the property, it is still possible to have a second mortgage from the lender using the same piece of real estate as security for the loan. However, if the borrower fails to make prompt payments and the property is sold in foreclosure, the first lender is entitled to receive its money first. The only time that a second mortgage holder will be paid is if the property is sold in foreclosure, the first mortgage holder is completely paid off, and there is still money left over. Because of the greater risk involved, interest rates on second mortgages tend to be significantly higher than those for first mortgages. Similarly, interest rates for third mortgages will be higher than those for second mortgages, since both the first and the second mortgage holders will be entitled to complete payment before the third mortgage holder receives anything. While there is no limit to the number of mortgages that one can have on a particular parcel of real estate, it is relatively uncommon for there to be more than two.

2.   Easements

An *easement* is a right to use in a particular way property that belongs to another. The owner of an easement does not have actual title to any portion of the property in question, but only has the right to use the property for a particular purpose. An example of an easement is the right of a utility company to run pipes and lines through a parcel of property. It is very difficult to destroy an easement once it is created, although it is possible for the owner of the property to destroy the easement by buying back the right from the easement holder. Easements can be created in several different ways.

a. In writing.   One can purchase easement rights from the owner of a parcel of property (if the seller is willing to grant such rights) by obtaining from the seller a document to that effect. Such easements are generally placed in the public records of the local county and can be found in the course of a normal title examination. Title examinations may also turn up municipal or county easements such as sewer and drainage easements that have resulted from local legislative action.

b. By implication.   An easement may exist as a result of the geographical layout of the land. Suppose, for example, that one owns a tract of land that is surrounded on three sides by water and is completely blocked from access to the road on the fourth side by an adjoining parcel of property. If the owners of the two parcels purchased their respective properties from a common grantor, the owner of the blocked property would have an implied common law right of access to the road. The property through which access would have to be given would be referred to as the *servient tenement* because its owner's interests would be subservient to those of the neighbor. The other property would be known as the *dominant tenement* because its owner's rights would dominate over those of the adjoining property owner. The word *tenement* in this context means a tract of land. While the servient tenement holder must provide the access, the holder of the servient tenement may choose the portion of the property through which the neighbor may travel. A title search of either the dominant or servient tenement will not disclose the easement since there will be no actual documentation transferring easement rights from one party to another.

c. By prescriptive right.   If one continually exercises a particular right of usage over the property of another for a long enough period of time in an open and notorious way, the law may recognize that right as a legally enforceable one in the future even though the owner of the property is opposed to the recognition of that right. For example, if a woman has allowed her next door neighbor to use a particular part of her property continuously and over an extended period for the parking of motor vehicles and she has never objected, it is possible that the neighbor may have a legally enforceable right to continue to use her property for that purpose in the future. The period of time required for the establishment of a prescriptive right varies from state to state.

SEC. 10-2
MULTIPLE OWNERSHIP

Sometimes, several parties hold title to a particular parcel of property together. For example, it is very common to see the title to real property held in the name of "John Smith and Mary Smith, his wife." There is no limitation as to how many parties may share real estate ownership. This very brief examination of the subject of multiple ownership is included to provide basic familiarity with these forms of ownership. There are three common ways in which parties hold property in more than one name. Those three ways are the following:

A. Tenancy In Common

This form of multiple ownership, which is also known as a *co-tenancy*, has certain characteristics:

1. Undivided Interest

When each party has an undivided interest in a parcel of property, none of the co-tenants owns any particular square foot of the property. Instead, each party owns a percentage interest in each square foot of the parcel. None of the co-tenants is therefore capable of selling any portion of the property without the concurrence of all other co-tenants. While the interests of the co-tenants are undivided, they are not necessarily equal. It is therefore possible for one co-tenant to own a 70 percent interest in the property while the other owns 30 percent. Unless it is specified otherwise, however, the interests of the co-tenants are presumed to be equal.

2. Transfer Rights

While it is not possible for a co-tenant to sell a specific portion of the property without the signatures of the other co-tenants, it is possible to transfer a percentage interest in the property to another without the approval of any other co-tenant. In the event of such a transfer, the buyer of the interest will become a co-tenant of the property. Similarly, it is possible for one to dispose of a percentage interest by will. The recipient of the real property interest in such an estate will likewise become a co-tenant with the other co-tenants of the property.

B. Joint Tenancy

Those classified as joint tenants have not only an undivided interest in the property but also a right of survivorship. This means that if one of the joint tenant dies, his or her interest passes by law to the remaining joint tenants. In order for two parties to be regarded as holding title to property as joint tenants with right of survivorship, the joint tenancy relationship must be clearly expressed in the title document such as in the case of a deed in the name of "Donald Wilkins and Patricia Snow as joint tenants with right of survivorship." If these two parties are the present title holders and Donald Wilkins dies first, his interest will pass to Patricia Snow. If Patricia Snow dies first, her interest will pass to Donald Wilkins. This would be true regardless of whether either Donald Wilkins or Patricia Snow left their interests in the property to other parties in their respective wills. The legal reason for this is that, in theory, at the moment of the death of the first party, the deceased's interest no longer exists, and it is therefore not the property of the deceased to dispose of by will.

It is recommended on occasion by some attorneys to their clients that the clients put their property in joint name with another party so that upon the death of the client, the property will automatically pass to the joint tenant, and the client's interest will not be tied up in probate proceedings. (For a further explanation of the effect of a joint tenancy upon probate, see the "Decedents' Estates" chapter of this book.) Placing property in joint name may affect other factors, however, such as the party's right to a total homestead taxation exemption. The determination of whether property in a particular transaction is to be held in joint tenancy is a legal judgment that a paralegal is not ethically empowered to make. It is also true that, even though the property passes directly to the surviving joint tenant, the deceased joint tenant's estate may be responsible for estate taxes on the entire value of the property. If the tenants are not married to each other and a joint tenancy or right of survivorship is not specifically indicated, then it will generally be presumed that a tenancy in common rather than a joint tenancy exists.

1. *Undivided Interest*

As in the case of a tenancy in common, a joint tenancy does not give the tenant the right to sell a particular portion of the real estate. It only gives the tenant a percentage interest in that property. While the interests of joint tenants are often equal, there is no legal requirement that the interests be the same. There is, however, a legal presumption that the interests are equal unless otherwise specified.

2. *Transfer Rights*

A joint tenant, like a tenant in common, does not have the right to sell a particular piece of the property. The tenant does, however, have the right to sell a percentage interest in the property during the tenant's lifetime. Nevertheless, in the event of such a transfer, the transferee acquires a tenancy in common rather than joint tenancy status. Any attempt by a joint tenant to transfer a percentage interest in the property by means of a last will and testament will be null and void since the remaining joint tenants automatically take the share by operation of law.

C.   *Tenancy by the Entirety*

A tenancy by the entirety is similar in many respects to a joint tenancy with its characteristic undivided interest and right of survivorship. However, in the case of a tenancy by the entirety, the tenants are married to each other. An example would be ownership held in the name of "Richard Johnson and June Johnson, his wife." In this situation, a right of survivorship would be presumed even though there is no reference either to a joint tenancy or a right of survivorship. The laws recognizing tenancies by the entirety should not be confused with community property laws which raise certain assumptions about property held in the name of the husband and the wife. Community property laws are only in effect in a few states, such as California, Texas, Louisiana, Arizona, New Mexico, Idaho, Nevada, and Wisconsin.

1.   *Undivided Interest*

As in the case of tenancies in common and joint tenancies, a husband and wife who hold property as tenants by the entirety have an undivided interest in the property, and neither one, therefore, owns any specific piece of the real estate.

2.   *Transfer Rights*

Unlike a tenancy in common or a joint tenancy in which the tenant can sell or transfer a percentage interest in the property, neither a husband nor a wife who hold an interest in tenancy by the entirety property can sell an interest in the property without the signature of the other party.

SEC. 10-3
CONDOMINIUMS

Condominiums have been created to accommodate the desires of those who are interested in the benefits of both apartment living and real estate ownership. The buyer who purchases a condominium is actually purchasing and taking title to the unit as well as receiving a percentage interest in the "common elements" of the complex such as the swimming pool or recreation hall. It is the responsibility of a potential buyer to obtain any needed loans or mortgages from a lender and approval from the condominium association for the purchase of the unit. The written condominium approval is placed along with the other key documents pertaining to the real estate transaction in the public records (see Recording in Sec. 10-4, subsection J).

There are both advantages and disadvantages to condominium ownership. One of the primary advantages is that the individual condominium unit owners are not personally responsible for maintenance of the common elements. The condominium association usually hires people for that purpose. Maintenance problems also pose one of the greatest disadvantages of condominium ownership. For example, in the event that the condominium association decides that a new roof for the entire complex is necessary, it may contract to have the work done and then charge each condominium unit owner a proportionate part of the bill whether or not the unit owner feels that the work is necessary. Similarly, if a unit owner feels that repair work is desperately needed and the other members of the condominium association object to such an expenditure, the work will not be done unless the unit owner is willing to pay for it. Under these circumstances, the unit owner may become part owner of a deteriorating property.

SEC. 10-4
TERMINOLOGY

A. Grantor

A *grantor* is a party who transfers an interest in real estate to another. (As in the case of many other legal terms, a party with an "or" at the end of its name is the one who is taking action. In this particular case, the grantor is the one who is granting or transferring the real estate interest.)

B. Grantee

A *grantee* is a party to whom an interest in real estate is transferred. (Again, as in the case of many legal terms, a party with an "ee" at the end of its name is the one to whom something is being done. In this particular case, the grantee is the one to whom a real estate interest is granted or transferred.)

C.   Deposit Receipt Contract

A *deposit receipt contract* is the initial contract for a residence signed by the buyer and seller that sets forth the terms of the real estate closing to take place at a future time. It is sometimes referred to by such other names as the *contract for sale and purchase* or the *receipt for deposit and purchase*. Because the documents transferring title will be signed at the closing and then recorded, it is not necessary for the parties to record the deposit receipt contract. (For a definition of "recording," see subsection J below.) An example of a deposit receipt contract can be found in Figures 10-3a, 10-3b, 10-3c, 10-3d, and 10-3e, pages 297–301. The following items are routinely included in the contract:

1. A listing of personal property (primarily tangible, movable property) that the parties agree to include in the sale. This might include such items as a refrigerator, stove, washer, dryer, or any one of a number of other pieces of personal property.

2. The purchase price.

3. The amount of the deposit.

4. A listing of any mortgages that are to be assumed by the buyer or given by the sellers as well as the basic terms and conditions of those mortgages.

5. A listing of any new mortgages that the buyer anticipates obtaining as well as the very basic terms and conditions of those mortgages.

6. The approximate amount of cash that the buyer will have to bring to the closing.

7. Special optional clauses such as those indicating that the particular property in question is being sold in an "as is" condition, or that the obligations under the contract are contingent upon the buyer obtaining *financing* such as approval for a loan.

8. The last possible date for the actual closing, at which time the actual title to the property will be transferred. This date can be extended by mutual agreement of the parties.

9. The amount of the real estate commission, if any, to be paid to the agent or broker.

10. The closing costs that will be borne by each of the parties. For the buyer, these are charges above and beyond the purchase price of the property. For the seller, these are charges that are to be deducted from the amount that would otherwise be received at the closing. Examples of closing costs are the title insurance premium (see subsection R below),

the cost of recording of the deed (see subsection J below), and the cost of the abstract (subsection K below). The parties may decide in the deposit receipt contract which of the expenses shall be borne by the buyer and which shall be borne by the seller.

D. Warranty Deed

A *warranty deed* is a document in which title to real property is transferred from one party to another. This document is the buyer's (or grantee's) actual proof of ownership. In this kind of a deed, the grantor is warranting or representing that the grantor has good title to the property being sold (except for specified exclusions). If the grantor does not have good title as represented in the deed, the grantee has a potential legal cause of action in a court of law. A warranty deed is signed only by the grantor or grantors since it is legally presumed that the grantee or grantees are willing to accept the real estate transfer. In most states, the warranty deed must contain a notarization and the signatures of a least two witnesses for each grantor in order for the document to be recorded, or placed in the public records of the county where the property is located. (See subsection J to follow.) An example of a warranty deed can be found in Figures 10-4a and 10-4b, pages 302–303.

E. Quitclaim Deed

Unlike the grantor of a warranty deed, the grantor of a *quitclaim deed* makes no warranties whatsoever as to his or her interest in the property. The grantor is only agreeing to transfer whatever interest he or she has in the property, if any, whether it be total or partial ownership, or other claim. Since the grantor is not making representations of ownership with this kind of document, it should, therefore, be clear that a buyer in an ordinary real estate transaction should not accept a quitclaim deed.

One may wonder then why quitclaim deeds would be used under any circumstances for the transfer of a real estate interest. This question can be most easily answered by two illustrations.

First, if a married couple owns a piece of real estate as tenants by the entirety and they subsequently seek a dissolution of their marriage, the postdissolution status of their real estate must be resolved. If part of their dissolution agreement is that the husband transfer his interest in the property to his wife, then a quitclaim deed would suffice. The wife's only concern would be to remove whatever interest the husband had in the title to the property at that time. Obviously, it would make little sense to require that a title search be made to examine the husband's interest in the property. All the wife would be concerned with would be a transfer to her of whatever interest the husband had in the property.

Second, if a title search of the property discloses that an heir of a previous owner of the property might possibly have an interest in the property but the actual claim of that heir is uncertain, the title problem could be cleared up by obtaining a quitclaim deed from the heir. In such a case, the heir who was unaware of even a potential interest in the property might be willing to sign off his or her interest in the property with a quitclaim deed, especially if some small compensation was given to the heir. An example of a quitclaim deed can be found in Figures 10-5a and 10-5b, pages 304–305.

F.   Bill of Sale

A *bill of sale* is a document that transfers title from the seller to the buyer of any personal property (tangible, movable property) that passes with the real estate. The items of personal property included in the bill of sale will generally be those listed in the deposit receipt contract. An example of a bill of sale can be found in Figure 10-6, page 306.

G.   No Lien Affidavit

A *no lien affidavit* is an affidavit or sworn statement signed by the seller that indicates that there are no liens or claims against the property that the seller knows of that would jeopardize the buyer's claim to the property upon sale, such as claims of workmen who had done recent construction work on the property. In this example, if the workmen were never paid, they would have a claim against the property regardless of who the owner might be. Furthermore, such potential claims might not show up in an ordinary title search of the property since there might not be any claim of record at that time. Since this document is an affidavit, and the party signing it, who is known as an *affiant*, is swearing to the truth of the statements made therein, the signature of the affiant must be notarized even though the instrument is not generally recorded. For a more extensive listing of the additional representations made in a standard no lien affidavit, see Figures 10-7a and 10-7b, pages 307–308.

H.   Assumption of Mortgage

When there is an assumption of mortgage by the buyer in a real estate transaction, the buyer is agreeing to assume the mortgage responsibilities of the seller who already has a mortgage on the property and to continue paying on the mortgage after the real estate closing. This may be an attractive option for the buyer especially if the seller has a mortgage with a low interest rate. A buyer would prefer to assume such a mortgage rather than to obtain a new mortgage at a higher interest rate. Some mortgages are written to prevent a future assumption. When the parties have agreed to an assumption of an existing mortgage, it is necessary to obtain from the lender a document known as an assumption letter which will indicate the exact amount of the debt that will be assumed by the buyer.

I.   Mortgage Payoff

If a seller still owes money on a pending mortgage at the time of the sale and there is not going to be an assumption of that mortgage, then there will generally be a *mortgage payoff*. Since it is the seller's mortgage, it will be the seller's responsibility to pay it off. The payment will come from the proceeds that the seller receives at closing. If a mortgage payoff is to take place, it is necessary to obtain from the lender a document that will indicate the exact amount of the debt outstanding at the time of closing. An example of a mortgage payoff letter can be found in Figure 10-8, page 309.

J.   Recording

If a document has been *recorded*, it has been filed in the public records. In real estate matters, this is generally done in the county where the land is located. Documents are recorded in order to give notice to the public that certain legal transactions, claims, or events have occurred.

Suppose, for example, that Wilmot sold a piece of real property to Baker on June 1 and Baker never recorded. Then on August 20, Wilmot fraudulently sold the same piece of property to Yancy. Yancy would have no way of knowing of Baker's interest in the property at the time of the purchase since Baker had never recorded. If Yancy then sold the property to Ziller, who bought the property innocently and without knowledge of Baker's claim, Ziller would generally have a claim to the property that was superior to that of Baker.

Recording is not necessary in order for Wilmot's deed to Baker to be valid, and consequently, Baker would have a legal cause of action against Wilmot in a court of law even though Ziller would still have a greater claim to the ownership of the property than Baker.[1]

In order for a document to be recorded in most states, it must be signed, notarized, and witnessed by at least two parties. Once an instrument is recorded, it should be found by the abstract company when preparing the abstract and included within any subsequent abstract of the property.

K. *Abstract*

An *abstract* (or abstract of title as it is known by its more complete name) is a compilation of copies of all of the real estate documents of record pertaining to a particular piece of real property. It would be examined by one searching the title to verify that the seller had clear title to the property, and it would include copies of such documents as warranty deeds, mortgages, and easements. Abstracts can be obtained from abstract companies which are in the business of researching the public records and compiling copies of the documents necessary for the creation of an abstract. A complete abstract could go back as far as there are documents of record for a particular tract.

If a couple purchased real estate in 1979, the abstract that they used in 1979 would include only those documents of record that existed up to that time. If they are now in the process of selling that same piece of property, the new buyers would want to have the abstract updated to include all documents of record since 1979. Such an update of the abstract would be called a *continuation* or *partial abstract*.

When an abstract company prepares an abstract, it does not in any way warrant that the title to the property is in the name of the seller or that the seller has clear title to the real estate. The abstract company is representing only that it has included within the abstract all of the documents of record for that particular parcel of property.

L. *Name Search*

At the time an abstract is prepared, a *name search* may also be done by the abstract company. Rather than just looking for legal documents pertaining to a particular parcel of property, the name or names of the seller or sellers are investigated. For example, if there is a recorded personal judgment against the seller in which the prevailing party was never paid by the seller, the creditor in that case would have a claim against the property that is being sold. If there is such an outstanding judgment in favor of a creditor, that creditor must generally be paid from the proceeds that the seller would otherwise receive at closing.

M. *Purchase Money Mortgage*

A *purchase money mortgage* is a mortgage in which the grantor or seller of the property also acts in the capacity of a lender or mortgagee. Rather than seeking a loan from an outside source such as a bank, the grantee or buyer agrees to make periodic payments to the grantor. The seller is, therefore, agreeing to accept periodic payments over an extended period of time rather than receiving the entire purchase price at the time of closing. The advantage to the buyer is that he or she does not have to come up with as much money all at once at the time of closing. The advantage to the grantor is that the grantor can get a much larger amount of money over the entire mortgage period than he or she would get in one lump sum since the grantor like any other lender would be entitled to charge interest on the loan. Whether or not a purchase money mortgage is created in a particular real estate transaction is a negotiable term to be agreed upon by the parties.

N. Balloon Mortgage

A *balloon mortgage* is a mortgage in which the last payment is much larger than the regular periodic payments and equals the entire remaining balance of the loan. For example, a mortgagor may be required to pay $750 each and every month for a period of five years and then make one final payment of $12,512.

A borrower might agree to such a loan arrangement for a variety of reasons. First of all, a balloon mortgage may be the only type of mortgage that the lender is willing to offer. Second, the borrower may feel certain of receiving a large sum of money during the mortgage period from an estate or from a sale of another piece of real estate. There is a significant risk to the borrower in this case, because if he or she is not able to make the balloon payment, the lender may foreclose on the property after the borrower has made all but the very last payment. Because of the potential risk to the consumer in these kinds of transactions, many states require that it be clearly stated across the top of the mortgage deed if the instrument is a balloon mortgage.

O. Amortized Loan

Most mortgages are *amortized*. This means that when the borrower makes the initial payments, a large percentage of the periodic (often monthly) payments is attributable to interest, while a small percentage is attributable to principal. If, for example, the loan is for an amount of $80,000 and payments are initially $750 per month, approximately $742 of the first payment might be attributed to interest and only $8 to principal. At the end of the first month, therefore, the total balance due on the mortgage would be $79,992 (only $8 less than the original loan amount even though the borrower had paid a total of $750). The lender is not receiving more interest than it would have if the interest had been distributed equally among each individual payment. Rather, the borrower is getting a greater proportion of the interest "up front." Note that regardless of the amortization of the loan, the monthly payment in this example remains constant. As the borrower approaches the end of the loan period, a very large proportion of each payment will be attributed to principal while the percentage attributable to interest will be accordingly smaller. The buyer in a standard real estate transaction often receives a computer printout of an amortization table showing what portion of each payment is interest and what portion is principal throughout the entire loan period. Such a table is useful to a buyer since the buyer may be able to deduct interest paid during the year on his or her income taxes.

P.   Satisfaction of Mortgage

A *satisfaction of mortgage* is a notarized statement from the lender that a mortgage has been paid off and satisfied. An example of a satisfaction of mortgage can be found in Figure 10-9, page 310.

Q.   Closing Statement

The *closing statement* is the document that gives the financial breakdown of all closing figures, and it will, therefore, indicate not only the total amount that must be brought to the closing by the buyer but also the total amount that the seller will receive at closing. Those two figures will not usually match since the buyer has to pay not only any amount still due to the seller, but also a number of other expenses associated with the real estate transaction such as stamp taxes, attorneys fees, and roof inspection costs. Similarly, it is also true that the seller will have certain expenses that must be subtracted from the gross amount to be received, such as attorneys fees and the real estate broker's commission. The closing statement should be signed by all grantors and all grantees. Multiple copies of the statement are usually signed at the closing so that each party, realtor, and attorney can have an original copy signed by the grantors and grantees.

Since this book is written as an introductory text, a more detailed analysis of the preparation of closing statements will be left to courses and texts dealing with real estate.

R.   Title Insurance

Just as one may purchase fire insurance to receive compensation in the event that one's home burns down, a person may purchase *title insurance* to cover the possibility that the title examiner has made an error during the title search. Rather than making periodic payments as in the case of some other kinds of insurance, the buyer of real estate who chooses to purchase title insurance will generally make a one-time, lump-sum payment at the time of closing. The purchase of title insurance is totally discretionary for the buyer. However, a mortgagee (lender) may require the mortgagor (borrower) to buy title insurance for the lender since the mortgagee would not want to lend money and accept the property as collateral if the seller's title to the property is questionable. A policy purchased for the lender would be called *mortgagee insurance,* while the owner's (buyer's) policy would be referred to as *mortgagor insurance.*

S. Claim of Lien

A *claim of lien* is a claim that is attached to a piece of real estate in order to force the owner to pay the amount due. The property cannot be sold until the debt is paid. A purchaser would want to verify that any claims of lien existing on the property prior to the sale are paid off before the closing. Any creditor with such a claim would record the document in the public records so that title examiners would be aware of the creditor's interest.

T. Release of Lien

A *release of lien* is a document signed by a creditor or the creditor's representative relinquishing the claim of lien. If a release of lien is obtained from the creditor, the buyer of the property will want to record the document (see subsection J above) so that subsequent title examiners will see that the creditor's claim has been canceled.

U. Satisfaction of Judgment

If the name search (see subsection L above) reveals that there are outstanding judgments against the seller that could become liens against the property and the creditors are paid in full, the debtor (seller) will be entitled to a written statement known as a *satisfaction of judgment* from the creditor acknowledging full payment. This document will then be filed in the public records of the county where the property is located.

V. Fee Simple Estate

This is the fullest ownership that one can have in a piece of property, which includes the right of the owner to sell the property during his or her lifetime, transfer the property by will, or leave the property to pass to heirs if there is no will. In many states, there is a statutory presumption that a fee simple estate is being conveyed in a real estate transfer unless the parties have indicated a contrary intent in the deed.

SEC. 10-5
STEPS IN A VERY BASIC STANDARD
RESIDENTIAL CLOSING

Obviously, the terms of every real estate transaction are going to be different, but this brief section is included in order to give a sense of the order in which certain events leading up to the closing actually occur. It should be clearly understood that this list should in no way be used as a format in preparing for a real estate closing since many more steps will probably be involved in any one transaction.

With the above precautionary statement in mind, the following is the order of the steps that might be followed from beginning to end in a very basic residential real estate closing.

A.   A Deposit Receipt Contract Is Signed

This initial contract is signed, and the buyer puts down a deposit.

B.   An Abstract Is Ordered

Whether this is the responsibility of the buyer or the seller will generally be indicated in the deposit receipt contract.

C.   The Buyer Applies for Credit Approval

Since credit approval takes time, application by the buyer for such approval should be initiated immediately upon the signing of the deposit receipt contract. The lender will require a copy of the contract since the real property will be the security for the loan.

D.   Roof, Pool, or Termite Inspections

Such inspections are generally optional on the part of the purchaser of the property. If the purchaser does exercise this option, it will normally be the purchaser's responsibility to pay for the inspection. If, however, the inspection indicates that repairs are necessary, any such repairs will have to be made at the expense of the seller unless the property is being sold in an "as is" condition.

The handling of roof, pool, and termite inspections is different when an FHA loan or a VA loan has been obtained for the sale. An *FHA loan* is one that has been insured by the Federal Housing Administration. A *VA loan* is one that has been insured by the Veterans' Administration. In both cases, however, the federal agency is not the actual lender; it only acts as an insurer of the loan. In order to obtain loan approval, representatives of the agency will have to appraise the property and indicate whether additional work, such as a roof repair, will be needed before FHA or VA approval can be given.

E. The Abstract Is Examined

Once an updated abstract of title is received, the attorney for the buyer searches the abstract and informs the seller's attorney of any title defects. The seller's attorney is responsible for clearing up any and all title defects.

F. A Request Is Sent for Assumption or Payoff Information

If a mortgage is to be assumed, a request for an assumption letter is sent to the mortgagee. If a mortgage is to be paid off at closing, a request for a payoff letter is sent to the mortgagee. Whether the mortgage is to be assumed or paid off, the buyer will need to know the exact amount of the outstanding balance and other related information from the lender.

G. Arrangement for the Transfer or Purchase of Insurance Policies

If the parties and the insurance company agree, the seller's insurance policy can be transferred to the buyer at the time of the sale. A buyer can also obtain insurance coverage from any other company.

H. A Closing Date Is Set, and Documents Are Prepared

Once the title has been examined and cleared, the financial information has been obtained from the lender, and all bills have been received from the inspectors, a closing date and time are established, and closing documents are prepared by the attorneys. The buyers are then told how much money to bring to the closing.

I. The Real Estate Closing Takes Place

At the closing, the documents are signed, the keys to the house are given to the buyer, and the seller and real estate agents get their checks. If the buyer has purchased title insurance, he or she may receive a binder indicating a commitment on the part of the title insurance company to issue the title policy.

J.   All Appropriate Documents Are Recorded

Examples of the kinds of documents that may be recorded in a simple real estate transaction include the warranty deed (see Sec. 10-4, subsection D), any quitclaim deeds (see Sec. 10-4, subsection E) if they have been executed in connection with the transaction, mortgage deeds (see Sec. 10-1, subsection C.1.), any satisfactions of mortgages (see Sec. 10-4, subsection P), any releases of liens (see Sec. 10-4, subsection T), a condominium approval when appropriate (see Sec. 10-3), and any satisfactions of judgments (see Sec. 10-4, subsection U).

K.   The Title Insurance Policy Is Sent to the Buyer

At the closing, the buyer who has agreed to purchase title insurance is usually given a *binder* which is a written commitment to issue the insurance policy at a later date. The reason that the policy is not given to the buyer at the closing is that information that will be stamped on such documents as the warranty deed and the mortgage deed at the recording office after the closing must be included in the policy.

This form is designed for
instruction, and <u>not</u> for use
in all jurisdictions.

$_____   Date: _____

60,000.00   **September 9, 1996**

MORTGAGE NOTE

IN RETURN FOR VALUE RECEIVED, the undersigned person(s) (jointly and severally if more than one) promise(s) to pay to the order of   **ABC Savings and Loan, 459 Financial Boulevard, Patterson, FL 19291**

the principal sum of **Sixty Thousand** --------------00/100 Dollars($ 60,000.00) together with interest thereon at the rate of **seven and a half** percent (7.5 %) per annum on the balance from   **October 1, 1996**   until the total principal amount plus accrued interest is paid in full. Said principal and interest shall be payable in lawful money of the United States of America at   **459 Financial Boulevard, Patterson, FL 19291**   , or such other place as the holder may designate in writing delivered to the maker. Payment(s) on this note shall be as follows:

The sum of $419.53, including principal and interest, shall be payable on the 1st day of November, 1996, and on the first of every subsequent month for 359 months; on October 1, 2026, the total remaining principal balance plus all interest accrued and unpaid, shall be payable in full.

This note may be prepaid in whole or in part at any time without penalty.

Any and all payments made on the obligation arising hereunder shall first be applied to interest accrued under this note, with all additional amounts paid serving to reduce the principal balance due.

The principal obligation under this note, together with the interest due under it, is secured by a mortgage executed on this same date and made by the Maker of this note in favor of the Payee. The terms of this Note and of the said Mortgage shall be construed and enforced according to the laws of the jurisdiction in which the subject real estate is situated.

In the event that there is a default in the payment of either principal or interest due under this Note, or in the performance of any of the other terms of this Note or of the said Mortgage, then the entire principal sum and all accrued interest shall, at the sole option of the holder hereof, become due and payable at once without notice; in such event, the total principal and accrued interest due hereunder shall bear the part of the holder to exercise this option shall not constitute a waiver of the holder's right to exercise such right at a later time, or in the event of a subsequent default.

Each person liable hereunder, either as a Maker, Endorser, or in any other way, hereby waives presentment, protest, notice or protest and notice of dishonor and agrees to pay all costs permitted under law, including attorney's fees reasonably necessary to collect amounts due, whether suit is brought or not.

8967 Winding Willows Lane

_____   _____(SEAL)
                                                   Jody Pasternak

Trenton, FL 19291

_____   _____(SEAL)
                                                   Beverly Pasternak

FIGURE 10-1

MORTGAGE DEED

THIS MORTGAGE DEED is being executed on this, the **9th** day of **September,** 19 **96**
by **Jody Pasternak and Beverly Pasternak, his wife,**
hereinafter in this document referred to as the Mortgagor(s), to and for the
Mortgagee(s), **ABC Savings and Loan, 459 Financial Boulevard, Patterson, FL
19291.**

WITNESSETH, That for good and valuable consideration, the receipt and sufficiency
of which is hereby acknowledged, and in consideration of the sum named in the
Mortgage Note of this same date, the Mortgagor(s) hereby grant, sell, bargain,
release and convey to the Mortgagee(s) and his/her/its/their heirs and assigns
in fee simple that certain real property which the Mortgagor(s) now own(s) and
possess(es), and which is located in the County of **Desdin**   , in the State
of **Florida**   , and which is described as follows:

**Lot 47, Block 14 of Blackacre Subdivision, according to the Plat thereof recorded
in Plat Book 76, page 722 of the Public Records of Desdin County, Florida.**

**Notwithstanding any provisions herein contained to the contrary, this mortgage
is non-assumable, and in the event any interest in the mortgaged property shall
be transferred, the note secured by this mortgage shall immediately become due
and payable in full.**

TO HAVE AND TO HOLD together with the tenements, hereditaments, and appurtenances
unto the said Mortgagee(s) and his/her/its/their heirs and assigns outright in
fee simple.

AND THE MORTGAGOR(S), for himself/herself/themselves and for his/her/their heirs
assigns and legal representatives do/does covenant with the Mortgagee(s),
his/her/its/their heirs, assigns and legal representatives, that the Mortgagor(s)
is/are indefeasibly seized of said land in fee simple; that the Mortgagor(s)
has/have the legal right to convey the real property; that the real property is
free and clear of all encumbrances, whether or not they are now of record; that
the Mortgagee(s) shall have the right at all times to enter upon, occupy and
enjoy the use of the real property and that the Mortgagor(s) does/do hereby
warrant the title to the real property and will defend against any and all
claims.

PROVIDED, HOWEVER, that if, and for as long as the Mortgagor(s) and his/her/their
heirs, assigns, and legal representatives shall continue to meet the obligations
of this Mortgage Deed and the terms and conditions of the Mortgage Note that it
secures, a copy of which is hereby attached and marked as Exhibit "A", then the

1

FIGURE 10-2a

estate created hereunder, and all rights created hereby shall be null, void, and of no effect whatsoever.

THE MORTGAGOR(S) FURTHER AGREE(S) on behalf of himself/herself/themselves and his/her/their heirs, assigns, and other legal representatives to do the following things:

1. To pay all principal and interest and all other amounts due and payable under the Mortgage Note and/or Mortgage Deed in a timely fashion when they become due.

2. To pay all taxes, assessments and other obligations of every nature on the real property. If such obligations are not promptly paid, then the Mortgagee(s), and his/her/their heirs, assigns, and legal representatives, shall have the right to pay those amounts on behalf of the Mortgagor(s) with every such payment bearing interest at the highest rate allowed by the jurisdiction from the date thereof until said amount is repaid to the Mortgagee(s) in full. Advancing such monies shall not limit in any way the right the Mortgagee(s) has/have to foreclose.

3. To commit or allow no waste, impairment or deterioration of said real estate or of any structure thereon at any time.

4. To maintain insurance in an amount at least equal to the balance remaining due under the Mortgage Note secured by this Mortgage Deed with a company or companies approved by the Mortgagee(s), with such policy or policies held by and payable to the Mortgagee(s) and his/her/its/their heirs, assigns, and legal representatives.

In the event that amounts become payable under the terms of such insurance policy or policies, then the Mortgagee(s) shall have the option to receive such amounts and apply them to the payment of the indebtedness or to permit the Mortgagor(s) to receive the said amount to use for any purpose agreed to by the Mortgagee(s). In the event that the Mortgagor(s) fail(s) to make payments on the premiums for such policy or policies, the Mortgagee(s) shall have the right to pay premiums on behalf of the Mortgagor(s), with every such payment bearing interest at the highest rate allowed by the jurisdiction from the date thereof until said amount is repaid to the Mortgagee(s) in full.

5. To comply with each and every requirement, condition, obligation and agreement contained in either this Mortgage Deed or the Mortgage Note(s) which it secures.

6. To pay any and all costs and expenses, even including attorney's fees, reasonable incurred by Mortgagee(s) or his/her/its/their heirs, assigns, or legal representatives as a result of the failure of the Mortgagor(s) to perform any of the obligations under this Mortgage Deed or the Mortgage Note it secures. All such amounts shall bear interest at the highest rate allowed by the jurisdiction from the date they become due until said amounts are paid to the Mortgagee(s) in full.

7. That, if any amounts due under this Mortgage Deed or the Mortgage Note(s) it secures, whether they are interest, principal, or other payments, are not paid in full within thirty day from the time they become due, then at the sole option of the Mortgagee(s), and upon his/her/its/their written notice delivered to the Mortgagor(s) at the location of the real property or elsewhere, the total of all obligations under the Mortgage Note(s) shall become immediately due, as if that total amount had been originally stipulated as being due on that day.

2

FIGURE 10-2b

IN WITNESS WHEREOF, the Mortgagor(s) has/have hereunto set his/her/their hand(s) and seal(s) on the date set out above.

_____   _____ (Seal)
Witness **Gerald Lipton**   **Jody Pasternak**
                                     8967 Winding Willows Lane
                                     Trenton, FL 19291

_____
Witness **Howard Garvey**

_____   _____ (Seal)
Witness **Gerald Lipton**   **Beverly Pasternak**
                                     8967 Winding Willows Lane
                                     Trenton, FL 19291

_____
Witness **Howard Garvey**

STATE OF **FLORIDA**

COUNTY OF **DESDIN**

I HEREBY CERTIFY that, on this day personally appeared before me, an officer duly authorized to administer oaths and take acknowledgements,

Jody Pasternak and Beverly Pasternak, his wife

They are personally known to me or have produced **valid Florida drivers' licenses** as identification. They have acknowledged before me that he/she/they executed the same freely and voluntarily for the purpose therein expressed.

WITNESS my hand and official seal in **Desdin** County, the State of **Florida** this the **9th** day of **September** , 19 **96** .

My commission expires: _____
                                     Clark H. Smith
                                     NOTARY PUBLIC, State of **Florida**

3

FIGURE 10-2c

296

This form is designed for
instruction, and _not_ for use
in all jurisdictions.

DEPOSIT RECEIPT
CONTRACT FOR SALE AND PURCHASE

THIS CONTRACT FOR SALE AND PURCHASE is being entered into by and between
Jody Pasternak and Beverly Pasternak, his wife   , whose address and telephone
number are: **8967 Winding Willows Lane, Trenton, FL 19291 / (954) 720-0110**
and who is/are hereinafter referred to as the Buyer(s) and
Arthur Bowles and Beatrice Bowles, his wife   whose address and telephone
number are: **5851 Panama Terrace, Trenton, FL 19291 / (954) 881-0445**
and who is/are hereinafter referred to as the Seller(s). Under this agreement,
the Seller(s) agree(s) to sell, and the Buyer(s) agree(s) to buy the real
property described below, together with any and all existing improvements
thereon, binding themselves by all of the terms and conditions of this agreement.

1. LEGAL DESCRIPTION The legal description of the real property which is the
subject of this agreement, and which is located in **Desdin**   County, in the
State of **Florida**   , is as follows:

**Lot 47, Block 14 of Blackacre Subdivision, according to the Plat thereof recorded
in Plat Book 76, page 722 of the Public Records of Desdin County, Florida**

Street Address: 919 Borders Drive, Trenton, FL 19291   Tax Folio #1609894

2. PURCHASE PRICE The purchase price in U.S. Dollars   100,000.00
shall be: $_____

3. METHOD OF PAYMENT The purchase price shall be paid
as follows(subject to the usual adjustments at the
time of closing):

    Deposit (receipt of which by the Seller or   10,000.00
    his/her/their agent(s) is acknowledged by $_____
    the execution of this document by the Seller)

    Additional Deposit to be paid within **15**   days.   5,000.00
    All deposits are to be held in trust by: $_____
    Carl Swaim Realty, 500 5th St., Trenton, FL 19291

    Principal balance of mortgage to be assumed by   0
    Buyer(s): $_____

    Principal balance of **first**   mortgage to be   60,000.00
    obtained by Buyer(s): $_____

    The balance of the purchase price, together with   75,000.00
    sufficient funds to pay for all of Buyer's closing $_____
    costs due in U.S. currency in the form of a cashier's or certified check
    drawn on a local banking institution, with such funds being placed in escrow
    if appropriate under this agreement.

4. EXPIRATION OF OFFER The offer whose terms are contained in this document
shall become null and void if not accepted by the Seller(s)/Buyer(s) on or before
the **4th**   day of **June**   , 19 **96** at **5:00**   o'clock **P.M.**

5. CLOSING DATE The Buyer(s) and Seller(s) agree that, unless the same shall be
extended by all parties in writing, the closing on the property shall take place
and be concluded on or before the **12th**   day of **September**   , 19 **96** .

1

FIGURE 10-3a

6. **TITLE** The Seller(s) agree(s) that he/she/they shall, at his/her/their own expense, order a complete abstract of title from a reputable title firm and have it delivered to the Buyer(s)(or an attorney or title company designated by the Buyer(s)) at least 14 days prior to the date for which the closing is scheduled. As an alternative, and at the sole option of the Seller(s), the Seller(s) may provide to the Buyer(s), at the expense of the Seller(s), an Owner's Title Insurance Policy in an amount equal to the purchase price under this contract. If the Seller(s) choose(s) this option, then, if the lending institution from which the Buyer(s) secure a mortgage requires a Mortgagee policy of the Buyer(s), then the Seller(s) shall cause such a policy to be issued (but the Buyer(s) shall be responsible for any expense above and beyond the cost of the owner's policy.)

If a defect in title shall be found, the Buyer(s) shall give the Seller(s) notice thereof in writing, after which the Seller(s) shall cure such title defects to the reasonable satisfaction of the Buyer(s). If such defect cannot be corrected, or if Seller(s) refuse(s) to correct the defect, the Buyer(s) shall have the option of either accepting the title as is or canceling the contract, receiving all monies deposited with the Seller(s) or his/her/their agent(s).

7. **ASSUMPTION OF CURRENT MORTGAGES** The Seller(s) shall provide the Buyer(s) with a statement from the current mortgagee(s) stating the principal, interest rate, amount of periodic payments, the status of the mortgage, and whether the mortgage can be assumed (and if so, on what terms); the cost of preparation for such a statement, as well as any mortgage transfer fee, shall be borne equally by the Seller(s) and the Buyer(s). In the event that a current mortgage is to be assumed by the Buyer(s), the Buyer(s) agree(s) to purchase the escrow balance held by the mortgagee, dollar for dollar, from the Seller(s).

8. **PURCHASE MONEY MORTGAGES** A Purchase Money Mortgage and Note may only be part of the agreement evidence by this writing if the Seller(s) explicitly grant(s) the Buyer(s) the right to do so. Any Purchase Money Mortgage shall require the Mortgagor(s) to provide proof of payment of taxes to the Mortgagee(s) annually. Mortgagor(s) shall also be required to annually prove to the Mortgagee(s) that any and all improvements on the property are fully insured to the total value of all secured indebtedness, and that payments on the policy are current. No Purchase Money Mortgage shall be assumed without the explicit written authority of the Mortgagee(s).

9. **RISK OF LOSS** All risk of loss or damage to the improvements on the property shall be with the Seller(s) until there has been actual delivery of the Deed to the Buyer(s) or his/her/their agent(s). If all, or a substantial portion of the improvements on the property shall be destroyed or rendered unsuitable for use after the execution of this agreement, then the Buyer(s) shall have the option of proceeding with the terms of this agreement, or declaring the contract null, void and of no effect, causing the return of all monies on deposit.

10. **SURVEY** At his/her/their own expense, the Buyer(s) may cause a survey of the property to be done. In the event that the survey shows an encroachment of the improvements on the property of others upon the land in question, or an encroachment of the improvements of this land upon adjoining property, then such encroachments shall be considered to be title defects, and shall be treated as such under paragraph 5 above.

11. **PRORATION OF TAXES** All real property taxes on the property to be conveyed, as well as any other taxes related to the property or the improvements thereon, shall be prorated as of the date of closing, based upon the most recent full year's tax billing. Buyer(s) and Seller(s) agree that the proration used for

2

FIGURE 10-3b

closing may later be adjusted at the request of either the Buyer(s) or the Seller(s) once the actual figures for the year in which the closing took place become available, and that this agreement shall continue in full force and effect after the closing.

12. LEASES AND RENT If the real property, or any part thereof, is leased for any term, then, at least one week prior to closing, the Seller(s) agree(s) to provide the Buyer(s) with copies of all leases, together with an estoppel letter from each tenant stating the nature and duration of each tenancy, the term thereof, the amount of any advance rents, the rental rate, and the amount and conditions of all deposits. Rents are to be prorated between the Buyer(s) and Seller(s) as of the date of closing, and the Seller(s) will credit an amount equal to all deposits to the Buyer(s) at closing.

13. INSPECTIONS The Buyer(s) shall have the right to pay to have the property and all structures thereon inspected. If the Buyer(s) elect(s) to do so, the Seller(s) shall cooperate by allowing full access to inspectors at reasonable times. Such inspections may include, *inter alia*, the following:

(a) **Termite Inspection** At his/her/their own expense, the Buyer(s) shall have the right to hire a licensed pest control company to inspect the premises for signs of damage to structures, and for signs of live, active termites. If either is found, the Seller(s) shall be responsible for all costs associated with treating infestations and for repairing all damage.

(b) **General and Structural Inspections** At his/her/their own expense, the Buyer(s) shall have the right to hire appropriate licensed inspectors to inspect pools, seawalls, electrical and plumbing systems, the roof and general structural soundness of any buildings, and any other reasonable feature of the property which is the subject of this agreement. If there shall be any material, functional defects (as opposed to aesthetic deficiencies) in any items inspected, then the Seller(s) shall be obligated to pay all costs of repairing such defects.

(c) **Personal Property Included in the Sale** The Seller(s) personally guarantee(s) that all personal property included in the sale of this real property is in good working order. This guarantee includes, but is not limited to ovens, stoves, refrigerators, freezers, heating and cooling systems, air conditioners, water softeners and treatment systems, and any and all appliances that are to be sold with the property. If any item of personal property being sold with the real property is not in good working order, then it shall be the Seller's responsibility to pay the cost of repairing the item; this can be accomplished either by having the Seller(s) repair the item prior to closing (with the Buyer(s) having a right to reinspect), or by placing sufficient funds in an escrow account for payment of repair bills after closing.

Notwithstanding the provisions of subparagraphs (a), (b), and (c) above, the Buyer(s) and the Seller(s) agree that the Seller(s) shall not be required by this agreement to make repairs totalling more than **two** percent (**2** %) of the purchase price under this contract. If the total repairs exceed that percentage, then the Seller(s) have the option to refuse to make such repairs in excess of the stated percentage; if Seller(s) refuse to make repairs under this provision, then the Buyer(s) may elect to declare the contract null, void, and without effect, and to have all deposits returned in full. (If the Buyer(s) choose(s), he/she/they may elect to have the Seller(s) make repairs up to the designated percentage of the purchase price, and then accept the property with remaining defects.)

3

FIGURE 10-3c

14. **DEFAULT** In the event that there is a default by either party, either in the payment of a required sum, or in the failure to meet any other requirement of this agreement, then the remedies for the non-defaulting party shall be as follows:

(a) **Default by Buyer(s)** If the Buyer(s) shall fail to make any payment or to fulfill in any other way the obligations under this agreement, then the Buyer(s) shall forfeit all deposits, which shall be given to the Seller(s) as agreed-upon liquidated damages for the breach.

(b) **Default by Seller(s)** If the Seller(s) shall fail to perform any obligation under this agreement, then the Buyer(s) shall have the option of either having all deposits returned to him/her/them and declaring the contract to be null, void, and without effect, or having the right of specific performance under the contract.

(c) **Attorneys Fees and Costs** In the event that it becomes necessary to litigate any question concerning a default (or any other aspect of this agreement) then reasonable attorneys fees and other costs of filing and maintaining the action shall be paid by the losing party to the prevailing party. This shall include all costs, fees, and necessary expenses associated with any action or appeal.

15. **FULL AND FINAL AGREEMENT** Buyer(s) and Seller(s) agree that this written document consisting of pages one, two, three, four, ---------------- and five, containing paragraphs numbered one through **sixteen** , constitutes the full and complete agreement between them, and that any further or additional agreements, as well as any amendments hereto, must be made in writing, and must be signed by both Buyer(s) and Seller(s) in order to be valid and enforceable.

16. **ADDITIONAL CLAUSES** (Additional clauses may be added here. If additional space is needed, extra pages can be added, numbering them 4.1, 4.2, 4.3, etc.)

A. In conjunction with the sale of this realty, the following personal property is included within the transfer: the refrigerator, the dishwasher, and dryer all located at 919 Borders Drive, Trenton, FL 19291 (which is the street address of the real property being sold.)

xxxxxxxxxxxx

READ THIS BEFORE SIGNING THIS CONTRACT! All parties should understand that once this document has been signed by the Buyer(s) and Seller(s), it becomes a legally-binding contract which can be dissolved only by mutual agreement of ALL the parties signing it or by a judge's order after a legal proceeding in civil

4

FIGURE 10-3d

court. Be sure you understand each and every provision of this contract before
you sign it. If you have any doubt about the meaning of any part of the
agreement, consult with an attorney who is looking out for *your* legal interests!

                                                                June 2, 1996
                                                 Date:_____

Buyer **Jody Pasternak**   Buyer **Beverly Pasternak**
      043-46-9110   872-45-5463

ACCEPTANCE AND AGREEMENT TO PAY BROKER'S COMMISSION The Seller(s)
hereby accept(s) the offer from the Buyer(s) to purchase the above-described real
property from the sellers. In accepting the offer, the Seller(s) confirm(s) and
agree(s) to pay **Carl Swaim Realty, Inc.,**   the real estate broker(s), the
7% commission agreed-upon in their separate listing agreement.

                                                                June 3, 1996
                                                 Date:_____

Seller **Arthur Bowles**   Seller **Beatrice Bowles**
       938-04-2746   246-97-5788

THIS IS TO CERTIFY that on this, the **3rd**   day of   **June**   , 19 **96**,
at   **2:00**   o'clock   **P.M.**, I have received a deposit in the amount of
   Ten   Thousand---**00/100**   Dollars ($
10,000.00) under the terms of this agreement, and that the disposition of the
deposit will henceforth be governed by the terms of this contract.

Carl Swaim Realty, Inc.

By: _____
    Carl Swaim

5

FIGURE 10-3e

This form is designed for
instruction, and not for use
in all jurisdictions

WARRANTY DEED

THIS INDENTURE is entered into on this the 8th day of September, 19 96, by
and between **Arthur Bowles and Beatrice Bowles, his wife,** hereinafter referred
to as the Grantor(s), of the County of **Desdin** and the State of **Florida,** and
Jody Pasternak and Beverly Pasternak, his wife whose mailing address is
8967 Winding Willows Lane, Trenton, FL 19291 in the County of **Desdin** , the
State of **Florida** , hereinafter referred to as the Grantee(s).'

WITNESSETH That the Grantor(s), for and in consideration of the sum of
Ten---------------------------00/100 Dollars ($ 10.00), and other good
and valuable consideration, the receipt and sufficiency of which is hereby
acknowledged does/do hereby forever grant and transfer unto the Grantee(s) and
to his/her/their/its heirs, assigns, and legal representatives, the following-
described real property located in the County of **Desdin** , State of **Florida,**
to-wit:

                Lot 47, Block 14 of Blackacre Subdivision,
                according to the Plat thereof recorded in Plat
                Book 76, page 722 of the Public Records of
                Desdin County, Florida; and

                SUBJECT TO taxes for the year 1996 and all
                subsequent years, and to easements, restrictions,
                applicable zoning, reservations, and limitations
                of record.

and the Grantor(s) does/do hereby fully warrant the title to said real property
and will defend the same against any and all lawful claims.

1

FIGURE 10-4a

IN WITNESS WHEREOF, the Seller(s) has/have hereunto set his/her/their hand(s) and seal(s) on the date set out above.

<table>
<tr><td>_____
Witness **Gerald Lipton**</td><td>_____ (Seal)
Arthur Bowles
5851 Panama Terrace
Trenton, FL 19291</td></tr>
<tr><td>_____
Witness **Howard Garvey**</td><td></td></tr>
<tr><td>_____
Witness **Gerald Lipton**</td><td>_____ (Seal)
Beatrice Bowles
5851 Panama Terrace
Trenton, FL 19291</td></tr>
<tr><td>_____
Witness **Howard Garvey**</td><td></td></tr>
</table>

STATE OF **FLORIDA**

COUNTY OF **DESDIN**

I HEREBY CERTIFY that, on this day personally appeared before me, an officer duly authorized to administer oaths and take acknowledgements,

Arthur Bowles and Beatrice Bowles, his wife

They are personally known to me or have produced **valid Florida drivers' licenses** as identification. They have acknowledged before me that he/she/they executed the same freely and voluntarily for the purpose therein expressed.

WITNESS my hand and official seal in **Desdin** County, the State of **Florida** this the **9th** day of **September** , 19 **96** .

My commission expires:

_____
Clark H. Smith
NOTARY PUBLIC, State of **Florida**

2

FIGURE 10-4b

Return to (enclose a self-
addressed stamped envelope

    Barber Hollings
    779 47th Way.
    Bakersville, FL 19292

This instrument prepared by:

    Barber Hollings
    779 47th Way
    Bakersville, FL 19292

Property Appraiser's Parcel
Identification Number

    #1609894

Grantee(s) SS#(s): **043-46-9110**
                    872-45-5463

This form is designed for
instruction, and <u>not</u> for use
in all jurisdictions

QUIT-CLAIM DEED
(Individual)

THIS TRANSFER OF THE SELLER'S INTEREST in real estate is entered into this **5th** day of **September** , 19 **96** , by and between **George Teller and Mary Teller, his wife** , hereinafter referred to as the Grantor(s), of the County of **Desdin** and the State of **Florida** , and **Jody Pasternak (SS# 043-46-9110) and Beverly Pasternak, his wife, (SS# 872-45-5463)** whose mailing address is **8967 Winding Willows Lane, Trenton, FL 19291** in the County of **Desdin,** State of **Florida** , hereinafter referred to as the Grantee(s).

WITNESSETH That the Grantor(s), for and in consideration of the sum of **Ten--------------------------------00/100** Dollars($ **10.00**), and other good and valuable consideration, the receipt and sufficiency of which is hereby acknowledged, does/do hereby forever grant and transfer unto the Grantee(s) and to his/her/their/its heirs, assigns, and legal representatives, any and all interest of which he/she is or may be seized in the following-described real property located in the County of **Desdin** , State of **Florida** , to-wit:

        Lot 47, Block 14 of Blackacre Subdivision,
        according to the Plat thereof recorded in Plat
        Book 76, page 722 of the Public Records of
        Desdin County, Florida.

FIGURE 10-5a

    IN WITNESS WHEREOF, the Seller(s) has/have hereunto set his/her/their hand(s) and seal(s) on the date set out above.

_____   _____(SEAL)

Witness **Miller Barnes**   George Teller
                                              99 Lexington Court
                                              Patterson, FL 19292

_____

Witness **Candace Rawlings**

_____   _____(SEAL)

Witness **Miller Barnes**   Mary Teller
                                              99 Lexington Court
                                              Patterson, FL 19292

_____

Witness **Candace Rawlings**

STATE OF **FLORIDA**

COUNTY OF **DESDIN**

I HEREBY CERTIFY that, on this day personally appeared before me, an officer duly authorized to administer oaths and take acknowledgements,

        George Teller and Mary Teller, his wife

They are personally known to me or have produced **valid Florida drivers' licenses** as identification. They have acknowledged before me that he/she/they executed the same freely and voluntarily for the purpose therein expressed.

WITNESS my hand and official seal in **Desdin** County, the State of **Florida** this the **4th** day of **September** , 19 **96** .

My commission expires: _____
                                          Clark H. Smith
                                          NOTARY PUBLIC, State of **Florida**

2

FIGURE 10-5b

This form is designed for
instruction, and not for use
in all jurisdictions.

BILL OF SALE

KNOW ALL YE BE THESE PRESENTS that I/We, **Arthur Bowles and Beatrice Bowles, his wife** of the **city** of **Trenton** , in the County of **Desdin** and the State of **Florida** , being the Seller(s) for and in consideration of the sum of **Ten------------------------00/100** Dollars ($ **10.00**) in U.S. currency paid to the seller(s) by **Jody Pasternak and Beverly Pasternak, his wife** , of **8967 Winding Willows Lane, Trenton, FL 19291** , the Buyer(s). The Seller(s) does/do hereby sell transfer and deliver to the Buyer(s) and his/her/their heirs, executors, administrators and assigns full and complete title to the following goods and chattels:

Refrigerator, dishwasher, and dryer all located at 919 Borders Drive, Trenton, FL 19291

AND BE IT FURTHER KNOWN that the Seller(s) does/do/hereby covenant to and with the Buyer(s), and with the heirs,executors, administrators and assigns of the Buyer(s) that the Seller(s) is/are the true and lawful owner(s) with the legal right and authority to sell such goods and chattels, and that they are free from all encumbrances. The Seller(s) further promise(s) to defend the sale of the goods and chattels against the claims and challenges of any third party.

IN WITNESS WHEREOF, I/We have set my/our hands and seal(s) this **9th** day of **September** 19 **96**.

_____   _____ (Seal)
Witness **Gerald Lipton**   Arthur Bowles
                                                    5851 Panama Terrace
_____   Trenton, FL 19291
Witness **Howard Garvey**

_____   _____ (Seal)
Witness **Gerald Lipton**   Beatrice Bowles
                                                    5851 Panama Terrace
_____   Trenton, FL 19291
Witness **Howard Garvey**

STATE OF **FLORIDA**
COUNTY OF **DESDIN**

I HEREBY CERTIFY that, on this day personally appeared before me, an officer duly authorized to administer oaths and take acknowledgements,

Arthur Bowles and Beatrice Bowles, his wife

They are personally known to me or have produced **valid Florida drivers' licenses** as identification. They have acknowledged before me that he/she/they executed the same freely and voluntarily for the purpose therein expressed.

WITNESS my hand and official seal in **Desdin** County, the State of **Florida** this the **9th** day of **September** , 19 **96** .

My commission expires: _____
                                                   Clark H. Smith
                                                   NOTARY PUBLIC, State of **Florida**

FIGURE 10-6

This form is designed for
instruction, and _not_ for use
in all jurisdictions.

"NO LIEN" AFFIDAVIT FROM SELLER(S)

STATE OF **FLORIDA**

COUNTY OF **DESDIN**

Before the undersigned authority, personally appeared **Arthur Bowles and Beatrice Bowles, his wife**   who, being first duly sworn by me on oath deposes and says:

1. THAT the Affiant(s) is/are the fee simple owner(s) of the real estate described as follows:

   Lot 47, Block 14 of Blackacre Subdivision, according to the Plat thereof recorded in Plat Book 76, page 722 of the Public Records of Desdin County, Florida.

   and they have been the owners since **November 22, 1983.**

2. THAT the property described above is free and clear of all taxes, liens, encumbrances and claims of every kind and description whatsoever, except for personal property and real estate taxes for the year **1996.**

3. THAT there have been no improvements, alterations, or repairs to the above-described property for which the costs remain unpaid during the 90 days that have immediately preceded this affidavit, and that there have been no claims for labor or material furnished for repairing or improving the same, which remain unpaid, unless such are listed herein.

4. THAT there are no mechanic's liens, materialmen's liens, or laborer's liens against the above-described property.

5. THAT any personal property being sold in conjunction with the sale of the above-described real property, if any, is also free and clear of all liens, encumbrances, and claims.

6. THAT said Affiant(s), in the use of the above-described property, has/have complied in all respects with applicable sales tax and other laws of the jurisdiction.

7. THAT no judgment or decree has been entered in any jurisdiction against the Affiant(s) that remains unsatisfied.

8. THAT there are no unrecorded easements pertaining to the property, nor has there been a history of boundary disputes or claims of title against the owner(s) affecting the property.

9. THAT affiants, whose taxpayer identification numbers are 938-04-2746 and 264-97-5788, are not residents of a foreign country.

10. THAT affiants have not executed any documents or done any acts since **August 15, 1996** that would in any way affect the title to the property, including the signing of any documents conveying interests in the property or causing liens to be placed on the property.

1

FIGURE 10-7a

11. THAT Affiant(s) know(s) of no violation of municipal ordinances pertaining
to the above-described property.

12. THAT this affidavit is being made (1) to induce the Buyer(s), **Jody Pasternak
and Beverly Pasternak, his wife** to purchase the above-described property
from the Affiant(s) and (2) to induce **ABC Savings and Loan** to make a
mortgage loan on the property and/or (3) to induce **Warren Kingsley**, as a
member of **XYZ Title Insurance Fund, Inc.** to issue a policy to insure the
title to the property.

_____ (Seal)   _____ (Seal)
Affiant **Arthur Bowles**   Affiant **Beatrice Bowles**

STATE OF **FLORIDA**

COUNTY OF **DESDIN**

I HEREBY CERTIFY that, on this day personally appeared before me, an officer duly
authorized to administer oaths and take acknowledgements,

Arthur Bowles and Beatrice Bowles, his wife

They are personally known to me or have produced **valid Florida drivers' licenses**
as identification. They have acknowledged before me that he/she/they executed
the same freely and voluntarily for the purpose therein expressed.

WITNESS my hand and official seal in **Desdin** County, the State of **Florida** this the
9th day of **September** , 19 **96** .

My commission expires: _____
                                                 Clark H. Smith
                                                 NOTARY PUBLIC, State of **Florida**

2

FIGURE 10-7b

308

This form is designed for
instruction, and <u>not</u> for use
in all jurisdictions.

WORLD SAVINGS AND LOAN ASSOCIATION
4444 Central Avenue
Queenstown, FL 19293
(954) 822-1001

August 20, 1996

Warren Kingsley, Esq.
23 125th Avenue
Patterson, FL 19292

Mortgagors:
Arthur and Beatrice Bowles
5851 Panama Terrace
Trenton, FL 19291
Loan #827731

Below you will find information concerning the amount necessary to pay this loan
in full subject to final verification by the Note Holder. Uncertified personal
checks are not acceptable.

Principal Balance as of August 1, 1996	$ 24,719.24
Interest to August 31, 1996	154.50
FHA Insurance Premium due the FHA	
Unpaid Late Charges	
Escrow Overdraft	
Trustee Fee	
Satisfaction Recording Fee	6.00
Prepayment Penalty	
Service Charge	
Total Due	$ 24,879.74

> This statement will **not** be verbally updated.
> Our office will require a written request for
> revised figures.
>
> The "per diem" or "Daily Rate" of interest on
> this loan is: $ 5.08

The balance in the Tax and Insurance Escrow/Impounds account is $845.47 as of the
date of this statement. This balance may change because of further receipts or
disbursements. When the release of lien is received from the Note Holder, the
balance will be refunded.

**If payment is not received on this loan by the date shown at "Interest to" and
in the amount listed on that line above, we will require additional interest
added that figure.**

Issuance of this statement does not suspend the contract requirement to make
monthly mortgage payments when due. If this property is sold please give us the
new address of the Seller. These figures will be adjusted if any check, money
order, or other negotiable instrument previously applied is rejected by the
institution on which it is drawn.

If you have any questions, please do not hesitate to contact us.

Sincerely,

Kathryn Elizabeth Johns
Loan Closing Agent

FIGURE 10-8

This form is designed for
instruction, and <u>not</u> for use
in all jurisdictions.

SATISFACTION OF MORTGAGE

KNOW ALL YE BY THESE PRESENTS, That I/We, **World Savings and Loan Association,**
4444 Central Avenue, Queenstown, FL 19293   am/are the owner(s) and holder(s)
of a Mortgage Deed executed by **Arthur Bowles and Beatrice Bowles, his wife**
to **Hathaway Manhattan Federal Savings and Loan, 100 Financial Drive, Atlanta,**
GA 42910 dated the **22nd** day of **November, 19 83** , and recorded in **Desdin**
County, in the State of **Florida,** in Official Records Book #**4115**, Page **217**,
in the office of the Clerk of Court, with such Mortgage Deed securing a Mortgage
Note in the amount of **Fifty Two Thousand----------------------00/100** Dollars
($ **52,000.00**), together with the promises and obligations set forth therein,
all related to the real property described as follows:

> **Lot 47, Block 14 of Blackacre Subdivision,**
> **according to the Plat thereof recorded in Plat**
> **Book 76, page 722 of the Public Records of**
> **Desdin County, Florida.**

And I/we hereby acknowledge full satisfaction of the obligations under the Note
and Mortgage deed, and hereby surrender(s) said Note, directing the Clerk of the
Court to cancel all such obligations under the Note and Mortgage Deed, and hereby
surrender(s) said Note, directing the Clerk of the Court to cancel all such
obligations of record.

WITNESS my/our hand(s) and seal(s) on this, the **1st** day of **November** , 19 **96**.

_____   _____ (Seal)
Witness **Mary Milner**   Ronald Goldenhauer
                                                    Treasurer
                                                    World Savings and Loan Assn.
_____
Witness **Stephen Unger**

STATE OF **FLORIDA**
COUNTY OF **CRAWFORD**

I HEREBY CERTIFY that, on this day personally appeared before me, an officer duly
authorized to administer oaths and take acknowledgements,

Ronald Goldenhauer, Treasurer, World Savings and Loan Association

He is personally known to me or has produced **a valid Florida driver's license**
as identification. He has acknowledged before me that he executed the same
freely and voluntarily for the purpose therein expressed.

WITNESS my hand and official seal in **Crawford** County, the State of **Florida** this
the **1st** day of **November** , 19 **96** .

My commission expires: _____
                                          Barnard Sims
                                          NOTARY PUBLIC, State of **Florida**

FIGURE 10-9

REVIEW QUESTIONS

1. In each of the following cases, circle either "x" or "y" to indicate the event that would generally occur first in a standard real estate transaction.

    a. x. abstract ordered

    y. warranty deed signed

    b. x. deposit receipt contract signed

    y. warranty deed signed

    c. x. recording

    y. closing

    d. x. abstract ordered

    y. title insurance policy prepared

    e. x. recording of closing documents

    y. deposit receipt contract signed

2. Indicate which of the three types of multiple ownership is applicable in the following factual circumstances. There may be more than one answer for each question. X and Y each own an equal undivided interest in a piece of real estate together.

    a. X dies. Y becomes automatic owner of the property.

    b. It does not indicate on the deed the manner in which the parties are holding the property. (We know for this part of the question that X and Y are not married.)

    c. X dies. X designates his son, A, as the recipient of his interest in the property. As a result of the will, A then owns the property together with Y.

    d. The deed reads "X and Y, his wife." X dies leaving the interest that he has in the property to his son, A. Nevertheless, Y receives a 100 percent interest in the property.

3. Which of the following documents must generally be notarized? Indicate "yes" next to those that have to be notarized and "no" next to those that do not.

    a. deposit receipt contract _____

    b. warranty deed _____

    c. bill of sale _____

    d. no lien affidavit _____

    e. mortgage deed _____

    f. mortgage note _____

    g. closing statement _____

4. Who signs the following documents—the grantor, the grantee, or both parties?

   a. deposit receipt contract _____

   b. warranty deed _____

   c. bill of sale _____

   d. no lien affidavit _____

   e. mortgage deed _____

   f. mortgage note _____

   g. closing statement _____

5. Prepare a deposit receipt contract based on the following fictitious information. Please use the format provided in this chapter.

   The property is located in [your county and state] and is referred to as "Lot 54, Block 11, Winding Trails Subdivision, according to the plat thereof as recorded in Plat Book 36, page 4555 of the public records of [your county and state]." The real estate is being sold by Sam and Sally Seller, husband and wife, to Bill Buyer, a single man. The Sellers' current address is 251 Northeast 83 Terrace, [your city, state, and zip code], and their telephone number is (987) 555-3210. Buyer's current address is 352 Kendlewood Drive, [your city, state, and zip code], and his telephone number is (987) 555-0466. Of the total purchase price of $100,000, a deposit of $500 is to be made at the time of the signing of the deposit receipt contract. Another $14,500 is to be paid within 10 days of the date of the contract. Ultimately, Arthur Attorney, counsel for the sellers, received the $14,500 on May 15, 1998, at 4:30 P.M. The buyer will come to the closing with an additional $20,000 in cash and will be assuming the balance of the sellers' mortgage in the amount of $47,000. He will also obtain a second mortgage from ABC Savings and Loan for the remaining amount. The contract is signed by both parties on May 12, 1998. There is no broker involved. The parties agree that the closing must take place on or before 5:00 P.M. on September 1 of that year unless they mutually agree otherwise at a later date. When the contract offer was originally made, the buyer gave the seller until 5:00 P.M. on May 16, 1998, to accept. The contract is to be contingent on the buyer obtaining the required financing within 30 days. If a mortgage commitment is not obtained with that time, the contract is to be declared null and void, and all deposits are to be returned to the buyer. The contract indicates that the witnesses for the buyer's signature were John Jones and Bill Pillsbury. The witnesses for the sellers' signatures are Bill and Betty Meyerson. The parties agree that the sellers shall not be responsible for repairs totaling more than 5 percent of the purchase price.

6. Prepare a warranty deed based on the following fictitious information. Use the format provided in this chapter.

The property, which is located in [your county and state] is being conveyed from Philip Grantor, a single man, to Grace Grantee, a single woman. The buyer is purchasing the property for her residence. The legal description for the real estate is "Lot 22, Block 7, Mayberry Estates South according to the plat thereof as recorded in Official Records Book 5405 at Page 32 of the public records of [your county and state]." The deed is executed on March 2, 1998. The property is being transferred subject to a mortgage in favor of the XYZ Savings and Loan Institution, dated August 8, 1985, and recorded in Official Records Book 4928 at Page 250 of the public records of [your county and state]. The original amount of the mortgage was $49,000. It is also transferred subject to all other easements and restrictions of record and taxes for the year 1998 and all subsequent years. Grantee lives at 453 Angler Street, [your city, state, and zip code]. Grantor lives at the property to be sold, which is located at 971 Park Drive, [your city, state, and zip code]. The purchase price of the property is $125,000. The deed is witnessed by Warren Halverson and Sandra Dawson. The document is notarized by John Panlow, whose notary seal expires on June 10, 1998.

7. Prepare a quitclaim deed based on the following fictitious information. Use the format provided in this chapter.

The property, which is located in your county and state, is being conveyed from Gail Chambers to Susan Carrington. The deed is executed on January 4, 1998. Carrington lives at 21 Saunders Way, [your city, state, and zip code]. Chambers lives at 333 43rd Drive, [your city, state, and zip code]. Both Chambers and Carrington live in your county. The legal description for the real estate is "Lot 13, Block 17, Manor Villa Subdivision, according to the plat thereof as recorded in OR 28889, page 9223 of the public records of [your county and state]." The deed is witnessed by Caroline Stevens and Donald Benson. The document is notarized by Phyllis Snoke, whose notary seal expires on October 10, 1998.

8. Prepare a bill of sale based on the following fictitious information.

This document, executed on July 9, 1998, is being used to convey the following personal property: a refrigerator, a stove, a washer, and a dryer. Cynthia Gaynor is purchasing Arthur Fell's real property as her residence simultaneously with the purchase of this personal property from Fell. Fell lives at 65121 Crossover Avenue, [your city, state, and zip code]. Gaynor lives at 989 11th Court, [your city, state, and zip code]. The deed is witnessed by Edward Simpson and George Carton. The document is notarized by Brian Masters, whose notary seal expires on April 14, 2000.

9. Prepare a mortgage note and a mortgage deed based on the following fictitious information. Use the forms provided in the book.

Both documents are executed on August 1, 1998. Bill Buyer, a single man, is borrowing $85,500.00 at 7.5 percent annual interest from ABC Savings and Loan. The debt is being secured by the real estate located in your county and state, and it has a legal description of "Lot 16, Block 8, Country Meadows Estates, according to the plat thereof as recorded in OR 78524, page 425 of the public records of [your county and state]." The payments are to be sent to 25 Main Street, [your city, state, and zip code]. The first payment on the mortgage is due September 1, 1998. The exact amount of each payment shall be $747.01. The final payment on the note is to be due and payable in full on July 1, 2023. The deed is witnessed by Walter Witness and Wilma Witness. It is notarized by Nancy Notary, whose notary commission expires on December 15, 1999. Buyer's address is 21 Hector Street, [your city, state, and zip code].

10. Prepare a satisfaction of mortgage based on the following fictitious information. Use the format provided in this chapter.

The original lender was Jeffrey Johanssen, but Ward Stack is the present owner of the mortgage. The borrower is Michael Reavers. Johanssen lives at 65 Pine Terrace, [your city, state, and zip code]. Reavers lives at 9995 Alastair Road, [your city, state, and zip code]. Stack lives at 622 Castleberry Lane, [your city, state, and zip code]. The satisfaction is dated December 29, 2000. The document is designed to satisfy a mortgage executed on January 11, 1991, in the amount of $78,000, as recorded in OR 4466 at page 1441 of the public records of [your county and state]. The real property securing the debt is known as "Lot 6, Block 6, Orangewood Manor, according to the plat thereof as recorded in OR 40132, page 2603 of the public records of [your county and state]." The deed is witnessed by Allison Pasque and Norma Daniels. It is notarized by Ben Pace, whose notary commission expires on December 31, 2000.

11. Prepare a no lien affidavit based on the following fictitious information. Use the format provided in this chapter.

This document, executed on May 22, 2000, is issued from the seller, Beatrice Crawford, to the buyer, Gregory Liston, in connection with a pending real estate transaction. The property in question has a legal description of "Lot 19, Block 24, Forest Hills Subdivision according to the plat thereof as recorded in OR 49022, page 2579 of the public records of [your county and state]." Taxes have been paid through the year 1999. There is one pending mortgage on the property in favor of QRS Savings and Loan in the initial principal amount of $85,000 dated April 24, 1988, and recorded in OR 36788, page 3255 of your county and state. The document is notarized by Pamela Evers, whose notary seal expires on November 8, 2001.

FOOTNOTE

[1]The whole issue of recording is considerably more complex than one might be led to believe by reading this example, and the illustration is given only to acquaint the reader with the effect of recording.

6 "prepare" exercises

nts' Estates

CHAPTER OVERVIEW

1. There Is a Surviving Spouse, but No Lineal Descendants
2. There Are Both Lineal Descendants and a Surviving Spouse
3. There Are Lineal Descendants, but No Surviving Spouse
4. There Are Neither Lineal Descendants Nor a Surviving Spouse
5. There Are Neither Lineal Descendants, Parents, Nor a Surviving Spouse
6. There Are No Remaining Claimants

11-3 Probate and Administration of Estates

A. The Circumstances under Which Probate or Administration Is Required
B. The Purpose of Probate and Administration Proceedings
C. The Typical Sequence of Events in Probate Proceedings
   1. A Petition for Administration Is Prepared
   2. An Oath of Witness to Will Is Prepared
   3. A Court File Is Opened in the Clerk's Office of the Probate Court
   4. A Notice of Administration Is Prepared and Filed
   5. An Inventory Is Prepared and Filed
   6. An Accounting Is Prepared and Filed
   7. Tax Statements Are Obtained and Filed
   8. The Property Is Transferred to the Beneficiaries
   9. The Closing Documents Are Prepared and Filed
      a. A petition for discharge
      b. Receipts of all beneficiaries
      c. A final accounting
      d. An order of discharge
D. Ancillary Administration

11-4 Living Wills

The subject of decedents' estates can be divided into three major areas for study:

1. Testate succession,
2. Intestate succession, and
3. Probate and administration of estates.

A fourth subject area pertaining to living wills is also addressed. Even though living wills are not technically wills at all, they are examined in this chapter because they are often prepared in conjunction with wills.

SEC. 11-1
TESTATE SUCCESSION

A. Definition

Anyone who has a valid last will and testament in effect at the time of death is said to die *testate*. The person making the will is known as the *testator*, if male, or *testatrix*, if female.

B. In General

1. The Ambulatory Nature of a Will

All wills are *ambulatory*, which means that while a will may be changed as many times as one likes during one's lifetime, the only one with legal effect is the most current valid will at the time of death.

2. Revocation by the Maker

Revocation by the maker can be accomplished in various ways in different states. These include the intentional destruction of the will by the testator or testatrix or the preparation of a superseding document such as a new will or a codicil. (See subsection B.4 for the meaning of the word "codicil.")

3. Capacity

To have a valid will, the testator or testatrix must generally be at least 18 years old, of sound mind, and under no duress or undue influence. Any will that was signed during minority is invalid even if the testator or testatrix died after reaching majority.

On the other hand, whether any beneficiary has legal capacity has no bearing whatsoever on the validity of the will. If a beneficiary is lacking legal capacity, the one making the will has the option of establishing a trust in the beneficiary's behalf. (See subsection D.6.)

4. Amendment of a Will

A will may be amended either by preparing a new legal document known as a *codicil*, which refers by date to the will it is amending, or by replacing the old will with an entirely new one. It is common in wills and codicils to begin with language that indicates an intention to revoke "any wills or codicils I formerly may have made." Attempts to amend a will by making handwritten alterations on it are generally ineffective.

For a codicil to be effective, it must comply with all of the requirements that have been established for the signing of wills.

C.   Form

The form required for a will can differ significantly from state to state, but certain basic requirements exist in all states. If the document does not conform to these requirements, then the last will and testament will be regarded as invalid, and upon the death of the testator or testatrix, the estate will pass according to the most recent valid will or, if there is no other valid will, according to the laws of intestate succession. (See Sec. 11-2 for an explanation of the law when a person dies without a will.)

1.   In Writing

As a general rule, attempts to make oral wills, which are also known as *nuncupative wills*, are ineffective.[1] For a will to be valid, it must generally be in writing. If the will is handwritten by the testator or testatrix, it is referred to as a *holographic will.*[2] The statutes of many states indicate that holographic wills are acceptable if they conform to the requirements of a valid will. In other states, the formalities that may be required for the execution of a holographic will are different from those required for wills that are not handwritten.

2.   Signed

To be valid, wills must be signed at the end of the document by the testator or testatrix.

3.   Witnessed

A significant majority of states require only two witnesses to sign a will for the will to be valid. A small minority require three. While wills generally need not be notarized, a self-proving affidavit accompanying a will must have a notary seal. (For a definition and discussion of self-proving affidavits, see subsection E.)

Paralegals should be aware of the fact that the laws of many states impose special rules on beneficiaries of the will who also serve as witnesses. State law may indicate that if a beneficiary signs as a witness to the will, that person's share of the estate may be reduced to the amount that the beneficiary would have gotten if no will had been signed.

D.   *Standard Clauses Found in Simple Wills*

An example of a last will and testament can be seen in Figure 11-1.[3]

1.   *Payment of Debts, Taxes, and Costs of Administration*

It is common to direct that all such obligations be paid by the estate, though such a requirement may be imposed by law even in the absence of such a clause.

2.   *Dispositive Clause*

The *dispositive clause* indicates to whom any money, property, or ownership rights will be given. As a general rule, if the testator or testatrix excludes individuals in the will, the exclusion will be effective. There are exceptional situations, however, in which certain parties may be able to receive a share of the estate even though they are not included in the will. One such example would be the right of a spouse to take a statutory elective share as discussed in subsection F, below.

Within the dispositive clause of all wills is a *residuary clause,* which indicates where all the remaining assets of the estate (if any) shall go after all other distributions under the will have been made.

3.   *Simultaneous Death Clause*

In most states, one can provide for the exact manner of distribution of the estate when the decedent and a beneficiary die either simultaneously or under circumstances in which there is insufficient evidence that they died other than simultaneously. Under such circumstances, the testator or testatrix may raise a presumption in the will by use of a *simultaneous death clause* that the beneficiary either did or did not survive.

4.   *Appointment of Personal Representative and Designation of Powers*

Any person making a will generally appoints a party to be responsible for the handling of the estate upon the death of the testator or testatrix. The one appointed can be either an individual or an institution such as a bank. In some states, this party will be referred to as the *executor* (or *executrix* if the party is a female), while in other states, the name of *personal representative* is used regardless of whether the party is male, female, or a business institution.[4]

LAST WILL AND TESTAMENT
OF

I, _____ , a resident
of _____ County, in the _____
State of _____ , do hereby make, publish, and declare this instrument to be my Last Will and
Testament, hereby revoking any and all wills and codicils I formerly may have made.

ARTICLE I
PAYMENT OF EXPENSES OF ADMINISTRATION

If my estate shall be subject to any estate, inheritance, succession or other death taxes of any nature that may be
levied under the law of any State, or of the United States, with respect to property passing under this will (or any
other property) , or any interest or penalties on such taxes, then I direct that payment of such shall be considered
a cost of administration of my estate. I further direct that my Executor, Executrix or Personal Representative shall
also pay all debts which I am legally obligated to pay at the time of my death, as well as expenses for my last illness,
funeral, and all other costs of administering my estate.

ARTICLE II
DISPOSITIVE CLAUSE

By and through this, my Last Will and Testament, I do hereby give all of my net estate, after payment of such items
as are necessary and appropriate under Article I of this will, in the following manner:

```
┌─────────────────────────────────────────────────┐
│ This form is designed for instruction, and       │
│ not for unmodified use in all jurisdictions       │
└─────────────────────────────────────────────────┘
```

ARTICLE III
SIMULTANEOUS DEATH

If any beneficiary and I die under such circumstances that it cannot be determined which of us died first, then it
shall be presumed for all purposes under this will that he/she predeceased me.

ARTICLE IV
APPOINTMENT OF EXECUTOR/EXECUTRIX/PERSONAL REPRESENTATIVE
AND POWERS

To be the Executor/Executrix/Personal Representative of my estate, I hereby nominate the following person(s):

In the event that the above-named Executor/Executrix/Personal Representative is unwilling or unable to serve,
then I appoint as Alternative Executor/Executrix/Personal Representative the following person(s):

I direct that the Executor/Executrix/Personal Representative herein appointed shall/shall not be required to
furnish bond in the relevant jurisdictions, and that such person(s) shall/shall not receive compensation for
services rendered in such capacity.

Page 1 of 2   _____
(Signature of Testator/Testatrix)

FIGURE 11-1a

I further grant unto my Executor/Executrix/Personal Representative full power and discretion to manage and control the assets of my estate during administration, with the power and authority to sell any portion thereof which the Executor/Executrix/Personal Representative shall deem necessary or advisable for the orderly administration and distribution of my estate and the payment of my just debts. My Executor/Executrix/Personal Representative shall also have full power and authority to compromise, settle or otherwise adjust all claims, debts or demands in favor of, or against my said estate.

IN WITNESS WHEREOF, I have hereunto subscribed my name and affixed my seal in the county of _____, in the State of _____, on this, the _____ day of _____, 19_____, in the presence of the subscribing witnesses whom I have asked to become attesting witnesses hereto.

```
This form is designed for instruction, and
not for unmodified use in all jurisdictions
```
_____
(Signature of Testator/Testatrix)

This instrument was on the date thereof signed, published, and declared by _____, the Testator/Testatrix, to be his/her Last Will and Testament, in our presence, and we, in the presence of the Testator/Testatrix and in the presence of each other, have at the same time hereunto signed our names as attesting witnesses.

_____   of   _____

Witness   _____

_____   of   _____

Witness   _____

_____   of   _____

Witness   _____

Page 2 of 2

FIGURE 11-1b

This form is designed for
instruction, and not for use
in all jurisdictions.

STATE OF

COUNTY OF

We, (the testator), and _____,
and _____, the testator and the witnesses,
respectively, whose names are signed to the attached or foregoing instrument,
having been sworn, declared to the undersigned officer that the testator, in the
presence of witnesses, signed the instrument as his last will, that he signed (or
directed another to sign for him), and that each of the witnesses, in the
presence of the testator and in the presence of each other, signed the will as
a witness.

_____
Testator

_____
Witness

_____
Witness

Subscribed and sworn to before me by (the testator), the testator, who is
personally known to me or who had produced ____(type of identification)____ as
identification, and by _____, a witness,
who is personally known to me or who has produced (type of identification) as
identification, and _____, a witness, who is
personally known to me or who has produced ____(type of identification)____ as
identification on this _____ day of _____,
19____.

Print, type or stamp   Signature of Notary Public
commissioned name of   (name of the notary)
notary public   My commission expires:

FIGURE 11-1c

It is customary to appoint an alternative personal representative in the will in case the primary personal representative is unwilling or unable to serve. In the absence of a valid appointment in the will, the court will appoint a personal representative at the initiation of probate proceedings.

Any individual named by a testator or testatrix must generally be domiciled in the state of the primary probate proceedings unless the designated party is an immediate relative. Immediate relatives in this context usually include spouses, lineal descendants, parents, brothers, sisters, and all the lineal descendants of these parties. Individual state statutes may differ, however, as to which out-of-state relatives may serve in this capacity.

The powers that the personal representative shall have, such as the power to sell real property, are generally included in the will. In addition to those stated in the will, there are also certain powers that all personal representatives have under statutory authority. While many jurisdictions require that the personal representative post a bond in order to serve, the testator or testatrix may waive the requirement in the will.

5. Guardianship Clause

When one of two parents dies, legal guardianship of any children under 18 years of age passes automatically to the surviving parent. In the event of simultaneous death of the parents (or the death of a single surviving parent), the parent or parents may wish to designate who the legal guardians of the minor children will be. They may be concerned that a court would appoint guardians whom they would not prefer. When no legal guardian of the minor children survives upon the death of the testator or testatrix, a probate court will generally honor the directions in the will concerning guardianship, although courts will also give considerable weight to the opinion of any minor child who is nearing the age of majority. The question of guardianship is irrelevant for children who are older than 18 years of age.

6. Trust Clause

One may choose to make gifts in a will indirectly by use of trusts. In a trust, one party receives legal title to the gift while a second party receives the benefit from it. For example, rather than leaving the sum of $15,000 outright to a minor child in the will, a testatrix may choose to leave the sum to her adult brother to spend only for the benefit of the child. The brother in this case would be known as the *trustee,* while the child would be referred to as the *beneficiary.* The testatrix who created the trust would be known as the *settlor.* In a trust, the trustee cannot spend the money for his or her own benefit.

The testator or testatrix may place conditions on the trust, such as the duration or purpose of the trust. In the illustration above, for example, the testatrix might provide that the money is to be spent only for college tuition expenses and that the unused portion is to be given to the child outright upon reaching the age of 21. The trust may indicate that it will only go into effect if the child is still a minor at the time of the death of the testator or testatrix. Such details are discretionary for the one making the will.

Trusts are established for many reasons. For instance, the beneficiary may be incapable of handling such affairs because of age or mental incompetency. A trust might be imposed because the testator or testatrix believes that the beneficiary is competent, but may not make an intelligent use of the gift if the entire amount is received all at one time. For example, a testator might feel that a beneficiary who was a drug abuser might squander the entire inheritance in a very short period of time in order to satisfy the drug dependency.

One may appoint either individuals or business entities such as banks as trustees. The testator or testatrix may designate in the will whether the trustee should serve with or without compensation, but the trustee always has the option of refusing acceptance of the appointment if no compensation is paid.

One responsibility of the trustee is to keep accurate records of the trust property in his or her care. State law generally requires the trustee of a *testamentary trust,* which is one that is created in a will, to file periodic reports in the court file during probate proceedings (see Sec. 11-3).

Not all trusts are found in wills. Many trusts, known as *inter vivos* trusts, are created to take effect during the lifetime of the settlor.

7.   Attestation Clause

At the end of a will, a short paragraph called an *attestation clause* is inserted between the signature of the testator or testatrix and the signatures of the witnesses. The clause indicates that the document was signed as the last will and testament of the testator or testatrix in the presence of the witnesses and that the witnesses signed in the presence of each other.

E.   Self-proving Affidavit

This is an optional affidavit signed by the testator or testatrix that relieves the witnesses of the necessity of having to swear to the validity of the will at the time of probate. (For an understanding of the meaning of the term "probate," see Sec. 11-3 of this chapter.) Even if the will is not accompanied by a self-proving affidavit, it may, nevertheless, be a valid document.

In states that allow for the use of self-proving affidavits, one of two things may happen if a probated will is not accompanied by the affidavit: one of the witnesses will have to go to the probate office in the courthouse and sign a document referred to as an *oath of witness to will*; or someone will have to be appointed by the probate court to obtain a similar sworn statement from one of the witnesses. In an oath of witness to will, the witness must swear to the fact that the witness saw the testator or testatrix sign and that the testator or testatrix and the witnesses all signed in the presence of each other. If none of the witnesses have survived the testator or testatrix, or none of them can be found, it is still possible to have the will admitted to probate if it can be established for the court that there was a diligent search for the witnesses. The affidavit is not required to make the will valid, but failure to execute a valid self-proving affidavit can delay probate.

The language to be used in the preparation of a self-proving affidavit is usually supplied by state statute, and it will be substantially as follows:

> We, Thomas Testator, and Wilma Witness and William Witness, the testator and witnesses, respectively, whose names are signed to the attached or foregoing instrument, having been sworn, declared to the undersigned officer that the testator, in the presence of witnesses, signed the instrument as his last will (or codicil), that he signed (or directed another to sign for him), and that each of the witnesses, in the presence of the testator and in the presence of each other, signed the will as a witness.

A location for the signatures of the testator and the witnesses is then provided. The "undersigned officer" referred to in the affidavit is the notary public.

The will itself need not be notarized, but it must be witnessed. Notarization and attestation of the self-proving affidavit, on the other hand, is required. The affidavit is normally signed at the same time as the will (although probate statutes indicate that it need not be), and it appears immediately after the signatures on the last page or on a separate sheet that is attached to the will.

An example of a self-proving affidavit for a testator can be found in Figure 11-1c.

F. *Statutory Elective Share*

Most states have passed statutes to protect widows and widowers in the event that their spouses provide little or nothing for them in their wills. While these statutes differ somewhat from state to state, they provide that a surviving spouse may receive a certain amount of the estate in spite of the provisions of the will. This is either a percentage of the estate, which is usually either one third or one half, or the amount that the spouse would have received if there had been no will at all. In order for a surviving spouse to take such a statutory share "against the will," that party must elect to do so within a specific period of time from the beginning of probate proceedings. A surviving spouse receiving less than the one third may apply for the statutory elective share. If the spouse does choose to exercise the right to claim the share, the remaining two-thirds of the estate will be distributed as directed under the will as though it were the entire estate.

G. The Concept of "Per Stirpes" Distribution

It is not uncommon to see language in a will that indicates that if a particular beneficiary dies before the testator or testatrix, the beneficiary's share shall pass to his or her *lineal descendants per stirpes.* The term *lineal descendants* refers to all those individuals who are directly related by blood and are lower on the family tree. It would, therefore, include children, the children of one's children, and so on, but it would not include the spouses of any children or those higher on the family tree, such as parents and grandparents. State statutes commonly provide that legally adopted children are to be regarded as natural children for the purpose of descent and distribution.

The term *per stirpes* means "by representation," and it can be most clearly understood by an examination of the following example:

Ann has three sons: B, C, and D. B has two daughters, who are E and F. C has one son whose name is G. D has three sons whose names are H, I, and J. None of Ann's grandchildren has lineal descendants. The testator (a person other than one of the parties indicated) leaves the sum of $3,000 to "Ann; in the event that she does not survive me, then her share shall pass to her lineal descendants per stirpes."

In this example, if Ann is surviving at the time, she receives the entire $3,000, and none of Ann's lineal descendants receive anything. If Ann is not surviving, her share will be divided equally between B, C, and D (assuming that all three are living). This means that each one of the three of them would receive $1,000 and Ann's grandchildren (E, F, G, H, I, and J) would receive nothing. If all parties but Ann and D were surviving, one third ($1,000) would pass to B, one third ($1,000) would pass to C, and the remaining one third would be divided equally between H, I, and J, who would each receive $333.33.

This kind of distribution can result in an unequal division of the property among the grandchildren if the grandchildren's parents are dead. For example, if Ann, B, C, and D all do not survive, then B's one third share would be divided equally between E and F, giving them $500 each. G would receive C's entire one third ($1,000) share, and D's one third ($1,000) share would be divided equally between H, I, and J, giving them each $333.33.

The testator or testatrix can, of course, leave shares of the estate to beneficiaries in any proportions that he or she chooses, and a per stirpes distribution is not required. Furthermore, any or all of one's relatives may as a general rule be entirely disinherited, although the surviving spouse may claim the statutory elective share.

SEC. 11-2
INTESTATE SUCCESSION

A. Definition

One who does not have a valid last will and testament in effect at the time of death is said to have died intestate. All states have statutes that dictate to whom property is to be distributed in the event that one dies intestate. All estate obligations must be paid first whether the estate is testate or intestate. If any assets are left over after the payment of estate obligations, the property will be distributed according to the will if the estate is testate or according to the state statute of intestate succession if the estate is intestate.

B. A Typical Order of Intestate Distribution

The order of intestate distribution differs from state to state, but it is likely to be similar to the following plan of distribution.

1. There Is a Surviving Spouse, but No Lineal Descendants

If one is survived by a spouse and leaves no lineal descendants, the entire estate generally passes to the spouse.

2. There Are Both Lineal Descendants and a Surviving Spouse

If a spouse survives and there are lineal descendants of the deceased all of whom are lineal descendants of the surviving spouse, the spouse under some state statutes receives the first $20,000 plus one half of the remainder of the estate. The other half of the estate passes to the lineal descendants per stirpes of the deceased. When there are any children of the deceased who are not children of the surviving spouse, some state statutes alter the plan of distribution.

There are other common plans of distribution in the event that there are both lineal descendants and a surviving spouse. One would give the surviving spouse one half or one third with the lineal descendants taking the remainder per stirpes.

For the purposes of determining who is or is not a lineal descendant of the deceased, the spouse of any deceased lineal descendant would not be entitled to inherit since that spouse would not be a blood-related lineal descendant of the deceased. Adopted children and illegitimate children are generally regarded as lineal descendants. In the case of illegitimate children, however, the child can qualify as an heir only if paternity can be proven. Generally, the deceased can, of course, disinherit a potential beneficiary by executing a valid will that leaves the property to others.[5]

3. *There Are Lineal Descendants, but No Surviving Spouse*

If there is no surviving spouse, the property passes per stirpes to the lineal descendants of the deceased. Under these circumstances, if one died intestate and left no spouse and only one grandchild, the grandchild would be entitled to the entire estate.

4. *There Are Neither Lineal Descendants Nor a Surviving Spouse*

If there is no surviving spouse and there are no lineal descendants, the estate generally passes to the parents of the deceased if they are still alive, or if one of them is deceased, to the survivor of the two.

5. *There Are Neither Lineal Descendants, Parents, Nor a Surviving Spouse*

If the spouse, lineal descendants, and parents all do not survive, the brothers and sisters of the deceased inherit. If the brothers and sisters are also deceased, their respective shares would pass to their lineal descendants per stirpes.

6. *There Are No Remaining Claimants*

The preceding listing of the order for intestate succession is a partial one. In some states, it also includes even the most remote heirs. In others, potential takers are cut off after the relationship is designated as being too remote, such as when the claimants are no more closely related to the deceased than first cousins. In any event, most states provide that potential beneficiaries must file claims with the court in order to receive cash or property from the estate.

If a party dies intestate and valid claims have not been filed for all of the estate property, then the unclaimed property *escheats*, or passes to the state by default.

SEC. 11-3
PROBATE AND ADMINISTRATION OF ESTATES

A. The Circumstances under Which Probate or Administration Is Required

Whenever a person dies testate and leaves property in his or her own name, some form of *probate* proceeding is necessary. Similarly, an administration of the estate is necessary in an intestate estate when a person owned property solely in his or her own name. If the property of the deceased is held in joint tenancy or tenancy by the entirety, the survivor takes automatically by operation of law, and probate may not be required. (See the "Real Estate" chapter for a definition of the terms "joint tenancy," "tenancy in common," and "tenancy by the entirety." In spite of the fact that these terms are in that chapter, they have applicability to personal property as well.) When all property is owned either in joint tenancy or tenancy by the entirety, some legal work of a relatively uncomplicated nature may still need to be done, but a formal opening of a probate file may not be necessary.

B. The Purpose of Probate and Administration Proceedings

The primary purposes of probate are to (1) verify the validity of the will, (2) provide creditors of the deceased with an opportunity to make claims against the estate, and (3) ensure that title to the deceased's property is transferred to the appropriate heirs or beneficiaries of the estate. When there is no will, administration is required for the latter two reasons. In the case of testate estates, the rightful beneficiaries are determined in general by the provisions of the will, while in intestate estates the heirs are determined on the basis of the state's statute of intestate succession.

Even though a person has indicated in the will that property should be divided among certain named individuals, the will cannot have any effect without the opening of probate proceedings.

C. The Typical Sequence of Events in Probate Proceedings

To illustrate common probate procedures, consider the following series of events in the probate of a testate estate. The requirements of probate are statutory in nature and will vary from state to state. The following, however, is a list of some of the kinds of steps that might occur in the probate of an estate.

1. A Petition for Administration Is Prepared

A *petition for administration* requests that probate proceedings be opened. This document normally includes statistical information concerning the deceased and interested parties, the name and address of the anticipated personal representative, a reference to the will by date, the nature and approximate value of the assets, and an initial determination as to whether estate tax returns will have to be filed.

2. An Oath of Witness to Will Is Prepared

This document must be executed only if the will did not include a self-proving affidavit (see Sec. 11-1, subsection E).

3. A Court File Is Opened in the Clerk's Office of the Probate Court

The petitioner is generally the personal representative, although state statutes commonly provide that the petition requesting an opening of the estate can be filed by any interested party. The initial papers to be filed include:

a. A petition for administration.

b. The original will.

c. An oath of witness to will (if necessary).

d. A certified death certificate. Death certificates can generally be obtained from the bureau of vital statistics in the county in which the party died. The certificates must be certified, which means that they must have a raised seal. Photocopies of previously certified death certificates are not sufficient. Probate courts may require that the certification be within a certain period of time such as six months prior to the filing of the document.

e. An order admitting the will to probate. This document is prepared and submitted for the judge's signature.

f. The *letters of administration*. This document, prepared for the judge's signature, appoints the personal representative and serves as the written authority for the personal representative to carry out those duties.

In some states, this document is known as the *letters testamentary* when testate estates are involved.

g. The *oath of personal representative, designation of resident agent, and acceptance.* This document has three main parts: a written agreement by the personal representative to serve; a designation of a resident agent, who is the party who receives legal papers such as summonses or subpoenas that are served upon the estate; and a written acceptance by the resident agent to serve in that capacity. The resident agent and the personal representative need not necessarily be the same party, although they generally can be. It is not uncommon for the testator or testatrix to designate a particular attorney to handle the legal affairs for the estate and to serve as resident agent while at the same time designating a different party to serve as personal representative.

In addition to the above documents, a check for the filing fee must be prepared.

4. A Notice of Administration Is Prepared and Filed

A notice to all potential creditors of the estate, called a *notice of administration,* must be published in the newspaper. It is required in many states that the notice be published several times. Creditors of the estate must present their claims within a certain period of time from the first date of publication or waive them. This brings a sense of finality to probate proceedings. Claim periods of three or four months are not uncommon, but the exact length of time to file such a claim will be determined by statute. Once the notice has run for the required number of weeks, a *proof of publication* obtained from the newspaper is filed in the probate file.

According to the U.S. Supreme Court case of *Tulsa Professional Collection Services, Inc. v. Pope,* 485 U.S. 478, 108 S.Ct. 1340, 99 L.Ed.2d 565 (1988), if the identity of creditors is known or reasonably ascertainable, actual notice by mail must be sent.

5. An Inventory Is Prepared and Filed

Within a certain period of time from the filing of the initial documents, the *petitioner,* who is the party who has requested the opening of the estate, must file an inventory of the property in which the deceased had an interest at the time of death. This includes real and personal property regardless of where it is situated.

6.   An Accounting Is Prepared and Filed

State laws commonly provide that if probate proceedings are still pending one year from the date that the letters were issued, the petitioner must submit to the court an accounting of all estate assets or obtain an extension for filing. In many states, the accounting can be waived as long as all interested parties agree to such a waiver.

7.   Tax Statements Are Obtained and Filed

Some states have no state estate taxes. If a state does impose estate taxes, the probate court will probably require proof that state death taxes have been paid before a closing of the estate will be permitted. While the citizens of all states are subject to federal estate taxes, payment is not due unless the estate is worth more than a certain amount.[6]

Even if the deceased was in a category exempt from taxes, it may be necessary for the personal representative to obtain a document verifying that no taxes were due. The original certificate is then placed in the probate file at the courthouse, and copies of the certificate may need to be recorded in the land records if the deceased owned any interest in real property.

8.   The Property Is Transferred to the Beneficiaries

A document called a *receipt of beneficiary* is obtained from each beneficiary as he or she receives the property. If real property is to be transferred, title has to be conveyed by the use of a *personal representative's deed.*

Like other deeds transferring title to real estate, a personal representative's deed generally makes reference to the fact that the property has been transferred "in consideration for the sum of _____ and other good and valuable consideration." As in the case of warranty deeds (see Sec. 10-4, subsection D), it is common practice in many states to insert a token amount, such as ten dollars, in the blank. A court order may be required to transfer real estate from the decedent's estate.

9.   The Closing Documents Are Prepared and Filed

They include at least the following:

a. A petition for discharge.   This document, which is signed by the petitioner, requests a closing of the probate of the estate. It usually includes such information as:

1. The date the letters of administration were issued.

2. A representation concerning the final accounting. The personal representative must either file a final accounting or submit waivers of accounting from all interested parties.

3. A representation that all estate obligations have been paid. The petitioner must represent that he or she has either paid all estate obligations or has made satisfactory provisions for payment.

4. A representation as to the payment of compensation. The amount of compensation paid to the personal representative, attorneys, accountants, appraisers, or other agents employed by the personal representative must be listed.

5. A representation that all estate taxes have been paid. (For a detailed discussion, see subsection C.7 above.)

6. A final plan of distribution of the remaining estate assets.

7. The names and addresses of all parties other than the petitioner who have an interest in the estate.

8. A notice of the procedure for objecting to the accounting, compensation paid, or proposed distribution of the assets. In most states, one has a certain statutory period for filing such objections, such as 30 days from the date of the service of either the petition for discharge or the final accounting, depending upon whichever is served latest.

b. Receipts of all beneficiaries. Each beneficiary of the estate must sign a document verifying receipt of his or her share.

c. A final accounting. The petitioner must either file a final accounting or submit waivers of accounting from all interested parties. Standard forms are available in most states for this purpose. Since it is the responsibility of the personal representative to prepare the final accounting, the personal representative or the estate's attorney may wish to prepare the waivers and obtain signatures from all interested parties to avoid the time and expense of preparing the accounting.

d. An order of discharge. This is the order that discharges the personal representative from duty and closes out the estate. The order includes a recitation that the decedent's property has been distributed and that all taxes and claims of creditors have been paid. It is usually prepared and submitted for the judge's signature.

D.   Ancillary Administration

If the deceased owned real property in a state other than the one in which the primary probate proceedings are taking place, a separate probate called an *ancillary administration* will have to be initiated in the state in which the real property is located.

SEC. 11-4
LIVING WILLS

Sometimes people may wish to indicate that if in the future they can no longer make decisions regarding medical care for a condition that is incurable and cannot significantly improve, no "heroic" medical treatments to prolong life are to be used. A signed statement to this effect is known as a *living will.*

Obviously, a person's desires as to medical treatment are not appropriate subjects for ordinary wills, because wills have no legal effect until after a person dies. A living will is therefore not a "will" at all. Nevertheless, it is a matter that is sometimes considered by people who are having wills prepared, and it is therefore an appropriate subject of discussion in this chapter.

One of the potential dangers of living wills is that there is always the possibility that the blanket authority to turn off life-sustaining machines and withhold other kinds of treatment may or may not be in conformity with what the maker of the living will would have done in any given case. It is therefore vital that the instructions given in a living will are clear, as specific as possible, and unequivocal.

Living wills are permitted under the laws of most states, and suggested language for living wills may appear in those statutes.

REVIEW QUESTIONS

1.   Arthur is married to Betty, and they have two sons, Charlie and Donald. Charlie has three daughters, who are Esther, Faye, and Gisela. Donald has two sons, who are Harry and Isadore. At the time of Arthur's death, his entire net estate is worth $30,000. Assume that all of the named parties survive Arthur. Arthur's will leaves his entire property to "my sons Charlie and Donald, and in the event that either one does not survive me, then to the lineal descendants per stirpes of such deceased son."

   a.   What is the amount that Charlie would get assuming Betty did not take a statutory elective share?

    b. What is the amount that Esther would get assuming Betty did not take a statutory elective share?

    c. What is the amount that Betty would receive if she did take a statutory elective share?

    d. What is the amount that Donald would receive if Betty took the statutory elective share?

2. Assume that all of the individuals named in the previous question were surviving at the time of Arthur's death, but assume that Arthur died without a will. How much would Betty receive?

3. After Barry signs a will in his hospital room in the presence of three signing witnesses, but before he can sign the self-proving affidavit, he dies. Is the will itself valid, and if so, what will be the ramifications of his failure to sign the self-proving affidavit? On what possible grounds, if any, might the validity of the will be challenged?

4. Ben has three daughters, who are Gail, Susan, and Julie. Gail is married to John, Susan is single, and Julie is married to Steven. John and Gail have one child, who is Larry. Steven and Julie have two children, who are Peter and Robert. Peter is married to Cathie, and they have one child, who is Dawn.

    a. Name all of Ben's lineal descendants.

    b. Name all of Julie's lineal descendants.

5. Give an example of a situation in which the grandchildren of a deceased testatrix might receive different percentages of her estate if the will provided for a distribution to "the lineal descendants per stirpes."

6. What parties may serve as personal representative in your state?

7. What is the purpose of a petition for administration, and what allegations must be in such a petition in your state?

8. What is the purpose of a petition for discharge, and what allegations must be in such a petition in your state?

FOOTNOTES

[1]Some statutes provide, however, that such wills made by members of the armed forces may be valid under limited circumstances.

[2]This term may imply that the document is not only handwritten, but also unwitnessed.

[3]Technically, the will is found in Figures 11-1a and 11-1b only. Figure 11-1c is the self-proving affidavit that accompanies the will. For an explanation of the purpose of a self-proving affidavit, see Sec. 11-1, subsection E.

[4]In this chapter, the term personal representative will be used from this point forward to include all of these titles. It may also include the party or institution appointed in an intestate estate (see Sec. 11-2).

[5]The statutory elective share that may be claimed by the spouse is a notable exception to this rule (see Sec. 11-1, subsection F).

[6]In 1995, this amount was $600,000. The estate for federal estate tax purposes includes not only property held solely in the name of the deceased, but also jointly held property, life insurance benefits payable on the death of the deceased, certain property transferred prior to the deceased's death, and other property.

12 *Domestic Relations*

CHAPTER OVERVIEW

SEC. 12-1
INTRODUCTION

This chapter analyzes some of the basic differences between an annulment and a dissolution of marriage. It then gives an example of the paperwork and procedure involved in the preparation of a simple, uncontested dissolution of marriage. It should be clearly understood that portions of any particular dissolution action may not be uncontested and that the procedure shown here is for illustrative purposes only. Domestic relations matters vary significantly across the country, so it is important to be thoroughly familiar with the rules and laws of one's own state.

SEC. 12-2
ANNULMENTS AND DISSOLUTIONS OF MARRIAGE

A. Annulment

When one requests an order of *annulment*, that person is asking the court to declare that a marriage was never valid. In contrast, orders for *dissolution of marriage* recognize that a valid marriage existed but that the bonds of matrimony are now terminated. The basis upon which an annulment is granted by a court of law may or may not be the same as that for an annulment from a religious institution such as the Roman Catholic Church. Courts are not ordinarily predisposed to grant annulments without substantial cause. Although grounds for an annulment may vary from state to state, they generally include most of the following:

1. *Sham Marriage*

    If it is clear that the parties participated in a marriage ceremony that neither one ever intended to have a binding effect and if one of those parties feels that it is necessary to clarify by court action the nonbinding nature of that ceremony, an annulment would be appropriate. This does not include situations in which the parties simply decide at a later time that they made a mistake in entering into the marriage relationship, since it is their intent at the time of the marriage ceremony that is controlling.

2. *Bigamy*

    If one of the parties is married at the time that he or she enters into a second marriage, the latter marriage would be invalid.

3. *Underage Party or Parties*

    The exact age at which a person is competent to enter into a marriage relationship depends upon state law.

4. *Incest*

    Any marriage based upon an incestuous relationship is invalid and subject to annulment. A marriage of a father and daughter, mother and son, brother and sister, grandfather and granddaughter, or grandmother and grandson would all be considered incestuous under most state statutes. Marriages between cousins may or may not be considered incestuous.

5. *Mental Incompetency*

    Annulment may be appropriate if one or both of the parties were incapable of understanding what they were doing when entering into a marriage.

6. *Intoxication*

    Not all marriages entered into during an intoxicated state will be subject to annulment. However, if the evidence strongly suggests that a person was intoxicated with either drugs or alcohol at the time of the ceremony to such an extent that the party was incapable of comprehending what he or she was doing, grounds for annulment may exist.

7.   Duress

If one of the parties was compelled against his or her will to participate in the wedding ceremony, that party may have grounds for annulment.

8.   Physical Incompatibility

Refusal to ever engage in normal sexual relations with the marriage partner is regarded by the law as an indication that the parties do not intend to live as husband and wife and that a valid marriage was, therefore, not intended.

B.   Dissolution of Marriage

Traditionally, specific grounds, such as adultery, loss of affection, irreconcilable differences, or abandonment had to exist in order to terminate a marriage. Experience proved, however, that parties anxious to terminate their marriages often perjured themselves in order to establish these grounds. Furthermore, proof of such grounds made the termination of a marriage difficult at a time when, at least in some cases, parties were attempting to avoid causing additional controversy.

1.   Minimal Grounds

In light of the difficulties created by the requirement of specific grounds, most states have now altered their domestic relations laws so that proof of the traditional grounds emphasizing fault on the part of one of the parties is no longer necessary. All that must generally be shown in order to obtain a *no-fault divorce* is that

    a. The marriage is "irretrievably broken;" and

    b. The minimal residency requirement has been met. The petitioner must show that he or she has been a resident of the state for a certain minimal period of time prior to the filing of the petition.

2.   Respondent's Lack of Defense

If one party petitions for a dissolution and the other party objects to the dissolution, there is relatively little that the objecting party can do. It is difficult for the respondent to argue that the marriage is not irretrievably broken if the other partner to the marriage is claiming that it is. Even if the respondent vehemently objects to the dissolution at the final hearing, the court might at the most issue an order that is not scheduled to go into effect for an additional 60 days, thereby giving the parties an opportunity to reconcile. The right of the petitioner to ultimately obtain the dissolution, however, may never be in doubt. Such a delay in the effective date of the order is certainly not required, and the granting of it would be entirely discretionary by the court.

In spite of the difficulties inherent in prohibiting a dissolution, a party can always contest the terms that will govern the final dissolution order, such as those pertaining to child custody or division of property. Dissolution actions are, therefore, not always without controversy.

3.   *Relevance of Traditional Grounds*

In a significant number of states, a dissolution of marriage may be obtained either on the basis of the no-fault laws or on the traditional grounds. Furthermore, some of the traditional grounds for terminating a marriage still have relevance to issues such as alimony. If the petitioner is shown to be guilty of adultery, for example, the court may reduce or deny the petitioner alimony even though the adulterous acts of the petitioner would not affect the petitioner's right to obtain the dissolution. Proof of adultery might also affect the court's decisions with respect to child custody and related issues.

SEC. 12-3
DOCUMENTS INVOLVED IN A SIMPLE, UNCONTESTED
SUIT FOR DISSOLUTION OF MARRIAGE

The following is a series of documents that might be filed in a simple, uncontested suit for dissolution of marriage. For the purpose of this example, it is assumed that both parties have agreed to all terms and have incorporated their understanding into a property settlement agreement. Especially in light of these assumptions, the following material is not intended to be regarded as applicable to all dissolutions. It is only included to give an appreciation for the kinds of pleadings and procedures that might be involved.

A.   *A Petition for Dissolution of Marriage*

In a dissolution of marriage action in which both parties have agreed to all key terms in a property settlement agreement, there is no particular advantage in being the party who actually files the suit. A standard petition for dissolution normally includes the following allegations:

1. A statement that this is an action for the dissolution of marriage.
2. A statement that the petitioner has fulfilled the residency requirement.
3. The date and place of marriage.
4. A statement that the marriage is now irretrievably broken.
5. The names and birthdates of minor children (if any) born during the marriage.
6. A statement that a property settlement agreement has been reached and that it is the desire of the parties to make the terms of the agreement a part of the final dissolution order.
7. A statement as to which party will have custody of minor children even if the subject is addressed in the property settlement agreement.
8. A request for restoration of the wife's maiden name if that is the wife's desire and if the wife is the petitioner in the action.

An example of a petition for dissolution of marriage based upon fictitious facts and a fictitious jurisdiction can be found in Figure 12-1.

B. A Declaration under the Uniform Child Custody Jurisdiction Act

Historically, many problems have arisen in custody matters as a result of contradictory orders issued by courts in different states. The awarding of custody to the husband in one state and to the wife in another can obviously create major problems for law enforcement officials. In order to address this problem, states have enacted the Uniform Child Custody Jurisdiction Act. This statute requires the party petitioning for a dissolution of marriage to include an affidavit with the papers filed if there are any minor children of the parties to the suit. In the affidavit, the petitioner represents the following:

1. Information concerning the minor children of the marriage, including names, dates, and places of birth, sex, the location at which each child has lived for the past five years (as well as the time of residency at each location), and the person with whom each child lived during those periods of time.
2. Whether or not the affiant (the one signing the affidavit) has participated as a party, witness, or in any other capacity in any state concerning custody of a child who is subject to the pending proceedings, and if so, the name of each child, the capacity of the declarant, the court and state, and the date of the court order issued, if any.

```
           IN THE CIRCUIT COURT OF THE 23RD JUDICIAL CIRCUIT
                  IN AND FOR WILSON COUNTY, FL


                                        Case No: 98-3754



       In re:  the Marriage of  )
                                )
       PATRICIA PETITIONER,      )
                                )
            Wife,                )
       v.                        )
                                )
       ROBERT RESPONDENT,        )
                                )
            Husband.             )
       _____)
```

PETITION FOR DISSOLUTION OF MARRIAGE

The petitioner, PATRICIA PETITIONER, shows:

1. This is an action for dissolution of the marriage between the petitioner and respondent, ROBERT RESPONDENT.

2. Petitioner has been a resident of Florida for more than six months before filing the petition.

3. Petitioner and respondent were married to each other on March 23, 1980 in Syracuse, New York.

4. The marriage between the parties is irretrievable broken.

5. During their marriage, the parties had two children: CYNTHIA RESPONDENT, born May 22, 1986, and MITCHELL RESPONDENT, born June 29, 1982.

6. The petitioner and respondent have agreed to and executed a property settlement agreement to be submitted to the court at the time of the final hearing and incorporated into the Final Judgment Dissolving Marriage if found to be acceptable to the court. A copy of the property settlement agreement is hereby attached to this petition.

FIGURE 12-1a

7. The petitioner and respondent have agreed that it would be in the best interest of the minor children of the parties for there to be shared parental responsibility, with the wife, PATRICIA PETITIONER, serving as the primary residential custodian.

8. It is the desire of the petitioner to have her maiden name of PATRICIA MARIA ESCOBAR restored at the time of the final dissolution of the marriage.

WHEREFORE, petitioner demands that:

1. The court grant her a judgment dissolving the marriage.

2. The court designate the petitioner as the primary residential custodian and grant the husband and the wife shared parental responsibility over the minor children.

3. The court adopt the property settlement agreement as it was agreed to by the parties.

4. The court restore to the petitioner her maiden name of PATRICIA MARIA ESCOBAR.

DATED this 19th day of November, 1998.

Collingwood and Davis
908 Cedar Road
Trumbull, FL 33519

By: _____
Sandra Davis, FL Bar #777421

STATE OF FLORIDA   )
)
COUNTY OF BROWARD   )

BEFORE ME, the undersigned authority, personally appeared PATRICIA

PETITIONER, who first being duly sworn, states that she is the

Petitioner in the above and foregoing Petition for Dissolution

FIGURE 12-1b

of Marriage; that she has read it, known the contents thereof, and that the same is true and correct to the best of her knowledge and belief.

_____
PATRICIA PETITIONER

SWORN TO AND SUBSCRIBED before me by _____ this day, the _____ day of _____, 19_____. I hereby certify that I relied upon the following form of identification:_____.

_____
NOTARY PUBLIC
My commission expires:

FIGURE 12-1c

3. Whether the affiant has any information of any such custody proceeding, and if so, the details of that information.

4. Whether the affiant knows of any person who is not a party to the proceeding, but who nevertheless has physical custody or claims to have custody or visitation rights with respect to any child subject to the proceeding. If so, the affiant is to provide the name and address of such person, and whether that person has physical custody, claims custody rights, or claims visitation rights.

This document must be notarized since the affiant is swearing to the truth of the statements made in the document.

There is presently no nationwide network that can easily establish the existence or nonexistence of conflicting custody orders in all jurisdictions. If the petitioner misrepresents information on the affidavit, however, any final order obtained in the accompanying proceedings is subject to attack on the basis of fraud. If the parties in a dissolution of marriage action have minor children and the petitioner fails to file the custody affidavit, the court may refuse to sign the final order until it is filed. An example of a declaration under the Uniform Child Custody Jurisdiction Act can be found in Figure 12-2.

C. An Answer

Just as in any other civil action, the respondent will have a certain number of days to file a response to the petition. If the dissolution is uncontested (as assumed in this illustration), and the husband and wife are interested in resolving the matter as quickly as possible, the respondent may wish to have the answer filed simultaneously with the petition. Under such circumstances, the answer would only have to indicate:

1. that the allegations of the petition were admitted; and

2. that all terms and conditions of the pending dissolution were to be governed by the terms of the property settlement agreement.

The format of an answer to a petition for dissolution of marriage is similar to that of an answer in any other civil action.

D. A Property Settlement Agreement

If the parties are truly willing to settle all terms between themselves in an uncontested dissolution, they can do so by entering into a contract. If the parties fail to reach an agreement on the key issues, such as alimony and custody of

IN THE CIRCUIT COURT OF THE **23rd** JUDICIAL CIRCUIT
IN AND FOR **Wilson** COUNTY, STATE OF **Florida**

In re: the Marriage of)
)
Patricia Petitioner,)
)   Case No. **98-3754**
            Wife,)
)
v.   )
)
)
Robert Respondent,)
)
            Husband.)

DECLARATION UNDER THE
UNIFORM CHILD CUSTODY JURISDICTION ACT

1..The number of minor children subject to this proceeding is **two** The name, place of birth, birthdate and sex of each child, the present address, periods of residence and the name, present address and relationship to the child of each person with whom the child has lived during that time are:

Child's Name	Place of Birth	Birthdate	Sex
MITCHELL RESPONDENT	New York, New York	June 29, 1982	M

Period of Residence	Address	Person Child Lived With
6/29/82 - 7/1/88	124 Easter Street Newport, FL	both parents
7/1/88 - present	124 Easter Street Newport, FL	mother

Child's Name	Place of Birth	Birthdate	Sex
CYNTHIA RESPONDENT	Bridgeport, CT	May 22, 1986	F

Period of Residence	Address	Person Child Lived With
5/22/86 - 7/1/88	124 Easter Street Newport, FL	both parents
7/1/88 - present	124 Easter Street Newport, FL	mother

FIGURE 12-2a

2.　　[**X**] I have not participated as a party, witness, or in any other capacity in any other litigation or custody proceedings, in this or any other state, concerning custody of a child subject to this proceeding.

　　　　[　] I have participated as a party, witness, or in some other capacity in other litigation or custody proceeding in this or some other state concerning custody of a child subject to this proceeding, as follows:

　　　a. Name of each child

　　　b. Capacity of declarant

　　　c. Court and State

　　　d. Date of Court Order of Judgment (if any):

3.　　[**X**] I have no information of any custody proceeding pending in a Court of this or any other state concerning a child subject to this proceeding, other than that set out in Item 2.

　　　　[　] I have the following information concerning a custody proceeding pending in a Court of this or some other state concerning a child subject to this proceeding, other that that set out in Item 2.

　　　a. Name of each child

　　　b. Nature of proceeding

　　　c. Court and State

　　　d. Status of proceeding:

4.　　[**X**] I do not know of any person, not a party to this proceeding who has physical custody or claims to have custody or visitation rights with respect to any child subject to this proceeding.

　　　　[　] I know that the following-named person, not a party to this proceeding, has physical custody or claims custody or visitation rights with respect to a child subject to this proceeding:

Name and Address of Person:　　　　　　　　　Name and Address of Person:

[　]　　has physical custody　　　　　　　　[　]　　has physical custody
[　]　　claims custody rights　　　　　　　　[　]　　claims custody rights
[　]　　claims visitation rights　　　　　　　[　]　　claims visitation rights

STATE OF　　**Florida**　　　　　）
　　　　　　　　　　　　　　　　　） SS:
COUNTY OF　**Wilson**　　　　　）

ON THIS DAY personally appeared before me　　　**PATRICIA PETITIONER**　, who, after being duly sworn, deposes and says:

I have read the foregoing declaration under the uniform child custody jurisdiction act, and the facts and allegations contained therein are true and correct to the best of my knowledge and belief.

　　　　　　　　　　　　　　　　　　　　PATRICIA PETITIONER
SWORN TO and SUBSCRIBED before me this　　**19th**day of　　**November**　, 19　**98**　.

My commission expires: **12/12/98**　　　　NOTARY PUBLIC **State of Florida**

FIGURE 12-2b

348

minor children, the terms will ultimately be decided at the final hearing. While it is regarded in many states as contrary to public policy for spouses to enter into property settlement agreements in contemplation of divorce or dissolution of marriage, settlement contracts can and often do ultimately control the terms and conditions of a dissolution when accepted by a court of law. These agreements can cover many different topics, but they may generally include most of the following terms when appropriate.

1.   *Separation*

The parties shall live separate and apart in the future.

2.   *Alimony*

Alimony may be payable by the husband to the wife or by the wife to the husband. When matters pertaining to a dissolution of marriage are contested, unlike the present example, courts are now more inclined than they used to be to grant the demands of husbands for alimony from their wives when the wife's income exceeds that of the husband. This is regarded as being consistent with equal treatment of the sexes under the law.

3.   *Custody of Children*

The question of custody is, of course, applicable only when the children are under 18 years of age. Many different arrangements can be made by the parents concerning the custody issue. For example, the parties may decide that one will have physical custody of the child while the other parent has regularly scheduled visitation rights. Joint custody arrangements, in which both parties share either legal or physical custody, are becoming more widespread.

4.   *Child Support*

Settlement agreements can require child support payments which generally provide for the termination of such support when the child reaches majority, marries, or becomes self-supporting.

5.   *Visitation Rights*

The parties may be specific with regard to this issue, but it is not uncommon to see relatively vague definitions of a party's visitation rights. Many agreements, for example, give one of the parties "reasonable" visitation rights. This can create difficulties at a later time if the husband and wife cannot agree on the meaning of that phrase in the contract.

6.   Children's Medical Expenses

Often spouses agree in the contract who will be responsible not only for medical bills but also for the continuation of medical insurance payments if any.

7.   Division of Property

This includes both real property (land, buildings, and so on) and personal property (tangible, movable property). Just as in the case of visitation rights, the division of property can be as specific or as general as the parties desire.

8.   Division of Indebtedness

The agreement should indicate which of the parties is responsible for each outstanding debt, such as any mortgage payments, unsecured loans, car payments, or credit card bills.

9.   Tax Issues

All relevant matters pertaining to taxes should be addressed, including such issues as which party is responsible for the payment of real estate taxes and which party is entitled to any pending tax refund.

10. Mutual Releases

The parties may agree to relinquish certain rights that each has in the property of the other as a result of the marital relationship, including the right to claim a statutory elective share if one of the parties dies while the two are still married (see the "Decedents' Estates" chapter of this book). Each may agree to waive any right to the proceeds of a life insurance policy based upon the spouse's life. This latter provision might be included to cover the situation in which the insured dies prior to changing the named beneficiary on the policy. The change of the beneficiary on the insurance policy itself is the appropriate manner in which to make such changes.

11. Full Disclosure

The agreement usually includes representations by the parties that each has made a complete disclosure to the other of all assets and debts.

12. Attorneys Fees

The parties may wish to include an agreement dealing with the payment of one party's attorneys fees by the other.

13. Execution of Subsequent Documents

Settlement contracts usually include an agreement by both parties to execute any documents necessary to fulfill the terms of the agreement. If, for example, the contract provides for a transfer of the title to the marital home into the sole name of the wife, the husband would be required by the contract to sign the deed necessary to accomplish the transfer of title.

Like any other contract, the terms of the property settlement agreement are negotiable between the parties and, therefore, can include an infinite variety of other terms. Such agreements also usually include other standard contract provisions such as restrictions on the manner in which the contract can be modified (if at all). If the parties fail to come to a written agreement, then many of the matters listed above will have to be determined by the court at the final hearing on the basis of testimony, financial affidavits, and other evidence.

Since each party is swearing to the truth of certain statements in the agreement such as the representation regarding full disclosure of assets, the signature of each party must be notarized.

E. A Motion for Final Hearing

This pleading is prepared by the petitioner's attorney and sent to the respondent's attorney in order to notify the respondent of the date, place, and time of the final hearing.

F. A Final Judgment of Dissolution of Marriage

This is the document that actually severs the bonds of matrimony when it is signed by the judge. If a property settlement is involved, the court may incorporate the terms of the agreement in its final order and include a duplicate original of the agreement in the court file. If there is no such agreement, then the order spells out all of the key terms governing the dissolution. In either event, it ordinarily states which party is entitled to custody of the minor children if there are any. In determining the issue of custody if it has not been agreed on by the parties, there is a modern trend for the courts to presume that each party should share responsibility for the raising of the children. In other words, courts are more willing to accept an arrangement in which there is shared responsibility even though only one party has actual physical custody of the minor children.

The court order may also restore the wife's maiden name if she requested it in her initial pleading. The order should also always contain a statement that the court retains jurisdiction over all matters pertaining to the dissolution.

An example of a final judgment dissolving marriage can be found in Figure 12-3.

SEC. 12-4
STEPS INVOLVED IN A SIMPLE SUIT FOR DISSOLUTION OF MARRIAGE

The following is a list of the steps that might be followed in a simple, uncontested dissolution of a marriage action in which the couple has minor children. It is presumed that the parties have executed a property settlement agreement covering all key issues.

A.   *The Property Settlement Agreement Is Signed*

If the husband and wife are in agreement as to division of property, custody of the children, child support, and other matters, they may enter into a legally binding agreement encompassing those terms.

B.   *The Suit Is Filed*

Such filing may include the petition, the declaration under the Uniform Child Custody Jurisdiction Act, and the answer.

C.   *A Court Date Is Set*

The judge's secretary is contacted for a date when the final hearing can be scheduled. Once a time is found that is favorable to all parties, a motion for final hearing can be prepared and sent to the attorney for the respondent.

IN THE CIRCUIT COURT OF THE 23RD JUDICIAL CIRCUIT
IN AND FOR WILSON COUNTY, FL

Case No 98-3754

In re: the Marriage of   )
)
PATRICIA PETITIONER,   )
)
     Wife,   )
)
v.   )
)
ROBERT RESPONDENT,   )
)
     Husband.   )
_____)

FINAL JUDGMENT DISSOLVING MARRIAGE

This action was heard before the court. On the evidence presented, IT IS ADJUDGED that:

1. The bonds of marriage between petitioner, PATRICIA PETITIONER, and respondent, ROBERT RESPONDENT, are dissolved.

2. The separation agreement between the parties, introduced in evidence and marked petitioner's exhibit 1, was executed voluntarily after full disclosure, and is in the best interests of the parties, and is approved and incorporated in this judgment by reference and the parties are ordered to comply with it.

3. Petitioner's former name is restored and she shall be known as PATRICIA MARIA ESCOBAR hereafter.

4. The petitioner and respondent shall have shared parental responsibility for the minor children who are CYNTHIA RESPONDENT, born on May 22, 1986, and MITCHELL RESPONDENT, born June 29, 1982. The wife, PATRICIA PETITIONER, shall serve as the primary residential custodian. The respondent, ROBERT RESPONDENT, shall have the right to visit the minor children at reasonable times and places after reasonable notice to the petitioner.

FIGURE 12-3a

5. The respondent shall pay to the petitioner the sum of one hundred dollars ($100) per week for each minor child.

6. The court retains jurisdiction to enforce the terms and conditions of the aforsaid property settlement agreement.

ORDERED in Duntze, Wilson County, Florida on January 6, 1999.

_____
Circuit Court Judge

FIGURE 12-3b

D. The Residency Witness Is Contacted

The petitioner will be required at the final hearing to prove by witness testimony that he or she has fulfilled the residency requirement. The petitioner's attorney should make sure that the petitioner brings the witness to the hearing.

E. The Final Hearing Is Held

At the final hearing, the petitioner's attorney will establish for the court by a relatively brief questioning of the petitioner that the requirements for dissolution have been met. The questions asked will generally follow the allegations of the client's petition. The attorney will ask the petitioner to identify the property settlement agreement and the signatures on the agreement and to verify whether the contract reflects the true agreement between the parties. The contract will then be offered into evidence. The residency witness will be asked to swear that the petitioner has been a resident for more than the required period of time. After all of the above has been established, the petitioner's attorney will hand to the judge for signature a prepared final judgment dissolving the marriage, and the judge will generally sign the order at that time. Copies of the order go to both the parties and their attorneys, and the original remains in the court file.

While the respondent is entitled to attend the final hearing, question the petitioner and residency witness, and address the court, he or she should recognize that the final terms may be predetermined by the answer and the property settlement agreement which were filed by the respondent.

SEC. 12-5
SIMPLIFIED DISSOLUTION PROCEDURES

While Sec. 12-4 describes the approach that might be taken in an uncomplicated dissolution, the procedure can be even more simplified in some jurisdictions[1] when the parties can certify for the court that "there are no minor or dependent children of the parties and the wife is not now pregnant; the parties have made a satisfactory division of their property and have agreed as to payment of their joint obligations; ..." and other factors.[2] Under this procedure, the state rule may require that the parties appear before the court before a dissolution will be granted.[3] Forms are often provided in the civil rules for the simplified petition, a residency affidavit or certificate of corroborating witness (which can relieve the residency witness of having to testify in court), a financial affidavit, a simplified property settlement agreement, and a final judgment. Examples of these forms can be found in Figures 12-4 through 12-8.

IN THE CIRCUIT COURT OF THE 17TH JUDICIAL CIRCUIT
IN AND FOR BROWARD COUNTY, FLORIDA

Case No.

In re: the Marriage of)
)
PATRICIA PETITIONER,)
)
Wife,)
)
v.)
)
)
ROBERT RESPONDENT,)
)
Husband.)
)
_____)

PETITION FOR SIMPLIFIED DISSOLUTION OF MARRIAGE

The petition of Husband and Wife shows:

1. This is a petition for dissolution of marriage.

2. The Husband and the Wife or one of them has been a resident of Florida for at least six (6) months immediately prior to filing this petition.

3. Husband and Wife were married to each other on _____, 19_____, at
_____.

4. The marriage between the parties is irretrievably broken.

5. There are no minor or dependent children of the parties and the Wife is not pregnant.

6. The parties have made provisions for the division of their property and the payment of their joint obligations. They are satisfied with those provisions.

[The property settlement agreement entered into by the parties and a financial affidavit from each party are attached.]

7. The parties understand that they may have legal rights against each other arising out of the marital relationship and that by signing this petition they may be giving up those rights.

FIGURE 12-4a

8. Each party certifies that he/she has not been threatened or pressured into signing this petition. Each understands that the result of signing this petition may be a final dissolution of the marriage with no further relief.

9. The parties understand that they are required to appear before the judge to testify as to the matters contained in this petition.

10. The address of each party is as stated below.

11. The Wife wished to have her former name restored to her. (Yes_____ No_____) If "Yes," state Wife's former name: _____.

Wherefore, Husband and Wife ask the Court to dissolve the marriage existing between them.

UNDER PENALTY OF PERJURY, WE CERTIFY THE FOREGOING FACTS ARE TRUE.

_____   _____
Wife's signature   Husband's signature

_____   _____
Wife's name typed   Husband's name typed

_____   _____
Wife's residence address   Husband's residence address

SWORN TO AND SIGNED before me this _____ day of _____, 19_____.

                                         CLERK OF THE CIRCUIT
                                         COURT

                                         by _____
                                         Deputy Clerk

FIGURE 12-4b

IN THE CIRCUIT COURT OF THE 17TH JUDICIAL CIRCUIT
IN AND FOR BROWARD COUNTY, FLORIDA

Case No.

In re: the Marriage of   )
)
PATRICIA PETITIONER,   )
)
Wife,   )
)
v.   )
)
ROBERT RESPONDENT,   )
)
Husband.   )
)
_____)

CERTIFICATE OF CORROBORATING WITNESS

UNDER PENALTY OF PERJURY I CERTIFY that I am a resident of the State of Florida; I have known (insert name of Husband or Wife) for more than six (6) months preceding this date and I know of my own personal knowledge that such person has resided in the State of Florida for at least that period of time.

_____
Witness' Signature

_____
Witness' Name Typed

_____

Witness' Residence Address

SWORN TO AND SIGNED before me this _____ day of _____, 19_____.

_____
CLERK OF THE CIRCUIT
COURT OR NOTARY PUBLIC

FIGURE 12-5

IN THE CIRCUIT COURT OF THE 17TH JUDICIAL CIRCUIT
IN AND FOR BROWARD COUNTY, FLORIDA

Case No.

In re: the Marriage of)
)
PATRICIA PETITIONER,)
)
Wife,)
)
v.)
)
)
ROBERT RESPONDENT,)
)
Husband.)
)
_____)

FINANCIAL AFFIDAVIT FOR
SIMPLIFIED DISSOLUTION OF MARRIAGE

STATE OF FLORIDA

COUNTY OF _____

Before me, the undersigned authority, personally appeared _____,
who was sworn and says that the following statement of affiant's income, assets, and liabilities is true:

Occupation _____

Employed by _____

Business address _____

Pay period _____

FIGURE 12-6a

ITEM 1: INCOME (Averaged on _____ Basis):
Average GROSS Wage
   Less Deductions
      Federal Income Tax $_____
      Social Security $_____
      Other $_____
      Total Deductions $_____
Average NET Wage $_____
Other Income _____
                                     $_____
_____ $_____

TOTAL NET INCOME $_____

ITEM 2: ASSETS
Cash on hand or in banks $_____
Stocks, bonds, notes $_____
Real estate
      Home $_____
      Other $_____
Automobiles $_____
Other personal property $_____
Other assets _____
                                     $_____
_____ $_____

    TOTAL ASSETS $_____

ITEM 3: LIABILITIES
Real estate mortgages $_____
Automobile loads $_____
Other Notes and Loans $_____
Other _____ $_____
                                       $_____
_____ $_____

    TOTAL LIABILITIES $_____

_____
                    Affiant

Sworn to and subscribed before me this _____ day of _____, 19_____.

_____
CLERK OF COURT OR NOTARY PUBLIC

FIGURE 12-6b

IN THE CIRCUIT COURT OF THE 17TH JUDICIAL CIRCUIT
IN AND FOR BROWARD COUNTY, FLORIDA

In re: the Marriage of	Case No.

In re: the Marriage of)
)
PATRICIA PETITIONER,)
)
Wife,)
)
v.)
)
)
ROBERT RESPONDENT,)
)
Husband.)
)
)
_____)

PROPERTY SETTLEMENT AGREEMENT FOR
SIMPLIFIED DISSOLUTION OF MARRIAGE

We, _____ (the Husband) and _____
(the Wife) were married on _____. Because irreconcilable
differences have caused the permanent breakdown of our marriage, we have made this agreement to settle
once and for all what we owe to each other and what we can expect from each other. Each of us states that
nothing has been held back, that we have honestly included everything we could think of in listing the
money and goods that we own; and each of us states that we believe the other one has been open and
honest in writing up this agreement. Each of us agrees to sign and exchange any papers that might be
needed to complete this agreement.

Division of Property

We divide our property as follows:
1. Husband transfers to Wife as her sole and separate property:
    A.
    B.
    C.
    D.
    E.
    F.
    G.

FIGURE 12-7a

2. Wife transfers to Husband as his sole and separate property:
   A.
   B.
   C.
   D.
   E.
   F.
   G.

Division of Debts

1. Husband shall pay the following debts and will not at any time hold Wife responsible for them:
   A.
   B.
   C.
   D.
   E.

2. Wife shall pay the following debts and will not at any time hold Husband responsible for them:
   A.
   B.
   C.
   D.
   E.

Dated: _____   Dated: _____

       _____   _____
       Husband   Wife

FIGURE 12-7b

IN THE CIRCUIT COURT OF THE 17TH JUDICIAL CIRCUIT
IN AND FOR BROWARD COUNTY, FLORIDA

Case No.

In re: the Marriage of   )
)
PATRICIA PETITIONER,   )
)
Wife,   )
)
v.   )
)
ROBERT RESPONDENT,   )
)
Husband.   )
)
_____)

FINAL JUDGMENT DISSOLVING MARRIAGE
UNDER SIMPLIFIED DISSOLUTION PROCEDURE

This action came before the Court upon the petition of the parties for dissolution of their marriage. Upon consideration thereof,

IT IS ADJUDGED that the bonds of marriage between Husband, ROBERT RESPONDENT, and Wife, PATRICIA PETITIONER, are dissolved.

IT IS FURTHER ADJUDGED that the Wife's former name is restored and she shall hereafter be known as PATRICIA MARIA ESCOBAR.

IT IS FURTHER ADJUDGED that the property settlement agreement filed in this proceeding as Exhibit 1 was executed voluntarily after full disclosure and is approved and incorporated in this judgment by reference, and the parties are ordered to comply with it.

ORDERED at _____, Florida, on this _____ day of _____, 19_____.

_____
CIRCUIT JUDGE

FIGURE 12-8

REVIEW QUESTIONS

1. What is the fundamental difference between an annulment and a dissolution of marriage?

2. What is the purpose of a Declaration under the Uniform Child Custody Jurisdiction Act?

3. Indicate whose signature you would expect to see on the following documents. (For the purposes of this question, assume that the answer is petitioner if either the petitioner or representing attorney signs the document. Make a similar assumption for the respondent.)

   a. petition

   b. answer

   c. Uniform Child Custody affidavit

   d. final judgment

4. Are there simplified dissolution of marriage procedures that are available in your state when certain requirements have been met such as the absence of minor children and the existence of a property settlement agreement signed by the parties? If so, what are those requirements, and what are the advantages of utilizing these simplified procedures?

5. Prepare a petition for dissolution of marriage and a declaration under the Uniform Child Custody Jurisdiction Act based upon the following fictitious information. Use the sample and format provided in this chapter. Assume that a property settlement agreement has been signed by the parties and that a copy of it is attached to and incorporated in the petition.

   > Barbara Moss is suing her husband, Robert Moss, for dissolution of their marriage. The suit (case number 96-55923) has been filed in your judicial circuit, county, and state. The petitioner does not desire to have her maiden name restored. The couple were married on July 31, 1986, in Canlon, New York, and have two children of the marriage: Bryan Moss, born on April 14, 1988, and Patricia Moss, born August 11, 1990. Bryan lived with both of his parents at 646 Orangeacre Lane, [your city, state, and zip code] from the time he was born until December 1, 1995. From that time until the present, he has lived with his mother at that same address. Patricia lived at the same address from the date of her birth until December 1, 1995, at which time she moved in with her father at 77 Mission Road, [your city, state, and zip code]. She has been at that address since that time. The petition and the affidavit are both dated May 4, 1996. The affidavit is notarized by Brad Nielson, whose commission expires on March 5, 1997. Both parties have been living in your county and state since the date of their marriage, and both children were born in your city and state.

2 prepare exercises (handwritten note)

agreed that the wife shall be the primary residential cus-
...or children although there is to be shared parental re-
...ara Moss's attorney is Frederick Whistler, who has an ad-
...eton Way, [your city, state, and zip code] and a telephone
...555-2295. Robert Moss's attorney is Tamara Manet, who
...of 2222 Epson Circle, [your city, state, and zip code].
...mber is #56745. Manet's Bar number is #22321. Barbara
...ticipated in any capacity in any other litigation or custody
...erning the children, nor does she have any information
...nding custody proceeding concerning them. She does
...who is not a party to the present proceeding who claims
...r visitation rights with regard to either of the children. The
...ized by Ken Palmer on May 4, 1996. His commission ex-
...1997.

...ent dissolving marriage based on the following fictitious information. Use the sample provided in this chapter.

Ann Campbell filed suit for a dissolution of marriage against Frank Campbell on September 19, 1997 in your judicial circuit, county, and state (case
number 97-67721). The petitioner did not request in her petition that her
maiden name be restored. Assume that a property settlement agreement,
dated September 16, 1997, has been signed by the parties and incorporated into the judgment. The judgment itself is dated December 4, 1997,
and is signed by Judge Megan Bailey. Ann is to be the primary custodian
of the minor children, but both parties are to have shared parental responsibility for them. The minor children are Elizabeth, born February 29,
1990; Sara, born January 31, 1994; and Kathryn, born April 19, 1996. The
respondent shall be responsible for paying $80 per week child support for
each of the children during their minority. Frank will have the right to visit
the children at reasonable times and places after reasonable notice to the
petitioner.

FOOTNOTES

[1]Rule 1.611 of the Florida Rules of Civil Procedure is being used as an example of this abbreviated approach which is available in some states.

[2]FLA. R. CIV. P. 1.611(c)(1).

[3]FLA. R. CIV. P. 1.611(c)(2).

13 *Contracts*

CHAPTER OVERVIEW

(a) Examples of offers that may not be revocable

[1] Options

[2] Situations involving detrimental reliance

[3] Firm offers

(3) Counteroffer

(4) Expiration of time

(5) Death of either party

(6) Insanity of either party

(7) Illegality after the offer but before the acceptance

2. The Acceptance

a. The offeree's discretion to accept or reject

b. Who may accept

c. The lack of a response does not constitute an acceptance

d. The means of acceptance

(1) The mailbox rule

B. Competent Parties

1. A General Presumption of Capacity

2. Parties with Special Kinds of Contractual Capacity Problems

a. Minors

(1) Voidable contracts

(2) Contracts for necessities

(3) Special examples in which minors' contracts are valid

(a) Release contracts

(b) Student loans

(4) When a minor can disaffirm the contract

(5) Whether the minor must return the property after disaffirming

(6) Misrepresentation of age by the minor

(7) Parents' responsibility for their minor children's contracts

(8) The liability of adults who cosign

b. Those intoxicated by drugs or alcohol

c. The insane

C. Consideration

1. Definition

a. Distinguishing gifts from contracts

2. Consideration in Unilateral and Bilateral Contracts

3. The Requirement of Consideration on Both Sides

a. Two examples of exceptions to the rule

(1) Pledges to charities

(2) Agreements to modify a contract for the sale of goods

b. Courts do not generally examine the sufficiency of consideration

(1) Some exceptional circumstances

[a] Illusory consideration

[b] Unconscionability

D. Legality
  1. Void Contracts
  2. Examples of Special Situations Pertaining to the Legality Issue
     a. Usury
     b. Licenses
     c. Agreements to not compete
E. Genuine Assent
  1. Mistake
     a. Unilateral mistake
     b. Bilateral (or mutual) mistake
  2. Coercion
     a. Duress
  3. Intentional or Unintentional Deceit
     a. Fraud
     b. Concealment
     c. Misrepresentation
     d. Undue influence

F. Sometimes, Evidence of a Writing
  1. A Writing Is Not Necessary for Most Contracts
  2. Exceptions to the General Rule
     a. Contracts for the sale of an interest in real estate
     b. Contracts that cannot be performed within one year
     c. Contracts in which one makes a promise to a creditor to pay a debtor's debts with the promisor's own money
     d. Contracts in consideration of marriage
     e. Contracts for the sale of goods over $500
  3. What Qualifies as a Valid Writing

SEC. 13-1
IN GENERAL

Any legal assistant who intends to seek employment, either in a law office with a specialty in contract law or a general practice law firm, should be thoroughly familiar with the basic elements of contracts and the common terminology associated with this specialization.

A *contract* is defined as a binding agreement. From the definition, it is clear that not all agreements are binding and that the existence of an agreement is only one factor that must be established to create an enforceable contract. For example, if one party agrees to pay another a sum of money if the other will commit an assault, the mere fact that the parties had such an agreement does not mean that a court will enforce the payment in a court of law.

A contract is not binding unless a variety of conditions are shown. The most basic requirements of a contract include all of the following elements:

1. The existence of an agreement
2. Competent parties

3. Consideration

4. Legality

5. Genuine assent

6. Sometimes, evidence of a writing

The bulk of this chapter is devoted to an examination of each of these elements in detail.

When there is a breach of an existing contract, the aggrieved party may seek redress in a number of ways. The most common is a suit for a specific dollar amount, which is also known as a *suit for damages*. When damages are sought, the amount claimed is normally equal to the amount that the claimant lost as a result of the breach including court costs, possibly attorneys fees, and other expenses. Another common remedy sought by the aggrieved party is an order of specific performance. In the context of contract law, this is a court order compelling a party to perform the obligations in the contract. As a general rule, any party seeking an order of specific performance to obtain property must establish that the property sought is unique.

To illustrate the various remedies available in the event of a breach of contract, consider the situation in which two parties have signed an agreement for the future sale and purchase of a house. If the current owner wrongfully refuses to transfer the title to the buyer, the buyer could seek damages from the seller or obtain an order of specific performance from the court compelling the seller to transfer title to the buyer. Even if there are similar or even apparently identical houses in the neighborhood, the buyer can successfully argue that an order of specific performance is appropriate because every piece of real estate is "one of a kind" due to its unique location.

The law of contracts emanates from courts, legislatures, and other sources. Contracts specifically pertaining to the sale of tangible and movable goods are governed by Article II of the Uniform Commercial Code (UCC). The UCC is a very lengthy statute dealing not only with the sale and purchase of goods, but also with many other matters.[1] It was the intent of the creators of the UCC to make the laws concerning commercial matters similar from state to state. Article II, which is the portion of the statute pertaining to the sale of goods, has been adopted by all states except Louisiana.[2]

SEC. 13-2
TYPES OF CONTRACTS

Contracts can be categorized in a number of ways. The most common ones include the following:

A.   Unilateral and Bilateral Contracts

In a *unilateral*[3] *contract offer,* the person promising or making the offer is calling for a performance on the part of the other party. A person who makes an offer is known as an *offeror,* and a person who receives an offer is known as an *offeree.*[4] A typical example of a unilateral contract offer is the promise of a reward to anyone who finds and returns a lost dog. The offeror is not looking for one who will promise to find the dog. The reward is due only when and if the dog is actually found and returned. If someone finds and returns the dog, a unilateral contract will be formed, and the finder of the dog will be entitled to the reward. The only way that unilateral contract offers can be accepted is by performance.

A *bilateral*[5] *contract offer* is one in which the offeror is making the offer and calling for a promise on the part of the other party. A typical example is a contract in which one party promises to transfer to the other a sailboat in return for a promise to pay $300. Once a promise is made to pay the $300, the two parties have a binding agreement. The offeree can accept the offer and create a binding contract either by promising to pay the $300 or by paying it. Since promising to pay the money is a valid acceptance of the offer, actual payment by the offeree indicates just as clearly that the offeree intends to be bound by the agreement. Therefore, bilateral contract offers can be accepted either by a promise or by performance.

B.   Executed and Executory Contracts

An *executed contract* is one that has been fully performed on both sides. In the example of the bilateral contract described above, the contract would be executed if the offeror had turned over the sailboat and the offeree had paid the money. The practical effect of a contract being executed is that neither party has remaining obligations on the contract. In contrast to executed contracts, an *executory contract* is one that is not yet fully performed on both sides. This would include contracts in which there has been performance on one side, but there has not been performance on the other.

C.   Express and Implied Contracts

An *express contract* is one that is openly stated in an oral or written fashion. An *implied contract* is an actual agreement between the parties that is not openly stated in an oral or written way, but can be discerned from the conduct of the parties. An example of an implied contract would be a situation in which Smith walks into a store and takes a can of paint off of the shelf for purchase. The owner and manager of the store is tied up with a customer, but she knows

Smith. After both parties nod to each other in a way that implies that Smith can come back to the store later to pay for the merchandise, Smith leaves the store. Even though no words were spoken, it was the clear understanding of both parties that a contract to pay for the merchandise existed.

It should be emphasized that the distinction between express and implied contracts is not the same as the distinction between written and oral ones since all oral contracts are by definition express.

D. Valid, Void, and Voidable Contracts

A *valid contract* is one that is fully enforceable by the parties.

A *void contract* is totally unenforceable and therefore not a contract at all. The absence of one of the required elements of a contract makes it void, such as when the agreement calls for the commission of an illegal act.

A *voidable contract* is one in which one of the parties has the option to enforce or not enforce the agreement. An example of this kind of contract is one that was signed by one of the parties because the other party was holding a gun to his or her head. In this case, the party who was forced to sign can either reject the contract by proving the duress or choose to enforce the agreement if he or she subsequently decides that the contract was a desirable one. In either event, the threatening party has no options and will have to abide by the decision of the other party.

E. Quasi Contracts

Even when a true agreement does not exist, a court may occasionally decide that an obligation of the parties must be imposed by law and enforced to prevent injustice because one party relied to his or her detriment on the other. In such cases, a court might declare that a *quasi contract* exists. The prefix "quasi" literally means "pretend." A quasi contract is not a true contract even though it is enforced as one.

In what type of situation might a court find the existence of a quasi contract? Assume that Carlson is hired by Lynch to trim the big tree on Lynch's lot for $75. Carlson goes to the wrong house by mistake and trims the one big tree on Hannover's property. Hannover watches Carlson from the house as Carlson does the work, but Hannover never stops him. When Hannover is presented with the bill, he refuses to pay on the ground that he never had an agreement with Carlson. Under these circumstances, most courts would say that while no technical contract existed, it would be unjust to allow Hannover to escape liability, and therefore the obligation to pay should be imposed by law.

It is important to emphasize that implied contracts and quasi contracts are distinctly different. Implied contracts are actual agreements between the parties as demonstrated by their conduct. Quasi contracts, on the other hand, are not technically contracts at all, but they are nevertheless enforced as binding agreements. In the case involving Hannover and Carlson, there was no implied contract because Hannover's conduct never led Carlson to believe that a contract existed.

SEC. 13-3
THE ELEMENTS OF A CONTRACT

As previously indicated, various elements must be established to create a contract. Those elements are A. an agreement, B. competent parties, C. consideration, D. legality, E. genuine assent, and F. sometimes, evidence of a writing. Each one will now be analyzed in detail.

A.   *An Agreement*

Every agreement is composed of two parts: an offer and an acceptance.

1.   *The Offer*

For an offer to be valid, it must show a present intention to create a contract if the offeree accepts. When a contract concerns the sale and purchase of property, the seller may approach the buyer and make an offer to sell, or the buyer may approach the seller and make an offer to buy. Sometimes, statements are made that appear to create offers and yet fail to show the requisite intent.

***a.** Examples of statements that do not constitute offers*

(1) *Offers made in jest.* When an "offer" is made under circumstances that would suggest to a reasonable person that no serious intention to form a contract existed, any attempted acceptance of the proposal will be regarded as ineffective. For example, if one party jokingly suggests that he or she would like to sell a brand new automobile for $10, a contract is not formed if the potential offeree "accepts." On the other hand, if the offeror makes a proposal that the offeror perceives as a joke, but a reasonable person in the position of the offeree would perceive it to be a real offer, the proposal might be regarded as a valid contract offer that could lead to a binding contract.

(2) *Social invitations.* Social invitations are not normally regarded as contract offers that can give rise to legally binding contracts. For example,

if one issues a dinner invitation to another party who accepts it, the one receiving the invitation obviously cannot ordinarily recover for breach of contract if the dinner invitation is withdrawn at the last minute.

(3) *Offers to negotiate or to receive offers from others.* An offer to enter into contract negotiations is obviously not an offer on the contract itself because it does not show the present intention to form a binding agreement. While this may be self-evident, it may be less obvious when drawing the distinction between actual offers and statements indicating an openness to receive offers from others. For example, when a merchant places an advertisement in the newspaper, is the merchant making an offer that can be accepted by members of the public or asking the public to make an offer to buy from the merchant? The answer to this question is critical, because if the advertisement is viewed as an offer, then the merchant is contractually bound to anyone who sees the advertisement and decides to purchase the product no matter how many people respond to the advertisement. In light of this problem, most advertisements are viewed by the courts as an indication of a willingness to receive offers from the general public. The purchasers are therefore the offerors and the merchants become the ultimate offerees. The general rule may change if the advertisement indicates the exact quantity available or limits the quantity by means of such statements as "first come, first serve."

b. *Special kinds of offers.*   As a general rule, offers must be sufficiently definite to form a contract if accepted by the offeree. Certain kinds of contract proposals, however, are lacking key terms and yet can be regarded as valid offers. Examples of such offers include the following:

(1) *Requirements contract offers.* If the offer includes a promise to buy all of the goods that the offeror will need in operating a business during the calendar year, an acceptance of the offer can result in a binding contract. This is true regardless of the fact that the exact quantity needed is not specified. While failure to abide by the terms of such an agreement may be difficult to ascertain in some cases, a breach of the contract would clearly be evident if it was discovered that the offeror had purchased the products elsewhere during the calendar year.

Not all requirements contract offers come from the buyer. An example of one emanating from the seller would be a promise to sell all of the goods that the offeree needed in operating a business during the calendar year. Regardless of whether the offer is coming from the seller or the buyer, a requirements contract offer is easily identified because the quantity is the amount needed by the buyer.

(2) *Outputs contract offers.* If the offer includes a promise to sell all of the goods that the offeror can produce, manufacture, or "put out" in a business during the calendar year, an acceptance of the offer can result in a binding contract. This is true regardless of the fact that the exact quantity needed is not specified. A breach would clearly be evident if it was discovered that the offeror had sold the products to other purchasers during the calendar year.

Not all outputs contract offers come from the seller. An example of one emanating from the buyer would be a promise to buy all of the goods that the offeree could produce, manufacture, or "put out" in a business during the calendar year. Regardless of whether the offer is coming from the seller or the buyer, an outputs contract offer is easily identified because the quantity is the amount that the seller can produce, manufacture, or "put out."

(3) *"Services as needed" contract offers.* When a contract calls for the rendering of a service rather than the sale of a product, the parties often agree on an hourly rate or payment whenever a particular task is performed. For example, suppose one party agrees to pay $20 every time the lawn is mowed by the other, and agrees that the lawn is to be mowed whenever it is needed. The agreement does not specify, however, whether this agreement shall continue for weeks, months, or years. Even though neither the contract duration nor the frequency of the work is specified, the contract is valid and the one mowing the lawn is obviously entitled to be paid for services rendered. Such an agreement is terminable, however, whenever either party so chooses.

(4) *"Cost plus" contract offers.* Sometimes a seller agrees to offer merchandise at a price that is equal to the amount that the item cost plus a profit or percentage. An example of this would be a proposal by an offeror to sell a specific automobile at "$100 over factory invoice." This would be a bona fide offer even though the exact dollar figure has not been stated, because a specific amount can be ascertained by referring to the invoice.

(5) *Contract offers referring to market price.* An offer to enter into a contract now to sell merchandise in the future at a price that will be established then can give rise to a binding contract provided that the price can be easily ascertained by the future date. A promise to buy 100 shares of J.C. Penny stock on October 1, 2008, at whatever price may exist for those shares on the New York Stock Exchange on that date is a valid contract offer because the price can easily be determined on that date simply by reading the stock reports in the newspaper.

c. Ways to terminate an offer. Offers may be terminated by the actions of the offeror, the actions of the offeree, operation of law, or by other means. If an offer is terminated before it is accepted, then there is no agreement and therefore no contract. The various ways to terminate an offer include the following:

(1) *Rejection.* The offer may be rejected by the offeree in any manner that indicates that the offeree has no intention of entering into a contract. No special words are required. As a general rule, if the offeree simply fails to respond to the offer, it will be assumed that this silence amounts to a rejection unless the circumstances suggest otherwise.

(2) *Revocation.* This occurs whenever the offeror takes back an offer prior to acceptance. If the offeree accepts the offer before the attempted revocation, a contract will then exist, and the attempted revocation will be regarded as ineffective. As a general rule, an offer can be revoked at any time prior to acceptance. This is true even when the offeror expressly promises not to revoke the offer prior to a certain date. There are, however, exceptions to the rule.

(a) *Examples of offers that may not be revocable*

[1] *Options.* An offer will be irrevocable during a specified period of time if the offeree pays the offeror money or transfers to the offeror something of value in exchange for the offeror's promise not to revoke. Such an agreement is known as an *option.* A common example of an option contract is a real estate contract in which the seller agrees to transfer title to the buyer in the future.[6] The buyer will place a deposit down with the real estate agent or attorney to verify that the seller will not change his or her mind and transfer the property to someone else.

[2] *Situations involving detrimental reliance.* If the offeror knows that the other party is relying on the fact that the offer will remain open, the right of the offeror to revoke an offer may be limited. This can be illustrated by a situation in which there is a contract for the sale of real estate, but the title to the property has not yet been transferred to the buyer. Assume that the seller has promised the buyer that she will not revoke her offer to sell. On the basis of this representation, the buyer then moves onto the property and starts spending large amounts on construction. If it can be shown that the seller is aware that the buyer is relying on the offer, many courts would say that the seller could not revoke the offer because the buyer had relied to his detriment on the seller's representation.

[3] *Firm offers.* According to the Uniform Commercial Code (see Section 13-1), when a merchant gives a potential purchaser a written, signed promise not to revoke an offer or not to revoke an offer for a specific period of time not to exceed three months concerning a contract for the sale of goods, the merchant is bound by the promise whether or not the merchant receives payment or property to keep the offer open.

(3) *Counteroffer.* Under traditional contract law, if the offeree responds to the offer in a way that significantly alters or adds to the terms of the offer, it is regarded both as a rejection of the original offer and a new offer, which can then be accepted or rejected. For example, if Burns offers to sell his CD player to Rodriguez for $200 and Rodriguez responds by indicating that he would buy it if the price was $175, Rodriguez has made a counteroffer that also rejected the original offer from Burns for $200. If Burns wishes to accept the counteroffer and form a binding contract for $175, he may do so.

(4) *Expiration of time.* If an offeror indicates that the offer will be open for no longer than March 1 of 2000, then the offer will expire on that date. If the offeror does not indicate how long the offer will be open, then it will be regarded as remaining open for no longer than a "reasonable time." One party may contend that the offer was accepted within the reasonable time period and that a contract was formed. The other party, however, may contend that the offer had expired prior to the acceptance and that there was therefore no contract. A court may ultimately have to define what a reasonable time is in the context of any particular case.

(5) *Death of either party.* If either the offeror or the offeree dies after the offer is made but before an acceptance is given, the offer will be regarded as automatically terminated.

(6) *Insanity of either party.* If either party loses sanity between the time of the offer and the time of the acceptance, the offer will be considered automatically terminated.

(7) *Illegality after the offer but before the acceptance.* If the action called for was legal at the time the offer was made, but a change in the law makes the action illegal, the offer is regarded as automatically terminated by operation of law, and it cannot be effectively accepted by the offeree.

2.   *The Acceptance*

When the offeree accepts the terms of the offer, an agreement is formed. If all other required elements are present (see Sec. 13-1), a contract results.

a. The offeree's discretion to accept or reject. As a general rule, the offeree cannot be compelled to accept an offer. Among the few but important exceptions to this rule are contracts pertaining to public utilities and public accommodations. Those wishing to purchase such services cannot be rejected on the basis of race, religion, or national origin. Other exceptions are situations in which merchants must accept offers from the general public to purchase goods advertised by the merchants because of consumer protection legislation.

b. Who may accept. The only one who can accept a contract offer is the one to whom the offer is directed. Consequently, if someone overhears an offer being made, that person does not have either the power or the right to accept it.

c. The lack of a response does not constitute an acceptance. As previously indicated in this chapter, a failure by the offeree to respond to an offer does not amount to an acceptance. This rule applies to unordered merchandise sent through the mail. Since no contract exists, the recipient is under no obligation to either pay for the merchandise or return it. This situation is to be distinguished, however, from one in which a consumer has entered into an agreement to receive merchandise periodically unless the consumer informs the merchant to stop all subsequent deliveries. Under these circumstances, the parties have both agreed by contract that silence will be regarded as an acceptance.

d. The means of acceptance. If the offeror indicates that the offer may be accepted in a specific way (such as by mail) and not by any other means, then that requirement will be regarded as a term of the offer, and the acceptance must be made in the prescribed manner. If no specific means of acceptance is required in the offer, acceptance may be made by any reasonable method. What is reasonable under the circumstances may depend on how the parties have dealt with each other in the past, or what is customary in contractual dealings of this nature.

When an acceptance is sent through the mail, it is critical to determine whether it is effective when it is mailed by the offeree or when it is received by the offeror.

(1) *The mailbox rule.* According to this rule, which is applicable in most states, an acceptance is valid when mailed assuming the letter is correctly addressed.[7] On the other hand, revocations of offers by offerors or rejections of offers by offerees are effective when received. To illustrate the effect of this rule, consider the following situation:

June 1   Mark mails an offer to Sally.

June 2   Sally receives Mark's offer.

June 3   Mark mails a revocation of his offer to Sally.

> June 4   Sally mails an acceptance to Mark.
>
> June 5   Sally receives Mark's revocation.
>
> June 6   Mark receives Sally's acceptance.

The acceptance was effective on June 4 since that was the date it was mailed. The revocation came too late since it was not effective until the day that it was received, which was June 5. Since there was a valid acceptance before there was a valid revocation, there was an agreement.

If offerors do not want the mailbox rule to apply, there is nothing that prohibits them from inserting a condition in the offer indicating that an acceptance is not valid until it is received by the offeror.

The increasing utilization and acceptance of fax machines in the world of business eliminates many of the problems associated with the sending of offers and acceptances through the mail because there is no significant gap from the time of the sending of any document until the time of its receipt.

B.   *Competent Parties*

As a general rule, a valid contract is not formed unless both parties are sufficiently competent to understand the nature of the agreement at the time the contract is formed. The fact that a party did not understand the terms of the contract does not, however, automatically mean that the party lacked contractual capacity.

Some incapacities in this context are based on the factual circumstances that may exist at the time, such as intoxication or insanity, while others may be based on a person's status, such as the fact that a person is a minor.

1.   *A General Presumption of Capacity*

Unless otherwise proven, the presumption is that the parties entering into the contract were sufficiently competent. This rule must be qualified with regard to certain kinds of parties who enter into contracts. The issues associated with a few of these parties are as follows:

2.   *Parties with Special Kinds of Contractual Capacity Problems*

a. Minors.   The contractual capacity of minors is a unique issue, because the laws are designed to protect the rights of minors entering into contracts with adults who have an inherent advantage over them. This special status of minors results in distinctive rules with regard to contractual capacity.

(1) *Voidable contracts.* As a general rule, most contracts of minors are voidable by the minor. This means that the minor has the option of either enforcing the contract that has already been formed or choosing to disaffirm and reject it. For example, suppose an adult enters into a contract with a 16-year-old for the sale of a bicycle. After the contract is actually formed, the minor may have the right to reject the contract, return the bicycle, and demand the return of the money given for the merchandise. The adult is not, however, given the same choice and is bound by the contract if the minor chooses to enforce it.

(2) *Contracts for necessities.* If a minor enters into a contract for the purchase of an item that would be regarded as a necessity, the minor can disaffirm the contract, but will have to pay for the value of whatever was received under the contract. While a determination of what constitutes a necessity may sometimes be debatable, the most common examples of necessities are food, shelter, and clothing. Whether an item is regarded as a necessity may still, however, depend on the circumstances. For example, a coat in a freezing climate would be regarded as a necessity, but a mink coat would not. There is a strong trend by the courts to increase the number of items that qualify as necessities.

(3) *Special examples in which minors' contracts are valid.* While most contracts of minors are voidable, in a number of situations minor's contracts will be regarded as valid (as opposed to voidable or void). Two examples are:

(a) *Release contracts.* A release contract is one in which one party releases the other by waiving the right to file a suit against that person in the future. Suppose, for example, that while an adult man is driving his automobile, he runs over a 17-year-old boy. The adult and the minor subsequently sign an agreement by which the adult is to pay the minor $10,000 as a settlement in exchange for a signed legal document from the minor that releases the adult from any further responsibility. The minor cannot return six months later and claim that the contract was voidable on the basis of his age. The release will be regarded as a valid rather than voidable contract as long as the other required elements of the contract are present.

(b) *Student loans.* Statutes commonly provide that minors are prohibited from avoiding repayment of student loans by disaffirming the loans as voidable contracts. If the rule were otherwise, students could receive the educational benefits provided and then refuse to make payments on their loans by disaffirming or rejecting the loan agreements.

(4) *When a minor can disaffirm the contract.* Traditional American case law indicates that a minor can disaffirm a contract at any time prior to "a reasonable time after his or her 18th birthday." To illustrate, a 16-year-old who enters into a contract has approximately two years to decide whether to disaffirm it. The reference to a "reasonable time" is obviously nonspecific and allows the court some leeway in the event that the disaffirmance takes place a few hours or days after the party reaches majority. If both parties disagree as to whether the disaffirmance took place within this "reasonable" time frame, the question may ultimately have to be decided by the court.

(5) *Whether the minor must return the property after disaffirming.* If the minor has entered into a contract for the purchase of goods and later wishes to disaffirm the contract and get the purchase money back, the minor must generally return the purchased property if the minor still has it. On the other hand, the fact that the minor no longer has the property does not necessarily mean that the minor cannot disaffirm the contract. If the property has been partially or completely destroyed, the minor still has the power to disaffirm. This means that even though the minor cannot return the property, the minor can disaffirm the contract by refusing to make further payments if any are due or by demanding the return of payments already made. Because this traditional rule has lead to apparent injustices in many situations, some courts refuse to follow the traditional rule.

If a minor cannot return the property because he or she intentionally disposed of it by selling it to another party, the minor will not be permitted to disaffirm the original contract. If the rule were otherwise, the minor could make a profit by disaffirming the original contract when he or she had already made money from the subsequent sale.

(6) *Misrepresentation of age by the minor.* Even when the minor represents to the adult that the minor is at least 18 years of age or older, the case law of many states indicates that the minor may still disaffirm the contract prior to a reasonable time after reaching majority. Because of the intentional and deceptive nature of the minor's statement, however, not all states have followed this rule. Regardless of the position taken by any given court with regard to this issue, the misrepresentation by the minor constitutes an act of fraud, and any attempt by the minor to disaffirm the contract may give rise to a suit for fraud by the adult. Many sellers include a statement above the buyer's signature line in their sales agreements stating that the buyer swears that he or she is at least 18 years of age or older. This will provide the seller with a cause of action for fraud in the event that the buyer is shown to be a minor.

(7) *Parents' responsibility for their minor children's contracts.* As a general rule, parents are not responsible for the contracts of their minor children unless the parents incur personal liability as cosigners or the child is acting as a direct agent of the parent. An illustration of the latter situation is when a parent directs a child to purchase goods for the parent using the parent's account at a store.

(8) *The liability of adults who cosign.* When adults enter into contracts with minors, they may require that an adult cosign the agreement with the minor for one of two primary reasons: (1) to avoid any problems associated with enforcement of voidable contracts with minors, and (2) to join a party who may have greater assets to fulfill any obligations under the contract. If the minor chooses to disaffirm the contract, the obligations of the cosigner are unaffected, and the cosigner will remain liable.

b. Those intoxicated by drugs or alcohol. The fact that a party entering into a contract is intoxicated does not automatically mean that the party lacked capacity and that the contract is therefore void and unenforceable. He or she will, however, be regarded as contractually incompetent if it would have been evident to a reasonable person at the time the contract was formed that the party was unaware of entering into a contract or understanding the basic nature of the agreement. Furthermore, it should be self-evident that, if one party "drugged" the other with alcohol or some other kind of narcotic, the one causing the intoxication cannot enforce the contract against the intoxicated party. If a person is intoxicated to the extent that he or she is unaware that an agreement is being made, the contract is voidable. In other words, the person who was intoxicated can choose to enforce or disaffirm it. If that person chooses to enforce it, the other party will be bound by the agreement.

c. The insane. The law of contracts makes a distinction between those who have been declared by a court of law to be insane and those who have not. When a court has issued a declaration of insanity and appointed a guardian to handle the legal affairs of the insane party, any contracts signed by the insane person after the declaration are void, and any contracts signed by the guardian on behalf of the insane person after the declaration are presumed valid.

More difficult problems arise when there has been no declaration of insanity and one of the parties may have lacked capacity at the time of the signing. Under such circumstances, a court may be called on to determine, through eye witness testimony and other forms of evidence, whether the party apparently understood the nature of the agreement and the fact that a contract was being formed. If the court is convinced by that evidence, the contract may be enforceable. The court is primarily concerned with the state of mind of the party at the time of contract formation. Evidence of a lack of capacity at other times is not necessarily conclusive if the court is convinced that the party was sane at that time.

C. Consideration

1. Definition

A party entering into a contract does so on the understanding that the party will receive something of value. The other party is entering the contractual relationship with similar expectations. Therefore, in any contract there must be something of value, known in the law as *consideration,* coming from both sides of the transaction. The consideration may be a promise, a performance, or a forbearance.

When performance is called for in a contract, the performance does not qualify as valid consideration if the performance has already taken place prior to the agreement or if the contract calls for an act that the party is already required to do by law. For example, a promise by a homeowner to pay a fireman for putting out a fire is not valid consideration because it is the fireman's duty to extinguish fires. Since the agreement has valid consideration on only one side, it would be unenforceable regardless of the fact that the parties agreed to it, and the homeowner would not be required to pay the money.

a. Distinguishing gifts from contracts.   Gifts involve situations in which consideration comes from one side only. The recipient of a gift may be receiving something of value, but consideration is not being transferred back to the donor as part of a bargain or exchange. Consequently, the laws pertaining to gifts made during the lifetime of the donor are distinct from those for contracts, and they focus on different issues, such as intent and delivery.

2. Consideration in Unilateral and Bilateral Contracts

Regardless of whether the contract is unilateral or bilateral, there is consideration on both sides even though the nature of the consideration is different in the two kinds of contracts. In a unilateral contract (which involves the exchange of a promise for a performance; see Sec. 13-2, subsection A), the consideration on one side of the transaction is the promise of the offeror, while the consideration on the other is the performance rendered by the offeree. In a bilateral contract (which involves the exchange of a promise for a promise), the consideration on each side is normally the promise rendered to the other.

3.   *The Requirement of Consideration on Both Sides*

The basic nature of a contract requires that there be consideration on each side of the agreement. Nevertheless, in a few exceptional situations courts will enforce the understandings of the parties with consideration coming from only one side of the transaction.

a. *Two examples of exceptions to the rule*

(1) *Pledges to charities.* When making a pledge to donate money to a particular charitable cause in the future, a party is not generally receiving anything of value from the recipient. In spite of the absence of consideration on both sides, courts may enforce the promise to donate, especially if there has been detrimental reliance. If a wealthy benefactor pledges a million dollars toward the construction of a new building on a university campus, for example, and the university begins construction relying on that pledge with the benefactor's full knowledge, the donor may be obligated as though there was a contract even though there was really only a statement of an intention to make a gift.

(2) *Agreements to modify a contract for the sale of goods.* Under the Uniform Commercial Code, a contract for the sale of tangible, movable property can be modified with new consideration on only one side. For example, if two parties have entered into an agreement for the sale and purchase of a video recorder, it is possible that the parties can agree to modify the terms of the sale at a subsequent date without each party transferring new consideration to the other. This assumes, however, that both parties have agreed to such a modification.

To modify a contract that does not deal with goods, such as contracts for the sale of services or real estate, the generally applied rule is opposite to the one for the sale of goods. New consideration is necessary on both sides of the transaction or the modification will be regarded as ineffective.

b. *Courts do not generally examine the sufficiency of consideration.*   While consideration is usually required on each side of the agreement, it is not the court's obligation in a breach of contract action to determine whether the considerations are of equal value. For example, assume that Jennifer promises to pay Michael $300 in exchange for Michael's promise to transfer his sofa to Jennifer. Under these circumstances, each party has made a promise of value to the other, and the requirement of consideration on each side has therefore been met. If there is a subsequent breach of contract action, it is immaterial that the sofa may only be worth $250.

(1) *Some exceptional circumstances*

(a) *Illusory consideration.* Sometimes consideration may appear to be present on both sides, but a closer inspection of the agreement shows that valuable consideration is coming from only one party to the transaction. If, for example, Perry offers to buy $800 worth of electronic equipment from Frank two years from the date of the agreement in the event Perry decides that he wants it at that time, Perry is really promising nothing of value. His promise would be regarded as *illusory consideration,* and the "agreement" would therefore be unenforceable in a court of law.

(b) *Unconscionability.* If the value of the consideration on one side is vastly greater than that on the other, a court in a breach of contract case may consider this fact to be evidence of fraud. To illustrate, if a heavy-handed salesperson sells an ordinary toaster to a poor, uneducated party for $400, a court would probably refuse to enforce the agreement on the basis that it shocked the conscience of the court. Courts are hesitant to find such agreements *unconscionable* and therefore unenforceable unless they are convinced that the considerations on each side are vastly different in value.

D. Legality

Even when the parties have a clear understanding, an agreement is unenforceable if the subject matter is illegal or if the agreement calls for an illegal performance by either party. Illegality must be proven, however, and there is a presumption that contracts are legal unless otherwise demonstrated.

1. Void Contracts

If an agreement is illegal, it will generally be regarded as void. The practical consequences of this are that neither party will have the option of obtaining recovery under the terms of the agreement. In a breach of contract action, if only part of the contract is illegal and the court is convinced that the legal and illegal portions are not so closely connected that enforcement of one part requires enforcement of the other, a court may declare the contract to be *divisible* and choose to enforce the legal part only. If enforcement is not appropriate or logical without enforcement of the entire agreement, the court will declare the agreement to be *indivisible* and declare the entire contract null and void.

2.   *Examples of Special Situations Pertaining to the Legality Issue*

Very often it is self-evident whether a contract is lacking the element of legality. For example, any contract calling for the commission of a crime would obviously be unenforceable. Similarly, contracts calling for the commission of a tort[8] would also be regarded as unenforceable. In many situations, however, the issue of enforceability may not be as clear. Such situations include:

a. Usury.   *Usury* is the charging of an illegal rate of interest. The maximum amount that may be charged (known as the "legal" rate of interest) may be either a specified rate or a rate tied to market indicators, and the rate may vary for different kinds of transactions. If an agreement contains a usurious rate of interest, the party being charged may request in any subsequent court proceeding that the legal rate of interest be substituted for the usurious one, or that the obligation to pay any interest be terminated, or that the contract itself be declared null and void.

b. Licenses.   If a party enters into a contract to perform services, can that party recover for services rendered if he or she did not have a license required by law to perform the services? For example, if Stinson and Thomas enter into an agreement whereby Stinson is to render medical services requiring substantial expertise to Thomas, can Stinson recover for services rendered even if he did not have a license to practice medicine? Whether recovery is allowed depends on the nature of that license. If proof of competence by examination would be necessary to obtain the license (such as in this example), one may not successfully sue to recover for services rendered. If, on the other hand, the primary purpose of the license is to raise revenue and no examination is required, then the failure to have the license will not prevent one from recovering for services rendered. Nothing in connection with this rule prevents the party who receives the services from suing the other party for negligence, whether or not the one performing the work had a license.

c. Agreements to not compete.   When a party enters into an employment contract, a provision may be included in the agreement that prohibits the party from competing against the company for a stated period of time after the employment contract ends. Similarly, when one sells a business, including its equipment, inventory, and customer list, the buyer may insist that the seller agree not to compete against the buyer's business in the area for a certain period of time. Both kinds of agreements are enforceable provided that they are reasonable as to area and time. Agreements to not compete under other circumstances are generally regarded as an illegal restraint of trade and therefore unenforceable.

E.   Genuine Assent

Even though the parties may have had an apparent agreement, it is possible that it was not binding because assent by the parties was not genuine. Three kinds of problems may arise that have a bearing on this matter.

1.   Mistake

To determine whether mistakes made by the parties have an effect on the enforceability of the contract, the nature of the mistake must be examined. The outcome may depend on whether the mistake was unilateral or bilateral.

a. Unilateral mistake.   A *unilateral mistake* is one that has been made on only one side of the contract. For example, a unilateral mistake has been made if one of the parties failed to read the contract or signed it without truly understanding what it meant. The general rule of law with regard to unilateral mistakes is that they have no effect on the enforceability of the contract. If a party fails to read the contract, that party must accept the consequences of such negligence. If the party did not have a true understanding of the contract, then an attorney should have been hired. Another common example of a unilateral mistake is a situation in which a party enters into a contract based upon a misunderstanding of the law. Under these circumstances, the party can be held liable on the contract regardless of the misunderstanding.

b. Bilateral (or mutual) mistake.   A *bilateral mistake* occurs when both parties make the same mistake about the same significant portion of the contract. For example, assume that two parties enter into a contract for the sale and purchase of a 1955 Buick. As it turns out, the seller actually owns two 1955 Buicks, and the seller was reasonably thinking of the green one while the buyer was reasonably thinking of the blue one. Under these circumstances, if one party attempts to enforce its interpretation of the contract on the other regardless of the misunderstanding, a court may decide that the parties never genuinely agreed to the same terms, and therefore an order of *rescission* declaring the contract to be null and void will be appropriate.

2.   Coercion

a. Duress.   Physical duress occurs when a party is forced to enter into a contract against the party's will, such as when one person is holding a gun at the head of the other and demanding a signature on an agreement. Contracts made under such duress are voidable at the option of the party who is being subjected to the coercion. In other words, that party can choose to disaffirm or enforce the contract while the party causing the duress is obligated if the other wishes to enforce the agreement.

In addition to physical duress, there are circumstances under which a threat of severe economic loss may be regarded by a court as a basis for finding a lack of genuine assent.

3.   *Intentional or Unintentional Deceit*

a. Fraud.   An act of fraud requires an intentional misrepresentation of facts under circumstances in which the defrauding party is expecting the other to rely on the misrepresentation to that party's detriment. For example, when a seller induces a buyer to purchase land under water after representing to the buyer, who has not seen the property, that it is ready to build on, the deceit is intentional and the sale is therefore fraudulent.

b. Concealment.   Concealment involves intentional fraud plus an overt act designed to further the fraud. This would occur in a situation in which a seller put wallpaper over a hole in order to intentionally conceal the defect and thereby trick the buyer into proceeding with the purchase of the house. Concealment should be distinguished from cases involving nondisclosure in which one party chooses not to disclose information that the other party would like to have known prior to entering into the agreement. Some types of nondisclosure may be a basis for granting a nullification of the contract, such as when a party sells a used car without telling the buyer that there have been eight major repairs on the automobile in the past three months.[9] Other kinds of nondisclosure may have no effect on the enforceability of the contract. To illustrate this kind of nondisclosure, suppose a major corporation hires someone to purchase real estate in the individual's own name and then immediately thereafter transfer the property to the corporation. In this case, the person is being hired so that the seller will not raise the price solely because the corporation's interest makes the property more valuable. Even though the seller would have liked to have known that the corporation was going to be the ultimate owner, the nondisclosure of that information to the seller would not generally form the basis for nullification of the agreement.

c. Misrepresentation.   Misrepresentation involves situations in which there is unintentional deception of another party. For example, assume Harold sells his house to Ben after he (Harold) paints the ceiling in the living room to disguise the fact that there is a major leak in the house. A week later, Ben sells the house to Susan and tells her that there are no leaks in the house. Harold's act was intentional deception and therefore constituted fraudulent concealment. On the other hand, Ben did not intend to mislead Susan, and his statement to her would therefore be classified as misrepresentation. Therefore, Susan would have a claim against Ben, and Ben would in turn have a claim against Harold.

d. *Undue influence.*   Undue influence occurs when one party coerces another into signing a contract by taking advantage of a *fiduciary* or confidential relationship. Examples of fiduciary relationships include those between doctors and patients, attorneys and clients, accountants and clients, and even family members dealing with other family members. To illustrate, if a patient agrees to have an operation because the doctor informed the patient that the operation was necessary even though it was not, a court will refuse to enforce the contract on the basis of undue influence. The underlying reason for refusing to enforce agreements when undue influence exists is that the party in the weaker bargaining position (the patient in the illustration) cannot obtain the information necessary to determine whether entering into the contract is in his or her best interest. This does not mean that the party in the stronger bargaining position can never recover on a contract for services rendered, but it does mean that a court will hesitate to enforce a contract if it becomes convinced that the party in the stronger position has taken unreasonable advantage of the weaker one. Contracts signed under duress are usually classified as voidable by the party who has been deceived.

F.   *Sometimes, Evidence of a Writing*

1.   *A Writing Is Not Necessary for Most Contracts*

As a general rule, most contracts need not be evidenced by a writing to be valid. Even when evidence of a writing is not required, however, it may be prudent for the parties to reduce their agreement to a written document so that proof of the contract terms is easier in the event of a dispute. Also, the process of reducing the agreement to a writing may force the parties to clarify their positions with regard to contract issues.

2.   *Exceptions to the General Rule*

Exceptional situations in which evidence of a writing is required are included in a legislative act that is commonly known as the *statute of frauds*.[10] This act does not necessarily refer to every situation in which a writing is needed. It does, however, normally include the following kinds of agreements:

a. *Contracts for the sale of an interest in real estate.*   Real estate includes land, buildings on the land, and fixtures such as bookcases that have been annexed to buildings. A writing is not required to evidence agreements that only lease rather than sell an interest in real property unless a writing is required under the statute of frauds for other reasons.

b. Contracts that cannot be performed within one year.   As a general rule, if it is possible to perform the contract within one year of the date of the agreement, it need not be in writing. It is immaterial whether the party ultimately exceeded the one-year period if, at the time of the agreement, it was possible to perform it within the required time.

c. Contracts in which one makes a promise to a creditor to pay a debtor's debts with the promisor's own money.   Suppose Ronald owes a debt of $1,000 to Rosa. If Martin (the promisor) promises Rosa (the creditor) that he will pay the debt that Ronald (the debtor) owes to her with his (Martin's) own money, that promise must be evidenced by a writing if it is to bind Martin. No writing is required if the promise is made to the debtor rather than to the creditor.

For a writing to be required, the promisor has to be promising to pay the debt with the promisor's own money. Assume, for example, that Linda owed $1,000 to Paul at the time of her death and that Steven was appointed the executor of her estate. If Steven (the promisor) promises to pay Paul (the creditor) the debt that Linda (the debtor) owed, but Steven is promising to make the payment out of Linda's funds in her bank account, he is not promising to pay with his own money, and the promise need not therefore be evidence by a writing.

d. Contracts in consideration of marriage.   These are contracts in which marriage is the consideration on one side of the agreement, such as when a person promises to leave money to someone whenever that person marries. This portion of the statute of frauds does not pertain to mutual promises to marry.

e. Contracts for the sale of goods over $500.   This portion of the statute of frauds pertains only to tangible, movable property with a contract price greater than or equal to $500. The price agreed on by the parties is determinative rather than the value of the goods on the open market.

Since this writing requirement is applicable only to the sale of goods, other agreements, such as those for services, need not be evidenced by a writing solely because the contract price exceeds $500.

3.   *What Qualifies as a Valid Writing*

For a writing to satisfy the statute of frauds, either the contract itself must be in writing, or there must be a written note or memorandum that confirms the existence of an oral agreement. If the writing is the contract itself, it must be signed by both parties. If the writing is a note or memorandum confirming the existence of an oral agreement, it need be signed only by the party being sued in the breach of contract action.

REVIEW QUESTIONS

1. Michael says to Pauline, "If you will mow my lawn, I will pay you $30."

   a. Is this an example of a unilateral or bilateral contract offer? Explain your answer. How can this offer be accepted?

   b. Is this an express or implied contract?

2. On May 1, Barbara promises to Henry that she will pay him $425 if he will promise to transfer to her his television. She gives him her word that she will not revoke the offer for 10 days. On May 8, Barbara gets a better deal and informs Henry that she is revoking her offer to buy. Henry files a suit demanding that Barbara follow through with the agreement.

   a. Will Henry be able to win his law suit? If not, what could he have done to ensure that Barbara would not be able to successfully revoke her offer?

   b. If Henry accepted the agreement prior to Barbara's revocation, would the agreement have to be evidenced by a writing in order to be enforceable?

3. A 15-year-old enters into a contract to purchase a bicycle for $400 by agreeing to pay $20 per month. At the time of the agreement, the seller insists that the contract be cosigned by one of the minor's parents.

   a. If the parent cosigns, can the minor still disaffirm the contract?

      (1) If so, is the parent still liable on the contract?

      (2) How long does the minor have to disaffirm the contract?

4. Theresa follows Victor's advice as to any and all matters and has had a close, personal, and trusting relationship with Victor for 40 years. Victor convinces Theresa that it would be in Theresa's best interest to transfer all her real estate holdings into Victor's name. Because Theresa trusts Victor, she does as he says not knowing that Victor is acting solely to benefit his personal interest. If Theresa wants a court of law to set aside the transfers, what argument should her attorney raise in court?

5. Indicate whether the following contracts are valid, voidable, or void.

   a. Rose, a 17-year-old, purchases a radio for her car from Ryan.

b. Spencer holds a gun up to the head of Maria and tells her that he will pull the trigger unless she signs a particular contract.

c. John promises to pay Carter $5,000 if he will kill John's next door neighbor.

d. Joshua signed a contract to purchase Melinda's entire set of *National Geographic* magazines. Melinda had not intended to sell the March 1987 issue with the collection, but no mention of that issue was made during negotiations or at the time of the signing of the contract.

e. Conrad enters into an agreement to clean Sam's swimming pool every three weeks, but the duration of the contract is not specified.

f. Jim signed an agreement with Bruce under circumstances in which Bruce was obviously intoxicated to the point that he didn't even know that he was entering into a contract.

6. What would question 5.d be an example of in the law of contracts?

FOOTNOTES

[1]These matters include among others the leasing of goods; commercial paper; bank deposits and collections; letters of credit; sales of businesses and bulk transfers; warehouse receipts, bills of lading, and other documents of title; investment securities; and secured transactions.

[2]An explanation for Louisiana's failure to pass the statute can be found in the state's historical roots. Because the Louisiana territory was a French possession during the early years of our nation, the Louisiana legal system is patterned after the one used in France and is significantly different from those of the other states.

[3]The word "unilateral" comes from two Latin stems. The prefix "uni" means "one," and we get the words "uniform" (one form, type, or appearance) and "unicycle" (one wheel) from the Latin term. The word "lateral" comes from the Latin word for "side." A lateral pass in football is a pass "to the side." Therefore, "unilateral" literally means "one-sided." In the law of contracts, a unilateral contract offer is one in which there is a promise on only one side. The other party is being asked to perform rather than simply promise to perform.

[4]In legal terminology, the "or" or "er" endings are common. A person who makes an offer is an "offeror." A person who vends (sells) is a "vendor." A person who grants (sells or conveys an interest in real property) is a "grantor." Similarly, the corresponding "ee" ending is frequently used. A person who receives an offer is an "offeree." A person to whom a sale is made (a buyer) is a "vendee." A person to whom an interest in real property is sold or conveyed is a "grantee."

[5]The word "bilateral" comes from two Latin stems. The prefix "bi" means "two," and we get the words "bicycle" (two wheels) and "biplane" (two wings) from the Latin term. Since the word "lateral" comes from the Latin word for "side," "bilateral" literally means "two-sided." In the law of contracts, a bilateral contract offer has two potential promises because one promise is calling for a promise from the other side.

[6]The property is not transferred immediately because each party wants to do various things prior to conveying the title from the seller to the buyer. For example, the buyer will want to search the land records to verify that the seller has legitimate ownership rights.

[7]If it is not correctly addressed, the acceptance is not valid until it is received.

[8]A *tort* is defined as a civil wrong other than breach of contract even though it may be associated with an underlying breach of contract as in the case of fraud (see Chapter 7).

[9]Under these circumstances, a court would nullify the contract on the basis that such a large number of repair attempts over a relatively short period of time demonstrates a continuing pattern of problems, and that the repairs should therefore be disclosed to any potential buyer.

[10]In spite of the name, the statute of frauds does not deal with the issue of fraud.

14 *The NALA CLA Examination*[1]

CHAPTER OVERVIEW[2]

SEC. 14-1
CERTIFICATION IN GENERAL

Certification bestows a measure of professional recognition on those persons who achieve significant competence in the field.

This opportunity for the legal assistant profession is provided by the National Association of Legal Assistants, Inc., through its national certification program. The CLA examination program consists of successful completion of a comprehensive two-day examination. Thereafter, evidence of continuing legal education must be submitted periodically in order to maintain certification. Those who achieve the CLA may pursue the CLA Specialist credential, an advanced certification offered in several practice areas.

Based on a foundation of twenty years of research and study, the program is administered by the national Certifying Board for Legal Assistants. The board consists of legal assistants who have achieved the CLA Specialty designation, attorneys, and legal assistant school program directors. At the close of 1994, approximately 7,000 legal assistants in 49 states, the District of Columbia, the Virgin Islands, and Puerto Rico had achieved the CLA credential.

Recognition of the Certified Legal Assistant program is nationwide. In fact, in the 1993 publication "Leveraging With Legal Assistants," published by the ABA Section of Law Practice Management, the certification program is discussed. On the subject of recruiting legal assistants:

> The legal assistant who can use the CLA designation has a number of advantages, not the least of which is that a hiring lawyer can assume from the CLA appellation that he or she is dealing with an experienced legal assistant who has performed to a high standard. It would be safe to assume that a CLA can immediately bring experience and capability to the practice.
>
> The hiring lawyer must be careful to distinguish between a legal assistant with a CLA designation and with a certificate from an educational institution. The latter certificate only implies that the legal assistant will perform well on the job because he or she has successfully completed the legal assistant course given at that institution. There is confusion within

the profession because of these two certificates. Legal assistants themselves often misconstrue the meaning of the certificate from the institution. The difference is that the CLA has proven experience and proven capabilities within the profession.

The CLA has been adopted in California, Florida, and Louisiana as the qualifying standard for legal assistants seeking advanced certification in state specialty practice areas.

Numerous bar associations offer guidelines for legal assistants and associate membership for legal assistants. Half of the bar associations and bar association sections offering this membership include the CLA credential among the alternate eligibility requirements for membership. The South Dakota Supreme Court has recognized the CLA as a means of identifying competent legal assistants and other courts have awarded higher fees to legal assistants with the CLA designation. Most recently, the Mississippi Bar Ethics Committee Opinion 223 (1/19/95) terms the CLA a reputable program and allows the use of the CLA and CLAS credentials on law firm letterhead listings.

The legal community has also been supportive of the credential economically. Legal assistants with the CLA receive higher salaries nationwide and their work is billed at higher rates. The CLA has been shown to be a statistically significant positive factor in salary and compensation levels (1993, National Utilization and Compensation Survey Report, National Association of Legal Assistants).

Now nearly 20 years old, the CLA and CLA Specialist credentials are national standards for legal assistant recognition.

SEC. 14-2
OUTLINE OF THE EXAMINATION

Each section of the examination contains objective questions, such as multiple choice, true/false, and matching. The sections on Communications and Judgment and Analytical Ability each contain short answer and/or essay questions.

As a standardized national examination, all sections are on the federal level—no state laws or procedures are tested.

A. Communications

This section of the Certified Legal Assistant examination covers the following areas of communications:

Word Usage	Correspondence
Punctuation	Concise Writing

Capitalization   Vocabulary

Grammar   Rules of Composition

Nonverbal Communication

B.   *Ethics*

This section deals with ethics in the legal assistant's contacts with employers, clients, coworkers, and the general public. Unauthorized practice, ethical rules, practice rules, and confidentiality are among the topics tested by this section.

Knowledge of the American Bar Association Rules of Professional Conduct and the National Association of Legal Assistants, Inc., Code of Ethics and Professional Responsibility is required by this examination.

C.   *Human Relations and Interviewing Techniques*

The Human Relations portion encompasses professional and social contacts with the employer, clients and other office visitors, co-workers, including subordinates, and the public outside of the law office. For this reason, the legal assistant should be familiar with: authorized practice, ethical rules, practice rules, delegation of authority, consequences of delegation and confidentiality.

Interviewing Techniques covers basic principles, as agreed upon by most authors on the subject, definitions of terms of basic principles, and handling of specialized interviews. Subject areas included in this section of the examination are:

General considerations for the interviewing situation: courtesy, empathy, physical setting, body language

Initial roadblocks: lapse of time, prejudice, etc.

Manner of questions

Use of checklists for specific matters

Special handling situations: the elderly, the very young

Both initial and subsequent interviews are included as are both client and witness interviews.

D.   *Judgment and Analytical Ability*

The sections of this part deal with (1) analyzing and categorizing facts and evidence; (2) the legal assistant's relationship with the lawyer, the legal secretary, the client, the courts, and other law firms; (3) the legal assistant's reaction to specific situations; (4) handling telephone situations; and (5) reading comprehension and data interpretation. The section also contains an essay question which requires analysis of a research request and applicable law and the writing of a responsive memo.

Familiarity with the Rules of Professional Conduct of the American Bar Association and the Code of Ethics and Professional Responsibility of the National Association of Legal Assistants, Inc., will also be helpful. Knowledge of logical reasoning and experience as a legal assistant are valuable assets.

E. Legal Research

It is extremely important for the legal assistant to be able to use the most important "tool" of the legal profession—the law library. The purpose of the Legal Research section of the CLA Certifying Examination is to test your knowledge of the use of state and Federal codes, the statutes, the digests, case reports, various legal encyclopedias, court reports, Shepardizing, and research procedure.

The amount of study and practice you will need to pass this section of the examination will depend on your current knowledge and experience with legal research. You can get excellent practice by researching various topics on your own.

F. Legal Terminology

The sections of this part deal with (1) Latin phrases; (2) legal phrases or terms in general; and (3) utilization and understanding of common legal terms.

The questions involve legal terminology and procedures used in general practice.

G. Substantive Law

The Substantive Law section of the CLA Certifying Examination is divided into nine parts:

1. General (includes the American Legal System)
2. Administrative Law
3. Bankruptcy
4. Contract
5. Business Organizations

6.   Criminal

7.   Litigation

8.   Probate & Estate Planning

9.   Real Estate

Each examinee will be required to take the general section and must select four out of the remaining eight specialty tests.

Those persons who are taking the examination, but have not had formal law courses, would benefit from study of a current textbook in the area.

A great deal of the material covered in this section of the examination is acquired through work experience in the legal field. The Substantive Law mini-tests are designed to test the legal assistant's general knowledge of the fields of law.

SEC. 14-3
SEMINARS AND MATERIALS USEFUL FOR
TEST PREPARATION

Many affiliated state and local legal assistant associations of the National Association of Legal Assistants sponsor study groups or review seminars for those interested in the CLA Certifying Examination. Notices of these programs are included in *Facts & Findings*, NALA's quarterly publication. Nonmembers may call NALA headquarters for this information or contact state or local associations directly.

The *NALA CLA Exam Preparation Manual* is available through West Publishing Company. Authored by Virginia Koerselman, J.D., in association with NALA, this manual is a useful tool for preparing to take the NALA Certifying Examination. Copies may be obtained by calling West Publishing Company at (800) 328-9352.

Compiled from sample tests and materials donated to the National Association of Legal Assistants, the *CLA Study Guide and Mock Examination* is one of the most extensive study guides for this professional certification program. It is an excellent companion to the *CLA Review Manual, A Practical Guide to CLA Exam Preparation*, authored by Virginia Koerselman, J.D., in cooperation with the National Association of Legal Assistants.

Single issues of the *CLA Study Guide and Mock Examination* are available from NALA Headquarters, 1516 S. Boston, #200, Tulsa, OK 74119. NALA members receive a discount off the purchase price. Quantity order and other inquiries should be directed to West Publishing Company.

Formal education courses are recommended, especially in assisting a candidate to prepare for the substantive law section. Should you choose this as a study option be sure to keep in mind that all substantive law sections are based on federal rules, codes, practice, and procedure. No state laws, codes, or procedures are tested.

SEC. 14-4
TESTING CENTER LOCATIONS

A list of possible locations for all testing sessions [is available from NALA]. All testing locations are subject to minimum registration requirements.

NALA reserves the right to cancel any testing center where fewer than ten people register. In the event a published center is canceled, all affected applicants will be notified and allowed to transfer to another center.

Any applicant desiring to change from one testing center to another must notify NALA headquarters at least thirty days prior to the examination date.

Applicants receive admission tickets approximately 15 days prior to the examination. The forms show the exact location of the examination center and the time schedule, and serve to reconfirm Social Security numbers and the four substantive law areas and/or retake or specialty sections. Exact testing center locations are not publicly announced.

The examinations are administered by members of the NALA Certifying Board or individuals designated by the Certifying Board.

SEC. 14-5
GRADING AND RETAKE POLICY

A passing score of 70 percent is required for each of the examination sections. The substantive law section is graded as a whole. From a total of 500 points, 350 points is a passing score regardless of the distribution of points among the five parts.

Results are announced by the Certifying Board in writing to all examinees. Results are not available by telephone or by FAX.

Of the seven sections of the CLA certifying examination, four sections must be successfully completed in order to retake only those sections failed.

Applicants in retake status may attend a maximum of five retake sessions within a three-year period. Applicants in retake status will be allowed to choose which sections will be retaken during any retake session. Again, an applicant may only attend a retake session five times within the three-year period. The examination must be successfully completed within five retake sessions in a three-year period, or credit for all passed sections will be forfeited. If fewer than four sections are successfully completed, the applicant must reapply for the full examination.

SEC 14-6
ELIGIBILITY REQUIREMENTS

An applicant for the Certified Legal Assistant examination must meet at least *one* [emphasis added] of the three eligibility requirements detailed in the Certified Legal Assistant application form [see Sections A, B, and C].

A.   *Graduation from a Legal Assistant Program*

Such a program should be:

1.   Approved by the American Bar Association; or
2.   An associate degree program; or
3.   A post-baccalaureate certificate program in legal assistant studies ...;[3] or
4.   A bachelor's degree program in legal assistant studies; or
5.   A legal assistant program which consists of a minimum of 60 semester (or equivalent quarter-) hours of which at least 15 semester hours (or equivalent quarter-hours) are substantive legal courses.[4]

The application form will be considered incomplete without a copy of the school's official transcript, and the post-baccalaureate statement if applying under Category A.3.

B.   *A Bachelor's Degree in Any Field Plus One (1) Year's Experience (or Legal Assistant Courses)*

If you are applying under this category, you must have a bachelor's degree in any field plus one (1) year's experience as a legal assistant. Successful completion of at least 15 semester hours (or 22½ quarter-hours or 225 clock hours) of substantive legal assistant courses is equivalent to the one year experience requirement.[5]

An application form will be considered incomplete without a copy of the school's official transcript, along with either verification of experience or official school transcript showing equivalent courses in lieu of experience.

C. A High School Diploma or Equivalent Plus Seven (7) Years' Experience and Continuing Legal Education Credits

If you are applying under this category, you must have a high school diploma or equivalent plus seven (7) years' experience as a legal assistant[6] plus a minimum of twenty (20) hours of continuing legal education completed within a two-year period prior to application for the examination.

Evidence of continuing education credit is documented by the attorney/employer attestation that must be signed to complete the application form. No further documentation is required.

SEC. 14-7
REQUIREMENTS FOR MAINTAINING CERTIFIED LEGAL ASSISTANT STATUS

In recognition of the continuing change in laws and procedures that have a direct impact on the quality of work performed by legal assistants, Certified Legal Assistants are required to maintain their certified status by submitting proof of continuing education. The CLA certifying designation is for a period of five years and if the Certified Legal Assistant submits proof of attendance in accordance with the requirements, the certificate is renewed for another five years and the process begins again. Lifetime certification is not available.

All Certified Legal Assistants must submit evidence of completion of five (5) units of Continuing Legal Assistant Education every five (5) years to maintain valid certification. A completed Recertification Audit Verification plus a fee of $50 will also be required at the time of recertification. Notice of one (1) year probation will be sent to the last known address of all Certified Legal Assistants failing to submit evidence of completion of the five (5) units of CLAE within the five- (5-) year period. If the Certified Legal Assistant fails to complete the above recertification requirements in this time, certification will be revoked, with notice to the legal assistant.

All requests for CLAE credit are subject to Certifying Board approval. Relevancy is subject to approval by the NALA Certifying Board who may request employer attestation.

A. Categories of Eligibility

The categories of CLAE with unit values are:

1. *Category A.* Successful completion of NALA Specialty Examination—2 units per Specialty Examination.

2. *Category B.* Successful completion (grade C or better) of a relevant course for a minimum of 3 quarter-hours or 2 semester hours at an accredited institution of higher education. Relevancy may be requested by employer attestation and NALA Certifying Board approval—2 units per course.

   Auditing of a relevant course, or completion of a relevant course not meeting above listed minimums—1 unit per course.

3. *Category C.* Attendance at conferences, seminars, workshops, etc., on relevant topics for working legal assistants, with actual hours recorded. Minimum content of one hour required for consideration. Actual educational hours will be recorded and copy of brochure and/or program indicating schedule must be attached (unless it is a NALA-sponsored event). Units will be recorded on the basis of ten hours of continuing education equaling one CLAE unit.

4. *Category D.* Certified Legal Assistants may petition NALA Certifying Board for credit for unusual experiences which may be considered for credit. Examples: teaching experience; extensive research beyond employment requirements on a topic related to the work of a practicing legal assistant which results in publication. Limited to 2 units per petition.

B. *Mechanics for Maintaining Eligibility*

It is the obligation of Certified Legal Assistants to secure supporting data (transcripts, employer and coordinator attestations, articles, etc.) to be submitted to NALA headquarters as events are attended. These documents will be reviewed by the full Certifying Board for action. Request forms are available from NALA Headquarters, 1516 South Boston, Suite 200, Tulsa, OK 74119-4464.

C. *Special Note*

Effective October 1982, for recertification purposes, except in Category A, units for attending seminars in areas other than substantive law are limited to one unit maximum for any five-year period.

SEC. 14-8
GROUNDS FOR REVOCATION OF CLA STATUS

The Certified Legal Assistant designation may be revoked for any one of the following reasons:

A. Falsification of information on application form.

B. Subsequent conviction of the unauthorized practice of law.

C. Failure to meet continuing legal education requirements as required by the Certifying Board.

D. Divulging the contents of any NALA examination questions.

E. Subsequent conviction of a felony.

F. Violation of the NALA Code of Ethics and Professional Responsibility.

Individuals currently serving a prison term are ineligible to sit for the CLA examination.

SEC. 14-9
ADDITIONAL NOTES

A. Applications must be received by January 15 for the spring examination; May 15 for the summer session; and October 1 for the winter session. Applications must be accompanied by a certified check or money order in the amount of $225 for NALA members; $240 for nonmembers. Applications mailed within ten working days after the deadline must be accompanied by a nonrefundable $25 late fee. Applications mailed after the ten working day allowance will not be accepted.

B. Testing centers will be offered throughout the United States in locations selected by the Certifying Board. NALA reserves the right to cancel any testing center where fewer than ten (10) applicants register.

C. Successful completion of a minimum of four of the seven sections permits the Certified Legal Assistant applicant to retake only those sections failed ($50 per section). If fewer than four sections are passed, one must reapply and retake the full examination. Applicants in retake status may attend a maximum of five retake sessions within a three-year period. Applicants in retake status will be allowed to choose which sections will be retaken during any retake session. The examination must be successfully completed within five retake sessions in a three-year period, or credit for all passed sections will be forfeited.

FOOTNOTES

[1]Reprinted with permission of the National Association of Legal Assistants, Inc., 1516 S. Boston, Suite 200, Tulsa, OK 74119, 1995. Subject to revision without notice.

[2]The headings are those of the author.

[3]Those applying under this category must attach "a course catalog or letter attesting this is a post-baccalaureate certificate program—that a bachelor's degree is necessary for course admission—along with a transcript showing completed coursework."

[4]Those applying under this category must "attach to [the] application a transcript which shows the semester, quarter or clock hours necessary to meet this qualification. If this is not shown on the transcript, a letter from the school registrar or program director will be necessary. The application will be incomplete without this information."

[5]All applicants under this category must submit with the application form a copy of the school's official transcript showing receipt of a bachelor's degree and date of completion. Those applying under the provision allowing for additional course work in lieu of the one year's work experience must submit with the application an official school transcript showing completed course work.

[6]Within this category, "legal assistant" is defined as follows: Legal assistants are a distinguishable group of persons who assist attorneys in the delivery of legal services. Through formal education, training and experience, legal assistants have knowledge and expertise regarding the legal system and substantive and procedural law which qualify them to do work of a legal nature under the supervision of an attorney.

Glossary

abstract (also known as an abstract of title). A compilation of copies of all public records and recorded documents pertaining to a particular piece of real property.

adjudication. The pronouncement of a judgment by a court.

administration of an estate. The process of preparing an inventory of a decedent's assets, paying all claims against the estate, and then making distribution to the appropriate beneficiaries.

administrator/administratix. The party appointed to handle the administration of the estate of a person who has died without a will.

advancement. A part or all of an inheritance given to an heir by the deceased before the death of the deceased.

affiant. One who swears to the truth of statements in an affidavit. *See* "Affidavit."

affidavit. A notarized statement in which a party swears to the truth of any matter.

affirmative defense. A defense that may be valid even if the allegations of a claim are presumed to be true.

alias summons. A second summons issued because the first one was ineffective due to misinformation in the document or defects in its form.

amicus curiae brief. A "friend of the court" brief filed by one who has no right to appear before the court, but who nevertheless wishes to bring to the court's attention legal arguments relevant to the resolution of the case.

amortized loan. A loan in which the percentage of each payment that is attributable to interest decreases throughout the duration of the loan.

ancillary administration. A second administration of an estate that is opened in a state other than the one in which the primary administration has been initiated.

answer. The pleading filed by the defendant in a civil case that responds to the allegations in the plaintiff's complaint.

arbitration, binding. The resolution of a legal dispute by the ruling of an independent individual or panel under circumstances in which both parties agree to be legally bound by the decision.

appellate jurisdiction. The power of a court to hear a case on appeal.

arraignment. A criminal hearing at which there is a formal notice to the accused of the charges that have been filed, a notice of the possible sentences that could be imposed by the court, and an entry of a plea of guilty, not guilty, or no contest by the accused.

articles of incorporation. The document that creates a corporation and indicates general information about the organization, such as the initial number of shares, the initial officers, the initial members of the board of directors, and other matters.

assignment of mortgage. A transfer of any rights that the lender may have on a loan to another party.

assumption of mortgage. An agreement by the buyer of real property to accept responsibility for the seller's mortgage after the purchase.

attestation. The witnessing by signature of a will or other document.

bailiff. The one who has responsibility for assistance in maintaining order in the courtroom, the custody of prisoners while in court, and the custody of jurors.

bequest. A gift of personal property by will.

bill of sale. The document that transfers title from the seller to the buyer of any personal property (tangible, movable property) that passes with real estate.

bylaws. Rules enacted by a corporation that pertain to its general operation.

caption. The top portion of a pleading, containing information such as the names of the parties, the case number, and the name of the court hearing the case.

case law. Law derived from the decisions of the courts, as opposed to law from statutes and other sources.

certiorari. A writ of a higher court ordering a lower court to provide it with a pending pleading, thereby resulting in the initiation of appellate proceedings.

chain of title. The sequence of transactions affecting a particular parcel of real property from the original title holder to the present.

civil law (v. criminal law). The branch of law that pertains to a private adjudication of rights by one party against another party.

class action. A suit brought against a party on behalf of all others who have similar claims against that party.

clerk of the court. The court officer who handles the court records, furnishes certified copies, enters judgments and orders, issues documents necessary for service of process, and performs other similar functions.

closing. The time at which the parties to a real estate transaction conclude the transfer of the interest in the property.

closing costs. Real estate costs other than the purchase price, such as taxes and insurance, that are chargeable either to the buyer or to the seller.

code. A compilation of laws (usually statutory or constitutional).

codicil. An amendment to a will.

collateral. Security for a loan.

common stock. A document indicating percentage ownership in a corporation and a right to dividends when and if declared.

comparative negligence. A doctrine applied in many states whereby the amount that a plaintiff can recover in a negligence action is reduced by the degree to which the plaintiff was responsible for the harm done.

compensatory damages. A money award in a civil suit that is designed to compensate the injured party for actual loss.

complaint. The plaintiff's initial pleading in most kinds of civil non-equity causes of action.

compulsory counterclaim. A type of counterclaim that must be raised by the defense in the cause of action or be waived.

condominium. A form of real estate ownership in which a party in a multi-unit complex owns an individual apartment, office, or other unit, and a percentage interest in the common areas such as a recreation hall or swimming pool.

contributory negligence. A doctrine applied in some states whereby a plaintiff in a negligence action can recover nothing if the defendant can show that the plaintiff was responsible to any degree for the harm done.

corporation. An artificial legal entity which is created by grant from the government and which exists as a legal entity independent of the identity of its members.

corpus delicti. The "body of the crime" necessary in order to establish that a crime was in fact committed, such as the cadaver of a murder victim.

cotenancy. *See* "Tenancy in common."

counterclaim. A claim that the defendant may raise in opposition to or as a set-off against the claim of the plaintiff.

criminal law (versus civil law). The body of law that designates certain kinds of punishment for behavior deemed by the government to unreasonably interfere with the rights of others or of society as a whole.

cross-claim. A claim by one party against a co-party, such as a defendant against a co-defendant; or, in some states, a claim brought by the defendant against the plaintiff.

damages. An award of money in a civil case.

default judgment. A judgment of the court on behalf of the plaintiff based upon a failure of the defendant to file responsive pleadings in a timely manner or appear in court.

defendant. The party against whom a suit or cause of action is brought in a civil case, or the party charged in a criminal case.

deposit receipt contract. The initial residential real estate sales contract which states such terms as the purchase price, the amount of any new mortgages to be taken out (if any), the personal property that is to pass with the sale, the cash required to close, and many other matters.

deposition. The oral pretrial or prehearing questioning in the presence of a court reporter of a party or witness under oath for the purpose of discovering information useful in the preparation of a case.

devise. A gift of real property by will.

devisee. A person to whom real property is given by will.

dicta. Statements found in previous court cases that were not necessary for a determination of the issues in the case.

discovery. Various methods, such as the use of depositions and interrogatories, that are available to attorneys for discovering facts and information concerning a case prior to the trial or final hearing.

dismissal with prejudice. A dismissal by the court of a claim which generally bars the claimant from ever bringing the same suit or cause of action again.

dismissal without prejudice. A dismissal by the court of a claim which allows the claimant to refile the same claim at a later time.

donee. The recipient of a gift or a power.

donor. The giver of a gift or a power.

duces tecum. *See* "Subpoena duces tecum."

easement. The right to use land belonging to another for a specific purpose, such as the right of a power company to run power lines under people's property.

eminent domain. The power of the government to seize private property for a public purpose provided that it pays the owner just compensation for the property.

equity. A system of jurisprudence based upon rules of fairness and justice applied by courts in cases where remedies other than damages may be sought.

escheat. The taking of a decedent's property by the state when there is no will and no heirs have claimed the property.

escrow. Money or property held by a disinterested third party on the request of two or more people until the third party is given instructions by all the people as to its disposition.

ethics. Principles of conduct that are deemed to be right based upon a sense of moral judgment.

ex parte hearing. A hearing which is upon the application of or for one party only.

ex post facto law. A law which attempts to hold the perpetrator responsible for violating a law which was not in force at the time of the purported violation.

executor/executrix. The man/woman (or institution) appointed in a will to handle the administration of a testator's or testatrix's estate according to the terms of the will.

F.H.A. loan. A home loan or loan for home repairs that is guaranteed by (rather than emanating from) the Federal Housing Administration, an administrative agency of the federal government.

fee simple. The fullest ownership that one can have in a piece of real property, which includes the right of the owner to sell the property during his or her lifetime, transfer the property by will, or leave the property to pass to heirs if there is no will.

felony. A serious criminal offense with substantial potential penalties.

final judgment. A judgment which terminates a suit or cause of action.

fixture. Any personal property that is so closely associated with real property due to annexation, adaptation, or the intent of the parties that it is regarded as real property.

foreclosure. Seizure of the mortgagor's interest in the real property subject to the mortgage as a result of his or her failure to abide by the terms of the mortgage, such as maintaining current payments.

fraud. A tort based upon a misrepresentation of a past or present fact, with knowledge of its falsity or reckless disregard for the truth, intent to cause reliance, actual reliance, and damages.

frivolous pleading. A pleading which on its face is so apparently insufficient that it cannot be regarded as controverting the pleading of the other party. *Compare* "Sham pleading."

G.I. loan. *See* "V.A. loan."

gift causa mortis. A gift, revocable under certain circumstances, which is made by the donor in contemplation of his or her impending death.

gift inter vivos. A gift not made in contemplation of the death of the donor which is made while both the donor and the donee are still living.

grand jury. A jury assembled for the purpose of hearing evidence and determining whether there is sufficient probable cause to formally charge or "indict" the accused.

grantee. A person or entity to whom an interest in real property is transferred in writing.

grantor. A person or entity who transfers an interest in real property in writing.

habeas corpus. A writ issued by a court requiring someone to "release the body," such as when a prisoner who is being held on unconstitutional grounds is ordered to be brought before a court of law.

headnote. A summary at the beginning of a written judicial decision of a primary legal issue addressed by the court.

hearsay. In-court evidence of an out-of-court statement used to prove the truth of a matter asserted in court; generally held to be second-hand evidence and, therefore, inadmissible although there are a number of exceptions.

heir. A person who would take as a beneficiary of an estate if the deceased died without a will.

impeachment of a witness. Examination of a witness or presentation of evidence in a court of law that questions the veracity of the witness.

in camera. Heard only in the judge's chambers (rather than in the presence of the jury).

in personam jurisdiction. Jurisdiction or power of a court to rule over a person, as opposed to jurisdiction purely over the person's property.

in re:. "Pertaining to," such as *In re:* the marriage of John Smith and Mary Smith."

in rem jurisdiction. Jurisdiction or power of a court to rule over a person's property, but not the person himself or herself.

indictment. A formal accusation by a grand jury that a specifically named party has committed a criminal offense.

injunction. A court order to refrain from committing a particular act.

inter vivos gift. *See* "Gift inter vivos."

inter vivos trust. A trust created during the lifetime of the settlor.

interlocutory judgment. A judgment rendered during the course of a suit or cause of action that does not terminate the case.

interrogatories. Written questions sent to an opposing party to be answered under oath in a civil action.

intestate/intestacy. Terms used to describe one who dies without a will.

involuntary dismissal. A dismissal of a claim by the court against the wishes of the claimant.

joint tenancy. Ownership of undivided interests in real or personal property by two or more parties with a right of survivorship.

jurisdiction. The power of a court to hear a case.

legacy. A gift of personal property by will.

legatee. A person to whom personal property is bequeathed in a will.

legal assistant. *See* "Paralegal."

lessee. A party who leases real property from another.

lessor. A party who leases real property to another.

letters of administration. The court order that gives the administrator or administratrix authority to act as representative of an intestate estate.

letters testamentary. The court order that gives the executor or executrix authority to act as representative of the testate estate.

lien. A claim that one may have on the property of another as a result of a judgment or other obligation.

life estate. The right to own and possess real estate for a person's lifetime.

lis pendens. A notice that legal proceedings are in progress with regard to a particular parcel of property, and a caution to anyone purchasing the property subsequent to the filing of the legal notice that they may take the property subject to the terms of the final judgment in those proceedings.

limited partnership. A partnership generally established under a format described by statute, in which the limited partner may contribute cash or property, but may not participate in the management of the business.

mala in se crimes. Acts designated as crimes because they are regarded as inherently evil and immoral.

mala prohibita crimes. Acts designated as crimes in spite of the fact that they are not regarded as inherently evil or immoral.

mens rea. The "guilty mind" of the accused that must be shown in order to make that party criminally responsible.

misdemeanor. A less serious criminal offense.

mortgage. A loan in which real property is used as collateral or security.

mortgage deed. The document that indicates among other things that the lender may seize the real estate or "foreclose" on the property that is the subject of the mortgage if the borrower fails to make timely payments on the mortgage.

mortgage note. The promissory note associated with a mortgage that indicates the exact amount of the financial obligation that the borrower has to the lender, the amount of interest to be charged, when it is to be paid, and other terms and conditions.

mortgagee. The lender of money whereby the debt is secured by a mortgage.

mortgagor. The borrower of money whereby the debt is secured by a mortgage.

motion for judgment on pleadings. A motion in which a party is claiming that he or she is entitled to recovery solely on the basis of the pleadings filed.

motion to dismiss. A motion in which the movant asks the court as a matter of law to dismiss the claim of the opposing party.

negligence. The failure to do an act that a reasonable person would do under the same circumstances, or, the failure to refrain from doing an act that a reasonable person would refrain from doing under the same circumstances; failure to use ordinary care.

no lien affidavit. A statement swearing to the fact that there are no liens or encumbrances on a particular piece of property.

nolo contendere. A plea of "no contest" in a criminal case.

nolo prosequi. The dropping of charges against the defendant by the prosecution in a criminal case.

nominal damages. A token award of damages to the claimant by the court.

notary public. An official who adds his or her signature and seal to a document in order to swear to the identity of another person signing the document.

note. *See* "Promissory note."

obiter dicta. *See* "Dicta."

original jurisdiction. The power of a court to hear a case for the first time.

paralegal. A person, qualified through education, training, or work experience, who is employed or retained by a lawyer, law office, governmental agency, or other entity in a capacity or function which involves the performance, under the ultimate direction and supervision of an attorney, of specifically delegated substantive legal work, which work, for the most part, requires a sufficient knowledge of legal concepts that, absent such assistant, the attorney would perform the task.

partnership. Two or more people in business for the purpose of sharing profits (as well as losses if they occur).

per curiam decision. An opinion of an entire court, as opposed to the opinion of only one of its judges or justices.

per stirpes. A term used in the descent and distribution of estates whereby the lineal descendants of a deceased ancestor take proportionate shares of that which the ancestor would have received if he or she had been alive.

permissive counterclaim. A type of counterclaim that can, but need not, be raised in the responsive pleadings of the defendant.

personal property. Tangible, movable property as well as, in some circumstances, claims and debts.

personal representative. A term that is used to include executor, executrix, administrator, and administratrix.

petitioner. One who files suit in equity, or, in appellate practice, one who initiates an appeal; also, in general, anyone who files a petition.

plaintiff. The party who initiates the suit or cause of action in a non-equity civil case.

pleadings. The written allegations and defenses of the parties that are submitted to the court for consideration of the case.

pluries summons. A third summons issued because the first one and the second one (the alias summons) were ineffective due to misinformation in the previous summonses or defects in their form.

points. A lump-sum amount charged by the lender at a real estate closing for making the loan, with each point equal to one percent of the total amount loaned.

power of attorney. A written agency agreement; a document in which one party, the principal, authorizes another, the agent, to act in the place of the principal under certain designated circumstances.

pocket parts. Paperback pamphlets prepared by the publisher and placed inside the back covers of law books for updating purposes.

preferred stock. Non-voting stock that gives the owner the right to be paid dividends before holders of common stock.

pretrial conference. A conference before the trial between the judge and all of the attorneys at which the parties attempt to narrow the issues, limit the number of expert witnesses, explore the possibilities of settlement, and deal with other issues.

probate. The process of proving the validity of a will to a court having jurisdiction over the administration of estates.

process server. One responsible for the delivery of documents compelling parties or witnesses to appear in court or at a deposition.

promissory note. An unconditional promise in writing made by one person to another, signed by the maker, agreeing to pay on demand or at a definite time a sum certain in money to order or to bearer.

punitive damages. A monetary award given by the court (above and beyond compensatory damages) for the purpose of punishing the wrongdoer.

purchase money mortgage. A mortgage in which the grantor or seller of the real estate also acts in the capacity of a lender or mortgagee.

quiet title. A suit brought for the purpose of removing any encumbrance on the title that adversely affects the owner's right to sell the property.

quitclaim deed. A real property deed that includes no warranties as to the grantor's interest in the property, but rather transfers whatever interest he or she may have in the property.

real property. Land, buildings upon the land, and anything annexed to or closely associated with the buildings or the land.

recording. Placing documents in the public records (usually in the county in which the pertinent property is located).

registered agent. The party designated by a corporation to receive service of process on behalf of the corporation.

release. A waiver of a right that one party may have against another, such as the relinquishment of the right to sue on a claim in exchange for a cash payment.

res judicata. A phrase used by courts to describe situations in which the court has already ruled upon the merits of the case, and that such a ruling is therefore binding in all later suits dealing with the same parties and cause of action.

respondent. One who filed an answer to any petition in equity, or, in appellate practice, one against whom an appeal is taken.

right of survivorship. The right of a joint tenant to receive a proportionate share of another joint tenant's share upon the death of that other joint tenant, or the right of a tenant by the entirety to receive the share of the other tenant upon the death of the latter.

satisfaction of mortgage. A notarized statement from the mortgagee that a mortgage has been paid off or satisfied.

settlor. One who establishes a trust.

sham pleading. A pleading that is apparently sufficient on its face, but is nevertheless known to be false by the pleader who is acting in bad faith.

share of stock. *See* "Common stock" or "Preferred stock."

specific performance. A court order compelling a party to perform his or her obligations on a contract.

statute. A legislative act.

statute of limitations. A statute that states the maximum time allowed by law from the date that a cause of action accrued until the filing of a suit.

style of a case. The title of the case, using the names of the parties on each side.

subpoena. A document served on a witness that compels the witness under threat of contempt to testify at a designated time and place.

subpoena duces tecum. A document served on a witness that compels the witness under threat of contempt to testify at a designated time and place and to bring along named documents, papers, or other tangible evidence.

summons. A document directing the sheriff or other official to notify a party that a suit or cause of action has been commenced against that party, and that such party is to appear at a designated time and place, or respond to the allegations in the complaint or petition.

tenancy by the entirety. Ownership by a husband and wife of undivided interests in real or personal property wherein a right of survivorship is presumed.

tenancy in common. Ownership by two or more parties of undivided interests in real or personal property wherein no right of survivorship by the surviving tenants is presumed.

testamentary trust. A trust created in a will.

testate. A term used to describe one who dies with a will.

testator. A man who executes or makes a will.

testatrix. A woman who executes or makes a will.

third-party complaint. A complaint initiated by a defendant (or counter-defendant) against a third party (one who is not already involved in the cause of action) which alleges that the third party rather than the defendant is responsible for the harm alleged in the plaintiff's complaint.

time share. Ownership of a unit in a multi-unit complex as well as a percentage interest in the common areas for a limited period of time each year, such as the ownership of a suite at a vacation resort for one week per year.

title insurance. Insurance that may be purchased in one lump-sum payment by a real estate owner or lender to provide coverage in the event of loss due to title defects.

tort. A civil wrong that is not based upon breach of contract.

trust. The transferal of property by one person (the settlor) to another (the trustee) with the understanding that the property is to be used or held by the transferee for the benefit of a third party (the beneficiary).

trustee. One to whom property is transferred with the understanding that the property is to be used or held by the transferee for the benefit of a third party (the beneficiary).

trustor. A creator, or settlor, of a trust.

U.S. Court of International Trade. The federal court that considers rulings made concerning the valuation of imported goods for the purposes of imposing customs duties.

U.S. Courts of Appeal. The federal courts of appeal immediately below the U.S. Supreme Court.

U.S. District Courts. The federal courts of original jurisdiction for most matters properly brought in the federal court system.

usury. The charging of an illegal rate of interest.

V.A. loan. A home loan that is guaranteed by (rather than emanating from) the Veteran's Administration, an administrative agency of the federal government.

vendee. A buyer of real or personal property.

vendor. A seller of real or personal property.

venue. The geographical location where a case is heard by a court.

voir dire. The jury selection process.

voluntary dismissal. A dismissal by a claimant of his or her own suit or cause of action.

warranty deed. A deed in which the seller guarantees expressly or implicitly among other things that he or she has good title and that the property is free from certain kinds of claims other than those specifically listed.

will. A person's declaration as to the disposition of his or her property upon death.

writ of certiorari. *See* "Certiorari."

Index